JAN 2 6 2015

N F T ™

Not For Tourists Guide to
WASHINGTON DC

Get more on
notfortourists.com

Keep connected with:
Twitter:
twitter/notfortourists

Facebook:
facebook/notfortourists

iPhone App:
nftiphone.com

www.notfortourists.com

Not For Tourists, Inc

Skyhorse Publishing

designed by:
Not For Tourists, Inc
NFT_{TM}—Not For Tourists_{TM} Guide to Washington DC
www.notfortourists.com

Publisher
Skyhorse Publishing

**Creative Direction and
Information Design**
Jane Pirone

Director
Stuart Farr

Managing Editor
Scott Sendrow
Production Manager
Aaron Schielke

Writing and Editing
Pamela Lalla
Scott Sendrow

**Graphic Design and
Production**
Aaron Schielke

**Information Systems
Manager**
Juan Molinari

Printed in China
Print ISBN: 978-1-62914-642-3 $21.95
Ebook ISBN: 978-1-63220-070-9
ISSN 2163-923X
Copyright © 2015 by Not For Tourists, Inc.
11th Edition

Every effort has been made to ensure that the information in this book is as up-to-date as possible at press time. However, many details are liable to change—as we have learned.
Not For Tourists cannot accept responsibility for any consequences arising from the use of this book.

Not For Tourists does not solicit individuals, organizations, or businesses for listings inclusion in our guides, nor do we accept payment for inclusion into the editorial portion of our book; the advertising sections, however, are exempt from this policy. We always welcome communications from anyone regarding ANYTHING having to do with our books; please visit us on our website at www. notfortourists.com for appropriate contact information.

Skyhorse Publishing books may be purchased in bulk at special discounts for sales promotion, corporate gifts, fund-raising, or educational purposes. Special editions can also be created to specifications. For details, contact the Special Sales Department, Skyhorse Publishing, 307 West 36th Street, 11th Floor, New York, NY 10018 or specialsales@skyhorsepublishing.com.

www.skyhorsepublishing.com

10 9 8 7 6 5 4 3 2 1

Dear NFT User,

Ah, Washington. You know you're an insider when you start using the word "insider" and calling the nation's capital "Washington" or "The District" and not "D.C."; when you begin to refer to lobbyists as "K Street," Congress as "The Hill" and get excited over the Senate vote on C-Span at happy hour. You find yourself ordering steak rare and snacking on crabcakes like potato chips. You always walk on the left but stand on the right, and huff with annoyance when a tourist does not. A celebrity sighting is seeing the Surgeon General in a restaurant. Your wardrobe starts to fill with pieces from Brooks Brothers, and you probably contemplated law school at one point. If you haven't yet moved to Maryland or Virginia, you might even start the battle cry etched on Washington license plates: No Taxation Without Representation!

Washington may seem dominated by politics like Los Angeles is by Hollywood, but it's really so much more. However, unlike Hollywood, Washington just never earned a "cool" vibe. But people don't come here to be cool. They come to change the world and perhaps to wear a bowtie or pearls. But that's okay, because Not For Tourists is designed to help change the world as well. Made with paper and ink and written for locals, by locals, NFT brings you the latest and greatest that Washington has to offer. Find everything—bowling alleys, museums, coffeeshops, bookstores, movie theaters and more. Discover parks to stroll with your dog, farmers markets to aid your farm-to-stomach efforts, local bars to cheer on the Nats or Redskins, or even one of those historic steak-and-mahogany institutions where President so-and-so once wrote a famous speech on a napkin. And believe it or not, Washington can be hip: once unlikely streets have become popular up-and-coming epicenters for bars, shops and edgy restaurants opened by *Top Chef* contestants. Even several 'burbs are flourishing as those residents grow up and move their over-educated families and organic tote bags into three-bedroom Craftsman bungalows. We got you covered.

The guidebook also works in tandem with the website and clever geo-targeted Smartphone App that keeps you up-to-date while on-the-go around the Beltway—whether by foot, metro, bus, car or bike (and if you're really an insider, a Capital Bikeshare bike). Our constantly updated website also lets you create a profile, write reviews, upload photos, make maps and submit new listings. So please, feel free to join the NFT crowd and voice your opinion. After all, this is Washington.

Didn't we say we wanted to help change the world? We're starting by changing yours.

Happy navigating!

—Jane, Scott, Pamela, et al.

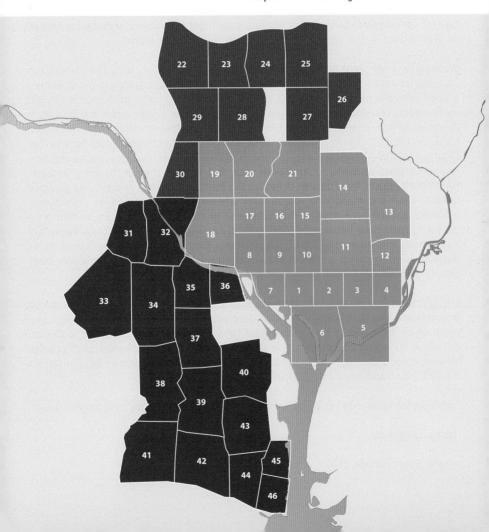

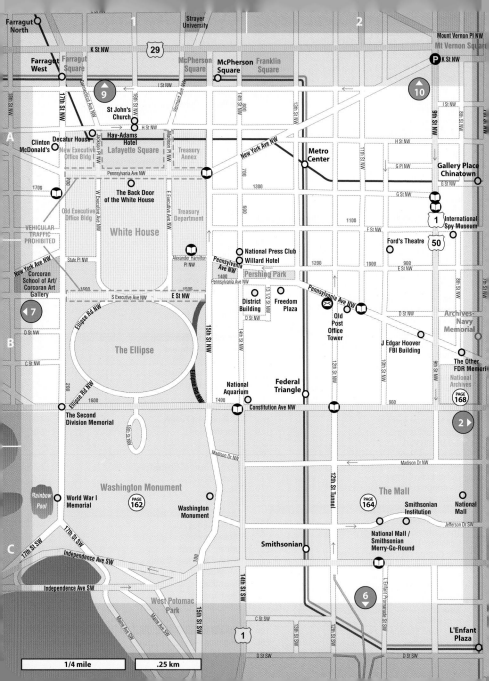

Here you'll find pretty much every reason DC is a top tourist destination: The White House, the **Washington Monument**, the Declaration of Independence, etc. If you didn't see them on a school trip, try to check them out on the weekdays. **The Mall**, on weekends, especially in warm weather, is a mob scene. Tip: When you've had enough of the white marble, photocopy this map and let it substitute as the tour guide when relatives arrive.

○ Landmarks

- **The Back Door of The White House** •
  1600 Pennsylvania Ave NW
  Free speech has never been so entertaining.
- **The Carousel on the National Mall** •
  900 Jefferson Dr SW
  202-633-1000
  Tacky, but quells crying children.
- **Clinton McDonald's** • 750 17th St NW
  202-347-0047
  Taste what Bill couldn't resist.
- **Decatur House** • 1610 H St NW
  202-965-0920
  Tour worth taking.
- **District Building** • 1350 Pennsylvania Ave NW
  DC's city hall. You can't fight it.
- **Ford's Theatre** • 511 10th St NW
  202-347-4833
  Lincoln's finale.
- **Freedom Plaza** • 1300 Pennsylvania Ave NW
  Downtown open space. Protesters and skaters unite.
- **The Hay-Adams** • 800 NW 16th St
  202-638-6600
  The luxury lap where Monica told all.
- **International Spy Museum** • 800 F St NW
  202-393-7798
  For all the future Aldrich Ames out there.
- **J. Edgar Hoover FBI Building** •
  935 Pennsylvania Ave NW
  202-324-3000
  Ask to see Hoover's cross-dressing dossier.
- **National Aquarium** •
  Constitution Ave NW & 14th St NW
  202-482-2825
  Save money, visit pet shop.

- **National Mall** • 3rd St SW & Jefferson Dr SW
  202-426-6841
  Shopping or something.
- **National Press Club** • 529 14th St NW
  202-662-7500
  Join the ink-stained hacks for a drink.
- **Old Post Office Tower** •
  1100 Pennsylvania Ave NW
  202-606-8691
  Best view of skyscraper-less Washington.
- **The Other FDR Memorial** • Pennsylvania Ave NW
  All FDR wanted was a stone outside the National Archives.
- **The Second Division Memorial** •
  17th St NW & Constitution Ave NW
  Overlooked history.
- **Smithsonian Institution Building (The Castle)** •
  1000 Jefferson Dr SW
  202-633-1000
  Storm the castle for information.
- **St. John's Church** • 16th St NW & H St NW
  202-347-8766
  Sit in the President's pew.
- **Washington Monument** • Independence Ave SW
  The phallus itself.
- **The Willard** • 1401 Pennsylvania Ave NW
  202-628-9100
  Historic hotel where the term "lobbyist" was born. And free HBO!
- **World War I Memorial** •
  Independence Ave SW & 15th St SW
  Often overlooked monument.

Map

6 5
40
9

Nightlife

- **Capitol City Brewing Company** •
  1100 New York Ave NW
  202-628-2222
  Great IPA.
- **Gordon Biersch Brewery** • 900 F St NW
  202-783-5454
  Five great lagers.
- **Grand Slam Sports Bar** • 1000 H St NW
  202-379-6646
  Sports bar perfection.
- **Harry's** • 436 11th St NW
  202-624-0053
  Downtown DC dining with a hometown corner
  restaurant feel.
- **Le Bar** • 806 15th St NW
  202-730-8700
  An oasis in a sea of offices.

- **Old Ebbitt Grill** • 675 15th St NW
  202-347-4800
  Try to spot your local congressman at this super-
  touristy Washington institution.
- **Proof** • 775 G St NW
  202-737-7663
  Wine bar. Fancy. Expensive. Of the moment.
- **Round Robin & Scotch Bar** •
  1401 Pennsylvania Ave NW
  202-628-9100
  Old style, old money DC. Herbal martinis.
- **Shelly's Back Room** • 1331 F St NW
  202-737-3003
  Cigars, scotch, strip streaks and middle-aged white
  men in suits.
- **Society of Wine Educators** • 1319 F St NW
  202-408-8777
  Non-profit educational organization with wine
  academies for groups.
- **Ultrabar** • 911 F St NW
  202-638-4663
  Best DJ's in the city on 4 different floors.

This neighborhood used to be seen as a place that catered mostly to tourists, with its many chain coffee shops and restaurants. But thanks to a booming food scene in Penn Quarter, things are changing and it seems that a new hyper-trendy spot opens daily, making this neighborhood a destination for White House staffers, K Street lobbyists and tourists alike. For a classic Washington experience, have a cocktail at **The Willard's** rooftop bar and enjoy the view.

🍴Restaurants

- **Aria Pizzeria & Bar** • 1300 Pennsylvania Ave NW
  202-312-1250 • $$
  Outdoor casual lunch spot.
- **Asia Nine** • 915 E St NW
  202-629-4355 • $$$
  Asian inspired in the heart of Chinatown
- **Astro Doughnuts & Fried Chicken** • 1308 G St NW
  202-809-5565 • $$
  The name says it all. Mmmmm, doughnuts.
- **Azur** • 405 8th St NW
  202-347-7491 • $$$$
  Seasonal, sustainable seafood.
- **Bistro D'Oc** • 518 10th St NW
  202-393-5444 • $$$$
  Homey Provençal with spotty service and an excellent pre-theater menu.
- **BLT Steak** • 1625 I St NW
  202-689-8999 • $$$$
  Super tasty and super pricey.

- **The Bombay Club** • 815 Connecticut Ave NW
  202-659-3727 • $$
  Terribly elegant Indian food in a reminiscent British colonization atmosphere.
- **Bourbon Steak** • 2800 Pennsylvania Ave NW
  202-944-2026 • $$$$
  Another branch of Michael Mina's steakhouse, in the Four Seasons.
- **Café Asia** • 1720 I St NW
  202-659-2696 • $$$
  Not quite as crowded as Asia but just as busy.
- **Café Mozart** • 1331 H St NW
  202-347-5732 • $$
  Walk past the deli into an authentic German restaurant.
- **The Caucus Room** • 2350 M St NW
  202-861-3450 • $$$$
  The taste of power. A favorite for DC's elite.
- **Cedar** • 822 E St NW
  202-637-0012 • $$$$
  Clean, Californianesque.

Map

9

Map

7
6 5
40
9

- **Ceiba** • 701 14th St NW
202-393-3983 • $$$$$
Brazilian indulgence, from the people who brought Tenpenh.
- **Chef Geoff's** • 1301 Pennsylvania Ave NW
202-464-4461 • $$$
Snooty service, great wine selection. Check out the jazz brunch.
- **Co Co. Sala** • 929 F St NW
202-347-4265 • $$$
Loungy, decadent dessert bar. Good if you like to peacock/spend money.
- **District of Pi Pizzeria** • 910 F St NW
202-393-5484 • $$
Rustic thin-crust pizza emphasized by the exposed brick setting.
- **Ella's Wood Fired Pizza** • 901 F St NW
202-638-3434 • $$
Tasty pizza in Chinatown
- **Equinox** • 818 Connecticut Ave NW
202-331-8118 • $$$$$
The finest food of the Chesapeake region.
- **The Hamilton** • 600 14th St NW
202-787-1000 • $$
Clyde's group opens another Washington favorite with crab cakes and steak frites.
- **Harry's** • 436 11th St NW
202-624-0053 • $$
Downtown DC dining with a hometown corner restaurant feel.
- **J & G Steakhouse** • 515 15th St NW
202-661-2440 • $$$$$
Washington steaks at Hotel W.
- **Le Grenier** • 502 H St NE
202-544-4999 •
Ooh la la! French on H Street!
- **Lincoln's Waffle Shop** • 504 10th St NW
202-638-4008 • $$
Greasy spoon deluxe in honor of Abe.
- **minibar** • 855 E St NW
202-393-0812 • $$$$$
DC's most avant-garde cooking. Foie gras and cotton candy, anyone?

- **MXDC** • 600 14th St NW
202-393-1900 • $$$$
Todd English takes on Mexican in DC.
- **Occidental Grill & Seafood** •
1475 Pennsylvania Ave NW
202-783-1475 • $$$$
Opulent White House classic.
- **Off the Record** • 800 16th St NW
202-638-6600 • $
Pricey hotel bar attracting DC's power players.
- **Old Ebbitt Grill** • 675 15th St NW
202-347-4800 • $$$
The quintessential Washington restaurant. Try to spot your local congressman.
- **Ollie's Trolley** • 425 12th St NW
202-347-6119 • $
1970s burger bliss.
- **OYA** • 777 9th St NW
202-393-1400 • $$
Mini food with big prices
- **Ping Pong Dim Sum** • 900 7th St NW
202-506-3740 • $$
"21st Century tea house" from London serves flash dim sum.
- **Proof** • 775 G St NW
202-737-7663 • $$$
Restaurant and wine bar. Fancy. Expensive. Of the moment.
- **Ristorante Tosca** • 1112 F St NW
202-367-1990 • $$$$$
Un ristorante tanto elegante.
- **Teaism** • 800 Connecticut Ave NW
202-835-2233 • $$
Need a teapot? Buy one with lunch!
- **Teaism** • 400 8th St NW
202-638-6010 • $$
Everything Zen at this hipster hangout.
- **Yogen Fruz** • 825 14th St NW
202-289-0078 •
Frozen yogurt with a healthy twist.
- **Zaytinya** • 701 9th St NW
202-638-0800 • $$$$
Tasty mezze menu offered by award-winning chef. Fabulous interior.

Hit up **BLT Steak** for steak, **Ristorante Tosca** for Italian, and **Old Ebbitt Grill** for a quintessential DC experience. **District of Pi** serves up quality 'za and **Proof** serves quality vino. For drinks, turn heads at **Poste Moderne Brasserie** and get a pint at either **Capitol City Brewing Company** or **RFD**.

Shopping

- **American Apparel** • 1090 F St NW
  202-628-0438
  Clothes that make your skin, wallet, and conscience feel good.
- **Anthropologie** • 950 F St NW
  202-347-2160
  Hippie chic finds in the heart of downtown.
- **Banana Republic** • 601 13th St NW
  202-638-2724
  Popular clothier's Chinatown site.
- **Barnes & Noble** • 555 12th St NW
  202-347-0176
  Mega bookstore.
- **Café Mozart** • 1331 H St NW
  202-347-5732
  Germanic treats.
- **Celadon Spa** • 1180 F St NW
  202-347-3333
  Great haircuts.
- **Central Liquor** • 625 E St NW
  202-737-2800
  Great prices on wide range of libations. Wine tastings Wed-Sat.
- **Coup de Foudre Lingerie** •
  1001 Pennsylvania Ave NW
  202-393-0878
  New high-end lingerie store.
- **Cowgirl Creamery** • 919 F St NW
  202-393-6880
  Cheese delights from all over the world
- **Fahrney's Pens** • 1317 F St NW
  202-628-9525
  Historic purveyors of pens, watches, and stationary.
- **Forever 21** • 1025 F St NW
  202-347-0150
  Trendy, cheap McFashions.
- **H&M** • 1025 F St NW
  855-466-7467
  New downtown outlet of European clothing giant.
- **International Spy Museum Store** • 800 F St NW
  202-654-0950
  James Bond would be jealous.
- **J. Crew** • 950 F St NW
  202-628-8690
  A prep paradise
- **Macy's** • 1201 G St NW
  202-628-6661
  Only full-service department store in downtown Washington.
- **Mia Gemma** • 933 F St NW
  202-393-4367
  High-end, trendy baubles.
- **Nancy's Flower Shop** • 1300 Pennsylvania Ave NW
  202-408-0677
  Fresh flowers for local delivery.
- **Penn Camera** • 840 E St NW
  202-347-5777
  Say cheese.
- **Political Americana** • 1331 Pennsylvania Ave NW
  202-737-7730
  Souvenirs for back home.
- **Radio Shack** • 615 12th St NW
  202-737-9480
  Great for headphones, batteries, and that special connection.
- **Radio Shack** • 1100 15th St NW
  202-296-2311
  Great for headphones, batteries, and that special connection.
- **T.J. Maxx** • 601 13th St NW
  202-637-1261
  Deceptively huge location offers best of bargain shopping.
- **Utrecht Art Supplies** • 1250 I St NW
  202-898-0555
  Channel Picasso.
- **The White House Gift Shop** • 529 14th St NW
  202-662-7280
  White House memorabilia and gifts.
- **Zara** • 1025 F St NW
  202-393-2810
  Euro trends at affordable prices.

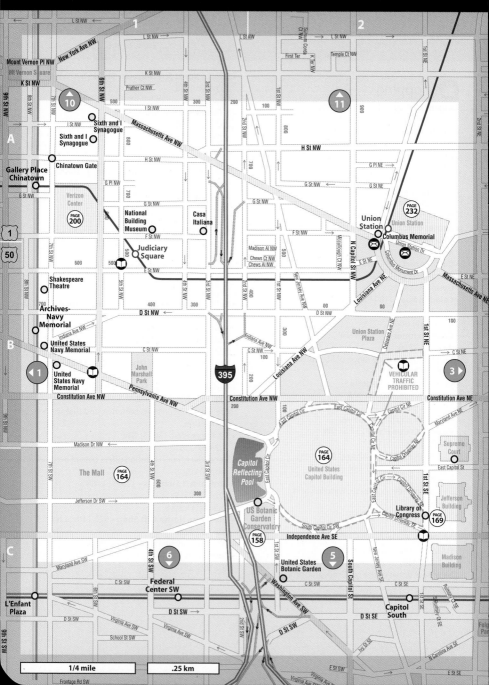

Map 2 · **Chinatown / Union Station**

Ⓝ

L St NW · L St NW · L St NW

Stursum Corda Ct NW

First Ter

K St NW · Temple Ct NW

New York Ave NW

Mount Vernon Pl NW
Mt Vernon Square

K St NW

9th St NW · 8th St NW · 7th St NW · 6th St NW

10

500

Prather Ct NW · 4th St NW · 3rd St NW

I St NW

200 · 100

1st St NE

Massachusetts Ave NW

Sixth and I
Synagogue

Sixth and I
Synagogue

I St NW

900

11

H St NW

H St NW

800

Chinatown Gate

G Pl NW · 700

G Pl NE

Gallery Place
Chinatown

G St NW

G St NW

G St NE · G St NE

Verizon
Center

PAGE
200

Union
Station

Union Station

PAGE
232

1
50

7th St NW · 600

National
Building
Museum

F St NW

Casa
Italiana

F St NW

500

N Capitol St NW

Columbus Memorial

Union Station Dr

Union Station Dr

Judiciary
Square

Madison Al NW
Chews Ct NW
Chews Al NW

Columbus Monument Dr

Massachusetts Ave NE

E St NE

Shakespeare
Theatre

8th St NW · 5th St NW

E St NW

400

4th St NW · 3rd St NW

300

D St NW · 00 · D St NW

Louisiana Ave NE

New Jersey Ave NW

100

Archives-
Navy
Memorial

Indiana Ave NW

United States
Navy Memorial

C St NW

C St NW · 100

John
Marshall
Park

300

Union Station
Plaza

Delaware Ave NE

1st St NE

100

C St NE

1

United
States Navy
Memorial

395

200

Louisiana Ave NW

**VEHICULAR
TRAFFIC
PROHIBITED**

3

9th St NW

Constitution Ave NW

Pennsylvania Ave NW

200

Constitution Ave NW · 100

East Capitol Cir

East Capitol Cir

Capitol Cir NE

Maryland Ave NE

Constitution Ave NE

1st St NE

Madison Dr NW

7th St SW

The Mall

PAGE
164

4th St NW · 600

300

Capitol
Reflecting
Pool

East Capitol Cir

Capitol Cir NE

PAGE
164

United States
Capitol Building

Capitol Driveway NE

Supreme
Court

East Capitol St

Jefferson
Building

Jefferson Dr SW

US Botanic
Garden
Conservatory

PAGE
158

South Capitol Cir SW

Independence Ave SE

1st St SE

Library of
Congress

PAGE
169

Madison
Building

L'Enfant
Plaza

9th St SW

C · Maryland Ave SW

6th St SW

4th St SW

6

Federal
Center SW

C St SW

1st St SW

United States
Botanic Garden

5

C St SW

South Capitol St

New Jersey Ave SE

Capitol
South

C St SE

1st St SE

Pennsylvania Ave SE

Madison
Building

D St SW

Virginia Ave SW

D St SW

D St SW

Washington Ave SW

D St SW · 2nd St SW

D St SE

Ivy St SE

N Carolina Ave SE

School St SW

E St SE · E St SE

Frontage Rd SW

Virginia Ave SW

| 1/4 mile | | .25 km |

Mostly white-collar business by day, Judiciary Square, Union Station, and the Capitol are full of politicians, lawyers, and other Washington DC fat cats. You really can see it all in this part of town: motorcades, suits feasting on steaks during weekday power lunches, credit card-happy consumers, fashion plates, hipsters, and sports fans, all set to go-go beats being pounded out on trash cans.

○ Landmarks

• **Casa Italiana** • 595 3rd St NW
202-638-1348
DC's half-block answer to Little Italy.
• **Chinatown Gate** • H St NW & 7th St NW
Ushers you in for cheap eats and cheaper pottery.
• **Columbus Memorial** •
1st St NE & Massachusetts Ave NE
Look for a big statue and fountain—the one with the carvings.
• **National Building Museum** • 401 F St NW
202-272-2448
Step inside and feel your jaw drop.
• **Shakespeare Theatre** • 450 7th St NW
202-547-1122
Where the Bard shows off.
• **Sixth and I Synagogue** • 600 I St NW
202-408-3100
Stunning, historic temple/event space welcomes all to its intimate sanctuary.
• **Supreme Court of the United States** • 1st St NE
202-479-3211
Bring your favorite protest sign.
• **United States Botanic Garden** • 245 1st St SW
202-225-8333
Flowers of freedom.
• **United States Botanic Garden Conservatory** •
100 Maryland Ave SW
202-225-8333
Relaxing refuge of tropical flora and primeval plants.
• **United States Navy Memorial** •
701 Pennsylvania Ave NW
Bronze reliefs depicting scenes from the Navy's distinguished history.
• **US Library of Congress** •
101 Independence Ave SE
202-707-5000
Lose yourself in letters.

🍸 Nightlife

• **Bar Louie** • 701 7th St NW
202-638-2460
Sandwiches, pizza, and bar food.
• **The Dubliner** • 4 F St NW
202-737-3773
Cozy, classy Irish pub.
• **Fadó Irish Pub** • 808 7th St NW
202-789-0066
Every beer imaginable.
• **Iron Horse Taproom** • 507 7th St NW
202-347-7665
Enormous, foodless "biker" bar with plenty of beer and bourbon.
• **Kelly's Irish Times** • 14 F St NW
202-543-5433
DC's only Irish pub with a swerve'dance club basement.
• **Lucky Strike Lanes** • 701 7th St NW
202-347-1021
Pricey bowling alley, but the martinis come with Pop Rocks.
• **My Brother's Place** • 237 2nd St NW
202-347-1350
Cheap, hole-in-the-wall CUA bar.
• **Poste Moderne Brasserie & Bar** • 555 8th St NW
202-783-6060
Full of fresh food, fresh faces, and fresh bank accounts.
• **RFD Washington** • 810 7th St NW
202-289-2030
Brickskeller's downtown sibling—hundreds of beers.
• **Rocket Bar** • 714 7th St NW
202-628-7665
The home of bar games.
• **Sixth Engine** • 438 Massachusetts Ave NW
202-629-2283
Perfect for after-work imbibing and eating.
• **Tel'veh** • 401 Massachusetts Ave NW
202-758-2929
Wine bar for people who use the word "aficionado."

Map 2

Chinatown / Union Station

8	9	10	11	12
36	7	1	2	3	4
7		6	5	
40				
9				

Restaurants

- **701** • 701 Pennsylvania Ave NW
202-393-0701 • $$$$
Posh food not worth the price.
- **Art and Soul** • 415 New Jersey Ave NW
202-393-7777 • $$$$
Southern hospitality for uptight Washingtonians
- **B. Smith's** • 50 Massachusetts Ave NE
202-289-6188 • $$$$
Creole elegance, jarring in Union Station.
- **Billy Goat Tavern & Grill** • 500 New Jersey Ave NW
202-783-2123 • $
Cheeseburger, cheeseburger, cheeseburger.
- **Bistro Bis** • 15 E St NW
202-661-2700 • $$$$
Pricey, but a solid place for an upscale lunch on the Hill.
- **Bistro Med** • 736 6th St NW
202-393-3300 • $$
Pizza on H St = last nail in Chinatown's coffin.
- **Burma** • 740 6th St NW
202-638-1280 • $$
Green tea leaf salad. We kid you not.
- **Cafe Grande** • 1775 K St NW
202-223-3636 • $
Coffee, espresso, sandwiches, and frozen yogurt near Farragut North metro.
- **Center Café** • 50 Massachusetts Ave NE
202-682-0143 • $$
Enjoy the scenery from the middle of the country's best RR station.
- **Charlie Palmer Steak** • 101 Constitution Ave NW
202-547-8100 • $$$$
Fine wine and world-famous steak—a splurge for wannabe high rollers.
- **Chinatown Express** • 746 6th St NW
202-638-0424 • $$
Watch food preperation from the street and decide for yourself.
- **District Chophouse** • 509 7th St NW
202-347-3434 • $$$$
Impressive roaring '20s atmosphere. Avoid Verizon game night.
- **The Dubliner** • 4 F St NW
202-737-3773 • $$
Hearty Irish pub grub for Washington bureaucracy.

- **Eat First** • 609 H St NW
202-289-1703 • $
Simple, no frills Chinese. Great for pre-theatre.
- **Fadó Irish Pub** • 808 7th St NW
202-789-0066 • $$
Antiquish décor and self-promoting gift shop. Disneyland for alcoholics.
- **Fiola** • 601 Pennsylvania Ave NW
202-628-2888 • $$$
Refined cooking goes rustic in a comforting yet elegant manner.
- **Full Kee** • 509 H St NW
202-371-2233 • $$
Chinatown can be overwhelming. We'll make it easier. Eat here.
- **Graffiato** • 707 6th St NW
202-289-3600 • $$$
Penn Quarter Italian hot spot to see and be seen.
- **Hill Country Barbecue** • 410 7th St NW
202-556-2050 • $$$
Texas style BBQ, brews, and live music.
- **Irish Channel Pub** • 500 H St NW
202-216-0046 • $$
The Irish Pub with Cajun flair.
- **Jaleo** • 480 7th St NW
202-628-7949 • $$$$
The tapas king of DC. Great for first dates.
- **Jerk Chicken Wrap Cart** • 4th St NW & E St NW
$
$5 for jerk chicken, citrus black beans, mango salsa, coconut rice.
- **Johnny's Half Shell** • 400 N Capitol St NW
202-737-0400 • $$$
Best crabcakes in Washington. Friendly barstaff attracts solo diners.
- **Kelly's Irish Times** • 14 F St NW
202-543-5433 • $$
Look to your left. See The Dubliner? Go there.
- **La Tasca** • 722 7th St NW
202-347-9190 • $$
Mexican tapas on a beer budget.
- **Matchbox** • 713 H St NW
202-289-4441 • $$$
Where martinis meet pizza.
- **Mitsitam Café** • Independence Ave SW & 4 St SW
202-633-1000 • $$
Cafeteria featuring American Indian cuisine.
- **Momiji** • 505 H St NW
202-408-8110 • $$
Great sushi. Great happy hour.

Once defined by its ethnic and culinary connections to China, a yuppie influx encouraged by the popularity of the Verizon Center has made Chinatown a haven for mid-career types looking to blow a wad on food, drink, and residence. Eat pizza at Matchbox, tapas at **Jaleo**, sushi at **Momiji**, grab a pint at **The Dubliner**, and an espresso at **Chinatown Coffee** (just don't ask for it over ice).

- **My Brother's Place** • 237 2nd St NW
  202-347-1350 • $$
  A lunchtime hole-in-the-wall.
- **Nando's Peri-Peri** • 819 7th St NW
  202-898-1225 • $$
  One more chain in Chinatown, this time
  Portuguese chicken via South Africa.
- **Oyamel** • 401 7th St NW
  202-628-1005 • $$$$
  Another outfit in Jose Andres's total tapas assault
  on DC.
- **Protein Bar** • 398 7th St NW
  202-621-9574 • $
  Feel good about yourself with their health-con-
  science offerings.
- **Rasika** • 633 D St NW
  202-637-1222 • $$$$
  Pricey, polished Indian.
- **Red Velvet Cupcakery** • 505 7th St NW
  202-347-7895 • $
  Aah! Another attack of the cupcakes!
- **Rosa Mexicano** • 575 7th St NW
  202-783-5522 • $$$$
  Squeeze past the perennial crowds for a pome-
  granate margarita.
- **SEI** • 444 7th St NW
  202-783-7007 • $$$
  Super-slick sushi, complete with glamorous
  cocktails.
- **The Source** • 575 Pennsylvania Ave NW
  202-637-6100 • $$$
  Wolfgang Puck cooks again.
- **Tony Cheng's Mongolian Restaurant** •
  619 H St NW
  202-842-8669 • $$
  No reason to dine here. Upstairs is where you want
  to be.
- **Tony Cheng's Seafood Restaurant** • 619 H St NW
  202-371-8669 • $$
  Overlook gaudy décor and enjoy best Chinese
  Washington offers.
- **Wok and Roll** • 604 H St NW
  202-347-4656 • $$
  Japanese and Chinese cuisine AND karaoke.
- **YO! Sushi** • 50 Massachusetts Ave NE
  202-408-1716 • $$
  Trendy, colorful, self-service sushi bar.
- **Zengo** • 781 7th St NW
  202-393-2929 • $$$
  Sleek Asian-Latin fusion.

Shopping

- **Alamo Flags Company** • 50 Massachusetts Ave NE
  202-842-3524
  Don't bring matches.
- **Appalachian Spring** • 50 Massachusetts Ave NE
  202-682-0505
  Pottery, jewelry, and other unique knick-knacks.
- **Aveda Institute** • 713 7th St NW
  202-824-1624
  Beauty on a budget for the willing guinea pig.
- **Bed Bath and Beyond** • 709 7th St NW
  202-628-0002
  Moderately priced home furnishings.
- **Chinatown Coffee Co.** • 475 H St NW
  202-559-7656
  Chinatown indie artisanal coffee.
- **Comfort One Shoes** • 50 Massachusetts Ave NE
  202-898-2430
  Beyond Birkenstocks.
- **Godiva Chocolatier** • 50 Massachusetts Ave NE
  202-289-3662
  Indulge.
- **LOFT** • 707 7th St NW
  202-628-1224
  Moderately priced womenswear shop.
- **Pua** • 701 Pennsylvania Ave NW
  202-347-4543
  Locally designed women's clothing.
- **Radio Shack** • 732 7th St NW
  202-638-5689
  Around the corner from the Spy Museum; not a
  coincidence.
- **Red Velvet Cupcakery** • 505 7th St NW
  202-347-7895
  Frosting is the best part.
- **Smithsonian National Air and Space Museum
  Store** • Independence Ave SW & 6th St SW
  202-633-4510
  Great plane-related stuff for the kids (or for you).
- **TangySweet** • 675 E St NW
  202-347-7893
  Green tea and other exotic flavors.
- **Urban Outfitters** • 737 7th St NW
  202-737-0259
  Slightly hipper than its Georgetown cousin.

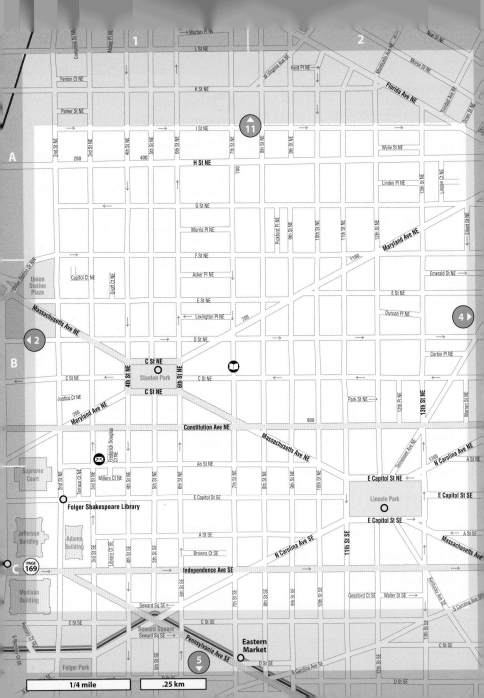

Few make it to the top, and when you get there, you're broke—unless you're a lobbyist. This area is home to an eclectic collection of folks and the burgeoning district known as Atlas. Here international moguls and hill staffers mix with rowdy interns and working stiffs to create an atmosphere that is uniquely DC. The controlling political party may change, but the charm of this historic neighborhood never will.

○ Landmarks

- **Folger Shakespeare Library** • 201 E Capitol St SE
  202-544-4600
  To go or not to go?
- **Lincoln Park** • E Capitol St SE
  High ratio of cute dogs per square foot.
- **Stanton Park** • C St NE & Maryland Ave NE
  Contemplate your freedom in a traffic circle.

▼ Nightlife

- **The 201 Bar** • 201 Massachusetts Ave NE
  202-544-5201
  Retro martini bar.
- **The Big Board** • 421 H St NE
  202-543-3630
  Beer prices drop with patron orders. And you thought PBR couldn't get any cheaper.
- **Capitol Lounge** • 229 Pennsylvania Ave SE
  202-547-2098
  Hill hangout, do-it-yourself Bloody Mary bar.
- **Cusbah** • 1128 H St NE
  202-506-1504
- **Granville Moore's** • 1238 H St NE
  202-399-2546
  Belgian Beers in the heart of DC
- **H Street Country Club** • 1335 H St NE
  202-399-4722
  Indoor mini golf with a DC theme, plus pool and skee-ball.
- **Pour House** • 319 Pennsylvania Ave SE
  202-546-0779
  Steelers fans and Irish accents.
- **The Pug** • 1234 H St NE
  202-388-8554
  Atlas District neighborhood bar.
- **Rock & Roll Hotel** • 1353 H St NE
  202-388-7625
  The Hill's indie rock hangout.
- **Sonoma** • 223 Pennsylvania Ave SE
  202-544-8088
  Sip wine in the upstairs lounge by the fireplace.
- **Top of the Hill** • 319 Pennsylvania Ave SE
  202-546-7782
  1 building=3 bars. This has pool and red vinyl.
- **TruOrleans** • 400 H St NE
  202-290-1244
- **Tune Inn** • 331 Pennsylvania Ave SE
  202-543-2725
  Dive bar option for an older Hill crowd.
- **Vendetta** • 1212 H St NE
  202-399-3201
  Play Bocce while drinking an Aperol Spritz and noshing on an antipasto plate. Perfetto!

Map

Map

7
40
9
6 5

Restaurants

- **Bearnaise** • 215 Pennsylvania Ave SE
  202-450-4800 • $$$
  Chef Spike does it again, this time a restaurant devoted to steak frites.
- **Bistro Cacao** • 320 Massachusetts Ave NE
  202-546-4737 • $$$$
  Romantic little Hill spot.
- **Boundary Road** • 414 H St NE
  202-450-3265 • $$$
  Obama-approved Americana fare and fancy cocktails; check out the chandelier.
- **Café Berlin** • 322 Massachusetts Ave NE
  202-543-7656 • $$
  For all your Oktoberfest needs.
- **Cusbah** • 1128 H St NE
  202-506-1504 • $$
  If you like your curry "hot" visit this "Spice Bar" in the Atlas District.
- **Ethiopic** • 401 H St NE
  202-675-2066 • $
  "Little Ethiopia" expands to the Atlas District.
- **Good Stuff Eatery** • 303 Pennsylvania Ave SE
  202-543-8222 • $
  Hickory burgers and rosemary fries.
- **H & Pizza** • 1118 H St NE
  202-733-1285 • $$
  Pizza. Plain and simple.
- **Horace & Dickie's** • 809 12th St NE
  202-397-6040 • $
  Standing in line around the block is worth the wait for this fried fish
- **Kenny's Smokehouse** • 732 Maryland Ave NE
  202-547-4553 • $
  BBQ with oodles of sides.
- **La Loma Mexican Restaurant** • 316 Massachusetts Ave NE
  202-548-2550 • $$
  They make you pay for refills. Enough said.

- **The Liberty Tree** • 1016 H St NE
  202-396-8733 • $$
  Masshole cuisine: clam chowder and fried Chatham cod.
- **Pete's Diner** • 212 2nd St SE
  202-544-7335 • $
  With a completely Asian staff, you wonder who "Pete" is.
- **Shawafel** • 1322 H St NE
  202-388-7676 • $
  Authentic Lebanese falafel and shawarma.
- **Smith Commons** • 1245 H St NE
  202-396-0038 • $$$
  Great food. Great beer. Great cocktails.
- **Sonoma** • 223 Pennsylvania Ave SE
  202-544-8088 • $$$
  40 wines by the glass.
- **Star and Shamrock** • 1341 H St NE
  202-388-3833 • $$
  Half Irish pub, half Jewish deli. Go figure.
- **Sticky Rice** • 1224 H St NE
  202-397-7655 • $
  A sushi bar with a kids menu.
- **Toki Underground** • 1234 H St NE
  202-388-3086 • $$
  Super-hip Taiwanese dumplings and ramen; almost always packed.
- **TruOrleans** • 400 H St NE
  202-290-1244 • $$$
  Hurricanes, gumbo and a roof-deck.
- **Union Pub** • 201 Massachusetts Ave NE
  202-546-7200 • $$
  Where everybody wants important Hill-types to know their name.
- **Vendetta** • 1212 H St NE
  202-399-3201 • $$
- **Zest** • 735 8th St NE
  202-544-7171 • $
  Family-friendly American bistro brings more yuppie fare to Barracks Row.

Wine connoisseurs dine at **Sonoma**, the hip crowd catches a show at the **Rock & Roll Hotel**, Hill staffers drink martinis at **The 201 Bar**, and interns take advantage of happy hour at **Capitol Lounge**. Don't underestimate a night out on the Hill. Here the best places to eat and drink are the real hot-button issues, because those who work hard, play hard, too.

🛍 Shopping

- **Capitol Hill Poultry** • 255 7th St SE
  202-544-4435
  Happy chickens go to Eastern Market.
- **Dangerously Delicious Pies** • 1339 H St NE
  202-398-7437
  Pies to die for.

- **Hunted House** • 510 H St NE
  202-549-7493
  Art-deco second-hand furnishings.
- **Jonathan Blum Art** • 225 7th St SE
  240-419-4151
  Doggy and kitty art at Eastern Market.

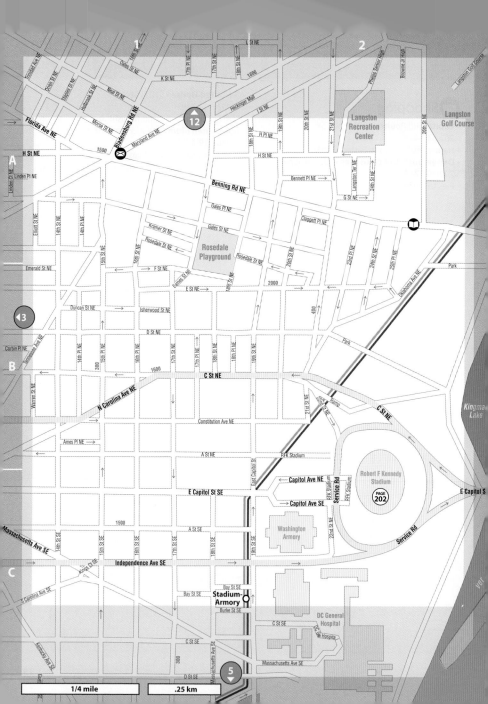

It used to be the home of the Skins, then the home of the Nats, and now DC United soccer fans finally have a stadium of their own. Feel free to join in for tailgating, samba music, and super-fan "black outs." This section of the Hill is less bourgie than Eastern Market, but still brims with neighborhood pride.

Nightlife

- **The Argonaut** • 1433 H St NE
  202-250-3660
  Atlas District's neighborhood tavern.

Restaurants

- **Biergartenhaus** • 1355 H St NE
  202-388-4085 • $$
  Brats, wheat beers, accordions = H Street Oktoberfest.
- **H Street Coffeehouse & Cafe** • 1359 H St NE
  $
  The Atlas District's coffee house.

Map 5 · **Southeast / Anacostia**

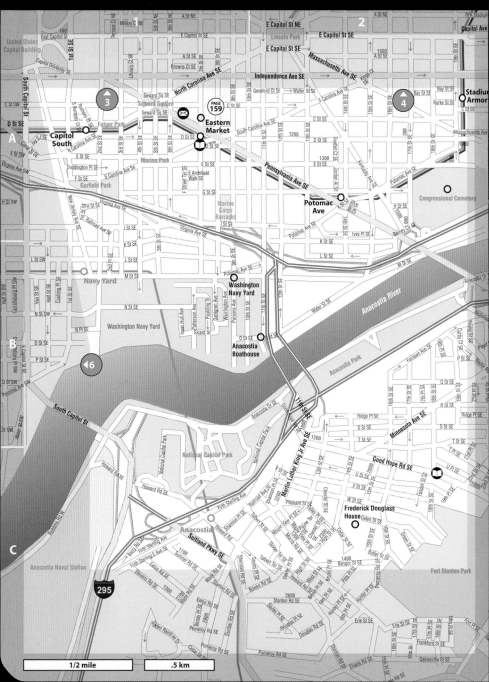

N

United States Capitol Building

East Capitol St

Capitol Driveway SE

A St SE

Seward Sq SE

Seward Square

Folger Park

Capitol South

Eastern Market

PAGE 159

Duddington Pl SE

Garfield Park

Marion Park

E Archibald Walk SE

Marine Corps Barracks

Pennsylvania Ave SE

Potomac Ave

Congressional Cemetery

Navy Yard

Washington Navy Yard

Washington Navy Yard

Anacostia Boathouse

Anacostia River

Anacostia Park

South Capitol St

National Capital Park

National Capital Park

Minnesota Ave SE

Good Hope Rd SE

Frederick Douglass House

Anacostia

Suitland Pkwy SE

Anacostia Naval Station

295

Fort Stanton Park

Stadium Armor

E Capitol St NE

E Capitol St SE

Lincoln Park

Massachusetts Ave SE

Independence Ave SE

North Carolina Ave SE

3

4

2

6

1/2 mile   .5 km

A microcosm of America itself, here you'll find life snippets ranging from urban decay to disturbin' decadence, with a splash of semi-suburban simplicity a stone's skip away from Anacostia. **Congressional Cemetery** is a lesser-known jewel in a city crowned with famous landmarks, where you can visit the final resting places of many forgotten congressmen from previous centuries and enjoy views of the river.

○ Landmarks

- **Anacostia Boathouse** • 1900 M St SE
  Take the dirty plunge.
- **Congressional Cemetery** • 1801 E St SE
  202-543-0539
  Individual graves, shared conditions.
- **Eastern Market** • 225 7th St SE
  202-698-5253
  Apples and art. Back in business after '07 fire.
- **Frederick Douglass House** • 1411 W St SE
  202-426-5951
  A man who showed up his neighborhood and his country.
- **Washington Navy Yard** • M St SE & 9th St SE
  202-433-4882
  Haven for men in tighty whites.

Nightlife

- **18th Amendment** • 613 Pennsylvania Ave SE
  202-543-3622
  Happy hour specials, live music and football. What more could you need?
- **Mr. Henry's** • 601 Pennsylvania Ave SE
  202-546-8412
  A spot for jazz lovers.
- **Pacifico Cantina** • 514 8th St SE
  202-507-8143
- **Remingtons** • 639 Pennsylvania Ave SE
  202-543-3113
  Country-Western gay bar.
- **Tortilla Coast** • 400 1st St SE
  202-546-6768
  Different special every night.
- **Trusty's** • 1420 Pennsylvania Ave SE
  202-547-1010
  Hole-in-the-wall with board games.
- **Tunnicliff's Tavern** • 222 7th St SE
  202-544-5680
  Cheers-esque.
- **The Ugly Mug** • 723 8th St SE
  202-547-8459
  TVs, pool, miniburgers, and beer.

Map

7 6 5
40
9

🍴 Restaurants

- **Banana Café & Piano Bar** • 500 8th St SE
  202-543-5906 • $$$
  Democrat-friendly Hill cabana.
- **Bistro La Bonne** • 1340 U St SE
  202-758-3413 • $$$
  Goodbye, Axis. Hello, French bistro.
- **Bluejacket** • 300 Tingey St SE
  $$$
  The Navy Yard's own brewery and tavern.
- **Cava Mezze** • 527 8th St SE
  202-543-9090 • $$
  Greek mezedes originally from Rockville.
- **DC-3** • 423 8th St SE
  202-546-1935 • $
  Creative Capitol Hill hot dogs (kimchi?!) and great fried pickles.
- **La Plaza** • 629 Pennsylvania Ave SE
  202-546-9512 • $$
  Pinatas, fried yucca, smooth margaritas, and friendly owner/chef Henry.
- **Matchbox** • 521 8th St SE
  202-548-0369 • $$$
  Where martinis meet pizza, now on Capitol Hill too.
- **Montmartre** • 327 7th St SE
  202-544-1244 • $$$$
  Comfortable French bistro.
- **The Old Siam** • 406 8th St SE
  202-544-7426 • $$
  Standard Thai favorites on the Hill. Bonus: patio seating.
- **Pacifico Cantina** • 514 8th St SE
  202-507-8143 • $$
  Fresh Mexican and a fresh roof deck.
- **Pizza Boli's** • 417 8th St SE
  202-546-2900 • $
  Cheap, gargantuan pizza.
- **The Pretzel Bakery** • 340 15th St SE
  202-251-0953 • $
  Fresh Philly-style pretzels and mustard.
- **Seventh Hill** • 327 7th St SE
  202-544-1911 • $
  Thin-crust pies with a French twist, from the owners of Montmartre.
- **Ted's Bulletin** • 505 8th St SE
  202-544-8337 • $$
  Throwback 1920s Americana comfort food.
- **Tortilla Coast** • 400 1st St SE
  202-546-6768 • $
  Favorite Hill non-power lunch spot.
- **We, The Pizza** • 305 Pennsylvania Ave SE
  202-544-4008 • $$
  Top Chef contestant Spike adds pizza, next door to Good Stuff's burgers.

Eighth Street (Barracks Row) is a nightlife epicenter that offers a variety of restaurants, bars, and a smattering of live music options. Check out **Eastern Market** on the weekends for arts and crafts outside and a mind-boggling selection of sausages inside. Feeling adventurous? Explore Anacostia and see the **Frederick Douglass House.**

Map 5

🛍️Shopping

- **AM Wine Shoppe** • 2122 18th St NW
  202-506-2248
  Wines, cured meats and specialty cheeses.
  Discounts for 20009 residents.
- **Capitol Hill Books** • 657 C St SE
  202-544-1621
  Plenty of page-turners.
- **Capitol Hill Sporting Goods & Apparel** •
  727 8th St SE
  202-546-8078
  Better believe it's a DC THANG.

- **Eastern Market** • 225 7th St SE
  202-698-5253
  Open-air stalls and weekend flea market. Back in business after '07 fire.
- **Greenworks Florist** • 1455 Pennsylvania Ave SE
  202-393-2142
  Modern arrangements for myriad occasions.
- **Harris Teeter** • 1350 Potomac Ave SE
  202-543-1040
  Teeter prevails where Lee failed.
- **Hill's Kitchen** • 713 D St SE
  202-543-1997
  Kitchen boutique sells octopus whisks and Eat, Pray, Love.
- **Woven History & Silk Road** • 311 7th St SE
  202-543-1705
  Visit Afghanistan without the war hassle.

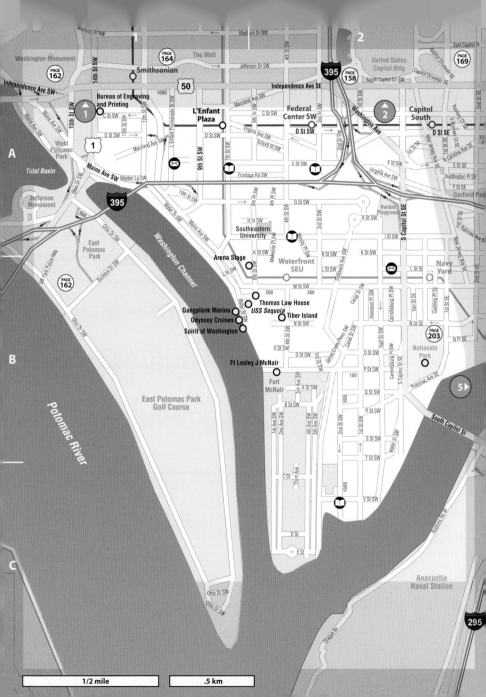

Once a relatively quiet section of town known for some of DC's funkiest residential architecture, that all changed when **Nationals Park** opened. DC's baseball stadium is the real deal---great views, friendly atmosphere, and it's even got a Ben's Chili Bowl! But as exciting as that is, much of this area is still a construction zone, with luxury condos going up faster than you can say "mixed use urban planning."

○ Landmarks

- **Arena Stage** • 1101 6th St SW
  202-488-3300
  Great theater.
- **Bureau of Engraving and Printing** •
  14th St SW & C St SW
  202-874-8888
  Where to get your dead presidents.
- **Fort Lesley J. McNair** • 4th St SW & P St SW
  For the Civil War buffs.
- **Gangplank** • 600 Water St SW
  202-554-5000
  A Washington Channel neighborhood of boat-dwellers.
- **Nationals Park** • 1500 South Capitol St SE
  202-547-9077
  Deep, I don't think it's playable: Parking garage!
- **Odyssey Cruises** • N Water St & W 6th Ave
  888-741-0281
  Dining and dancing on the Potomac river.
- **Spirit of Washington** • 6th St SW & Water St SW
  202-484-2320
  Experience Washington by boat.
- **Thomas Law House** • 1252 6th St SW
  Impressive house, not open to the public.
- **Tiber Island** • 429 N St SW
  202-554-4844
  Looking for an apartment?
- **USS Sequoia** • Maine Ave SW & 6th St SW
  202-333-0011
  Rent it when the VP isn't in the mood to play Mr. Howell.

🍸 Nightlife

- **Cantina Marina** • 600 Water St SW
  202-554-8396
  Ordering advice: avoid the cantina; go with the marina.
- **Half Street Fairgrounds** • 1299 Half St SE
  202-646-0045
  Pretend you're a Nationals relief pitcher and get blitz.

🍴 Restaurants

- **Cantina Marina** • 600 Water St SW
  202-554-8396 • $$
  Cantina Marina-Island Vacation in the City.
- **CityZen** • 1330 Maryland Ave SW
  202-787-6148 • $$$$$
  The most expensive place you might dine
- **Jenny's Asian Fusion** • 1000 Water St SW
  202-554-2202 • $$$
  Good food but depressing atmosphere, regardless of the water view
- **Justin's Café** • 1025 1st St SE
  202-692-1009 • $
  "Fast casual" food and fancy drinks, near the ballpark.
- **Phillip's Seafood** • 900 Water St SW
  202-488-8515 • $$$
  Fresh Atlantic fish not worth pathetic portions and lousy service.
- **The Pier 7** • 650 Water St SW
  202-554-2500 • $$
  Showy waterfront seafood.
- **Sou'Wester** • 1330 Maryland Ave SW
  202-787-6148 • $$$
  Homestyle Southern food replace Cafe MoZu at the Mandarin Oriental.

🛍 Shopping

- **Maine Avenue Fish Market** • 1100 Maine Ave SW
  202-484-2722
  Fresh off the boat.
- **Safeway** • 1100 4th St SW
  202-554-9155
  Swank newly renovated store is a welcome addition to SW.

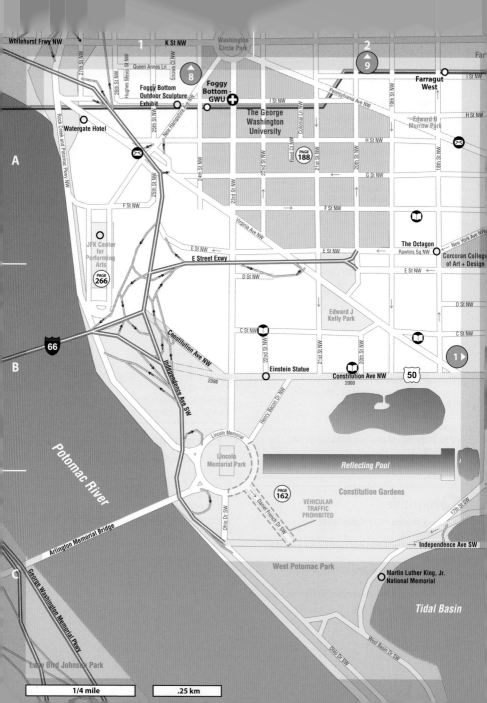

Map 7

This neighborhood is populated by a mix of George Washington University students, government employees, and "old money" Washingtonians. Nevertheless, there isn't much entertainment, but at least there's a plethora of high-end restaurants for those Federal employees looking to impress dignitaries.

○ Landmarks

- **Einstein Statue** •
  Constitution Ave NW & 22nd St NW
  At his rumpled best.
- **Foggy Bottom Outdoor Sculpture Exhibit** •
  New Hampshire Ave NW
  Everyone likes sculptures.
- **Kennedy Center** • 2700 F St NW
  202-467-4600
  High-brow culture.
- **Martin Luther King, Jr. National Memorial** •
  1964 Independence Ave SW
  MLK emerges from the Stone of Hope at Tidal Basin.
- **The Octagon** • 1799 New York Ave NW
  202-626-7439
  Peculiar floor plan.
- **The Watergate Hotel** • 2650 Virginia Ave NW
  202-965-2300
  Location of the most infamous Washington scandal yet; still a great design.

Nightlife

- **The Exchange** • 1719 G St NW
  202-393-4690
  DC's oldest saloon just steps from the White House.
- **Froggy Bottom Pub** • 2021 K St NW
  202-338-3000
  GW student hangout.
- **Funxion / Dysfunxion** • 1309 F St NW
  202-386-9466
  Funxion = daytime smoothies. DysFunxion = nighttime cocktails.
- **Nick's Riverside Grill** • 3050 K St NW
  202-342-3535
  Mediocre food, excellent view, copious seagulls.

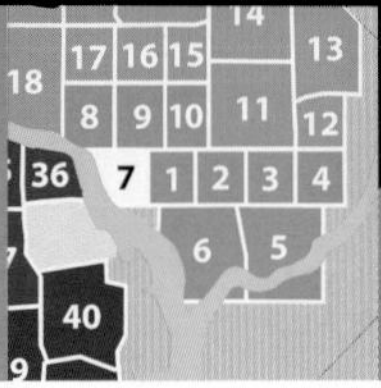

Map 7

Foggy Bottom

🍴 Restaurants

- **Bread Line** • 1751 Pennsylvania Ave NW
  202-822-8900 • $$
  Screw South Beach if it means you can't eat here.
  (Lunch only.)
- **Cabanas** • 3000 K St NW
  202-944-4242 • $$
  Upscale Latin ceviches, ensalatas, ad nauseum.
- **DISH + drinks** • 924 25th St NW
  202-383-8707 • $$$$
  Southern infusion for inquisitive palates.
- **Finemondo** • 1319 F St NW
  202-737-3100 • $
  Casual, Italian country cooking.
- **Founding Farmers** • 1924 Pennsylvania Ave NW
  202-822-8783 • $$$
  Ingredient-driven, farmer-owned farm-to-table
  cuisine.
- **Kaz Sushi Bistro** • 1915 I St NW
  202-530-5500 • $$$
  Impress your date by ordering the *omasake*.
- **La Taberna Del Alabardero** • 1776 I St NW
  202-429-2200 • $$$$
  Wide-open menu dares you to be bold.
- **Lindy's Red Lion** • 2040 I St NW
  202-466-6000 • $
  Burgers on GW campus; so good, so collegiate.
  Avoid the crowd by ordering to-go.
- **Nick's Riverside Grill** • 3050 K St NW
  202-342-3535 • $$$
  Mediocre food, excellent view, copious seagulls.
- **Notti Bianche** • 824 New Hampshire Ave NW
  202-298-8085 • $$$$
  Full or half portion pasta dishes perfect for lunch.
- **Pret a Manger** • 1825 I St NW
  202-828-6971 • $
  UK stronghold crosses the pond.
- **Primi Piatti** • 2013 I St NW
  202-223-3600 • $$$$
  Eat like an Italian, but you'll want to dress up like
  one too.
- **Roof Terrace** • 2700 F St NW
  202-416-8555 • $$$$
  Book Sunday brunch instead of fighting theater-
  goers for the last split of wine.
- **Roti** • 1747 Pennsylvania Ave NW
  202-466-7684 • $
  Mediterannean grill with roti, falafel, kabob.

The mix of upscale and college dives is obvious. **Notti Bianche** and **DISH + drinks** are reserved for the power players and parents visiting GW students. If you forgot your jacket, duck into a gyro joint, or head for the nearest neon window to mingle with the co-ed crowd. And for weekend brunches, you can't beat **Founding Farmers**.

Shopping

• **Peruvian Connection** • 950 F St NW
202-737-4405
World fashions for the modern woman.

• **Whole Foods Market** • 2201 Eye St NW
202-296-1660
Maybe we can apply its meat rating system to Congress…

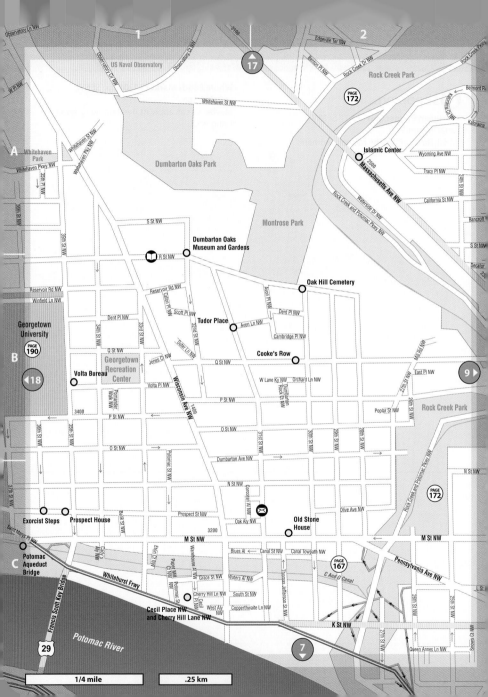

Precious townhouses and stately mansions, cobblestone streets and garden tours—
yes, this is very Washington indeed. The peons cluck though the main drags of M and
Wisconsin searching for trendy outfits and the traffic is jam-packed by car and foot day
and night. Leave your heels at home as the cobblestones will gobble them right up.

○ Landmarks

- *Exorcist* **Steps** • 3600 Prospect St NW
  Watch your balance and LOOK UP! LOOK UP!
- **Cecil Place NW and Cherry Hill Lane NW** •
  Cecil Pl NW & Cherry Hill Ln NW
  Pretty, secluded street of hundred-year-old homes.
- **Cooke's Row** • 3007 Q St NW
  Romantic row.
- **Dumbarton Oaks Museum and Gardens** •
  1703 32nd St NW
  202-339-6401
  An absolute treasure.
- **Islamic Center** • 2551 Massachusetts Ave NW
  202-332-8343
  Oldest Islamic house of worship in the city.

- **Oak Hill Cemetery** • 3001 R St NW
  202-337-2835
  Old and gothic.
- **Old Stone House** • 3051 M St NW
  202-895-6070
  Old. And Stone. It's the oldest building this town's
  got.
- **Potomac Aqueduct Bridge** • 3530 Water St NW
  Oasis in Georgetown.
- **Prospect House** • 3508 Prospect St NW
  Spectacular view of the Potomac.
- **Tudor Place** • 1644 31st St NW
  202-965-0400
  Bring a picnic.
- **Volta Bureau** • 1537 35th St NW
  202-337-5220
  HQ of the Alexander Graham Bell Association for
  the Deaf.

Map

7
6 5
40
9

Nightlife

- **51st State Tavern** • 2512 L St NW
  202-625-2444
  An unpretentious watering hole, plus 10-cent wings on Tuesdays.
- **A Bar + Kitchen** • 2500 Pennsylvania Ave NW
  202-333-8060
  Chic scene-y hotel lounge in Georgetown with small plates and outdoor seating.
- **Blues Alley** • 1073 Wisconsin Ave NW
  202-337-4141
  THE place for live jazz.
- **Capitol Prague** • 3277 M St NW
  202-333-0434
- **Chadwicks** • 3205 K St NW
  202-333-2565
  Georgetown dive. (Read: nicer than half the bars in DC.)
- **Clyde's** • 3236 M St NW
  202-333-9180
  Reliable wood-themed bar.
- **Degrees Bistro** • 3100 South Street NW
  202-912-4100
  Pretty ritzy.
- **L2 Lounge** • 3315 Cady's Alley NW
  202-965-2001
  A members preferred sweet spot catering to the elite.
- **Martin's Tavern** • 1264 Wisconsin Ave NW
  202-333-7370
  Gin-and-tonic crowd.
- **Maté** • 3101 K St NW
  202-333-2006
  Posh Latin hangout on K Street.
- **Modern** • 3287 M St NW
  202-338-7027
  If you're smart, keep walking.
- **Mr. Smith's** • 3104 M St NW
  202-333-3104
  WASPs invade hole-in-the wall bar.
- **Old Glory** • 3139 M St NW
  202-337-3406
  Great for daytime drinking.
- **Paper Moon** • 1073 31st St NW
  202-965-6666
  Italian restaurant by day and sometimes dance place by night.

- **Rhino Bar & Pumphouse** • 3295 M St NW
  202-333-3150
  Cheap beer, dance music, and pool tables.
- **Sequoia** • 3000 K St NW
  202-944-4200
  Where type As meet before getting married and divorced.
- **The Tombs** • 1226 36th St NW
  202-337-6668
  Georgetown institution.

Restaurants

- **1789** • 1226 36th St NW
  202-965-1789 • $$$$
  1789: Age of the patrons, or total for your bill?
- **Bandolero** • 3241 M St NW
  202-625-4488 • $$
  Top Chef-winner Mike Isabella's trendy, star-powered, gothic Mexican eatery.
- **Bangkok Joe's** • 3000 K St NW
  202-333-4422 • $$$$
  Chinese at a quick lunch spot
- **Birreria Paradiso** • 3282 M St NW
  202-337-1245 • $$
  Indulge in some beer snobbery. And pizza.
- **Bistrot Lepic** • 1736 Wisconsin Ave NW
  202-333-0111 • $$$
  Wine bar and lounge with a French flair
- **Booeymonger** • 3265 Prospect St NW
  202-333-4810 • $$
  Serious about mediocre sandwiches.
- **Café Bonaparte** • 1522 Wisconsin Ave NW
  202-333-8830 • $
  Fine French-onion soup.
- **Café Divan** • 1834 Wisconsin Ave NW
  202-338-1747 • $$$
  It's Turkish, so anything with the word "Kebab" is safe bet.
- **Café La Ruche** • 1039 31st St NW
  202-965-2684 • $$
  Great food for great prices.
- **Café Milano** • 3251 Prospect St NW
  202-333-6183 • $$$$
  Would you care for a celebrity sighting with your tiramisu?

Hands down, the most comprehensive shopping strip in the city is here. Once the sun sets, the human traffic jams continue as Georgetown plays host to a predominantly preppy and collar-popping nightlife scene. **Rhino Bar**, **Old Glory**, and **The Tombs** are college kid madness. **Blues Alley** and **Maté** are hot spots. And **Morton's**, **1789**, and **Café Milano** will set you back a few hundred each.

- **Café Romeo's** • 2132 Wisconsin Ave NW
  202-337-1111 • $
  Most college kids order Domino's; Georgetown kids order Romeo's.
- **Capitol Prague** • 3277 M St NW
  202-333-0434 • $$$
  Your only DC destination for Czech beer and food.
- **Chadwicks** • 3205 K St NW
  202-333-2565 • $$
  Go strictly for a burger.
- **Ching Ching Cha** • 1063 Wisconsin Ave NW
  202-333-8288 • $$
  Tea, dumplings.
- **Clyde's** • 3236 M St NW
  202-333-9180 • $$$
  Famous Georgetown saloon made less notable through suburban franchising.
- **Crisp & Juicy** • 4533 Wisconsin Ave NW
  202-966-1222 • $
  Succulent Peruvian-roasted chicken spices up Tenleytown.
- **Degrees Bistro** • 3100 South Street NW
  202-912-4100 • $$$$
  Italian-American in the deco Ritz-Carlton hotel.
- **Georgetown Cupcake** • 3301 M St NW
  202-333-8448 • $
  Mediocre cupcakes with ridiculous frostings
- **HomeMade Pizza Co.** •
  4857 Massachusetts Ave NW
  202-966-1600 • $
  Take-out pizza for when you want to pretend you cooked.
- **Il Canale** • 1063 31st St NW
  202-337-4444 • $$
  Neapolitan pies canal-side in Georgetown.
- **J. Paul's** • 3218 M St NW
  202-333-3450 • $$$
  Wanna feel like a pompous Georgetown loudmouth? It's kinda fun!
- **La Chaumiere** • 2813 M St NW
  202-338-1784 • $$$
  Mon Dieu! Are we in Georgetown or Paris?
- **Martin's Tavern** • 1264 Wisconsin Ave NW
  202-333-7370 • $$$
  Cubbyholed tables add flair to this old-school saloon.

- **Morton's the Steakhouse** • 3251 Prospect St NW
  202-342-6258 • $$$$
  Steaks a la carte will make converts out of vegetarians.
- **Mr. Smith's** • 3104 M St NW
  202-333-3104 • $$$
  Mr. Smith, you have an ordinary name and an ordinary restaurant.
- **Old Glory** • 3139 M St NW
  202-337-3406 • $$
  Southeast-style BBQ, with hoppin' john on the side.
- **Peacock Cafe** • 3251 Prospect St NW
  202-625-2740 • $$
  "Contemporary"
- **Pie Sisters** • 3423 M St NW
  202-338-7437 • $
  Who needs a cupcake when you can have pie!
- **Puro Cafe** • 1529 Wisconsin Ave NW
  202-787-1937 • $
  Be Bold…Be Hot…Be Calm…Be Branded…Be Georgetown.
- **Sea Catch Restaurant & Raw Bar** •
  1054 31st St NW
  202-337-8855 • $$$$
  Fresh and raw seafood on the C&O Canal.
- **Sequoia** • 3000 K St NW
  202-944-4200 • $$$$
  A Georgetown see-and-be-seen hotspot.
- **Smith Point** • 1338 Wisconsin Ave NW
  202-244-0592 • $$$
  Pretend-pretentious.
- **Sweetgreen** • 3333 M St NW
  202-337-9338 • $
  Old Little Tavern space, fast food becomes fresh and gourmet salads.
- **Tackle Box** • 3245 M St NW
  202-337-8269 • $$$
  Top-notch seafood dishes. And eco-friendly too!
- **The Tombs** • 1226 36th St NW
  202-337-6668 • $$
  An underground GU favorite.
- **Wisemiller's Grocery & Deli** • 1236 36th St NW
  202-333-8254 • $
  Two words: Chicken Madness.
- **Wisey's** • 1440 Wisconsin Ave NW
  202-333-4122 • $
  Affordable, yummy food in Georgetown!

Map
40
7 6 5
9

🛍 Shopping

- **Abercrombie & Fitch** • 1208 Wisconsin Ave NW
  202-333-1566
  Quintessemtial college kids' clothes.
- **Anthropologie** • 3222 M St NW
  202-337-1363
  Pretty, super-feminine women's clothing.
- **Apple** • 1229 Wisconsin Ave NW
  202-572-1460
  iParadise for Mac fanatics.
- **Banana Republic** • 3200 M St NW
  202-333-2554
  It is what it is.
- **BCBGMAXAZRIA** • 3210 M St NW
  202-333-2224
  B well-dressed.
- **Blue Mercury** • 3059 M St NW
  202-965-1300
  Spa on premises.
- **BoConcept** • 3342 M St NW
  202-333-5656
  Modern décor.
- **CUSP** • 3030 M St NW
  202-625-0893
  Max out your credit card with one dress.
- **Dean & DeLuca** • 3276 M St NW
  202-342-2500
  Dean and delicious.
- **Design Within Reach** • 3306 M St NW
  202-339-9480
  Furniture showroom.
- **Diesel** • 3033 M St NW
  202-747-7855
  Hip designer jeans.
- **Dolcezza** • 1560 Wisconsin Ave NW
  202-333-4646
  Sleek Argentinian gelato nook.
- **Georgetown Running Company** • 3401 M St NW
  202-337-8626
  Gear up for a race.

- **Georgetown Tobacco** • 3144 M St NW
  202-338-5100
  Celebrate smoke.
- **Georgetown Wine & Spirits** • 2701 P St NW
  202-338-5500
  Gorgeous wine store; great selection, friendly
  owners.
- **H&M** • 3222 M St NW
  855-466-7467
  Cheap Euro clothes for the college crowd.
- **Hu's Shoes** • 3005 M St NW
  202-342-0202
  Sexy and sexier.
- **Hu's Wear** • 2906 M St NW
  202-342-2020
  Popular Hu's Shoes spawns nearby clothing
  boutique.
- **Illuminations** • 3323 Cady's Aly NW
  202-965-4888
  Hot flashes.
- **Intermix** • 3300 M St NW
  202-298-8080
  Cutting-edge women's designer fashions.
- **J. Chocolatier** • 1039 33rd St NW
  202-333-4111
  A Georgetown rowhouse chock full of truffles.
- **J. Crew** • 3222 M St NW
  202-965-4090
  Inoffensive yuppie casual gear.
- **J. McLaughlin** • 3278 M St NW
  202-333-4333
  Jet-setting to the Hamptons?
- **Jaryam** • 1631 Wisconsin Ave NW
  202-333-6886
  Lacy lingerie.
- **Jinx Proof Tattoo** • 3285 M St NW
  202-337-5469
  The best place in town to get inked.
- **Jonathan Adler Georgetown** •
  1267 Wisconsin Ave NW
  202-965-1416
  Eclectic furniture and housewares from the A-List
  designer.

Nothing beats watching million-dollar yachts pulling up to the pier at **Seqouia** while you sip outdoor drinks. If you're feeling hipsterific, try Top Chef Mike Isabella's goth-like Mexican restaurant, **Bandolero**. If you're shopping, there's **Kate Spade**, mainstream mainstay **Banana Republic**, and trendy boutiques like **Sherman Pickey**. For the best of the chains, try the palatial three-story **Anthropologie**.

- **Kate Spade** • 3061 M St NW
202-333-8302
Preppy polish.
- **Keith Lipert Gallery** • 2922 M St NW
202-965-9736
Unique global gifts.
- **Lush** • 3066 M St NW
202-333-6950
Handmade soap and cosmetics; stratospheric prices.
- **MAC** • 1201 G St NW
202-628-6661
Sephora's main rival in the cosmetics biz.
- **Marvelous Market** • 3217 P St NW
202-333-2591
Try the blueberry muffins.
- **The Old Print Gallery** • 1220 31st St NW
202-965-1818
The name says it all.
- **Paper Source** • 3019 M St NW
202-298-5545
Heaven for scrapbookers and greeting card seekers alike.
- **Papyrus** • 1300 Wisconsin Ave NW
202-337-0720
Scrapbook materials, stationery, journals, wedding invitations…
- **Patisserie Poupon** • 1645 Wisconsin Ave NW
202-342-3248
Old-world-style bonbons.
- **The Phoenix** • 1514 Wisconsin Ave NW
202-338-4404
Georgetown stalwart boutique of Mexican artisanal wares.
- **Ralph Lauren Polo Shop** •
1245 Wisconsin Ave NW
202-965-0905
Where Dad should shop, but probably doesn't.
- **Relish** • 3312 Cadys Alley
202-333-5343
For your bod, not your hot dog.
- **Restoration Hardware** • 1222 Wisconsin Ave NW
202-625-2771
High-end home goods.
- **Sassanova** • 1641 Wisconsin Ave NW
202-471-4400
The latest and greatest in shoes.
- **Secret Garden** • 3222 M St NW
202-337-0833
Romantic flowers and plants store.
- **See** • 1261 Wisconsin Ave NW
202-337-5988
Fashionable, cheap eyewear.
- **Sephora** • 3065 M St NW
202-338-5644
Popular high-end cosmetics chain.
- **Sherman Pickey** • 1647 Wisconsin Ave NW
202-333-4212
Pet-friendly attire.
- **Thomas Sweet Ice Cream** • 3214 P St NW
202-337-0616
Known to provide the White House with desserts.
- **Toka Salon** • 3251 Prospect St NW
202-333-5133
Relax.
- **Trader Joe's** • 1101 25th St NW
202-296-1921
If only the folks shopping there were as laid back as the décor.
- **Urban Chic** • 1626 Wisconsin Ave NW
202-338-5398
Super chic if you have serious cash
- **Urban Outfitters** • 3111 M St NW
202-342-1012
More like dorm outfitters.
- **Wink** • 3109 M St NW
202-338-9465
Fun Georgetown boutique.
- **Zara** • 1238 Wisconsin Ave NW
202-944-9797
A step up from H&M.

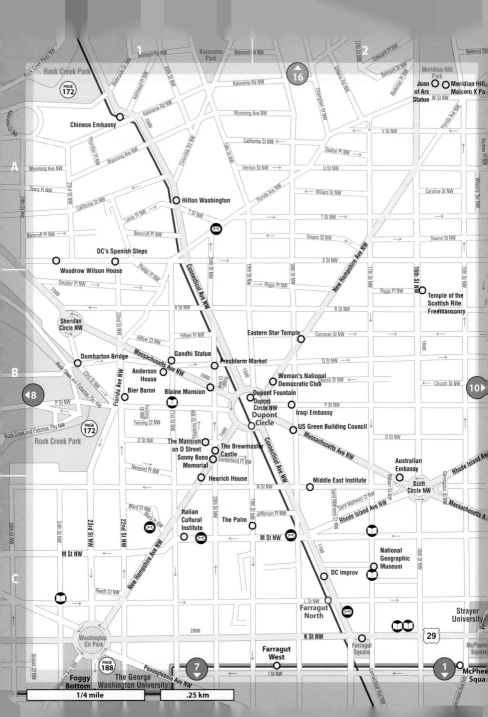

Rock Creek Pkwy NW

Rock Creek Park

PAGE 172

1

Belmont Rd NW

Kalorama Park

Belmont Rd NW

Crescent Pl NW

Belmont St NW

2

Belmont St

Meridian Hill Park

16

Joan of Arc Statue

Meridian Hill/ Malcom X Pa

Chinese Embassy

Kalorama Rd NW

W St NW

Wyoming Ave NW

Champlain St NW

Florida Ave NW

Partner Pl NW

California St NW

V St NW

Waverly Ter NW

A

Wyoming Ave NW

Wyoming Ave NW

Thornton Pl NW

23rd St NW

Vernon St NW

Seaton Pl NW

Caroline St NW

Tracy Pl NW

California St NW

U St NW

24th St NW

California St NW

Leroy Pl NW

Hilton Washington

Florida Ave NW

Willard St NW

T St NW

Caroline St NW

Bancroft Pl NW

Bancroft Pl NW

T St NW

✉

Swann St NW

Swann St NW

DC's Spanish Steps

S St NW

2000

Woodrow Wilson House

Pinds Pl NW

20th St NW

Connecticut Ave NW

Riggs Pl NW

19th St NW

18th St NW

New Hampshire Ave NW

S St NW

Riggs Pl NW

16th St NW

Temple of the Scottish Rite Freemasonry

Decatur Pl NW

22nd St NW

Hillyer Ct NW

R St NW

R St NW

Corcoran St NW

15th St NW

Sheridan Circle NW

Hillyer Pl NW

Eastern Star Temple

Q St NW

1600

B

Dumbarton Bridge

Massachusetts Ave NW

Gandhi Statue

Freshfarm Market

Woman's National Democratic Club

Church St NW

Church St NW

10

Florida Ave NW

2000

Anderson House

Riggs Ct NW

1500

Dupont Fountain

Dupont Circle NW

Iraqi Embassy

P St NW

Rock Creek and Potomac Pkwy NW

23rd St NW

Bier Baron

Blaine Mansion

21st St NW

N St NW

Dupont Circle

US Green Building Council

Massachusetts Ave NW

O St NW

8

Twining Ct NW

Twining Ct NW

20th St NW

P St NW

Rock Creek and Potomac Pkwy NW

PAGE 172

O St NW

The Mansion on O Street

The Brewmaster Castle

Sunderland Pl NW

Australian Embassy

Babcat St NW

Rhode Island Ave

Rock Creek Park

Newport Pl NW

Sonny Bono Memorial

Heurich House

N St NW

Middle East Institute

Saint Mathews Ct NW

Scott Circle NW

Connecticut Ave NW

Massachusetts A

C

25th St NW

Ward Ct NW

Ward Pl NW

Italian Cultural Institute

20th St NW

The Palm

Jefferson Pl NW

19th St NW

Rhode Island Ave NW

Saint Mathews Ct NW

16th St NW

24th St NW

23rd St NW

22nd St NW

✉

✉

M St NW

✉

National Geographic Museum

M St NW

New Hampshire Ave NW

DC Improv

1100

📖

Reeds Ct NW

📖

L St NW

Farragut North

✉

Strayer University

Washington Cir Park

📖

2000

📖 📖

29

McPhe Squa

PAGE 188

7

Foggy Bottom

The George Washington University

Pennsylvania Ave NW

Farragut West

I St NW

K St NW

Farragut Square

Connecticut Ave NW

1

McPhe Squa

16th St NW

1/4 mile

.25 km

Neither tourist trap nor chain store-stuffed, boutique-filled Dupont is a standard destination for locals. North and east of the circle, toward club-crazed Adams Morgan and the trendy Logan Circle/U Street areas, is where the scene really is: shops, cafes, and great people-watching. Dupont is a little too settled to be considered bohemian or edgy any more, though, and anywhere south of the circle is office territory.

○ Landmarks

- **Anderson House** • 2118 Massachusetts Ave NW
  202-785-2040
  One of the premiere gems in the crown of the Society of the Cincinnati.
- **Bier Baron** • 1523 22nd St NW
  202-293-1887
  Get drunk on the world's largest beer list.
- **Blaine Mansion** • 2000 Massachusetts Ave NW
  Large, red, and brick.
- **The Brewmaster's Castle** •
  1307 New Hampshire Ave NW
  202-429-1894
  German beer-themed bling rules in this 1892 crib.
- **Chinese Embassy** • 3505 International Pl NW
  202-495-2266
  Look for the Falun Gong protesters.
- **Consulate of Iraq** • 1801 P St NW
  202-483-7500
  Watch the hated old shell come alive.
- **DC Improv** • 1140 Connecticut Ave NW
  202-296-7008
  Chortle in a city that doesn't laugh enough.
- **Dumbarton Bridge** • Q St NW & 23rd St NW
  Four fantastic buffalos guide you from Dupont to Georgetown.
- **Dupont Fountain** • Dupont Cir
  Top spot for people-watching.
- **Eastern Star Temple** •
  1618 New Hampshire Ave NW
  202-667-4737
  National Women's Party HQ.
- **Embassy of Australia** •
  1601 Massachusetts Ave NW
  202-797-3000
  Look out for the Christmas kangaroos.
- **Farragut Square** • K St NW & 17th St NW
  Share park benches with K Street suits and the homeless.
- **Freshfarm Market** • 20th St NW
  202-331-7300
  Where yuppies get their fruit.
- **Gandhi Statue** •
  Massachusetts Ave NW & 21st St NW
  Don't peek under the skirt.

- **Heurich House** • 1307 New Hampshire Ave NW
  It sure feels haunted.
- **Hilton Washington** • 1919 Connecticut Ave NW
  202-483-3000
  Where Reagan took a bullet.
- **Italian Cultural Institute** • 3000 Whitehaven St NW
  202-518-0998
  Learn how to whistle at babes like the Romans did.
- **Joan of Arc Statue** • Meridian Hill Park
  You'd think she conquered Washington.
- **The Mansion on O Street** • 2020 O St NW
  202-496-2020
  Hidden passageways, celeb guests, and Grey Goose Martini happy hours.
- **Meridian Hill Park** • 16th St NW & Euclid St NW
  202-895-6070
  Sunday drum circle + soccer!
- **Middle East Institute** • 1761 N St NW
  202-785-1141
  A Middle East Mecca…er, you know what we mean.
- **National Geographic Museum** • 1145 17th St NW
  202-857-7588
  It holds the world and all that's in it, apparently.
- **The Palm** • 1225 19th St NW
  202-293-9091
  A.k.a., The Institute For Power Lunching.
- **Scottish Rite of Freemasonry** • 1733 16th St NW
  202-232-3579
  So that's what that is.
- **Sonny Bono Memorial** •
  New Hampshire Ave NW & 20th St NW
  Rest In Peace, babe.
- **Spanish Steps** • S St SE & 22nd St SE
  A mini-Roman Holiday.
- **US Green Building Council** • 2101 L St NW
  800-795-1747
  Non-profit promotes earth-friendly building approaches plus tours of 'Ocean 13' movie set.
- **Woman's National Democratic Club** • 1526 New Hampshire Ave NW
  202-232-7363
  Presidents and First Ladies on walls.
- **Woodrow Wilson House** • 2340 S St NW
  202-387-4062
  Another president's crib.

Nightlife

- **Bar Rouge** • 1315 16th St NW
  202-232-8000
  Super laid back in a trendy hotel.
- **Beacon Bar & Grill** • 1615 Rhode Island Ave NW
  202-872-1126
  Great for happy hours and bar treats.
- **Bier Baron** • 1523 22nd St NW
  202-293-1887
  Try a beer from Timbuktu—possibly the best beer selection on the planet.
- **The Big Hunt** • 1345 Connecticut Ave NW
  202-785-2333
  Should be called the big dump. Local favorite.
- **Black Fox Lounge** • 1723 Connecticut Ave NW
  202-483-1723
  Practice raising your pinky with your glass.
- **Black Rooster Pub** • 1919 L St NW
  202-659-4431
  Dark as a black rooster inside. Good darts.
- **The Board Room** • 1737 Connecticut Ave NW
  202-518-7666
  Like a rec room with good beer.
- **Bravo! Bravo!** • 1001 Connecticut Ave NW
  202-223-5330
  Salsa and Merengue.
- **Buffalo Billiards** • 1330 19th St NW
  202-331-7665
  Relaxed poolhall.
- **Café Citron** • 1343 Connecticut Ave NW
  202-530-8844
  Sweat in the crowd downstairs, or dance on chairs upstairs.
- **Camelot Show Bar** • 1823 M St NW
  202-887-5966
  Honey, they're professional dancers.
- **Chi-Cha Lounge** • 1624 U St NW
  202-234-8400
  Informal (ties forbidden) Ecuadorian hacienda.

- **CIRCA at Dupont** • 1601 Connecticut Ave NW
  202-667-1601
  Sophisticated wine bar and cafe.
- **Cobalt** • 1639 R St NW
  202-232-4416
  Smoke-free 30 Degrees, smoky Cobalt.
- **DC Improv** • 1140 Connecticut Ave NW
  202-296-7008
  Don't laugh up your weak rum and Coke.
- **Eighteenth Street Lounge** • 1212 18th St NW
  202-466-3922
  Hip, mature and the deck is always packed.
- **Elephant & Castle** • 900 19th St NW
  202-296-2575
  North American chain wants to be British.
- **Firefly** • 1310 New Hampshire Ave NW
  202-861-1310
  Sophisticated drinking.
- **The Fireplace** • 2161 P St NW
  202-293-1293
  Landmark gay bar.
- **Floriana** • 1602 17th St NW
  202-667-5937
  Friendly subterranean bar.
- **Fox and Hounds Lounge** • 1537 17th St NW
  202-232-6307
  Where uptight people go to relax.
- **The Front Page** • 1333 New Hampshire Ave NW
  202-296-6500
  Pre-10 pm: businessman's grill; post-10 pm: strictly t & a.
- **Gazuza** • 1629 Connecticut Ave NW
  202-667-5500
  Best mango mojitos in town.
- **HR-57 Center for the Preservation of Jazz and Blues** • 1007 H St NE
  202-253-0044
  Cool BYOB jazz joint. A real gem.
- **James Hoban's** • 1 Dupont Cir NW
  202-223-8440
  Washington's architect has a bar.

This is about as complete a neighborhood as you can find in DC. Just a short walk down the street will put you in reach of a tofu wrap, Advil for the hangover, and a copy of the London Daily Mirror, all on the same block. All Dupont needs is a three-story IKEA and the yuppies would never have to leave.

Map

- **Japone** • 2032 P St NW
202-223-2573
Serious sake and karaoke.
- **JR's** • 1519 17th St NW
202-328-0090
Don't miss the daily drink specials and theme nights.
- **Kramerbooks & Afterwords Café** •
1517 Connecticut Ave NW
202-387-3825
Fun eats amidst café/bar/bookstore environs. The Perfect Weapon.
- **La Frontera Cantina** • 1633 17th St NW
202-232-0437
Have a Corona and people-watch.
- **Lauriol Plaza** • 1835 18th St NW
202-387-0035
Order a pitcher of margaritas for a lounge day.
- **Local 16** • 1602 U St NW
202-265-2828
Great deck spring/summer/fall. Lounge atmosphere without a cover.
- **Lucky Bar** • 1221 Connecticut Ave NW
202-331-3733
Lucky not to get beer spilled on you.
- **Maddy's Bar and Grille** •
1726 Connecticut Ave NW
202-483-2266
Slick lounge with 14 beers on tap.
- **Madhatter** • 1319 Connecticut Ave NW
202-833-1495
A midtown dive bar with character.
- **McClellan's** • 1919 Connecticut Ave NW
202-483-3000
Hilton Hotel sports bar.
- **McFadden's** • 2401 Pennsylvania Ave NW
202-223-2338
Wall-to-wall Tues/Thurs/Fri/Sat nights.
- **Ozio** • 1813 M St NW
202-822-6000
Grown and sexy hip-hop scene.

- **Recessions Lounge** • 1823 L St NW
202-296-6686
Basement bar.
- **Rumors** • 1900 M St NW
202-466-7378
After-work drinks downtown.
- **Russia House Restaurant and Lounge** •
1800 Connecticut Ave NW
202-234-9433
Swanky joint beloved by eurotrash.
- **Science Club** • 1136 19th St NW
202-775-0747
Laid-back lounge that caters to cocktails and conversation.
- **Sign of the Whale** • 1825 M St NW
202-785-1110
Cozy and cheap.
- **Soussi** • 2228 18th St NW
202-299-9313
Outdoor wine bar.
- **Stetson's Famous Bar & Restaurant** •
1610 U St NW
202-667-6295
Popular and crowded U Street destination.
- **Tabard Inn Restaurant** • 1739 N St NW
202-331-8528
Romantic rendezvous.
- **Topaz Bar** • 1733 N St NW
202-521-2113
Go for the drinks.
- **Townhouse Tavern** • 1637 R St NW
202-234-5747
Get your Schlitz in a can.
- **Twist Dupont** • 1731 New Hampshire Ave NW
202-234-3200
Carlyle Suites lounge.
- **Urbana** • 2121 P St NW
202-956-6650
Multiple rushes of wine pleasure.

Map 9

Dupont Circle / Adams Morgan

🍴Restaurants

- **15 Ria** • 1515 Rhode Island Ave NW
202-742-0015 • $$$$
New York chic dining in the nation's capital.
- **Al Tiramisu** • 2014 P St NW
202-467-4466 • $$$$
Romantic climate, friendly Italian service will make
it a *bella notte*.
- **Alberto's Pizza** • 2010 P St NW
202-986-2121 • $$$
Especially flat specialty pizzas.
- **Annie's Paramount Steak House** •
1609 17th St NW
202-232-0395 • $$
24-hour gay (straight-friendly) steak joint; packed
Sunday brunch.
- **Bagels, Etc.** • 2122 P St NW
202-466-7171 • $
Bagels served with a smile.
- **Bier Baron** • 1523 22nd St NW
202-293-1887 • $$
Renowned beer selection overshadows some
damn fine eats.
- **Bistro Bistro** • 1727 Connecticut Ave NW
202-328-1640 • $
What is this again?
- **Bistrot du Coin** • 1738 Connecticut Ave NW
202-234-6969 • $$$$
French joint, sans the stuffiness.

- **Black & Orange** • 1300 Connecticut Ave NW
202-296-2242 • $
Half-pound wood-grilled burgers until 5am.
- **Blue Duck Tavern** • 1201 24th St NW
202-419-6755 • $$$
Fry anything in duck fat and it tastes good.
- **Bobby's Burger Palace** • 2121 K St NW
202-974-6260 • $
Yes, as in Flay. "Crunchify" your burger for authen-
ticity.
- **Bread & Brew** • 1247 20th St NW
202-466-2676 • $
Café and coffeehouse upstairs, beers and cocktails
downstairs.
- **Bua** • 1635 P St NW
202-265-0828 • $$
The food far outclasses the décor, as it should be.
- **Café Citron** • 1343 Connecticut Ave NW
202-530-8844 • $$$
South American cuisine sets stage for serious
dance party.
- **Café Luna** • 1633 P St NW
202-387-4005 • $$$
Always busy, yet always intimate. Enjoy the
Dupont open air.
- **Cake Love** • 1506 U St NW
202-588-7100 • $
Give your sweet tooth a fix with a gourmet
cupcake.
- **Chi-Cha Lounge** • 1624 U St NW
202-234-8400 • $$$
Kick off an evening on U with tapas, sangria, and
a hookah.

Dupont Circle / Adams Morgan

Map 9

This is where DC bubbles over with nightlife options. Although Dupont is frequently labeled the hub of DC's gay community, even Evangelicals can find a place to party here. From beer-soaked sports bars to painfully hip clubs to sticky-floored dives and late-night-snack spots, it's no surprise that this neighborhood has a vibrant singles scene. But despite **Bistrot du Coin**, no one will ever mistake Connecticut Avenue for the Champs-Elysées.

- **Circle Bistro** • 1 Washington Cir NW
  202-872-1680 • $$$
  Hooray for $5 Martini happy hour.
- **City Lights of China** • 1731 Connecticut Ave NW
  202-265-6688 • $$$
  Standard Chinese food that can't go wrong.
- **Daily Grill** • 1200 18th St NW
  202-822-5282 • $$$
  A 40-entrée menu.
- **Darlington House** • 1610 20th St NW
  202-332-3722 • $$$$
  Upstairs fancy restaurant vs. downstairs laid back bar.
- **Duplex Diner** • 2004 18th St NW
  202-265-7828 • $
  Comfort food.
- **Eye Street Grill** • 1575 I St NW
  202-289-7561 • $
  Sandwich and salad lunch spot.
- **Ezmè** • 2016 P St NW
  202-223-4303 • $$
  Bites of Turkish mezedes paired with sips of wine.
- **Farragut Fridays: DC Food Trucks** • 1700 K St NW
  $
  Sample DC's booming food truck scene Fridays at Farragut Square.
- **The Front Page** • 1333 New Hampshire Ave NW
  202-296-6500 • $$$
  Respectable dark wood-paneled Americana restaurant by day, seedy intern meat-market by night.
- **Grillfish** • 1200 New Hampshire Ave NW
  202-331-7310 • $$
  Perfect happy hours specials and excellent food.

- **Hank's Oyster Bar** • 1624 Q St NW
  202-462-4265 • $$
  60 min happy hour features 1-for-$1 oysters!
- **Hanoi House** • 2005 14th St NW
  202-747-2377 • $$$
  Trendy Asian fare.
- **Henry's Soul Cafe** • 1704 U St NW
  202-265-3336 • $$
  Ultimate take-out spot for serious soul food.
- **i Ricchi** • 1220 19th St NW
  202-835-0459 • $$$$
  Restaurants in Italy aren't this upscale.
- **Julia's Empanadas** • 1221 Connecticut Ave NW
  202-861-8828 • $
  So good and so cheap. Cash only.
- **Kababji Grill** • 1351 Connecticut Ave NW
  202-899-0909 • $$
  Charcoal-grilled Lebanese kebabs, straight from Beirut.
- **Kellari Taverna** • 1700 K St NW
  202-535-5274 • $$
  White tablecloth moussaka comes to K Street.
- **Komi** • 1509 17th St NW
  202-332-9200 • $$$$$
  Absolutely the best in DC!
- **Kramerbooks & Afterwords Café** •
  1517 Connecticut Ave NW
  202-387-3825 • $$
  Restaurant? Bookstore? All-night pancake joint? A must-visit.
- **La Tomate** • 1701 Connecticut Ave NW
  202-667-5505 • $$
  Delicious contemporary Italian.

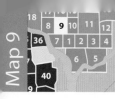

- **Lauriol Plaza** • 1835 18th St NW
202-387-0035 • $$$
Ritzy architecture doesn't match run-of-the-mill dishes.
- **Levante's** • 1320 19th St NW
202-293-3244 • $$
Great Middle Eastern served by happy waiters.
- **Local 16** • 1602 U St NW
202-265-2828 • $$$$
The classiest place on U.
- **Luna Grill & Diner** • 1301 Connecticut Ave NW
202-835-2280 • $$
Great brunch.
- **Mackey's Public House** • 1823 L St NW
202-331-7667 • $$
Another O'Whatever's.
- **Mai Thai** • 1200 19th St NW
202-452-6870 • $$
Thai-riffic.
- **Malaysia Kopitiam** • 1827 M St NW
202-833-6232 • $$
Menu offers extensive notes for the uninitiated Malaysian diner.
- **Marcel's** • 2401 Pennsylvania Ave NW
202-296-1166 • $$$$
Sheer decadence.
- **Mari Vanna** • 1141 Connecticut Ave NW
202-783-7777 • $$$$
A taste of old Russia in DC with a slightly hefty price tag.
- **Marrakesh Palace** • 2147 P St NW
202-775-1882 • $$
Cool, laid back vibe and great Moroccan eats.
- **McCormick & Schmick's** • 1652 K St NW
202-861-2233 • $$$
A K Street staple. Exploit the happy hour food specials.

- **Meat in a Box** • 2005 18th St NW
703-533-9070 • $
An intriguing combination of kebabs and pizza.
- **Meiwah** • 1200 New Hampshire Ave NW
202-833-2888 • $$$
The lighter side of Chinese food.
- **Nage** • 1600 Rhode Island Ave NW
202-448-8005 • $$$
Surf and surf.
- **Newton's Noodles** • 1129 20th St NW
240-328-8942 • $$
Noodles eat with a "chork", that's chopstick + fork.
- **Nooshi** • 1120 19th St NW
202-293-3138 • $$
We recommend everything but the cheeseball name.
- **Obelisk** • 2029 P St NW
202-872-1180 • $$$$
Put your reservation in now for next March.
- **The Palm** • 1225 19th St NW
202-293-9091 • $$$$
If you're an elitist and you know it clap your hands!
- **Pesce** • 2002 P St NW
202-466-3474 • $$$
Perhaps the best of the half-dozen fish joints on the block.
- **The Pig** • 1320 14th St NW
202-290-2821 • $$
Four legs good, especially when it's pork, at this Logan Circle establishment.
- **Pizzeria Paradiso** • 2003 P St NW
202-223-1245 • $$
The toppings are meals themselves. Pray there's no line.
- **Plume** • 1200 16th St NW
202-448-2300 • $$$$$
For when you really want to splurge.

Fleece the taxpayers at **Smith and Wollensky**, **The Palm**, or **Prime Rib**. For French decadence, try **Marcel's**. If Italian is your indulgence, it's **Obelisk**. **Blue Duck Tavern** is a DC institution. and **Komi** makes it onto every food critic and lay foodie's Top 10. Get sushi at **Sushi Taro** and experience Morocco at **Marrakesh Palace**.

- **The Prime Rib** • 2020 K St NW
  202-466-8811 • $$$$
  Voted Washington's No.1 steakhouse.
- **Public Bar** • 1214 18th St NW
  202-223-2200 • $$
  Bar for the public.
- **Raku** • 1900 Q St NW
  202-265-7258 • $$
  Hip Asian bistro with comforting udon. Great croissant pudding dessert.
- **Restaurant Nora** • 2132 Florida Ave NW
  202-462-5143 • $$$$
  Nora keeps her own herb garden in back. Every ingredient organic.
- **RIS** • 2275 L St NW
  202-730-2500 • $$$$
  Signature restaurant from Ris Lacoste of 1789 fame.
- **Rosemary's Thyme** • 1801 18th St NW
  202-332-3200 • $$$
  Mediterranean, meet Creole. Great people watching patio.
- **Sacrificial Lamb** • 1704 R St NW
  202-797-2736 • $
  Afghan, Indian, and Pakistani specialties…and pizza.
- **Sette Osteria** • 1666 Connecticut Ave NW
  202-483-3070 • $$
  As simple as Italian gets. Pastas are all the rave.
- **Shake Shack** • 1216 18th St NW
  202-683-9922 • $
  New York's celebrity burger and custard shakes takes up a Washington residence.
- **Smith and Wollensky** • 1112 19th St NW
  202-466-1100 • $$$$
  Sleek setting makes you forget it's a chain.
- **Sushi Taro** • 1503 17th St NW
  202-462-8999 • $$
  Traditional sushi above a CVS.

- **Sweetgreen** • 1512 Connecticut Ave NW
  202-387-9338 • $
  Baby arugula, "guac deconstructed," and yogurt dressings on the go.
- **Tabard Inn Restaurant** • 1739 N St NW
  202-331-8528 • $$$$
  Fireplace, brick walls, outdoor tables, and elegant dishes.
- **Teaism** • 2009 R St NW
  202-667-3827 • $$
  Would you like dinner with your cup of tea?
- **Teddy & The Bully Bar** • 1200 19th St NW
  202-872-8700 • $$$$$
  Fine dining, cocktail and taxidermy and Teddy.
- **Thai Chef** • 1712 Connecticut Ave NW
  202-234-5698 • $$
  Comfy Thai food (and sushi).
- **Thaiphoon** • 2011 S St NW
  202-667-3505 • $$
  A curry lover's paradise.
- **Triple B Fresh** • 1506 19th St NW
  202-232-2338 • $
  Think "Korean Chipotle."
- **Vapiano** • 1800 M St NW
  202-640-1868 • $$
  Fancy restaurant food and feel but on the cheap.
- **Veritas Wine Bar** • 2031 Florida Ave NW
  202-265-6270 • $$
  Not your cheesy "I'm such a wino" bar
- **Vidalia** • 1990 M St NW
  202-659-1990 • $$$$
  A taste of dixieland refinery. Brilliant.
- **Washington Deli** • 1990 K St NW
  202-331-3344 • $
  Perfect take-out lunch spot.
- **Zorba's Cafe** • 1612 20th St NW
  202-387-8555 • $$
  Greek DC mainstay; sort of like the Jefferson Memorial.

Map 9
36 7 1 2 3 4
6 5
7
40
9

🛍 Shopping

- **Adam & Eve** • 1723 Connecticut Ave NW
202-299-0440
Hint: don't go here looking for a nice jacket.
- **Andre Chreky, the Salon Spa** • 1604 K St NW
202-293-9393
Fancy trims.
- **Ann Taylor** • 1140 Connecticut Ave NW
202-659-0120
Corporate duds that are budget-friendly.
- **Bang Salon** • 1612 U St NW
202-299-0925
Cool trims.
- **Beadazzled** • 1507 Connecticut Ave NW
202-265-2323
Make your own jewelry.
- **Bell Wine & Spirits** • 1821 M St NW
202-223-4727
Wide variety and knowledgeable staff.
- **Betsy Fisher** • 1224 Connecticut Ave NW
202-785-1975
Expensive casual Fridays.
- **Blue Mercury** • 1619 Connecticut Ave NW
202-462-1300
Cosmetics for maidens and metrosexuals alike.
- **Books-A-Million** • 11 Dupont Cir NW
202-319-1374
If you can't bear to hold out for Amazon Prime.
- **Brooks Brothers** • 1201 Connecticut Ave NW
202-659-4650
DC's uniform supply shop.
- **Burberry** • 1155 Connecticut Ave NW
202-463-3000
Fashionistas and foreign correspondents and plaid.
- **Caramel** • 1603 U St NW
202-265-1930
Clothes and art in one.
- **Chocolate Moose** • 1743 L St NW
202-463-0992
Great candies and cards.
- **Comfort One Shoes** • 1630 Connecticut Ave NW
202-328-3141
Beyond Birkenstocks.

- **Commonwealth** • 1781 Florida Ave NW
202-265-1155
New and established street and fashion sports-wear.
- **The Custom Shop Clothiers** •
1033 Connecticut Ave NW
202-659-8250
Design your own button-down.
- **De Vino's** • 2001 18th St NW
202-986-5002
A yuppie wine shop.
- **Doggie Style Bakery, Boutique and Pet Spa** •
1825 18th St NW
202-667-0595
Irreverent pet gifts.
- **Dupont Market** • 1807 18th St NW
202-797-0222
Upscale stuff you won't find at Safeway.
- **Fatty's Custom Tattooz** •
1333 Connecticut Ave NW
202-452-0999
Custom Tats for those who can afford it.
- **Gap** • 1120 Connecticut Ave NW
202-429-0691
Affordable, inoffensive, basic gear.
- **Ginza** • 1717 Connecticut Ave NW
202-332-7000
Japanica.
- **Godiva Chocolatier** • 1143 Connecticut Ave NW
202-638-7421
Indulge.
- **Grooming Lounge** • 1745 L St NW
202-466-8900
Feed your inner metrosexual.
- **Hello Cupcake** • 1361 Connecticut Ave NW
202-861-2253
Expensive, highly attractive sweets.
- **Human Rights Campaign** •
1633 Rhode Island Ave NW
202-232-8621
Gifts and cards for a cause.
- **J. Press** • 1801 L St NW
202-857-0120
Conservative conservative.
- **JoS. A. Bank** • 1200 19th St NW
202-466-2282
For professional types who can't afford Brooks Brothers.

Proper Topper has unique pieces and Betsy Fisher is geared toward expensive shoes and fashions from labels you've never heard of. Hit up Thomas Pink and Brooks Brothers when the school year is about to begin. U-Street boutique Caramel has great one-of-a-kind merchandise. For home furnishings, try Tabletop or Millennium Decorative Arts.

- **Junction** • 1510 U St NW
  202-483-0261
  Vintage and resale clothing store.
- **Kramerbooks & Afterwords Café** •
  1517 Connecticut Ave NW
  202-387-3825
  Scope for books and dates.
- **Legendary Beast** • 1520 U St NW
  202-797-1234
  U-Street jewelry shop. Vintage, of course.
- **LOFT** • 1611 Connecticut Ave NW
  202-299-9845
  Last year's corporate duds.
- **Marvelous Market** • 1511 Connecticut Ave NW
  202-332-3690
  Bread and brownies.
- **Meeps** • 2104 18th St NW
  202-265-6546
  Vintage clothes.
- **Millennium Decorative Arts** • 1528 U St NW
  202-483-1218
  Cool stuff for your crib.
- **Mr. Yogato** • 1515 17th St NW
  202-629-3531
  Thank you very much Mr. Yogato for helping me escape just when I needed to! Thank you!
- **National Geographic Headquarters Store** •
  1145 17th St NW
  202-857-7591
  Travel the world in a shop.
- **Nordstrom Rack** • 1800 L St NW
  202-627-3650
  A bargain hunters delight.
- **Pasargad** • 1217 Connecticut Ave NW
  202-659-3888
  Beautiful rugs.
- **Proper Topper** • 1350 Connecticut Ave NW
  202-842-3055
  Cutesy hats and gifts.
- **Q West Nails** • 1919 18th St NW
  202-332-3001
  Nail care. Reasonably priced. What what.
- **Radio Shack** • 1830 K St NW
  202-467-5052
  Great for headphones, batteries, and that special connection.

- **Radio Shack** • 1150 Connecticut Ave NW
  202-833-3355
  Great for headphones, batteries, and that special connection.
- **Red Onion Records & Books** • 1901 18th St NW
  202-986-2718
  Great vinyl selection.
- **Rizik's** • 1100 Connecticut Ave NW
  202-223-4050
  Designer department store.
- **Salon Cielo** • 1741 Connecticut Ave NW
  202-518-9620
  Early morning karaoke with your clip. Ask for Jamie.
- **Second Story Books** • 2000 P St NW
  202-659-8884
  Largest outlet of this used and antiquarian book operation.
- **Secondi** • 1702 Connecticut Ave NW
  202-667-1122
  Consignment shop so chic you forget the clothes are used.
- **Skynear Designs** • 2122 18th St NW
  202-797-7160
  Funky décor.
- **Tabletop** • 1608 20th St NW
  202-387-7117
  Dress up your dinner table.
- **Thomas Pink** • 1127 Connecticut Ave NW
  202-223-5390
  The perfect dress shirt.
- **Tiny Jewel Box** • 1147 Connecticut Ave NW
  202-393-2747
  Ready to pop the question?
- **United Colors of Benetton** •
  1666 Connecticut Ave NW
  202-232-1770
  Generic clothing.
- **Violet Boutique** • 2439 18th St NW
  202-621-9225
  Cute new boutique offers Sex-in-the-City like trends.
- **The Wine Specialist** • 1133 20th St NW
  202-833-0707
  Bone up on your grapes.

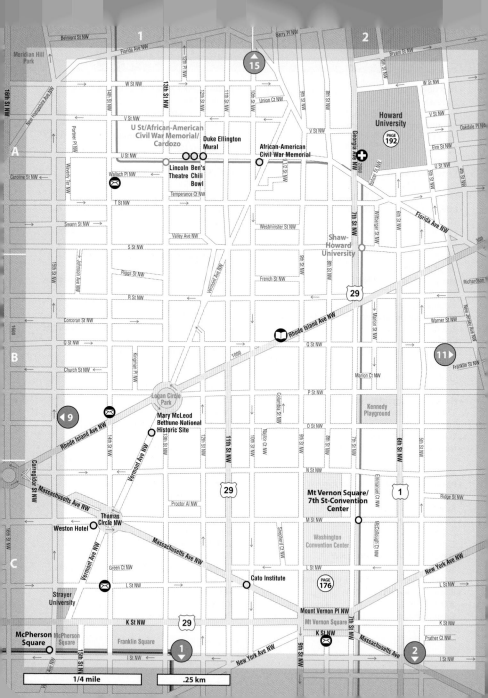

It's a river of bars, restaurants, and shops in this culturally vibrant part of town. U Street is a great place for indie rockers, hip-hoppers, and street-stoppers. Thanks to an eye turned toward the past—once called Black Broadway—jazz joints that once famously lined the streets in the '20s are making a comeback.

○ Landmarks

- **African-American Civil War Memorial** •
  1000 U St NW
  202-667-2667
  A belated thanks.
- **Ben's Chili Bowl** • 1213 U St NW
  202-667-0909
  Half-smokes and milkshakes beloved by locals and celebs.
- **Cato Institute** • 1000 Massachusetts Ave NW
  202-842-0200
  Conservative temple.

- **Duke Ellington Mural** • 1200 U St NW
  He's watching.
- **Lincoln Theatre** • 1215 U St NW
  202-328-6000
  Renovated jewel.
- **Mary McLeod Bethune Council House** •
  1318 Vermont Ave NW
  202-673-2402
  History without propaganda.
- **Westin Washington DC City Center** •
  1400 M St NW
  202-429-1700
  Back when it was the Vista International, Marion Barry got caught smoking crack here.

Map
36 | 7 | 1 | 2 | 3 | 4
6 | 5
40
9

Nightlife

- **9:30 Club** • 815 V St NW
  202-265-0930
  A DC music institution.
- **Bar Pilar** • 1833 14th St NW
  202-265-1751
  A laid-back hangout.
- **Black Cat** • 1811 14th St NW
  202-667-4490
  The OTHER place in DC to see a band.
- **Bohemian Caverns** • 2001 11th St NW
  202-299-0800
  Cavernous underground U st. jazz club is authentic DC.
- **Busboys and Poets** • 2021 14th St NW
  202-387-7638
  Shabby chic leftist bookstore/restaurant, proletarian prices.
- **Café Saint-Ex** • 1847 14th St NW
  202-265-7839
  Once-cool bistro overrun by the khaki crowd.
- **Cause Philanthropub** • 1926 9th St NW
  202-588-5220
- **Columbia Room** • 1021 7th St NW
  202-393-0220
  Hand-crafted bitters, tinctures and ice at The Passenger.
- **Cork Wine Bar** • 1720 14th St NW
  202-265-2675
  The favorite of all the DC wine bars.
- **DC9** • 1940 9th St NW
  202-483-5000
  Rock club.
- **Dickson Wine Bar** • 903 U St NW
  202-322-1779
  Organic, bio-dynamic booze, anyone?
- **Duffy's** • 2106 Vermont Ave NW
  202-265-3413
  $1 domestic cans 4 pm-12 am.
- **The Gibson** • 2009 14th St NW
  202-232-2156
  OMG a line?! but masterful cocktails.
- **Helix Lounge** • 1430 Rhode Island Ave NW
  202-462-9001
  New trendy neighborhood addition.
- **Lima** • 1401 K St NW
  202-789-2800
  Head downstairs for DJs and bottle service.
- **Lotus Lounge** • 1420 K St NW
  202-289-4222
  An underground oasis that is always empty
- **Marvin** • 2007 14th St NW
  202-797-7171
  Tribute to Marvin Gaye's Belgium detox in the 80s. No joke. Sweet rooftop deck.
- **Old Dominion Brewhouse** • 1219 9th St NW
  202-289-8158
  A fab selection of ales, lagers, and stouts from a local microbrewery.
- **The Park at Fourteenth** • 920 14th St NW
  202-737-7275
  Decadent club with four levels of pleasure
- **The Passenger** • 1021 7th St NW
  202-393-0220
  Brothers Derek Brown (Gibson) and Tom Brown (Cork) come together, finally.
- **Patty Boom Boom** • 1359 U St NW
  202-629-1712
  Jamaican patties downstairs, reggae lounge upstairs.
- **The Saloon** • 1205 U St NW
  202-462-2640
  European appeal—go for the beer.
- **The Satellite Room** • 2047 9th St NW
  202-506-2496
- **Shaw's Tavern** • 520 Florida Ave NW
  202-518-4092
- **Solly's U Street Tavern** • 1942 11th St NW
  202-232-6590
  Good sports bar. Watch for runaway cabs.
- **Tabaq Bistro** • 1336 U St NW
  202-265-0965
  Chillin' hookah bar with a killer view of downtown.
- **Tattoo Bar** • 1413 K St NW
  202-408-9444
  Bangin' beats and babes in this edgy bar.
- **Twins Jazz** • 1344 U St NW
  202-234-0072
  Intimate bar with Ethiopian food.
- **Vegas Lounge** • 1415 P St NW
  202-483-3971
  Blues joint keeps the Gen Y's jumpin'.

The current surge of activity hearkens back to U Street's heyday as an African American cultural destination. Also in the mix are Mediterranean joints like **Tabaq Bistro**, upscale coffee shops like **Busboys and Poets**, speakeasy types like **The Gibson**, and party spots like **DC9**, the **Black Cat**, and **Café St. Ex**.

- **Velvet Lounge** • 915 U St NW
  202-462-3213
  Get your lounge on with the likes of punk rock to alt-folk.
- **Warehouse** • 645 New York Ave NW
  202-783-3933
  Live music alongside a gallery, theater, and café.

Restaurants

- **1905** • 1905 9th St NW
  202-332-1905 • $$$
  Cosy, dark and inviting with great food.
- **Acadiana** • 901 New York Ave NW
  202-408-8848 • $$$$
  Southern bayou classics at a price
- **Al Crostino** • 1324 U St NW
  202-797-0523 • $$$$
  Wine bar and homey Italian restaurant. Try the lamb ragu.
- **Bar di Bari** • 1401 R St NW
  202-222-2222 • $$
  A European sidewalk cafe in the heart of DC.
- **Ben's Chili Bowl** • 1213 U St NW
  202-667-0909 • $
  A District chili institution.
- **Birch & Barley** • 1337 14th St NW
  202-567-2576 • $$$
  Rustic American grub with a range of brews.
- **Brasserie Beck** • 1101 K St NW
  202-408-1717 • $$$$
  Feast on hearty bistro fare in generous portions, and sample some 50 Belgian beers
- **Busboys and Poets** • 2021 14th St NW
  202-387-7638 • $$
  Shabby chic leftist bookstore/restaurant, proletarian prices.
- **Café Saint-Ex** • 1847 14th St NW
  202-265-7839 • $$$
  Once-cool bistro overrun by the khaki crowd.
- **Cause Philanthropub** • 1926 9th St NW
  202-588-5220 • $$
  Eat, drink and support a cause.
- **Chix** • 2019 11th St NW
  202-234-2449 • $
  Affordable, eco-conscious take-out, open late.

- **Commissary** • 1443 P St NW
  202-299-0018 • $$
  Very proud-to-be-American, organic eatery.
- **Corduroy** • 1122 9th St NW
  202-589-0699 • $$$$$
  Sleek, innovative restaurant gives hotel dining a good name.
- **Creme Café** • 1322 U St NW
  202-234-1885 • $$$$
  Upscale southern home cooking.
- **DC Coast** • 1401 K St NW
  202-216-5988 • $$$
  Another sterile, upscale American establishment.
- **Dukem** • 1114 U St NW
  202-667-8735 • $$
  Authentic Ethiopian. Special weekend outdoor grill menu.
- **Eatonville** • 2121 14th St NW
  202-332-9672 • $$
  Busboys and Poets owner serves Southern cooking.
- **El Centro D.F.** • 1819 14th St NW
  202-328-3131 • $$
  Tacos, dancing and rooftop cocktails at this busy, Manhattan-esque taqueria/tequileria .
- **Estadio** • 1520 14th St NW
  202-319-1404 • $$
  Spanish tapas favorites with surprising ingredients for a fun twist.
- **Georgia Brown's** • 950 15th St NW
  202-393-4499 • $$$$
  Upscale Southern features a scandalous brunch.
- **Great Wall Szechuan House** • 1527 14th St NW
  202-797-8888 • $$
  Spicy, numbing, delicious "ma la."
- **Juice Joint Cafe** • 1025 Vermont Ave NW
  202-347-6783 • $
  Healthy, good-for-you lunches and juices for K Street folks
- **Le Diplomate** • 1601 14th St NW
  202-332-3333 • $$$$
  France meets U Street.
- **Logan Tavern** • 1423 P St NW
  202-332-3710 • $$$$
  Eclectic comfort food with juicy ribs

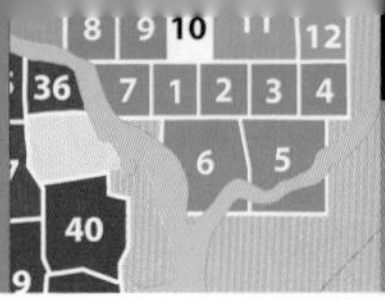

Map 10

8 9 10 11 12
36 7 1 2 3 4
6 5
40

Logan Circle / U Street

- **Lost Society** • 2001 14th St NW
  202-618-8868 • $$$$
  Swanky U St. lounge/steakhouse with city views from rooftop bar.
- **Manny & Olga's Pizza** • 1841 14th St NW
  202-387-0025 • $$
  Home of the heavy pizza.
- **Marvin** • 2007 14th St NW
  202-797-7171 • $$
  Amazing roof top bar and indoor dining.
- **Masa 14** • 1825 14th St NW
  202-328-1414 • $$$
  Fusion is back! And tequila is in!
- **Mio** • 1110 Vermont Ave NW
  202-955-0075 • $$$
  Inventive, expensive, personable, loud.
- **Next Door** • 1211 U St NW
  202-667-8880 • $$
  Historic Ben's expands next door with crab cakes and alcohol.
- **Oohs and Aahs** • 1005 U St NW
  202-667-7142 • $
  The District's best soul food.
- **Pearl Dive Oyster Palace** • 1612 14th St NW
  202-319-1612 • $$$
  Delicious Louisiana gourmet favorites with bocce ball upstairs while-u-wait.
- **Policy** • 1904 14th St NW
  202-387-7654 • $$$
  Blended fusion swank.
- **Post Pub** • 1422 L St NW
  202-628-2111 • $$
  Best burgers in city. Shhh! A secret!
- **Posto** • 1515 14th St NW
  202-332-8613 • $$$
  Loud Italian dining room with no reservations.
- **Rice** • 1608 14th St NW
  202-234-2400 • $$$
  Swanky minimalist Thai. Try the green tea dishes.
- **Rogue 24** • 922 N St NW
  202-408-9724 • $$$$
  Elegant New American; enter through rear on Blagden Alley.
- **The Saloon** • 1205 U St NW
  202-462-2640 • $$$
  Go there for the beer. Just be sure to eat beforehand.

- **The Satellite Room** • 2047 9th St NW
  202-506-2496 • $$$
  Before 930, after 930 or anytime really. Don't skip the shakes!
- **Shaw's Tavern** • 520 Florida Ave NW
  202-518-4092 • $$
  Gastropub with a great weekend brunch and trivia night.
- **Siroc** • 915 15th St NW
  202-628-2220 • $$$
  Pasta is back back back!
- **Sweetgreen** • 1461 P St NW
  202-234-7336 • $
  Baby arugula, "guac deconstructed," and yogurt dressings on the go.
- **Tabaq Bistro** • 1336 U St NW
  202-265-0965 • $$$$
  Mediterranean tapas joint with a hopping glass-top roof deck.
- **Table** • 903 N St NW
  202-588-5200 •
  Casual, seasonal, sustainable.
- **Thai Tanic** • 1326 14th St NW
  202-588-1795 • $$
  Probably best Thai restaurant in the country.
- **Thai X-ing** • 515 Florida Ave NW
  202-332-4322 • $$
  Great Thai but you have to take it home.
- **U & Pizza** • 1250 U St NW
  202-733-1286 • $$
  Pizza. Plain and simple.
- **Ulah Bistro** • 1214 U St NW
  202-234-0123 • $$$
  American, sterile
- **Utopia** • 1418 U St NW
  202-483-7669 • $$$
  Reasonably priced eclectic international cuisine.
- **Vinoteca** • 1940 11th St NW
  202-332-9463 • $$
  vino! vino!
- **Yellow Bulgogi Cart** • 14th St NW
  $
  Bulgogi and bibimbap, at your service.
- **Zentan** • 1155 14th St NW
  202-379-4366 • $$$
  Trendy Asian at the Donovan House Hotel.

In the boutique-industrial complex, there's **Muleh**, **Treasury Vintage**, **Ginger Root**, **Passport Fashion**, and **Zina**. Turn to **Home Rule** for kitschy fun, and if you like a little adventure when you shop, don't miss **Ruff & Ready**. For vintage, check out the **Hunted House** and **Miss Pixie's**. If you're boozing, iconic **Barrel House** in Logan Circle, and **Modern Liquors** in Mount Vernon both have you covered.

🛍Shopping

- **Barrel House** • 1341 14th St NW
202-332-5999
Iconic Logan Circle liquor store.
- **Blink** • 1431 P St NW
202-234-1051
Wear your sunglasses at night.
- **Cork Market & Tasting Room** •
1805 14th St NW
202-265-2674
High-end wine shop with gourmet foodstuffs to match.
- **Gallery Plan B** • 1530 14th St NW
202-234-2711
Gallery for up-and-comers.
- **Ginger Root** • 1530 U St NW
202-567-7668
Hot boutique specializes in fixing up vintage items.
- **Good Wood** • 1428 U St NW
202-986-3640
Antique furniture built from, you guessed it.
- **Home Rule** • 1807 14th St NW
202-797-5544
Kitchen treasures.
- **HomeMade Pizza Co.** • 1522 14th St NW
202-588-0808
Ready-to-bake pizza pies with fresh, all-natural ingredients.
- **INARI Salon & Spa** • 1425 K St NW
202-898-6350
Salon and spa.
- **Logan Hardware** • 1416 P St NW
202-265-8900
Super-friendly, sort-of-hipster hardware joint.
- **Miss Pixie's Furnishing and What-Not** •
1626 14th St NW
202-232-8171
Second-chance finds.

- **Modern Liquors** • 1200 9th St NW
202-289-1414
Wide variety and knowledgeable staff.
- **Muleh** • 1831 14th St NW
202-667-3440
Javanese furniture.
- **Passport Fashion** • 2003 11th St NW
202-332-4111
One-of-a-kind finds for all women.
- **Pulp** • 1803 14th St NW
202-462-7857
Dirty birthday cards.
- **Redeem** • 1734 14th St NW
202-332-7447
Badass clothes, expected for U-Street.
- **Rue 14** • 1803 14th St NW
202-462-6200
Dress like a true fashionista.
- **Ruff & Ready Furnishings** • 4722 14th St NW
202-726-2600
Find a diamond in the ruff.
- **Treasury** • 1843 14th St NW
202-332-9499
Another "vintage" store.
- **U Street Flea Market** • 13th St NW & U St NW
202-296-4989
Find a gem and make an offer.
- **Urban Essentials** • 1401 14th St NW
202-299-0642
Lust-worthy décor.
- **Vastu** • 1829 14th St NW
202-234-8344
Upscale contemporary furnishings.
- **Whole Foods Market** • 1440 P St NW
202-332-4300
Expensive organic food chain store.
- **Zina** • 1526 U St NW
202-629-4181
Boutique offers unique finds and great silver jewelry.

Map 11 · **Near Northeast**

Lamont St NW
Irving St NW
Irving St NE
Lawrence St NE
Kearney St NE

1

2

Kenyon St NW
Washington Hospital Ctr Rd
Jackson St NE
Irving St NE
Hamlin St NE
Girard St NE

500
Irving St NW

Columbia Rd NW
5th St NW
Hobart Pl NW
Michigan Ave NW
US Soldiers' &
Airmen's Home
Hawthorne Dr NW
Hawthorne St NE
9th St NE
10th St NE
12th St NE
13th St NE

US Soldiers' &
Airmen's Home

Trinity
College

Girard St NE
**Chocolate
City Beer**

A

cMillan
1servoir
McMillan
Park

15

5th St NE
6th St NE
7th St NE
Girard St NE
Franklin St NE

Howard Pl NW
4th St NW
McMillan Dr NW
Girard St NW
Franklin St NW
Evarts St NW
Douglas St NW
Glenwood
Cemetery
Evarts St NE
Edgewood St NE
Evarts St NE
Evarts St NE
1300

College St NW
Channing St NW
Channing St NW
Cromwell Ter NE
Douglas St NE
Channing St NE
Douglas St NE

14

**Howard
University**
Bryant St NW
Bryant St NE
Channing St NE
Bryant St NE
Saratoga Ave NE
14th St NE
Montana

Adams St NW
Lincoln Rd NE
Ascot Pl NE
**Rhode
Island
Ave**
Rhode Island Ave NE
Bryant St NE
13th St NE
Adams

PAGE
192
W St NW
Prospect
Hill
Cemetery
Saint Mary's
Cemetery
1st St NW
Adams St NE
W St NE
Brentwood Rd NE
W St NE

V St NW
Oakdale Pl NW
Elm St NW
V St NW
Crispus Attucks
Ct NW
Upland Ter NE
U St NE
U St NE
Summit Pl NE
3rd St NE
4th St NE
5th St NE
V St NE
13

W St NW
Todd Pl NE
T St NE

Anna J Cooper
Cir NW
**Crispus
Attucks
Park**
Thomas St NE
T St NE
9th St NE
1200

**LeDroit
Park**
Rhode Island Ave NW
Seaton Pl NW
Seaton Pl NE
Seaton Dr NE
Seaton Pl NE
Langley Community
Park NE
Randolph Pl NE

Richardson Pl NW
5th St NW
4th St NW
3rd St NW
Florida Ave NW
S St NW
S St NE
Randolph Pl NW
Randolph
Pl NE

B
R St NE

Quincy Pl NW
Quincy Pl NE
400

Q St NW
1600
Q St NE

Franklin St
NW
Bates St NW
Q St NE
Q St NE
Brentwood Park

O St NW
Porter St NE
P St NW
P St NE

New Jersey Ave NW
Hanover Pl NW
O St NW
O St NE
Gallaudet University
PAGE
186

10
Ridge St NW
N St NW
N St NE
N St NE
**Florida Ave
Market**

1
M St NW
North Capitol St NE
Morgan St NW
**Florida Ave –
New York Ave –
Gallaudet University**

New York Ave NW
1st Ter
NW
McKinley St NW
Patterson St NE
Pierce St NW
800

Kirby St NE
Sursum
Corda Ct NW
Pierce St NE
Orleans Pl NE
Morton Pl NE
W Virginia Ave NE
1000
Holbrook St NE
Owen Pl NE
Penn St NE
Neal Pl NE
Morse St NE

6th St NW
395
Pierce St NW
L St NW
L St NE
**Washington
Coliseum**
Abbey Pl NE
Kent Pl NE
Trinidad Ave NE

Prather Ct NW
4th St NW
1st St NW
Temple Ct NW
Fenton Ct NE
Morse St NE

C
K St NW
K St NE
12

Massachusetts Ave NW
3rd St NW
First Ter NW
Parker St NE
Florida Ave NE

I St NW
I St NE
Wylie St NE

1
G Pl NW
G Pl NE
H St NW
H St NE
Linden Pl NE
Linden Ct NE

2
3

1
50
G St NW
G St NW
Madison Al
NW
Chews Ct NW
F St NE
G St NE
Morris Pl NE
F St NE
Acker Pl NE
800
Emerald St NE

Maryland Ave NE
Union Station Dr NW
**Union
Station**
Massachusetts Ave NE
Capitol Ct NE
Groff Ct NE
Lexington Pl NE
Duncan Pl NE

E St NW
E St NE

1/4 mile
.25 km

Ledroit Park and Bloomingdale are at the edge of the gentrification craze pushing east from Shaw, which is predicted to be the next Dupont Circle, and historic homes, including some breathtaking Victorians, are being restored block by block. Unfortunately, the huge swath of railroad tracks slicing through does little for unification or aesthetics, however, and certain areas require an extra bit of caution.

○ Landmarks

- **Chocolate City Beer** • 2801 8th St NE
  DC's first microbrewery melts Chocolate City's heart.
- **Crispus Attucks Park** • V St NW & U St NW
  Neighborly public space in the heart of Bloomingdale.
- **LeDroit Park** •
  Rhode Island Ave NW & Florida Ave NW
  Race relations/green space.
- **Washington Coliseum** • 1140 3rd St NW
  DC's performance venue.

Nightlife

- **Boundary Stone** • 116 Rhode Island Ave NW
  202-621-6635
  Where hipsters go to meet and make baby hipsters.
- **Fur** • 33 Patterson St NE
  202-842-3401
  You like sweaty 18-year-old girls?
- **Lux Lounge** • 649 New York Ave NE
  202-347-8100
  Too cool for school.

Restaurants

- **The Atlas Room** • 1015 H St NE
  202-388-4020 • $$$
  Global fusion taken to a new art form.
- **Bacio Pizzeria** • 81 Seaton Pl NW
  202-232-2246 • $$
  If this were Connecticut, it'd be called Mystic Pizza.
- **Beau Thai** • 1700 New Jersey Ave NW
  202-536-5636 • $
  Continuing the tradition of terribly punny Thai restaurant names.
- **Cookie's Corner** • 1970 2nd St NW
  202-986-2793 • $
  Part take-out, part convenience store. Ask about Cookie.
- **DC Empanadas** • 1309 5th St NE
  703-400-5363 • $
  Once, these gourmet empanadas only came from a truck.
- **Kushi** • 465 K St NW
  202-682-3123 • $$
  Izakaya and sushi restaurant with plenty of small-batch sake.
- **Mandu** • 453 K St MW
  202-289-6899 • $$$
  Upscale Korean fare with a twist.
- **Menomale Pizza Napoletana** • 2711 12th St NE
  202-248-3946 • $$
  Chef's a master pizza maker from Italy.

- **Rappahannock Oyster Bar** • 1309 5th St NE
  202-544-4702 • $$
  Renowned raw bar and small plates.
- **The Red Hen** • 1822 1st St NW
  202-525-3021 • $$$
  Seasonal, fresh, Italian-influenced American cuisine.
- **Takorean** • 1309 5th St NE
  $
  The Korean BBQ Taco truck goes brick-and-mortar.
- **Thaaja** • 1335 2nd St NE
  202-289-4200 • $
  It's like Chipotle only for Indian food.
- **Uncle Chip's** • 1514 N Capitol St NW
  202-999-4990 • $
  Cookies. Sandwiches. Coffee.

Shopping

- **A. Litteri, Inc.** • 517 Morse St NE
  202-544-0184
  Fine Italian grocery and deli.
- **Anna's Linens** • 1060 Brentwood Rd NE
  202-529-3402
  Nicely priced linens and curtains.
- **Capitol Hill Premium Cigars & Tobacco** •
  1006 Florida Ave NE
  202-396-8006
  Cigarette shop below members' only smoking lounge.
- **City Cleaners** • 84 Rhode Island Ave NW
  202-299-0009
  Standard drycleaners in Bloomingdale.
- **Curbside Cupcakes** • 1309 5th St NE
  202-495-0986
  The roving food truck's Union Market brick-and-mortar store.
- **Giant Food** • 1050 Brentwood Rd NE
  202-281-3900
  Washington DC's first supermarket.
- **Harris Teeter** • 1201 1st St NE
  202-589-0351
  Teeter prevails where Lee failed.
- **Home Depot** • 901 Rhode Island Ave NE
  202-526-8760
  You know, Home Depot.
- **Le Droit Park Market** • 1901 4th St NW
  Beloved community convenience shop.
- **Lyon Bakery** • 1309 5th St NE
  202-484-2100
  Artisan breads of every sort.
- **Red Apron Butcher** • 1309 5th St NE
  202-524-6807
  An American butcher with a European twist.
- **Trickling Springs Creamery** • 1309 5th St NE
  717-816-3622
  Find out what dairy is supposed to taste like.

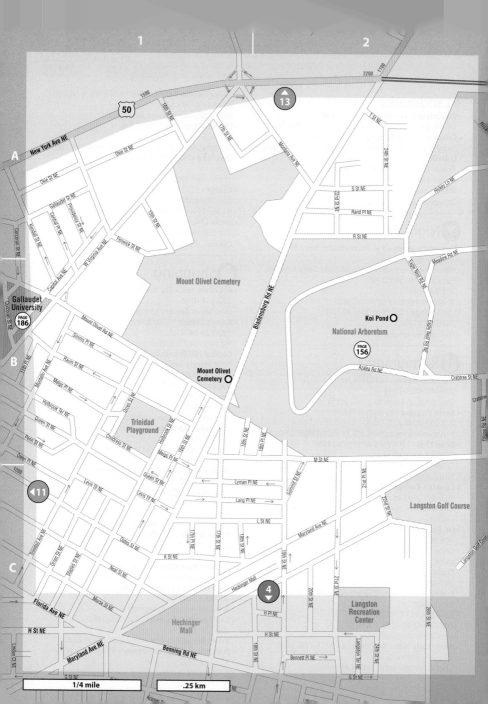

Map 12

On the NE outskirts of the District, Trinidad is one of DC's last affordable neighborhoods... and it shows. But outside speculators are coming in with business concepts that longtime residents would rather fend off, and between **Mount Olivet Cemetery** and the **National Arboretum**, green spaces are plentiful.

○ Landmarks

- **Koi Pond** • 3501 New York Ave NE
  202-245-2726
  Feed and pet humongo Japanese fish!
- **Mount Olivet Cemetery** •
  1300 Bladensburg Rd NE
  Visit Mary Suratt, hanged for her part in killing Lincoln.

Nightlife

- **Jimmy Valentine's Lonely Hearts Club** •
  1103 Bladensburg Rd NE
  No Phone
  No sign, no phone, and red lights.
- **Love Nightclub** • 1350 Okie St NE
  202-746-1736
  Huge nightclub straight out of a rap video.

Map 13 • Brookland / Langdon

Leafy streets with big lots provide an affordable alternative to nearby Maryland suburbs—while still allowing residents to proudly claim a DC address. The neighborhood's annual home and garden tour connects residents and draws visitors who delight in turn of the century mansions and quaint 1920s bungalows.

Landmarks

- **DC Brau** • 3178 Bladensburg Rd NE
  202-621-8890
  Local brewery does a neighborhood good. Free tours.
- **Franciscan Monastery** • 1400 Quincy St NE
  202-526-6800
  Beautiful gardens.

Nightlife

- **Aqua** • 1818 New York Ave NE
  202-832-4878
  Asian dance club at a Korean restaurant.

Restaurants

- **Rita's** • 2318 Rhode Island Ave NE
  202-636-7482 • $
  Italian ice, frozen custard and gelato.

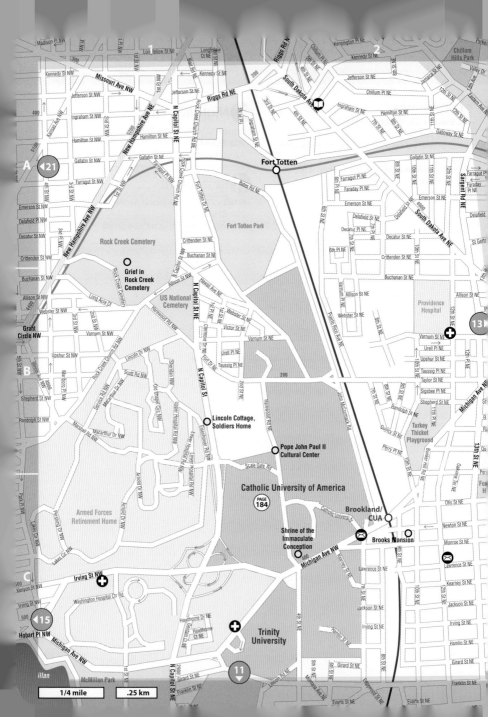

College town meets Little Vatican in this sleepy corner of the District. Here, the largest church in the western hemisphere, the Basilica of the National Shrine of the Immaculate Conception, serves the region's most devoted Catholics, while Catholic University has taught young minds for over 125 years.

○ Landmarks

- **Blessed John Paul II Shrine** •
  3900 Harewood Rd NE
  202-635-5400
  When you can't get to The Vatican.
- **Brooks Mansion** • 901 Newton St NE
  A Greek revival.
- **President Lincoln's Cottage at the Soldiers' Home** • 300 Randolph St NW
  202-829-0436
  Lincoln's summer residence; where he drafted the Emancipation Proclamation.
- **Rock Creek Cemetery** •
  Webster St NW & Rock Creek Church Rd NW
  Memorial to Adam's wife is best in the city.
- **Shrine of the Immaculate Conception** •
  400 Michigan Ave NE
  202-526-8300
  Humungo Catholic Church.

🍴 Restaurants

- **Askale Cafe** • 3629 12th St NE
  202-758-0077 • $$
  Come for the food, stay for the traditional coffee ceremony.
- **Brookland Grill** • 3528 12th St NE
  202-526-7419 • $
  Dive restaurant serves up breakfast all day.
- **Hitching Post** • 200 Upshur St NW
  202-726-1511 • $$
  Southern fried chicken, crab cakes.
- **Little Ricky's** • 3522 12th St NE
  202-525-2120 • $$
  Get your Cuban fix for lunch, dinner and weekend brunch.
- **Murray & Paul's** • 3513 12th St NE
  202-529-4078 • $
  Old school breakfast dive with lots of grease.
- **Pete's New Haven Style Apizza** •
  1400 Irving St NW
  202-332-7383 • $
  New Haven-style pies have quickly become a DC favorite.
- **San Antonio Bar and Grill** • 3908 12th St
  202-832-8080 • $$
  New Tex-Mex spot for Brookland.

🛍 Shopping

- **Yes! Organic Market** • 3809 12th St NW
  202-832-7715
  For all your organic food needs.

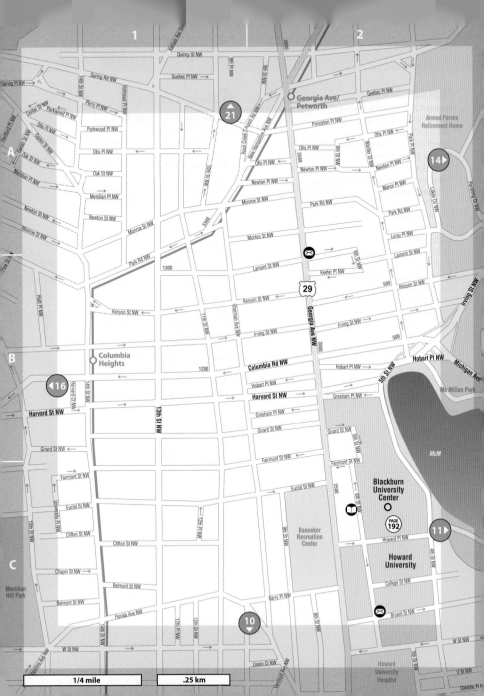

Columbia Heights has a well-earned reputation as a hipster mecca and vegan ghetto. It's true, there's no shortage of skinny jeans, fixies or soy cheese here. But there's also amazing Latin and African American culture and eats. Traveling away from the main drag reveals that the neighborhood's full transformation isn't yet complete.

oLandmarks

- **Blackburn University Center** • 2400 6th St NW
  202-806-5983
  Howard University's living room.

Nightlife

- **Acre 121** • 1400 Irving St NW
  202-328-0121
  Low Country BBQ and craft beer.
- **Chuck & Billy's** • 2718 Georgia Ave NW
  202-234-5870
  Malcolm X adorns the wall, elder statesmen hold court, circa 1992 decor prevails.
- **The Coupe** • 3415 11th St NW
  202-209-3342
  Full-service bar with cocktails.
- **Maple** • 3418 11th St NW
  202-588-7442
- **Meridian Pint** • 3400 11th St NW
  202-588-1075
  Pour your own beer and indulge in brined pork chops.
- **Mothership** • 3301 Georgia Ave NW
  202-629-3034
  Late-night food and drinks.
- **Room 11** • 3234 11th St NW
  202-332-3234
  The fanciest feather in CH's gentrification cap: a wine bar.
- **The Wonderland Ballroom** • 1101 Kenyon St NW
  202-232-5263
  Crowded, smoky, fun neighborhood dive. Great bratwurst.

Map 1

🍴Restaurants

- **Acre 121** • 1400 Irving St NW
202-328-0121 • $$
Low Country BBQ and craft beer.
- **The Coupe** • 3415 11th St NW
202-209-3342 • $$
Breakfast all day and late night, diner style.
- **DC Reynolds** • 3628 Georgia Ave NW
202-506-7178 • $
Patio gets a new definition, plus summer dinner and a movie.
- **El Chucho** • 3313 11th St NW
202-290-3313 • $
Taqueria dishing out Mexican staples and margaritas, por favor.
- **El Pollo Sabroso** • 1434 Park Rd
202-986-0022 • $
Two El Pollo Sabrosos within half a mile of each other = high demand.
- **El Rinconcito II** • 1326 Park Rd NW
202-299-1076 • $
Small, unassuming spot with a lot of character.
- **Fast Gourmet** • 1400 W St NW
202-448-9217 •
Don't fear the gas station setting; these sandwiches are unbelievable.
- **Fish in the Neighborhood** • 3601 Georgia Ave NW
202-545-6974 • $$
So good, you won't tell anyone else about this place.
- **Five Guys** • 1400 Irving St NW
202-332-8060 • $
The smell of cajun fries by Columbia Heights Metro is irresistible.
- **Florida Avenue Grill** • 1100 Florida Ave NW
202-265-1586 • $$
Greasy spoon from the dirty south.
- **G** • 2201 14th St NW
202-234-5000 • $$
Mike Isabella does it again, this time with sandwiches.
- **The Heights** • 3115 14th St NW
202-797-7227 • $$
Upscale homestyle food: fried chicken, meatloaf, burgers, rotisserie chicken.
- **Kangaroo Boxing Club** • 3410 11th St NW
202-505-4522 • $
From the BBQ geniuses behind the PORC food truck.
- **Kapnos** • 2201 14th St NW
202-234-5000 • $$$
Mike Isabella dishes out Northern Greek fare.
- **The Looking Glass Lounge** •
3634 Georgia Ave NW
202-722-7669 • $$
New owners change name, but keep all the 1920s charm.
- **Maple** • 3418 11th St NW
202-588-7442 • $$$
New Italian fare in Columbia Heights.
- **Mothership** • 3301 Georgia Ave NW
202-629-3034 • $$
Community tables, weekend brunch and family-friendly foods.
- **Negril** • 2301 Georgia Ave NW
202-332-3737 • $
Local Caribbean quick-eats chain.
- **Panda Express** • 3100 14th St NW
202-986-0292 • $
Definitely not Chinese. Make no mistake about that.
- **Pollo Campero** • 3229 14th St NW
202-745-0078 • $
Addictive fried chicken born in Guatemala.
- **Red Rocks** • 1036 Park Rd NW
202-506-1402 • $$
Brick-oven pizza in a red-brick dining room.
- **Rita's West Indian Carry-Out** •
3322 Georgia Ave NW
202-722-1868 • $$
Authentic Caribbean carryout, recently refurbished without the bullet-proof glass.
- **Ruby Tuesday** • 3365 14th St NW
202-462-7681 • $$
All you've heard, and nothing more.
- **Taqueria Distrito Federal** • 3463 14th St NW
202-276-7331 • $
Trying to describe the deliciousness feels like food porn.
- **Thai Tanic** • 3462 14th St NW
202-387-0882 • $$
Popular Thai restaurant opens second location farther north on 14th Street.

The only **Target** in the District means plenty of visitors hauling toilet paper and lumpy bull's-eye shopping bags. Chicks in granny glasses and guys with sleeve tattoos chow down on vegan eats at **Sticky Fingers Bakery**. Catch them washing it all down with a beer at **Wonderland Ballroom.**

Shopping

- **Best Buy** • 3100 14th St NW
  202-387-6150
  Gadgets, gadgets, gadgets.
- **Mom N' Pop Antiques** • 3534 Georgia Ave NW
  202-722-0719
  Perhaps the last affordable antique store in DC.
- **Palace 5ive** • 2220 14th St NW
  202-299-9008
  DC meets Dogtown.

- **Sterling Cleaners** • 3106 Georgia Ave NW
  202-723-9535
  The sole dry cleaner within 20 blocks, and the service to go with it.
- **Sticky Fingers Bakery** • 1370 Park Rd NW
  202-299-9700
  Vegan bakery.
- **Target** • 3100 14th St NW
  202-777-3773
  DC's first. Is that bull's eye aimed at small and local business?

Map 10 • **Adams Morgan (North) / Mt Pleasant** Ⓝ

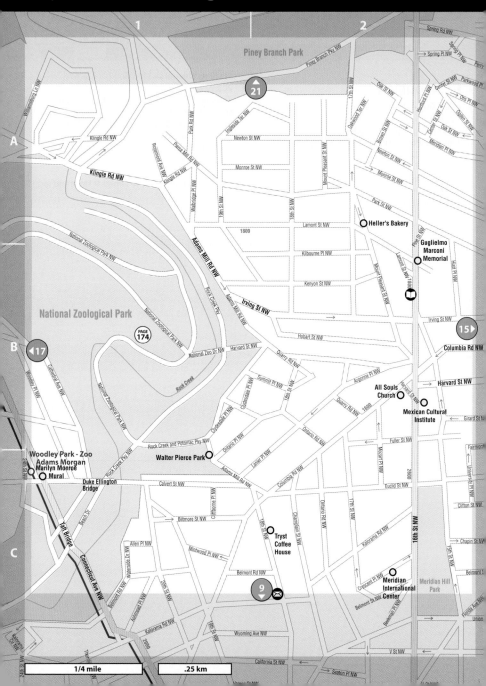

Piney Branch Park

Spring Rd NW
Spring Pl NW
Perry

21

Klingle Rd NW

Klingle Rd NW

A

Williamsburg Ln NW

Rosemont Ave NW

Klingle Rd NW

Walbridge Pl NW

Pierce Mill Rd NW

Park Rd NW

Ingleside Ter NW

19th St NW

Newton St NW

Monroe St NW

Mount Pleasant St NW

Oak St NW

Brown St NW

17th St NW

Oakmont Ter NW

Spring Pl NW

Center St NW
Parkwood Pl NW

Harvard Pl NW

Otis Pl NW

Ogden St NW

Newton St NW

Meridian Pl NW

Oak St NW

National Zoological Park NW

1800

Park St NW

Lamont St NW

Kilbourne Pl NW

Kenyon St NW

Heller's Bakery

Guglielmo Marconi Memorial

Lamont St NW 1800

Hiatt Pl NW

Adams Mill Rd NW

Rock Creek Pkwy

Irving St NW

National Zoological Park NW

National Zoological Park

PAGE 174

National Zoo Dr NW

Harvard St NW

Rock Creek

Hobart St NW

Quarry Rd NW

Mount Pleasant St NW

Irving St NW

Columbia Rd NW

15▶

◀17

B

Woodley Pl NW

Cathedral Ave NW

Summit Pl NW

Clydesdale Pl NW

18th St NW

Argonne Pl NW

Quarry Rd NW 1900

All Souls Church

Harvard St NW

Mexican Cultural Institute

Girard St NW

Fairmont

University Pl NW

2600

Clydesdale Pl NW

Rock Creek and Potomac Pky NW

Ontario Pl NW

Lanier Pl NW

Adams Mill Rd NW

Ontario Rd NW

Fuller St NW

Mozart Pl NW

Walter Pierce Park

Woodley Park - Zoo
Adams Morgan
Marilyn Monroe
Mural

Duke Ellington Bridge

24th St NW

Rock Creek Pkwy

Calvert St NW

Columbia Rd NW

Euclid St NW

16th St NW

Clifton St NW

2600

Clifton St NW

◀Chapin St NW

Beach Dr

Taft Bridge

Connecticut Ave NW

Biltmore St NW

Cliffbourne Pl NW

Allen Pl NW

Waterside Dr NW

29th St NW

Mintwood Pl NW

18th St NW

Champlain St NW

Ontario Rd NW

17th St NW

Kalorama Rd NW

19th St NW

Belmont St NW

C

Tryst Coffee House

Belmont Rd NW

Crescent Pl NW

Meridian International Center

Meridian Hill Park

Florida Ave NW

Union

9▼

✉

Belmont Rd NW

Ashmead Pl NW

Belmont St NW

Beekman Pl NW

Biltmore St NW

Kalorama Rd NW

2000

Wyoming Ave NW

19th St NW

California St NW

Seaton Pl NW

24th St NW

24th St NW

Thornton

Belmont Rd NW

| 1/4 mile | .25 km |

1

2

From the Salvadoran pupuserias to the glut of Ethiopian eats to the frat house scene along 18th Street, these two neighborhoods are a microcosm of the District. Adams Morgan has long been the nightlife destination for college students and Hill interns. Mount Pleasant has fewer offerings, but those there are laid-back sanctuaries.

○ Landmarks

- **All Souls Church** • 1500 Harvard St NW
202-332-5266
Progressive Unitarian Church.
- **Guglielmo Marconi Memorial** •
16th St NW & Lamont St NW
Art Deco tribute to the Fascist inventor.
- **Heller's Bakery** • 3221 Mt Pleasant St NW
202-265-1169
For generations, a doughnut destination.
- **Marilyn Monroe Mural** •
Connecticut Ave NW & Calvert St NW
A tiny bit of glamour for DC.
- **Meridian International Center** •
1630 Crescent Pl NW
202-667-6800
Look out for the exhibits.
- **Mexican Cultural Institute** • 2829 16th St NW
202-728-1647
Top-notch work by Mexican artists.
- **Tryst Coffeehouse** • 2459 18th St NW
202-232-5500
Canoodle here the way Chandra and Gary did.
- **Walter Pierce Community Park** •
2630 Adams Mill Rd NW
202-588-7332
Former cemetery now boasts colorful mural and new-fenced dog park.

▼ Nightlife

- **Angles Bar and Billiards** • 2339 18th St NW
202-462-8100
Dive bar with great burgers; a favorite of reporters.
- **Bedrock Billiards** • 1841 Columbia Rd NW
202-667-7665
Pool hall with extensive alcohol choices.
- **The Black Squirrel** • 2427 18th St NW
202-232-1011
90 bottles of beer on the menu.
- **Bossa** • 2463 18th St NW
202-667-0088
Cool downstairs, samba upstairs.

- **Bukom Café** • 2442 18th St NW
202-265-4600
West African music and a diverse crowd.
- **Chief Ike's Mambo Room** • 1725 Columbia Rd NW
202-332-2211
Dirty dance 'til dawn.
- **Club Timehri** • 2439 18th St NW
202-518-2626
Reggae, Calypso, R&B.
- **Columbia Station** • 2325 18th St NW
202-462-6040
More jazz and blues in an intimate setting.
- **Federal Restaurant** • 2477 18th St NW
202-506-4314
If you are looking for bottle service, visit the lounge.
- **Grand Central** • 2447 18th St NW
202-986-1721
Looks more like a Metro station than Grand Central.
- **Last Exit** • 3155 Mt Pleasant St NW
202-986-7661
Hidden speakeasy style cocktail bar in the basement between Tonic and Radius.
- **Madam's Organ** • 2461 18th St NW
202-667-5370
Redheads get a discount; best blues in DC.
- **Meze** • 2437 18th St NW
202-797-0017
Salsa and Mediterranean goodness.
- **Pharmacy Bar** • 2337 18th St NW
202-483-1200
Low-key alternabar.
- **The Raven** • 3125 Mt Pleasant St NW
202-387-8411
Neighborhood bar.
- **The Reef** • 2446 18th St NW
202-518-3800
Jellyfish and drinks.
- **Rumba Café** • 2443 18th St NW
202-588-5501
Cuban treats.
- **Tonic** • 3155 Mt Pleasant St NW
202-986-7661
Local tavern.

Map key numbers: 30 19 20 21 14 17 16 15 13 18 8 9 10 11 12 35 36 7 1 2 3 4 37 6 5

🍴 Restaurants

- **Adam Express** • 3211 Mt Pleasant St NW
  202-328-0010 • $$
  Unassuming but delicious Korean/Chinese/
  Japanese.
- **Amsterdam Falafel Shop** • 2425 18th St NW
  202-234-1969 • $
  Best falafel in the city on the cheap
- **Angelico La Pizzeria** • 3205 Mt Pleasant St NW
  202-234-2622 • $$
  Local take-out/cafe chain gets a second DC loca-
  tion.
- **Astor Mediterranean** • 1829 Columbia Rd NW
  202-745-7495 • $
  Great falafel sandwich and subs.
- **Bardia's New Orleans Café** • 2412 18th St NW
  202-234-0420 • $
  Perfect brunch with great Cajun takes on poached
  egg classics.
- **Bukom Café** • 2442 18th St NW
  202-265-4600 • $$$
  West African food, feel, and music.
- **Cashion's Eat Place** • 1819 Columbia Rd NW
  202-797-1819 • $$$$
  Chelsea Clinton known to have played the dating
  game here.
- **The Diner** • 2453 18th St NW
  202-232-8800 • $
  Self-explanatory. Open 24 hours.
- **Don Jaime** • 3209 Mt Pleasant St NW
  202-232-3875 • $
  World's best waiter makes for a lovely, down-to-
  earth brunch.
- **Dos Gringos** • 3116 Mt Pleasant St NW
  202-462-1159 • $
  Proving that classy Salvadorean establishment is
  not an oxymoron.
- **El Pollo Sabroso** • 3153 Mt Pleasant St NW
  202-299-0374 • $
  Roasted chicken and yucca fries just can't go
  wrong.
- **El Tamarindo** • 1785 Florida Ave NW
  202-328-3660 • $$
  Delighting taste buds with Latin cuisine for 30
  years.

- **Federal Restaurant** • 2477 18th St NW
  202-506-4314 • $$
  Craft beer and cocktails served with local, organic
  pub foods.
- **The Grill From Ipanema** • 1858 Columbia Rd NW
  202-986-0757 • $$$
  Killer caiphirinas that scream "Brazil!"
- **Haydee's** • 3102 Mt Pleasant St NW
  202-483-9199 • $
  Cheap but awful Salvadorean food. Beware the
  salsa.
- **Heller's Bakery** • 3221 Mt Pleasant St NW
  202-265-1169 • $
  Start your morning off with donuts and coffee.
- **Himalayan Heritage** • 2305 18th St NW
  202-483-9300 • $$
  Himalayan fare at fair prices, with great service.
- **Julia's Empanadas** • 2452 18th St NW
  202-328-6232 • $
  Filling, cheap, and open late.
- **La Fourchette** • 2429 18th St NW
  202-332-3077 • $$$$
  Casual creperie.
- **Little Fountain Café** • 2339 18th St NW
  202-462-8100 • $$
  Charming oasis on Adams Morgan's Drunkards
  Row.
- **Mama Ayesha's** • 1967 Calvert St NW
  202-232-5431 • $$
  Middle Eastern good enough for Bill Clinton.
- **Marx Café** • 3203 Mt Pleasant St NW
  202-518-7600 • $$$
  Quasi-hipster Mount Pleasant standout.
- **Meskerem Ethiopian Restaurant** •
  2434 18th St NW
  202-462-4100 • $$$
  Authentic Ethiopian meets DC posh.
- **Millie & Al's** • 2440 18th St NW
  202-387-8131 • $$
  A dive's dive for pizza and pitchers.
- **Mintwood Place** • 1813 Columbia Rd NW
  202-234-6732 • $$
  A serious menu for serious Washingtonians who
  aren't sure how to handle the laid-back atmo-
  sphere.
- **Mixtec** • 1792 Columbia Rd NW
  202-332-1011 • $$
  Originally a grocery store, this Mexican beanery is
  superb.

Adams Morgan (North) / Mt Pleasant

Start your day by jockeying for a seat at **Tryst**, where you can linger all day over one cup of joe. Save your appetite for the legendary food of **Meskerem Ethiopian Restaurant**. Afterwards you'll be ready for the live music at **Madam's Organ**, where redheads always drink half price, before heading to one of the neighborhood pizza joints at bar time, for a requisite jumbo slice.

Map 16

- **Napoleon Bistro** • 1847 Columbia Rd NW
  202-299-9630 • $$$
  Because crepes always go better with champagne in hand.
- **Pasta Mia** • 1790 Columbia Rd NW
  202-328-9114 • $$
  Queue up early or wait for hours to be told how and when you may eat your perfect pasta
- **Perry's** • 1811 Columbia Rd NW
  202-234-6218 • $$$
  A punk sushi experience. Killer city views.
- **Pho 14** • 1436 Park Rd NW
  202-986-2326 • $
  Go Pho in Mt. Pleasant.
- **Pi Pizzeria & The Bottom's Up Bar** •
  2309 18th St NW
  202-232-6146 • $$
  Wood fired pizza is 3.14 times better than others.
- **Pica Taco** • 1629 Columbia Rd NW
  202-518-0076 • $
  Taqueria tucked into the Argonne apartment building.
- **Radius Pizza** • 3155 Mt Pleasant St NW
  202-234-0202 • $
  A slice of New York.
- **Rumba Café** • 2443 18th St NW
  202-588-5501 • $$
  Eat steak and watch tango. (Wednesday nights.)
- **Sawah Diner** • 2222 18th St NW
  202-232-2377 • $
  American diner with Mediterranean bent tries to do it all.
- **Smoke & Barrel** • 2471 18th St NW
  202-319-9353 • $$
  Tasty, tasty bbq in AdMo.
- **Sutra Lounge** • 2406 18th St NW
  202-299-1113 • $$
  Upstairs-downstairs set up offers one-stop restaurant, lounge and bar.
- **Tonic** • 3155 Mt Pleasant St NW
  202-986-7661 • $$
  Comfort food and a can't-be-beat happy hour.
- **Tono Sushi** • 2605 Connecticut Ave NW
  202-332-7300 • $$
  Serviceable sushi, $1/piece happy hour special.
- **Tryst Coffeehouse** • 2459 18th St NW
  202-232-5500 • $$
  Excellent Wi-Fi cafe. A central DC spot.

🛍 Shopping

- **A Little Shop of Flowers** • 2421 18th St NW
  202-387-7255
  Great name, good flowers.
- **The Brass Knob** • 2311 18th St NW
  202-332-3370
  Architectural antiques from doors to knobs.
- **Crooked Beat Records** • 2116 18th St NW
  202-483-2328
  Off-beat, hard to find selections.
- **Dollar Star** • 3129 Mt Pleasant St NW
  202-462-7900
  For the fashionable thrifty.
- **Fleet Feet** • 1841 Columbia Rd NW
  202-387-3888
  No referee uniforms here and maybe you'll see Mayor Fenty.
- **Idle Time Books** • 2467 18th St NW
  202-232-4774
  Disorganized lit.
- **Radio Shack** • 1767 Columbia Rd NW
  202-986-5008
  Great for headphones, batteries, and that special connection.
- **Radio Shack** • 3100 14th St NW
  202-265-0514
  Great for headphones, batteries, and that special connection.
- **Smash! Records** • 2314 18th St NW
  202-387-6274
  Vintage punk vinyl, new punk clothes.
- **So's Your Mom** • 1831 Columbia Rd NW
  202-462-3666
  Äœber-deli with great sandwiches, imported NY bagels.
- **Trim** • 2700 Ontario Rd NW
  202-462-6080
  If you need hip bangs.
- **Yes! Organic Market** • 1825 Columbia Rd NW
  202-462-2069
  Yes! Wheat germ!

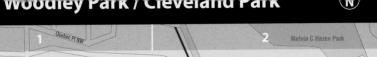
Map 17 • Woodley Park / Cleveland Park

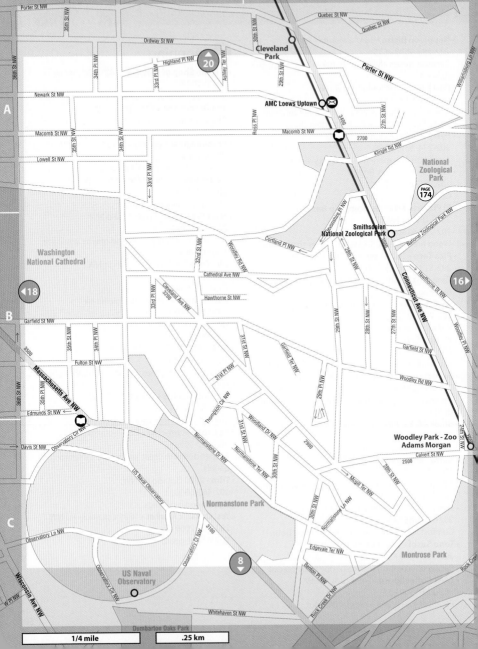

Quebec Pl NW
Melvin C Hazen Park
Porter St NW
Quebec St NW
Quebec St NW
Ordway St NW
Highland Pl NW
Cleveland Park
20
Porter St NW
Newark St NW
AMC Loews Uptown
Ross Pl NW
A
Macomb St NW
Macomb St NW
2700
Lowell St NW
Klingle Rd NW

National Zoological Park
PAGE 174
Cortland Pl NW
Smithsonian National Zoological Park
Washington National Cathedral
Cathedral Ave NW
18
Hawthorne St NW
16
B
Garfield St NW
Garfield St NW
Fulton St NW
Woodley Rd NW
Massachusetts Ave NW
3500
31st Pl NW
Garfield Ter NW
Edmunds St NW
Thompson Cir NW
Davis St NW
Woodland Dr NW
Woodley Park - Zoo Adams Morgan
Calvert St NW
2500
Normanstone Dr NW
Normanstone Ter NW
C
Observatory Ln NW
Normanstone Park
Montrose Park
US Naval Observatory
Edgevale Ter NW
8
Benton Pl NW
Wisconsin Ave NW
Whitehaven St NW
Rock Creek
Dumbarton Oaks Park

1/4 mile   .25 km

Woodley Park and Cleveland Park have long stood proud as safe, residential neighborhoods with good retail. Sandwiched between the imposing **National Cathedral** and bamboo-crunching Pandas at the **National Zoo**, the gorgeous single-family homes cost a pretty penny.

○ Landmarks

- **AMC Loews Uptown 1** • 3426 Connecticut Ave NW
  202-966-5401
  Red velvet curtains over a 40-foot screen; this is the Art Deco queen of DC movie houses.
- **Smithsonian National Zoological Park** •
  3001 Connecticut Ave NW
  202-633-4800
  Two words: baby panda.
- **US Naval Observatory** •
  3450 Massachusetts Ave NW
  202-762-1467
  VP's disclosed location and the best place to ask what time it is.

Nightlife

- **Ardeo + Bardeo** • 3311 Connecticut Ave NW
  202-244-6750
  Ardeo's chi-chi wine bar, where well-heeled yuppies tote glasses of chardonnay.
- **Atomic Billiards** • 3427 Connecticut Ave NW
  202-363-7665
  Subterranean pool, darts, and beer.
- **Cleveland Park Bar & Grill** •
  3421 Connecticut Ave NW
  202-806-8940
  Watch the game with a popped collar.
- **Murphy's** • 2609 24th St NW
  202-462-7171
  Irish pub with summertime patio and wintertime fireplace.
- **Nanny O'Brien's** • 3319 Connecticut Ave NW
  202-686-9189
  Legendary Celtic jam sessions.
- **Ripple** • 3417 Connecticut Ave NW
  202-244-7995
  Aroma, stripped of the smoke, is reborn as Ripple the wine bar.
- **Zoo Bar Cafe** • 3000 Connecticut Ave NW
  202-232-4225
  Low-key with live blues bands.

Map

18
8 9 10 11 12
35 36 7 1 2 3 4
37 6 5

Restaurants

- **Alero** • 3500 Connecticut Ave NW
  202-966-2530 • $$
  Margarita before a movie at the Uptown.
- **Ardeo + Bardeo** • 3311 Connecticut Ave NW
  202-244-6750 • $$$
  New American bistro boasting a Who's Who clientele.
- **Byblos Deli** • 3414 Connecticut Ave NW
  202-364-6549 • $
  Mediterranean yumminess.
- **The Cereal Bowl** • 3420 Connecticut Ave NW
  202-244-4492 • $
  From Grape Nuts to Trix, plus parfaits and oaties.
- **Dino** • 3435 Connecticut Ave NW
  202-686-2966 • $$$
  Try the boar pasta.
- **District Kitchen** • 2606 Connecticut Ave NW
  202-238-9408 • $$$
  Big prices, small portions.
- **Fresh Med** • 3313 Connecticut Ave NW
  202-244-3995 • $
  Med means Mediterranean.
- **Lavandou** • 3321 Connecticut Ave NW
  202-966-3003 • $$$$
  Casual French sidewalk-style bistro.
- **Lebanese Taverna** • 2641 Connecticut Ave NW
  202-265-8681 • $$$
  Delicious.

- **Mr. Chen's Organic Chinese Cuisine** •
  2604 Connecticut Ave NW
  202-797-9668 • $$$
  Cult favorite of munchies-stricken health-conscious hipsters.
- **Nam Viet** • 3419 Connecticut Ave NW
  202-237-1015 • $$
  No frills pho.
- **New Heights** • 2317 Calvert St NW
  202-234-4110 • $$
  A cute garden-like eatery tucked away in Woodley Park for dates of all kinds.
- **Open City** • 2331 Calvert St NW
  202-332-2331 • $$
  Hipper-than-thou diner with round-the-clock brunch.
- **Petits Plats** • 2653 Connecticut Ave NW
  202-518-0018 • $$$
  Reliable French.
- **Pulpo** • 3407 Connecticut Ave NW
  202-450-6875 • $$
  Funky fusion tapas with colorful cocktails and atmosphere.
- **Sorriso** • 3518 Connecticut Ave NW
  202-537-4800 • $$$
  Artisanal Italian with an awesome Nutella pizza.
- **Spices** • 3333 Connecticut Ave NW
  202-686-3833 • $$$
  Dependably tasty pan-Asian. Try the suicide curry.

This stretch of Connecticut Avenue has commercial clusters surrounding Metro stations that can provide you with basic necessities. As for nightlife, the strip boasts a number of top-notch restaurants that cater to a variety of palates, a few hopping bars, and the Art Deco **Uptown Theater**, a single-screen DC institution. Arrive early to get a front-and-center balcony seat at the latest high-grossing blockbuster.

Shopping

- **All Fired Up** • 3413 Connecticut Ave NW
  202-363-9590
  Local version of Color Me Mine.
- **Allan Woods Flowers** • 2645 Connecticut Ave NW
  202-332-3334
  Gorgeous buds and blossoms.
- **Guitar Gallery** • 3400 Connecticut Ave NW
  202-244-4200
  Flamenco and classical guitars, plus lessons.
- **Manhattan Market** • 2647 Connecticut Ave NW
  202-986-4774
  Upscale cornerstore.

- **Transcendence-Perfection-Bliss of the Beyond** •
  3428 Connecticut Ave NW
  202-363-4797
  Children's toys and gift cards with inexplicable name.
- **Vace** • 3315 Connecticut Ave NW
  202-363-1999
  Best pizza in town.
- **Wake Up Little Suzie** • 3409 Connecticut Ave NW
  202-244-0700
  Wacky gifts and knick-knacks for the home.
- **Yes! Organic Market** • 3425 Connecticut Ave NW
  202-363-1559
  A healthy lifestyle will cost you.

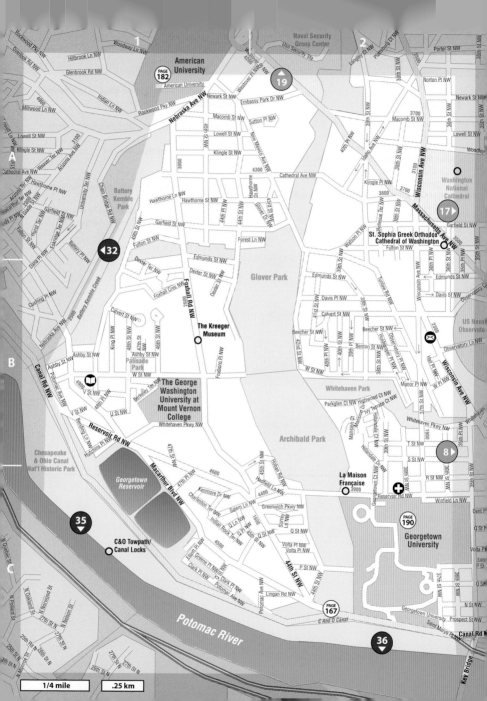

Bordering one of DC's most unappreciated green spaces, Glover Park is populated largely by well-heeled couples. The Palisades, which hugs the river, is off in its own little world of twee front porches. But Foxhall, on the extreme and unapologetic end, is so exclusive that it's completely inaccessible by public transportation.

○ Landmarks

- **C&O Canal** • Canal Rd NW
  301-739-4200
  Scenic views minutes from cityscape.
- **The Kreeger Museum** • 2401 Foxhall Rd NW
  202-337-3050
  Residence turned private museum houses a stunning art collection.
- **La Maison Francaise** • 4101 Reservoir Rd NW
  202-944-6400
  Learn what *savoir faire* truly means.
- **Saint Sophia Greek Orthodox Cathedral of Washington** •
  Massachusetts Ave NW & 36th St NW
  202-333-4730
  Sometimes there are Greek festivals here. Otherwise, just worshipping.
- **Washington National Cathedral** •
  Massachusetts Ave NW & Wisconsin Ave NW
  202-537-6200
  Newly-constructed old cathedral. Pure American.

Nightlife

- **Bourbon** • 2348 Wisconsin Ave NW
  202-625-7770
  Great bourbon, of course.
- **Breadsoda** • 2233 Wisconsin Ave NW
  202-333-7445
  How do you make roast beef sandwiches and pool classy? Breadsoda knows.
- **District 2 Bar & Grille** • 3238 Wisconsin Ave NW
  202-362-0362
  One time wine bar resurrects as beery tavern with sports.
- **Good Guys** • 2311 Wisconsin Ave NW
  202-333-8128
  Friendly, low-bling rock-and-roll strip club.

Map

18

8 9 10 11 12
35 36 7 1 2 3 4
37 6 5

Restaurants

- **2 Amys** • 3715 Macomb St NW
  202-885-5700 • $$
  Pizza Napolitana. Romantic or just for kicks.
- **Angelico La Pizzeria** • 2313 Wisconsin Ave NW
  202-333-8350 • $
  Affordable Italian with bonus of homemade bread.
- **BlackSalt** • 4883 MacArthur Blvd NW
  202-342-9101 • $$$
  Gorgeous seafood with a posh bar.
- **Cactus Cantina** • 3300 Wisconsin Ave NW
  202-686-7222 • $$$
  Same as Lauriol Plaza, minus courtly architecture.
- **Café Deluxe** • 3228 Wisconsin Ave NW
  202-686-2233 • $$$
  A greasy spoon with absolutely no grease.
- **Chef Geoff's** • 3201 New Mexico Ave NW
  202-237-7800 • $$$
  Forgive snotty waiters by chowing down.
- **Figs Lebanese Cafe** • 4828 MacArthur Blvd NW
  202-333-7773 • $
  Tasty Middle Eastern food with lots of veggie and
  vegan options.
- **Heritage India Georgetown** •
  2400 Wisconsin Ave NW
  202-333-3120 • $$$
  Heritage India spinoff. Still gourmet.
- **Jetties** • 1609 Foxhall Rd NW
  202-380-9298 • $
  Every neighborhood deserves such an ice cream
  shop.
- **Kotobuki** • 4822 MacArthur Blvd NW
  202-281-6679 • $$
  Price: low. Quality: high.

- **Makoto Restaurant** • 4822 MacArthur Blvd NW
  202-298-6866 • $$$
  Sushi a la carte. You'll never need to visit Japan.
- **Old Europe** • 2434 Wisconsin Ave NW
  202-333-7600 • $$$
  Forget Atkins: try the Rindergoulasch ungarische
  Art and Apfelstrudel.
- **Palisades Pizzeria & Clam Bar** •
  4885 MacArthur Blvd NW
  202-338-2010 • $$
  NY thin crust, Philly cheesesteaks, fried clams, and
  soft serve, then, angina.
- **Rocklands** • 2418 Wisconsin Ave NW
  202-333-2558 • $$
  Cooking 150,000 pounds of pork a year, and
  counting.
- **Something Sweet** • 3706 Macomb St NW
  202-380-9368 • $
  More cupcakes
- **Sprig & Sprout** • 2317 Wisconsin Ave NW
  202-333-2569 • $
  Pho and Viet sandwich shop with craft beer.
- **Surfside** • 2444 Wisconsin Ave NW
  202-380-9353 • $$
  Dude, eat up
- **Sushiko** • 2309 Wisconsin Ave NW
  202-333-4187 • $$$$
  Washington's first sushi bar, since 1976.
- **Town Hall** • 2340 Wisconsin Ave NW
  202-333-5640 • $$$
  Soul food without the soul.
- **Z Burger** • 2414 Wisconsin Ave NW
  202-965-7777 • $$
  Burger, dogs, and milkshakes—and a bazillion
  ways to have them.

This area of DC is home to some of the finest eats in the city, including **2 Amys'** heavenly Neapolitan pizza pies and **Sushi Ko's** delectable sashimi. Of course, there are more salacious options here too, including one of the city's most popular strip clubs, **Good Guys**. Despite the name, the dancers are female.

 18 8 9 10 11 12 35 36 7 1 2 3 4 37 6 5

👜 Shopping

- **Ann Hand** • 4885 MacArthur Blvd NW
  202-333-2979
  Top-notch jewelry boutique.
- **Encore Resale Dress Shop** • 3715 Macomb St NW
  202-966-8122
  Second-hand glitzy gowns.
- **Inga's Once Is Not Enough** •
  4830 MacArthur Blvd NW
  202-337-3072
  Chanel, Valentino, and Prada, for example.

- **The Kellogg Collection** • 5215 Wisconsin Ave NW
  202-363-6879
  Local chain of upscale home furnishings.
- **Marvelous Market** • 4885 MacArthur Blvd NW
  202-625-5110
  Treat yourself to gourmet cheeses, breads, and olives.
- **Sullivan's Toys & Art Supplies** •
  4200 Wisconsin Ave NW
  202-362-1343
  Narrow aisles crammed with every toy imaginable. Leave kids home.
- **Theodore's** • 2233 Wisconsin Ave NW
  202-333-2300
  Funky décor.

It you want the feel of a wealthy suburb without sacrificing your DC address, this is your neighborhood. Upscale retail and casual dining line the major streets, while the close proximity of the neighborhoods allows you to easily get around on foot. Brick colonials and fancy Victorians contrast with more modern apartment high rises, and there's a brand new sleek library branch in the heart of Tenleytown.

○ Landmarks

- **Fort Reno** • Chesapeake St NW
  Civil War fort, highest point in DC; summer punk shows.

Nightlife

- **The Dancing Crab (The Malt Shop)** •
  4615 Wisconsin Ave NW
  202-244 1882
  A dozen large crabs and beer. Popular with AU students.
- **Guapo's** • 4515 Wisconsin Ave NW
  202-686-3588
  Tortillas + margaritas = stumbling to Tenleytown Metro.

Map 1

Restaurants

- **Angelico La Pizzeria** • 4529 Wisconsin Ave NW
  202-243-3030 • $$
  You know you want some cheap, greasy Italian food.
- **Café of India** • 4909 Wisconsin Ave NW
  202-244-1395 • $$
  Worst copyedited menu ever.
- **Café Ole** • 4000 Wisconsin Ave NW
  202-244-1330 • $$$
  Fun neighborhood Spanish-style tapas.
- **The Dancing Crab** • 4611 41st St NW
  202-244-1882 • $$$
  Grab a bib and mallet and get cracking.
- **FroZenYo** • 5252 Wisconsin Ave NW
  $
  Self-serve frozen yogurt inside Booeymonger.
- **Guapo's** • 4515 Wisconsin Ave NW
  202-686-3588 • $$$
  Nothing better than drinking tequila outside.
- **Le Chat Noir** • 4907 Wisconsin Ave NW
  202-244-2044 • $$$
  For all you Belle Epoque and Art Nouveau fans.

- **Maggiano's Little Italy** • 5333 Wisconsin Ave NW
  202-966-5500 • $$
  Opposite of this book's title.
- **Masala Art** • 4441 Wisconsin Ave NW
  202-362-4441 • $$
  Contemporary Indian cuisine from the Heritage India folks.
- **Matisse** • 4934 Wisconsin Ave NW
  202-244-5222 • $$$$
  French and Mediterranean with all the details.
- **Murasaki** • 4620 Wisconsin Ave NW
  202-966-0023 • $$$
  Wide range of Japanese cuisines.
- **Neisha Thai** • 4445 Wisconsin Ave NW
  202-230-2788 • $$
  Decent Thai in a place that really needs it.
- **Osman and Joe's Steak 'n Egg Kitchen** •
  4700 Wisconsin Ave NW
  202-686-1201 • $
  This greasy spoon hasn't changed a thing in over 60 years.
- **Z Burger** • 4321 Wisconsin Ave NW
  202-966-1999 • $$
  AU student hang-out for grilled burgers and 75 flavors of milkshakes.

Friendship Heights could double for Orange County, with its mall-style shopping (J. Crew) and speciously upscale dining (Cheesecake Factory, Maggiano's). Tenleytown fought big-box stores for years, but tiring of Chinese takeout and mattress outlets, went with the niche shops (**Hudson Trail Outfitters**, **Container Store**) and eateries like **Guapo's** and **Neisha Thai**.

🛍 Shopping

- **Best Buy** • 4500 Wisconsin Ave NW
  202-895-1580
  Gadgets, gadgets, gadgets.
- **Bloomingdale's** • 5300 Wisconsin Ave
  240-744-3700
  182,458 square feet of $$$.
- **The Container Store** • 4500 Wisconsin Ave NW
  202-478-4000
  Buckets, shelves, hangers.
- **Hudson Trail Outfitters** • 4530 Wisconsin Ave NW
  202-363-9810
  Tents and Tevas.
- **Johnson's Florist & Garden Centers** •
  4200 Wisconsin Ave NW
  202-244-6100
  For those of you with a yard.
- **Loehmann's** • 5333 Wisconsin Ave NW
  202-362-4733
  An exciting melange of trash and treasures.
- **Middle C Music** • 4530 Wisconsin Ave NW
  202-244-7326
  Home of the Jack Black-less rock camp every summer.

- **Neiman Marcus** • 5300 Wisconsin Ave NW
  202-966-9700
  Ultra-upscale department store.
- **Red Door Spa** • 5225 Wisconsin Ave NW
  202-362-9890
  Serious pampering.
- **Roche Bobois** • 5301 Wisconsin Ave NW
  202-686-5667
  African traditions.
- **Rodman's** • 5100 Wisconsin Ave NW
  202-363-3466
  Luggage, wine, scented soaps, and other necessities.
- **Serenity Day Spa** • 4000 Wisconsin Ave NW
  202-362-2560
  Name says it all.
- **Tempo Book Distributors** •
  4905 Wisconsin Ave NW
  202-363-6683
  Language books.
- **Tenley Wine and Liquor** • 4525 Wisconsin Ave NW
  202-363-0484
  Wine, liquor and kegs, plus free parking & delivery.

Map 20 Cleveland Park, Upper Connecticut 🌐

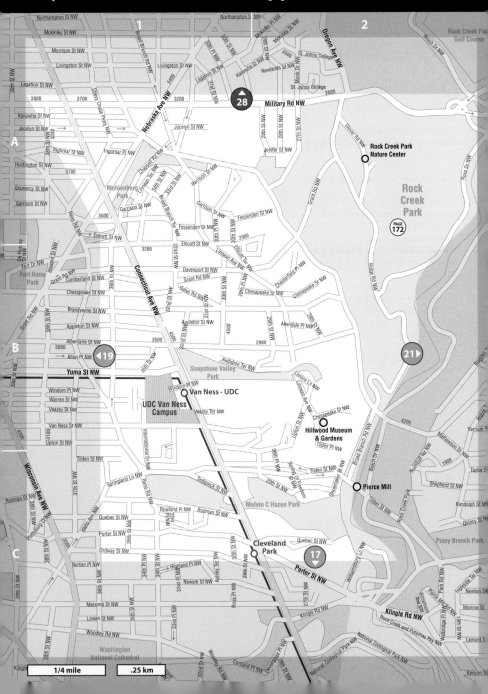

1

2

Northampton St NW
McKinley St NW
Morrison St NW
Livingston St NW

Legation St NW
3800   3700

Kanawha St NW
Jocelyn St NW
5300

A   Ingomar St NW
38th St NW
3700

Huntington St NW

Gramercy St NW
Garrison St NW
3800

Chesapeake St NW

Brandywine St NW

Appleton St NW

Albemarle St NW
3800

Alton Pl NW

B   Yuma St NW

Windom Pl NW
Warren St NW
Veazey St NW
Van Ness St NW
4100
Upton St NW

Tilden St NW

Wisconsin Ave NW

Rodman St NW
38th St NW
37th St NW
4200

Quebec St NW
Porter St NW
Ordway St NW

C   Norton Pl NW

38th St NW
38th Pl NW

Macomb St NW
Lowell St NW
Woodley Rd NW

Klingle

Washington
National Cathedral

Northampton St NW
McKinley Pl NW
29th St NW
5500
St Johns College

St Johns College
2600

Nebraska Ave NW
3200

Military Rd NW

Jocelyn St NW

Jenifer St NW

Muhlenberg
Park

Garrison St NW
3600

Fessenden St NW

Ellicott St NW
3200

Davenport St NW
Grant Rd NW
Gates Rd NW

Appleton St NW
4500

Audubon Ter NW

Soapstone Valley
Park

Windom Pl NW

Van Ness - UDC

UDC Van Ness
Campus

Veazey Ter NW

International Dr NW

Springland Ln NW
Reno Rd NW

Sedgwick St NW

Rowland Pl NW
Rodman St NW

Melvin C Hazen Park

Cleveland
Park

Quebec St NW

Porter St NW

Highland Pl NW

Ashley Ter NW

Newark St NW

Ross Pl NW

Klingle Rd NW

Cortland Pl NW

28

19

17

Chapman Rd NW
Linnean Ter NW
34th St NW
Broad Branch Rd NW

Garrison St NW
Fessenden St NW
30th Pl NW
30th St NW
2900

Linnean Ave NW
29th St NW
Chesapeake St NW

31st St NW

Karhavha St NW
Newlands St NW
29th St NW
Monk St NW
28th St NW

28th St NW

Connecticut Ave NW
3500
4500
4600

Harrison St NW

Fessenden St NW

Chesterfield Pl NW

Chesapeake St NW

Allendale Pl NW
2900

Lenore Ln NW
Linnean Ave NW

Chesapeake St NW
28th St NW

Hillwood Museum
& Gardens

Sons Of Freedom

Tilden Pl NW

Tilden St NW
29th St NW

Sons Of Freedom

Shoemaker St NW

Sutton Pl NW

Oregon Ave NW

Grant Rd NW

Rock Creek Park
Nature Center

Glover Rd NW

Ridge Rd NW

Rock
Creek
Park

PAGE
172

Beach Dr NW

4200

Broad Branch Rd NW

Shoemaker St NW

Pierce Mill

Tilden St NW
Williamsburg Ln NW

Porter St NW

Quebec St NW

Rock Creek Park Golf Course

Ross Dr NW

Beach Dr NW

Rock Creek Park and Potomac Pkwy NW

21

Buggan

Blagden

Argyle

Varnum

Mathewson Dr NW
1900
Taylor St

Shepherd St NW

Randolph St NW

Quincy St NW

Piney Branch Park

Pierce Mill Rd NW
Ingleside Ter NW
Newton St
Monroe St

Lamont St NW

National Zoological Park NW

Kenyon

1/4 mile   .25 km

Self-satisfied liberals unite! These blocks are dominated by well-meaning professionals who carry their own bags to the organic market, shun fancy restaurants, and enjoy the debates at **Politics & Prose**. But they like their coffeehouses sans the grunge.

o Landmarks

- **Hillwood Estate, Museum & Gardens** •
  4155 Linnean Ave NW
  202-686-5807
  Home of heiress Marjorie Merriweather Post is simply exquisite.
- **Pierce Mill** • 2401 Tilden St NW
  202-895-6070
  Doesn't everyone love a 19th-century grist mill?
- **Rock Creek Park Nature Center and Planetarium** • 5200 Glover Rd NW
  202-895-6070
  Nature in the city.

Nightlife

- **Comet Ping Pong** • 5037 Connecticut Ave NW
  202-364-0404
  Go for ping pong and Paul.
- **St. Arnold's of Cleveland Park** •
  3433 Connecticut Ave NW
  202-621-6719
  Hits all three Belgian mainstays: beer, mussels, waffles.

Restaurants

- **Acacia Bistro** • 4340 Connecticut Ave NW
  202-537-1040 • $$
  Small plates and wine from the Wellness Cafe folks.
- **Buck's Fishing & Camping** •
  5031 Connecticut Ave NW
  202-364-0777 • $$$$
  More sophisticated than the name suggests.
- **Indique** • 3512 Connecticut Ave NW
  202-244-6600 • $$$$
  Wrap your mind around an inside-out samosa.
- **Medium Rare** • 3500 Connecticut Ave NW
  202-237-1432 • $$
  Concept steakhouse does one thing and does it well; vegetarians beware.
- **Palena** • 3529 Connecticut Ave NW
  202-537-9250 • $$$$
  Continental food and an engrossing dessert menu.
- **Paragon Thai** • 3507 Connecticut Ave NW
  202-237-2777 • $$
  No-frills Thai.
- **St. Arnold's of Cleveland Park** •
  3433 Connecticut Ave NW
  202-621-6719 • $$
  Hits all three Belgian mainstays: beer, mussels, waffles.

Shopping

- **Calvert Woodley** • 4339 Connecticut Ave NW
  202-966-4400
  Paradise for the snooty but cheap booze hound.
- **Marvelous Market** • 5035 Connecticut Ave NW
  202-686-4040
  Try the blueberry muffins.
- **Politics & Prose** • 5015 Connecticut Ave NW
  202-364-1919
  Bookstore mecca, great readings too!
- **Weygandt Wines** • 3519 Connecticut Ave NW
  202-362-9463
  Imported Euro wines for sale, plus a tasting bar.

Map 21 • **16th S** orth

It was only a matter of time before the neighborly charm of Petworth's ticky-tack rowhouses was "discovered" by upstarts. This incursion has led to spiking real estate costs and some grumbling from the old timers. But come on, where are all the liberals priced out of Logan Circle and Dupont supposed to go?

Nightlife

- **Mad Momos** • 3605 14th St NW
  202-829-1450
  Don't call it a "beer garden," it's a beer deck and it's got momos!
- **Red Derby** • 3718 14th St NW
  202-291-5000
  Everyday specials, Charlie Chaplin on the walls.

Restaurants

- **Chez Billy** • 3815 Georgia Ave NW
  202-506-2080 • $$
  Old school posh in the heart of Petworth.
- **Domku** • 821 Upshur St NW
  202-722-7475 • $$$
  East European and Scandinavian comfort food.
- **El Torogoz** • 4231 9th St NW
  202-722-6966 • $$
  Salvadoran sit-down with Spanish TV and outdoor seating.
- **Fusion** • 4815 Georgia Ave NW
  202-726-2210 • $$
  Fused Indian and American flavors nestled in Petworth.
- **Mad Momos** • 3605 14th St NW
  202-829-1450 • $$
  Don't call it a "beer garden," it's a beer deck and it's got momos!
- **Sweet Mango Café** •
  3701 New Hampshire Ave NW
  202-679-1333 • $$
  Slow-roasted jerked chicken on the bone. Best in the city.

Shopping

- **Bentley's Vintage Furniture and Collectibles** •
  810 Upshur St NW
  202-251-0527
  Gentrifantiques: Great finds are just a little pricey.
- **Flip It Bakery** • 4532 Georgia Ave NW
  202-291-3605
  Chef Rodriguez bakes up donuts, mini cupcakes, and Salvadoran turnovers.

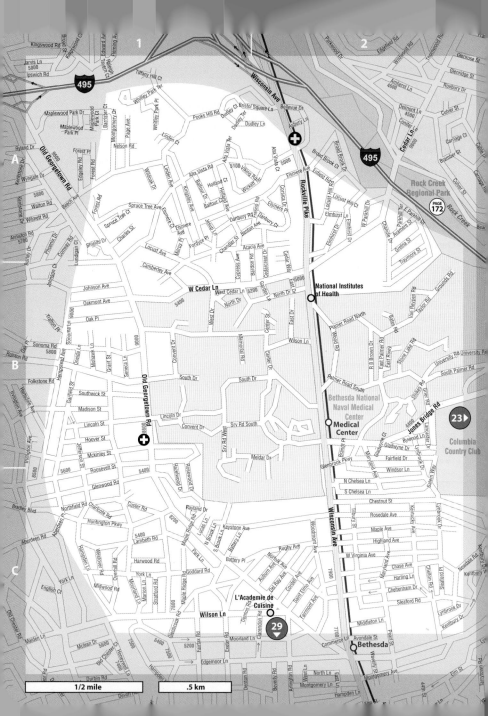

Centered around the NIH and Bethesda National Naval Medical Center, the northern end of Bethesda caters to NIH, NIH's employees, and their homes in the very quaint, suburban setting (but still within the Beltway!!!). It's where Washingtonians ditch their Dupont Circle apartments and move to grow up, and to have their kids grow up, but in public school.

○ Landmarks

- **L'Academie de Cuisine** • 5021 Wilson Ln
  301-986-9490
  One step up from learning to make french fries.
- **National Institutes of Health** • 9000 Rockville Pike
  301-496-4000
  Monkeys and rats beware.

❤ Nightlife

- **Caddies on Cordell** • 4922 Cordell Ave
  301-215-7730
  "The 19th hole," with an outdoor patio and plenty of screens.
- **Flanagan's Harp and Fiddle** • 4844 Cordell Ave
  301-951-0115
  Authentic Irish bartenders.
- **Rock Bottom Brewery** • 7900 Norfolk Ave
  301-652-1311
  Worth the wait.
- **Saphire Cafe** • 7940 Wisconsin Ave
  301-986-9708
  Average bar.
- **Union Jack's** • 4915 St Elmo Ave
  301-652-2561
  A real faux-British pub.

Restaurants

- **Assaggi Mozzarella Bar** • 4838 Bethesda Ave
301-951-1988 • $$
Casual Italian deliciousness in the form of mozzarella, more mozzarella, and more.
- **Bacchus of Lebanon** • 7945 Norfolk Ave
301-657-1722 • $$$$
Lebanese menu with lots of twists and turns.
- **BGR: The Burger Joint** • 4827 Fairmont Ave
301-358-6137 • $$
Gigantic burgers for gigantic people.
- **BlackFinn American Saloon** • 4901 Fairmont Ave
301-951-5681 • $
Do you like sports, beer, and not much else?
- **Delicias Carry Out** • 4708 Highland Ave
301-654-7887 • $
Mom-and-pop burritos in a land of Chipotles.
- **Faryab** • 4917 Cordell Ave
301-951-3484 • $$$
Premier DC metro area Afghan stop.
- **Grapeseed** • 4865 Cordell Ave
301-986-9592 • $$$$
Spanish cuisine to go with wine list al grande.
- **Haandi** • 7905 Norfolk Ave
301-718-0121 • $$$
Super-tasty Indian.
- **Louisiana Kitchen & Bayou Bar** •
4907 Cordell Ave
301-652-6945 • $$
Get your Muffuletta fix here.
- **Matuba** • 4918 Cordell Ave
301-652-7449 • $$$
Basic sushi and buffet.

- **Mia's Pizzas** • 4926 Cordell Ave
301-718-6427 • $$
Pizza pies from a wood-burning oven.
- **Olazzo** • 7921 Norfolk Ave
301-654-9496 • $$$
Italian with a brick oven (and yet no pizza!).
- **The Original Pancake House** •
7700 Wisconsin Ave
301-986-0285 • $
Oh, go ahead. Bring back a few childhood memories.
- **Passage to India** • 4931 Cordell Ave
301-656-3373 • $
Sudhir Seth's top-notch culinary aromatherapy.
- **Peter's Carry-Out** • 8017 Wisconsin Ave
301-656-2242 • $
Best greasy spoon according to some people.
- **Tako Grill** • 7756 Wisconsin Ave
301-652-7030 • $$$
Traditional and nontraditional Japanese for the enthusiast.
- **Tastee Diner** • 7731 Woodmont Ave
301-652-3970 • $
Surly waitresses, free refills, clogging arteries, and a whole lotta pies
- **Tia Queta** • 4839 Del Ray Ave
301-654-4443 • $$
Margaritas on a rooftop. Need we say more?
- **Tout de Sweet** • 7831 Woodmont Ave
301-951-0474 • $
French macarons and patisseries make this delectable shop a must-visit.
- **Yamas Mediterranean Grill** • 4806 Rugby Ave
301-312-8384 • $$
Small Greek plates in the Bethesda 'burbs.

Sure, it's the cringingly picture-perfect suburbs complete with overeducated moms pushing their MacLaren strollers to/from the gelateria and the yoga studio in Lululemon outfits, but Bethesda does have its claim to fame as the most restaurants per square mile in the country. Some of our favorites: **Rock Bottom Brewery**, **Passage to India**, and **Faryab**. There's the weekly **farmers market** as well, and a good shopping strip in downtown Bethesda families like to visit by bike along the Capitol Crescent Trail.

🛍Shopping

• **Big Planet Comics** • 4849 Cordell Ave
301-654-6856
Superhero genealogy experts on hand.

• **Ranger Surplus** • 8008 Wisconsin Ave
301-656-2302
Smaller than the Fairfax branch but worth a look.

• **Wiggle Room** • 4924 Del Ray Ave
301-656-5995
Consignment shop for kids' clothes. Why spend more?

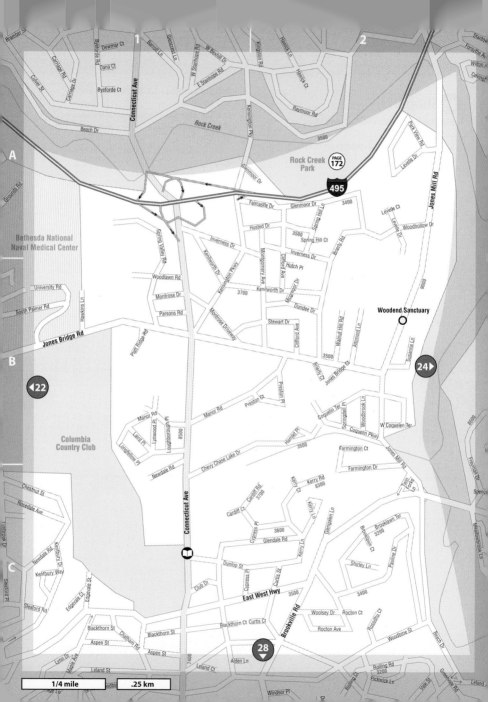

You might as well be on location at a Smith & Hawken catalog shoot. The fussy homes and landscaping here make Maryland's side of Chevy Chase a sought-after, practically unreachable suburb. Your kids will go to one of the area's best public schools…but of course you would never send them to public school.

○ Landmarks

• **Woodend Sanctuary** • 8940 Jones Mill Rd
301-652-9188
Quiet National Audubon property tucked within Chevy Chase.

Restaurants

• **Tavira** • 8401 Connecticut Ave
301-652-8684 • $
Wonderful Portuguese in subterraneon Chevy Chase MD.

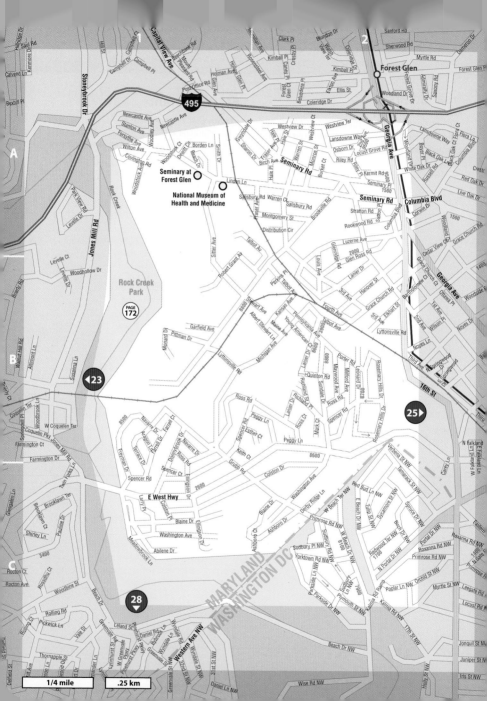

If you ever follow **Rock Creek Park** to its northern end, you'll stumble upon a quiet sanctuary of beautiful homes, seemingly far away from the gritty city. Sandwiched between the Beltway and the District line, between Chevy Chase and Silver Spring, life here is green and lovely. The **Forest Glen Seminary**'s architecturally eclectic buildings are a must-see, however, even if you don't call this hilly neighborhood home.

Map

○ Landmarks

- **National Museum of Health and Medicine** •
  2500 Linden Ln
  301-319-3300
  One of the greatest medical oddity collections on the planet.
- **Seminary at Forest Glen** • Beach Dr & Linden Ln
  Creepy complex of crumbling faux pagodas and French chateaux soon to become creepier housing development.

Restaurants

- **Parkway Deli** • 8317 Grubb Rd
  301-587-1427 • $$
  Another rare high-quality Jewish deli.

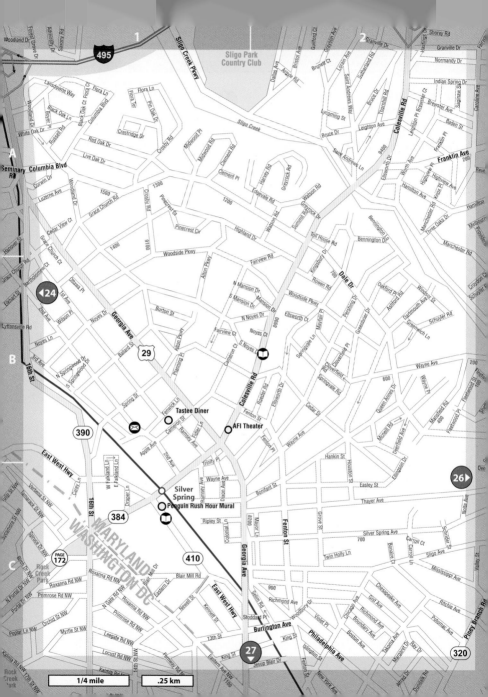

Bordering the District and with good public transportation links (Ride-On, Metrobus, Metro, and MARC), Silver Spring is an older suburb that has seen its share of hard times. Following its "Silver Sprung" redevelopment, Silver Spring's downtown underwent several facelifts until it was finally rewarded with a **Whole Foods** (as well as a Red Lobster—who says you can't have it all?). But the neighborhood does boast an ethnically diverse population, and Sligo Creek is pleasant for biking and playing.

o Landmarks

- **AFI Silver Theatre** • 8633 Colesville Rd
  301-495-6700
  You don't have to see artsy films in crappy movie houses anymore.
- **Penguin Rush Hour Mural** • 8400 Colesville Rd
  Stop elbowing your way onto the Metro to appreciate a piece of Silver Spring.
- **Tastee Diner** • 8601 Cameron St
  301-589-8171
  A thorn in the side of corporate development.

Nightlife

- **The Fillmore Silver Spring** • 8656 Colesville Rd
  202-960-9999
  DC's newest live music venue hosts myriad international acts.
- **Galaxy Billiards** • 8661 Colesville Rd
  301-495-0081
  City Place pool hall for betting suburbanites.
- **Piratz Tavern** • 8402 Georgia Ave
  301-588-9001
  Part Renaissance Fair, part pirate-themed.
- **Quarry House** • 8401 Georgia Ave
  301-587-8350
  Great neighborhood bar but a true hole-in-the-wall.

Restaurants

- **8407 Kitchen Bar** • 8407 Ramsey Ave
  301-587-8407 • $
  "Organic-Modern" American from ex-Nicaro.
- **Addis Ababa** • 8233 Fenton St
  301-589-1400 • $$
  Authentic Ethiopian. Ask to sit on the rooftop.
- **Austin Grill** • 919 Ellsworth Dr
  240-247-8969 • $$
  Down-home grub at down-home prices. Yee-haw.
- **Cubano's** • 1201 Fidler Ln
  301-563-4020 • $$$
  Fountain and foliage make the décor cheesissimo.

- **Eggspectation** • 923 Ellsworth Dr
  301-585-1700 • $$
  So many eggs you wonder where they hide their hens.
- **El Aguila** • 8649 16th St
  301-588-9063 • $$
  Better than its location would have you believe.
- **Jackie's** • 8081 Georgia Ave
  301-565-9700 • $$
  Wine and food at your neighborhood hot spot.
- **Lebanese Taverna** • 933 Ellsworth Dr
  301-588-1192 • $$
  Fast, decent Middle Eastern food.
- **Mandalay** • 930 Bonifant St
  301-585-0500 • $$
  Addictive Burmese food next door to a gun shop.
- **Mi Rancho** • 8701 Ramsey Ave
  301-588-4872 • $$
  Quite cheap Mexican/Salvadorean.
- **Mrs. K's Tollhouse** • 9201 Colesville Rd
  301-589-3500 • $$$$
  Quaint country inn.
- **Ray's The Classics** • 8606 Colesville Rd
  301-588-7297 • $$$
  Need a steak in your life?
- **Roger Miller Restaurant** • 941 Bonifant St
  301-562-7050 • $$
  Unique Cameroonian fare, named after a soccer star. Try the goat.
- **Romano's Macaroni Grill** • 931 Ellsworth Dr
  301-562-2806 • $$$
  Good standard Italian.

Shopping

- **Cakelove** • 8512 Fenton St
  301-565-2253
  High-end and tasty.
- **Color Me Mine** • 823 Ellsworth Dr
  301-565-5105
  Do-it-yourself pottery.
- **Dale Music Company** • 8240 Georgia Ave
  301-589-1459
  Amazing collection of sheet music. Open since 1950.

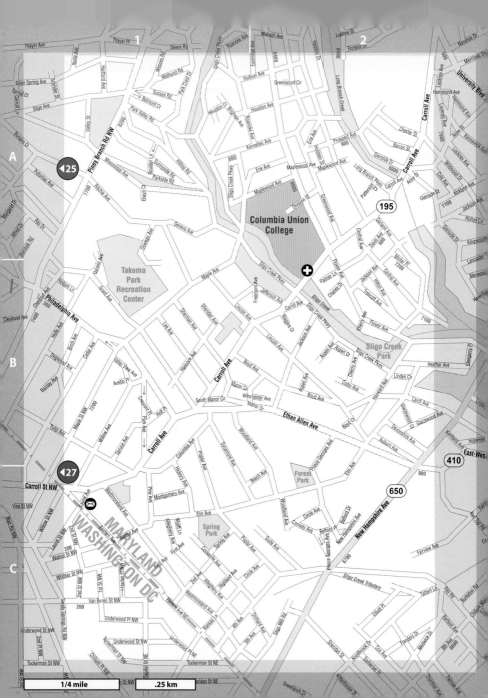

The surfeit of aging activists, neo-hippies, and left-leaning yuppies has earned this town the nickname "The People's Republic of Takoma Park." Proletariat they are not, however. Residents enjoy all the benefits of suburban living: big houses, fancy lattes, locally grown produce. But don't get too cynical—Takoma Park is fiercely loyal to local businesses and has successfully resisted development and corporate "revitalization."

Restaurants

- **Capital City Cheesecake** • 7071 Carroll Ave
  301-270-7260 • $
  Cheesecakes and so much more!
- **Mark's Kitchen** • 7006 Carroll Ave
  301-270-1884 • $$
  Green-friendly American and Korean fare.
- **Olive Lounge & Grill** • 7006 Carroll Ave
  301-270-5154 • $$
  Middle Eastern cuisine.
- **Roscoe's Pizzeria** • 7040 Carroll Ave
  301-920-0804 • $
  New Neapolitan pies for TkPk.

Shopping

- **AMANO** • 7034 Carroll Ave
  301-270-1140
  Casual clothing.
- **Artful Framing and Gallery** • 7050 Carroll Ave
  301-270-2427
  Archival & custom framing.
- **The Covered Market** • 7000 Carroll Ave
  301-270-1219
  Turkish bazaar by way of Takoma Park.
- **Fair Day's Play** • 7050 Carroll Ave
  301-270-4999
  Fair trade and American made apparel.
- **House of Musical Traditions** •
  7040 Westmoreland Ave
  301-270-9090
  Looking for a new skakuhachi or hurdy-gurdy? They've got it.
- **The Magic Carpet** • 6925 Laurel Ave
  301-270-5623
  Eclectic gifts, home décor, jewelry, furniture, imports.
- **Now and Then** • 6927 Laurel Ave
  301-270-2210
  Eclectic gifts, children's clothing and toys, yarn, jewelry, home décor.
- **Park Florist** • 6921 Laurel Ave
  301-270-1848
  Where to get all your flowers since 1935!
- **Polly Sue's** • 6915 Laurel Ave
  301-270-5511
  Vintage heaven.
- **S & A Beads** • 6929 Laurel Ave
  301-891-2323
  Beads and jewelry. Classes, too!
- **The Still Point** • 1 Columbia Ave
  301-920-0801
  Massage, acupuncture and therapeutic bodywork.
- **Takoma Picture Framers** • 7312 Carroll Ave
  301-270-4433
  Archival & custom framing.

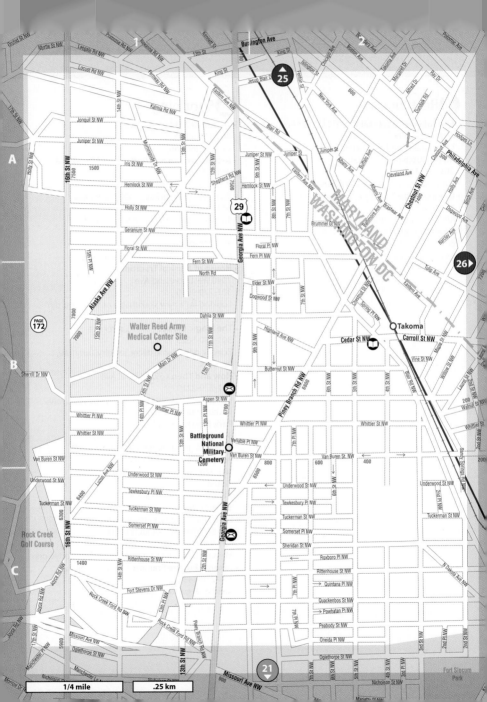

Until 2011, when the Walter Reed Army Medical Center was consolidated with nearby Bethesda Naval Medical Center, the neighborhood catered to military families and veterans using its services. The grounds are the neighborhood's diamond in the rough, and it remains to be seen how the 100-plus acre site will be redeveloped.

Map

○ Landmarks

- **Battleground National Military Cemetery** •
  6625 Georgia Ave NW
  Check out the entrance.
- **Walter Reed Army Medical Center Site** •
  6900 Georgia Ave NW
  202-782-3412
  Site of Army's main medical center from
  1909–2011.

Nightlife

- **Charlie's Bar & Grill** • 7307 Georgia Ave NW
  202-726-3567
  Soul food and contemporary jazz.
- **Takoma Station Tavern** • 6914 4th St NW
  202-829-1999
  Jazz haven.

Restaurants

- **Blair Mansion** • 7711 Eastern Ave
  301-588-1688 • $$$$
  Waiter, there's a dead body in my soup!
- **Cedar Crossing** • 341 Cedar St NW
  202-882-8999 • $$
  Bistro and bar on the other side of the Takoma
  tracks.
- **Teddy's Roti Shop** • 7304 Georgia Ave NW
  202-882-6488 • $
  West Indian curries with ginger drink…mmm…

Shopping

- **Georgia Avenue Thrift Store** •
  6101 Georgia Ave NW
  202-291-4013
  A landmark DC thrift store.

Map 28

This extremely wealthy pocket of upper northwest DC and suburban Maryland is green, well manicured and lily white—reminiscent of a Norman Rockwell cross-stitch. It's picture-perfect in spring when cherry blossoms drop pink petals all over your car, and drivers obey the 30 mph speed limit on Connecticut or get caught by the camera. And no, the town is not named for the star of Fletch.

Landmarks

- **Avalon Theatre** • 5612 Connecticut Ave NW
  202-966-6000
  Beloved neighborhood movie house.

Nightlife

- **Chevy Chase Lounge** • 5510 Connecticut Ave NW
  202-966-7600
  Parthenon Restaurant's wood-panelled lounge.
- **The Tasting Room** • 5330 Western Ave
  301-664-9494
  Vino vending machines from Boxwood Winery in Middleburg.

Restaurants

- **American City Diner** • 5532 Connecticut Ave NW
  202-244-1949 • $
  1950s drive-in themed diner, complete with movies.
- **Arucola** • 5534 Connecticut Ave NW
  202-244-1555 • $$$$
  Straightforward Italian.
- **Bread & Chocolate** • 5542 Connecticut Ave NW
  202-966-7413 • $
  Can't go wrong with this combination.
- **La Ferme** • 7101 Brookville Rd
  301-986-5255 • $$$$
  Charming (if bizarre) French bistro in a residential area.
- **Pumpernickels Deli** • 5504 Connecticut Ave NW
  202-244-9505 • $
  Top-notch local bagels, sandwiches, and attitude.

Shopping

- **Broad Branch Market** • 5608 Broad Branch Rd NW
  202-249-8551
  High-end corner store for exclusive upper NW hood.
- **Chevy Chase Wine & Spirits** •
  5544 Connecticut Ave NW
  202-363-4000
  Charming, expert boozologists.

Map 29 · **Bethesda (South)**

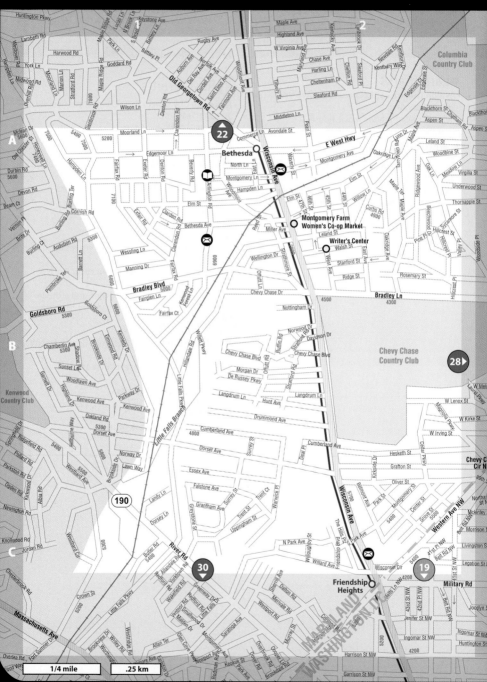

Every young DC couple yearns to become one of those suburban families clustered around Bethesda, with easy access to the metro, restaurants and top school systems. If they're lucky and their government salary permits, they can enter the Chevy Chase Country Club; if not, they can dress the part by shopping at the high-end stores along Wisconsin near Friendship Heights.

Map

o Landmarks

- **Montgomery Farm Women's Co-op Market** •
  7155 Wisconsin Ave
  301-652-2291
  Indoor country market.
- **The Writer's Center** • 4508 Walsh St
  301-654-8664
  Take a class, write for NFT.

Nightlife

- **The Barking Dog** • 4723 Elm St
  301-654-0022
  Decent frat-boy bar.
- **Bowlmor** • 5353 Westbard Ave
  301-652-0955
  Not your average bowling alley.
- **Tommy Joe's** • 4714 Montgomery Ln
  301-654-3801
  Frat boy central.

Restaurants

- **Bethesda Crab House** • 4958 Bethesda Ave
  301-652-3382 • $$
  More like "basement" than "house" with excellent crabs year-round and little else.
- **The Brown Bag** • 7272 Wisconsin Ave
  301-654-4600 • $$
  Outstanding sandwiches.
- **Clyde's** • 5441 Wisconsin Ave NW
  301-951-9600 • $
  All-American fare amidst Orient Express décor.
- **Dolcezza** • 7111 Bethesda Lane
  301-215-9226 • $
  Gelato on Bethesda Row fits right in.
- **Georgetown Cupcake** • 4834 Bethesda Ave
  301-907-8900 • $
  From Georgetown to Bethesda Row, these are the fanciest cupcakes in town.
- **Hinode** • 4914 Hampden Ln
  301-654-0908 • $$$
  No-surprises Japanese.
- **Indique Heights** • 2 Wisconsin Cir
  301-656-4822 • $$
  Fusion Indian.
- **Jaleo** • 7271 Woodmont Ave
  301-913-0003 • $$$$
  Good, if overpriced, tapas.
- **Moby Dick House of Kabob** • 7027 Wisconsin Ave
  301-654-1838 • $
  Mind your manners or "No kebob for you!"

- **Mon Ami Gabi** • 7239 Woodmont Ave
  301-654-1234 • $$$$
  Authentic French atmosphere: expensive and snooty. Half-price wines on Wednesday evenings.
- **Persimmon** • 7003 Wisconsin Ave
  301-654-9860 • $$$$
  Superlative Bethesda continental experience.
- **Potomac Pizza** • 19 Wisconsin Cir
  301-951-1129 • $
  Much-loved pizza parlor for 30+ years.
- **Raku** • 7240 Woodmont Ave
  301-718-8680 • $$$
  Pan-Asian delight with lovely outdoor patio.
- **Redwood** • 7121 Bethesda Ln
  301-656-5515 • $$$$
  Seasonal, new American food from the Sonoma folks.
- **Sushiko** • 5455 Wisconsin Ave
  301-961-1644 • $$$
  Sexy second edition of DC's first sushi spot includes a room just for sake swilling.
- **Sweetgreen** • 4831 Bethesda Ave
  301-654-7336 • $
  Baby arugula, "guac deconstructed," and yogurt dressings on the go.
- **Tara Thai** • 4828 Bethesda Ave
  301-657-0488 • $$
  Well-known for bold Thai.
- **Uncle Julio's** • 4870 Bethesda Ave
  301-656-2981 • $$$
  Great free chips and salsa, good Tex Mex.
- **Vace** • 4705 Miller Ave
  301-654-6367 • $
  Queue up for the best pizza in town.

North of the Friendship Heights glitzy, high-end shopping and restaurants is a brief residential pause before entering the arts end of Bethesda. Check out the **Montgomery Farm Women's Co-op Market**, where you can get your handbags handmade and Turkish rugs for cheap. Head to **Bethesda Crab House** to shell some Maryland blue crabs and knock back some cold ones.

Shopping

- **Bethesda Tattoo Company** •
  4711 Montgomery Ln
  301-652-0494
  It wouldn't hurt you to commit to something.
- **Brooks Brothers** • 5504 Wisconsin Ave
  301-654-8202
  DC's uniform supply shop.
- **Bruce Variety** • 8011 Woodmont Ave
  301-656-7543
  Structured mishmash of costumes, school supplies, pipe cleaners and more!
- **Cartier** • 5471 Wisconsin Ave
  301-654-5858
  Tiffany?! Go classic with Cartier.
- **Chico's** • 5418 Wisconsin Ave
  301-986-1122
  Clothing for stylish women with professional bank accounts.
- **Georgetown Bagelry** • 5227 River Rd
  301-657-4442
  Pick up a warm one every morning.
- **Knit and Stitch Equals Bliss** • 4706 Bethesda Ave
  301-652-8688
  Knit and crochet supplies.
- **Luna** • 7232 Woodmont Ave
  301-656-1111
  Small boutique carrying expensive designer labels.
- **Mustard Seed** • 7349 Wisconsin Ave
  301-907-4699
  Not your typical resale store.
- **Parvizian Fine Rugs** • 7924 Wisconsin Ave NW
  301-654-8989
  Serious rugs.
- **Pirjo Boutique** • 4821 Bethesda Ave
  301-986-1870
  Because soccer moms need Finnish clothes.
- **Saks Fifth Avenue** • 5555 Wisconsin Ave
  301-657-9000
  Where rich people shop.
- **Saks Jandel** • 5510 Wisconsin Ave
  301-652-2250
  For the well-dressed socialite.
- **Strosniders Hardware** • 6930 Arlington Rd
  301-654-5688
  Serious hardware store with an irascible and knowledgeable staff.
- **Sylene** • 4407 S Park Ave
  301-654-4200
  Fine lingerie.
- **Tiffany & Co.** • 5481 Wisconsin Ave
  301-657-8777
  Pop the question.
- **Trader Joe's** • 6831 Wisconsin Ave
  301-907-0982
  If only the folks shopping there were as laid back as the décor.
- **Urban Country** • 7117 Arlington Rd
  301-654-0500
  Country furniture with an urban twist.
- **The Writer's Center** • 4508 Walsh St
  301-654-8664
  Funky bookstore with literary journals.

It's hard to believe you're in a city when all that surrounds you are single-family homes with portable basketball nets lining the streets, tons of flowering trees that beat fighting the crowds downtown in spring, chirping birds, and the infamous **Mushroom House** across the city line. Nearby is the Dalecarlia Reservoir and Capital Crescent Trail.

○ Landmarks

- **Little Falls Parkway Trail** •
  Massachusetts Ave & Little Falls Pkwy
  Nature trail for Marylandites.
- **Mushroom House** • 4940 Allan Rd
  Private residence is a life-sized smurf house.
- **Spring Valley Park** •
  49th St NW & Hillbrook Ln NW
  A mini stretch of woodland populated by wood-peckers, red-tailed hawks, and dogwalkers.

🍴 Restaurants

- **DeCarlo's** • 4822 Yuma St NW
  202-363-4220 • $$$
  The geriatric crowds feasts on tasty Italian here, the definition of a neighborhood joint.
- **Le Pain Quotidien** • 4874 Massachusetts Ave NW
  202-459-9141 • $$$
  Deliciously French-y food, with French-y portions.

👜 Shopping

- **Crate & Barrel** • 4820 Massachusetts Ave NW
  202-364-6100
  Wedding registry HQ.
- **Ski Center** • 4300 Fordham Rd NW
  202-966-4474
  Umm, skis.
- **Spring Valley Patio** • 4300 Fordham Rd NW
  202-966-9088
  Furniture for your expansive, green, upper NW lawn.
- **Wagshal's Market** • 4845 Massachusetts Ave NW
  202-363-5698
  Gourmet foodstuffs.
- **Western Market** • 4840 Western Ave
  301-229-7222
  Lonesome general store.

Map 31 • Chest

Potomac River

Fort Marcy Park

George Washington Memorial Pkwy

Chainbridge Rd

Marie Butler Leven Preserve

Kirby Rd

Chesterbrook Rd

Old Dominion Dr

Little Pimmit Run Stream Valley Park

N Chesterbrook Rd

Fort Ethan Allen Park

Gleb Road Park

32▶

Golf Branch Nature Center

Jamestown Park

N Glebe Rd

Williamsburg Blvd

33▼

Little Pimmit Run

Old Dominion Dr

Washington Country Club

34▼

Marymount University

FAIRFAX COUNTY
ARLINGTON COUNTY

1/4 mile   .25 km

This residential 'burb is home to senators, Supreme Court justices, and former White House spokesmen, complete with the oldest golf and country club in the DC area. With its large homes and spacious leafy yards, Chesterbrook is old-school wealthy, with none of the crammed together McMansions found in newer parts of NoVa. If you live here, expect to drive your kids' lacrosse team-stickered Lexus SUV elsewhere for essentials.

○ Landmarks

• **Fort Marcy** •
George Washington Memorial Parkway
703-289-2500
Grass and some cannons.

Restaurants

• **Amoo's House of Kabob** • 6271 Old Dominion Dr
703-448-8500 • $$
Go for the great kabobs; ignore the bland décor.
• **Café China** • 6271 Old Dominion Dr
703-821-8666 • $
Pick up little white boxes on the way home from work.
• **Pizza Hut** • 6263 Old Dominion Dr
703-448-3535 • $
You get what you pay for.
• **Subway** • 6216 Old Dominion Dr
703-532-3700 • $
If it's good enough for Jared, it's good enough for me.

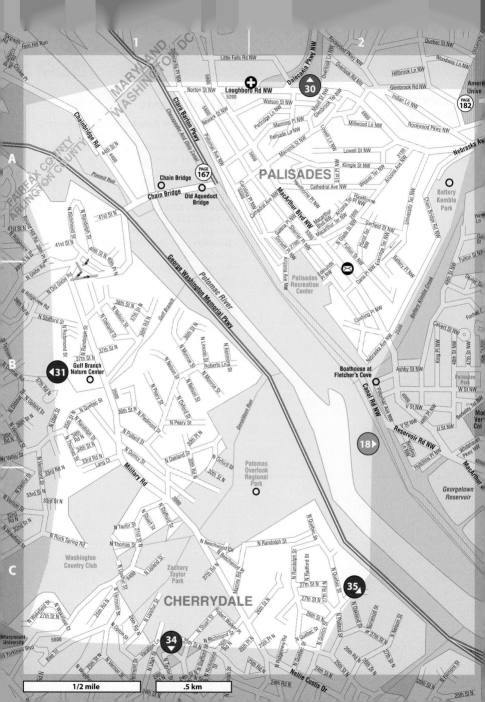

Palisades is one of DC's overlooked neighborhoods—oh-so-quiet and with a mix of modest to magnificent homes, some with fantastic views of the Potomac. A smattering of local shops line MacArthur Boulevard, including essentials like the adorable **Palisades Post Office. Battery Kemble Park** is an often overlooked treasure, with expansive grassy hills and running/walking trail access, but picnickers beware, the spot is popular with local dog owners as a place for an off-leash romp. Across the river in Virginia, it's an outdoor wonderland of nature parks, hiking trails, and fishing holes.

○ Landmarks

- **Battery Kemble Park** • Battery Kemble Park
  Top sledding spot on snow days.
- **The Boathouse at Fletcher's Cove** •
  4940 Canal Rd NW
  202-244-0461
  Boats, angling, and info.
- **Chain Bridge** • Chain Bridge Rd NW
  Completed in 1939 but full history goes back to
  1797.
- **Gulf Branch Nature Center** • 3608 N Military Rd
  703-228-3403
  Family favorite with log cabin, pond, live critters,
  and Potomac trail.
- **Old Aqueduct Bridge** • Chesapeake & Ohio Canal
  All that remains of this former cargo-carrying
  structure has been overtaken by graffiti. Nice.
- **Potomac Overlook Regional Park** •
  2845 Marcey Rd
  703-528-5406
  Nature center, 100 acres with easy walks and challenging trails.

Restaurants

- **Bambu** • 5101 MacArthur Blvd NW
  202-364-3088 • $$$
  Reliable Asian fusion.
- **DC Boathouse** • 5441 MacArthur Blvd NW
  202-362-2628 • $$$$
  Don't crack your skull on the skull.
- **Et Voila!** • 5120 MacArthur Blvd NW
  202-237-2300 • $$$
  Straightforward French cuisine for the Palisades.
- **Listrani's** • 5100 MacArthur Blvd NW
  202-363-0620 • $$$
  A real neighborhood-y pizza & pasta place.
- **Sur La Place** • 5101 MacArthur Blvd NW
  202-237-1445 • $$$
  Cozy Palisades neighborhood Belgian bistro with
  mussels by the kilo.

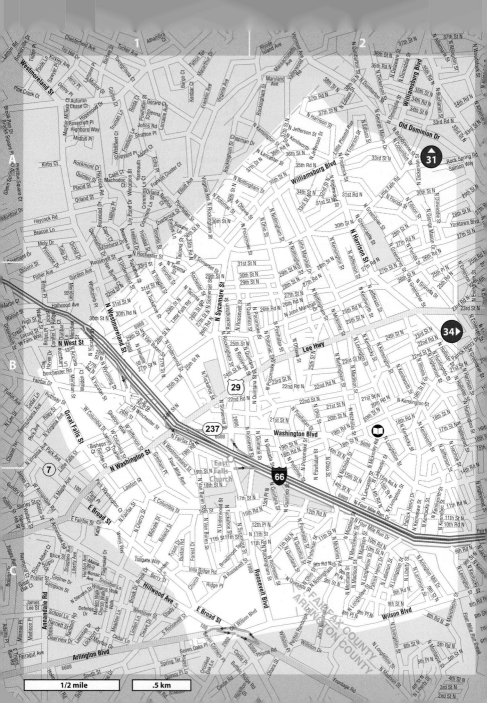

Falls Church is a quiet little suburban paradise with all the right amenities, including the Orange Line, halfway proximity between DC and Dulles, the year-round open-air **Falls Church Farmers Market**, mini-golf, public pool, live music venues, Safeways, schools, and easy access to the 45-mile **Washington & Old Dominion (W&OD) Trail** running from Arlington to Purceville. It's almost an ideal place for families and those who want to get away from the city, if you're okay with raising kids in the South.

Nightlife

- **Chasin' Tails** • 2200 N Westmoreland St
  703-538-2565
  Specializes in crawfish.
- **Dogwood Tavern** • 132 W Broad St
  703-237-8333
  Pub style menu is inspired by regional Virginia dishes.

- **Ireland's Four Provinces** • 105 W Broad St
  703-534-8999
  Why are you in Falls Church? (A good bar, nonetheless.)
- **The State Theatre** • 220 N Washington St
  703-237-0300
  Grab a table, a beer, and listen.
- **Westover Beer Garden and Haus** •
  5863 Washington Blvd
  703-276-7826
  Beer garden offering menu supplied by in-house butcher.

33 34 35 36 37 38 40 7 8 9

🍴Restaurants

- **Asian Kitchen** • 5731 Lee Hwy
  703-538-4888 • $$
  Heavily Japanese inspired Asian fusion offers inventive sushi combos.
- **Caribbean Grill** • 5183 Lee Hwy
  703-241-8947 • $
  Cuban style home cooking perfected. Popular for takeout.
- **Chasin' Tails** • 2200 N Westmoreland St
  703-538-2565 • $$$
  Simple, Cajun style seafood, shrimp bags are generous deal.
- **Clare & Don's Beach Shack** • 130 N Washington St
  703-532-9283 • $$
  Low key patio seating, seafood, sandwiches and live music.
- **District Taco** • 5723 Lee Hwy
  703-237-1204 • $
  Neighborhood taqueria, everything fresh made from scratch.
- **Elevation Burger** • 2447 N Harrison St
  703-300-9467 • $
  Grass fed beef, organic ingredients, fast food style burgers.
- **Ghin Na Ree** • 2509 N Harrison St
  703-536-1643 • $$
  Family run, for three generations, cozy neighborhood Thai restaurant.

- **Huong Viet** • 6785 Wilson Blvd
  703-538-7110 • $$
  Over 163 items! All Vietnamese!
- **Joe's Pizza** • 5555 Lee Hwy
  703-532-0990 • $
  Pizza by New York transplants is a team/school favorite.
- **La Cote D'Or** • 2201 N Westmoreland St
  703-538-3033 • $$$
  Classic French, offers changing daily set price ($25) three-course special.
- **Lebanese Taverna** • 5900 Washington Blvd
  703-241-8681 • $$$
  Family-style Lebanese. Everyone shares.
- **Little Saigon** • 6218 Wilson Blvd
  703-536-2633 • $$
  Easily overlooked restaurant offers authentic, extensive, and well prepared menu.
- **Lost Dog Cafe** • 5876 Washington Blvd
  703-237-1552 • $$
  Specializes in pizza, sandwiches, and wide array of beer.
- **Nhu Lan Sandwich Shop** • 6763 Wilson Blvd
  703-532-9009 • $
  Tucked away neighborbood secret, fairly price, handmade sandwiches.
- **Peking Pavilion Chinese Restaurant** •
  2912 N Sycamore St
  703-237-6868 • $
  Hidden Chinese gem in strip mall Arlington hell.

Falls Church

The cheap eats in this neighborhood compensate for the strip-mall aesthetic. Westover Village on Washington Boulevard is a handy place to grab a beer and dinner at the **Lost Dog Café** (or wine, salad, and the feline perspective at the **Stray Cat**), chicken shawarma at **Lebanese Taverna**, or coconut soup with lemongrass at **Thai Noy**. Nightlife is sparse, but in Westover you can find local music and craft beer until midnight. Also, Broad Street in Falls Church has **The State Theatre**, which hosts an eclectic array of performers, **Ireland's Four Provinces**, **Clare & Don's Beach Shack**, and the **Dogwood Tavern**.

Map 33

- **Pho 88** • 232 W Broad St
  703-533-8233 • $
  Traditional Vietnamese perfected, at a fair price.
- **Pie-Tanza** • 2503 Harrison St
  703-237-0200 • $$
  Wood-fired pizzas and herb infused traditional Italian fare.
- **Pines of Florence** • 3811 Fairfax Dr
  703-243-7463 • $$
  Classic Italian restaurant offers familiar favorites.
- **Public House No. 7** • 6315 Leesburg Pike
  703-942-6383 • $$
  A British recreation offers pub inspired food.
- **Rice Paper** • 6775 Wilson Blvd
  703-538-3888 • $
  Simplicity but multi-flavored Vietnamese establishment.
- **Stray Cat Café** • 5866 Washington Blvd
  703-237-7775 • $
  Kitty kat décor with great sandwiches, burgers and salads.
- **Sushi-Zen** • 2457 N Harrison St
  703-534-6000 • $$$
  Sushi and sashimi served in hand-carved wooden boats draw families—lots of them.
- **Taqueria El Poblano** • 2503 N Harrison St
  703-237-8250 • $$
  As predictable as it is cheap.
- **Thai Noy** • 5880 N Washington Blvd
  703-534-7474 • $$
  Above-average Thai in arty, Buddha-filled space.

Shopping

- **Best Buy** • 5799 Leesburg Pike
  703-671-0184
  Gadgets, gadgets, gadgets.
- **Calico Corners** • 6400 Williamsburg Blvd
  703-536-5488
  Reams of fabric and helpful guidance.
- **Westover Market** • 5863 Washington Blvd
  703-536-5040
  Old-timey village feel, almost everything you need.

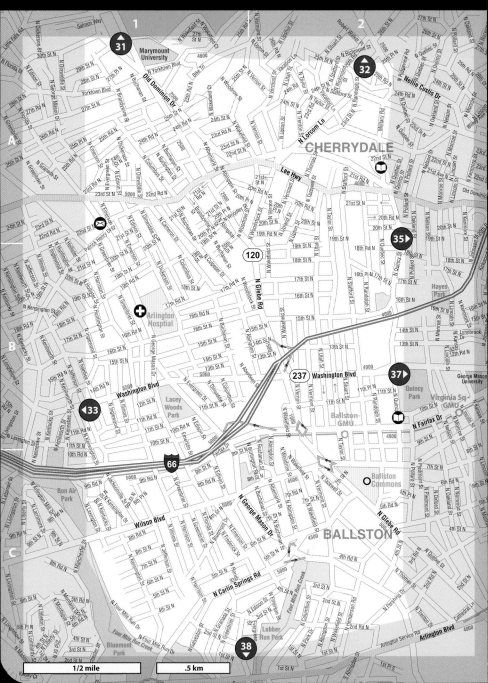

Map 34 • **Cherrydale / Ballston**

GoRemy's "Arlington Rap" described Ballston perfectly: malls, pricey condos, and townhouses filled with Pottery Barn furniture, and aging frat boys in brown flip-flops drinking coffee at the Starbucks (at the Starbucks, at the Starbucks, etc.). Yes, Ballston has a bit of a college town feel, what with all the twenty- and thirty-somethings who flock to the area. But families and more mature adults are part of the community, too: after all, who else can afford the half-million dollar (and up) townhouses and condos?

○ Landmarks

- **Ballston Commons** • 4238 Wilson Blvd
  703-243-8088
  Big box invasion.

◯ Nightlife

- **Bailey's Pub and Grill** • 4238 Wilson Blvd
  703-465-1300
  A sports superbar with a gazillion TVs.
- **Carpool** • 4000 Fairfax Dr
  703-532-7665
  Pool, darts, and beers on the patio.
- **Cowboy Café** • 4792 Lee Hwy
  703-243-8010
  Neighborhood bar and burgers.
- **The Front Page** • 4201 Wilson Blvd
  703-248-9990
  Restaurant with two bars. Great happy hour Monday-Friday.
- **Rock Bottom Brewery** • 4238 Wilson Blvd
  703-516-7688
  Go for happy hour.

Map 34

Cherrydale / Ballston

31 32 18 17 16
8 9
33 35 36 7
34
37
38 40

🍴 Restaurants

- **America Seafood** • 4550 Lee Hwy
  703-522-8080 • $$
  Beachy feel, casual outdoor seating, simple fresh seafood.
- **Buzz Bakery** • 818 N Quincy St
  703-650-9676 • $
  Cheerful and colorful bakery/coffee spot.
- **Crisp & Juicy** • 4540 Lee Hwy
  703-243-4222 • $$
  Latino-barbecued chicken.
- **Café Tirolo** • 4001 N Fairfax Dr
  703-528-7809 • $$
  Hidden European treasure with modest prices.
- **Cassatt's** • 4536 Lee Hwy
  703-527-3330 • $$
  Head over on Kiwi Mondays for interesting dinner fare and an art lesson downstairs.
- **Crisp & Juicy** • 4540 Lee Hwy
  703-243-4222 • $$
  Latino-barbecued chicken.
- **Grand Cru Wine Bar and Bistro** • 4401 Wilson Blvd
  703-243-7900 • $
  If you like to pretend you're a wine snob. Food—not so grand cru.
- **Heidelberg Pastry Shoppe** • 2150 N Culpeper St
  703-527-8394 • $
  A tasty German bakery "Shoppe" fit for a president. Move over, cupcakes.
- **Hunan Gate** • 4233 Fairfax Dr
  703-243-5678 • $
  Cheap Chinese. Good.
- **La Union** • 5517 Wilson Blvd
  703-522-0134 • $$
  Cozy, low-key Salvadorian place offers generous plates.
- **Layalina** • 5216 Wilson Blvd
  703-525-1170 • $$$
  Middle Eastern rugs adorn walls. Straight out of *Aladdin*.
- **Linda's Cafe** • 5050 Lee Hwy
  703-538-2542 • $
  Neighborhood greasy spoon diner serves heaping breakfast plates.
- **Matsutake Hibachi Steak & Sushi** •
  4121 Wilson Blvd
  703-351-8787 • $$$
  Well-executed Japanese cuisine, quick lunchtime sushi fix.
- **Me Jana** • 2300 Wilson Blvd
  703-465-4440 • $$$
  Elegant, classic Lebanese cuisine.
- **The Melting Pot** • 1110 N Glebe Rd
  703-243-4490 • $$$
  Mmmm overpriced melted cheese.
- **Metro 29 Diner** • 4711 Lee Hwy
  703-528-2464 • $$
  Diner breakfast with some Greek touches.
- **P.F. Chang's** • 901 N Glebe Rd
  703-527-0955 • $$$
  Tasty posh Chinese; lettuce wraps are a crowd pleaser.
- **Ruffino's Spaghetti House** • 4763 Lee Hwy
  703-528-2242 • $$
  Casual, reasonably priced pasta house.
- **Rustico** • 4075 Wilson Blvd
  571-384-1820 • $$$
  Amazing beer list to go with the good food.
- **Super Pollo** • 550 N Quincy St
  571-970-3431 • $
  They don't call it "World Famous" for nothing.
- **Super Pollo Charcoal Chicken** • 5011 Wilson Blvd
  703-351-7666 • $
  Charcoal chicken and generous portions of diverse side dishes.
- **Ted's Montana Grill** • 4300 Wilson Blvd
  703-741-0661 • $$
  Upscale, red-state buffalo meat chain.
- **Tutto Bene** • 501 N Randolph St
  703-522-1005 • $$$
  Italian cuisine, when not Bolivian. We love America.
- **Uncle Julio's Rio Grande Café** • 4301 N Fairfax Dr
  703-528-3131 • $$
  We don't know what café means anymore.
- **Vapiano** • 4401 Wilson Blvd
  703-528-3113 • $$
  Dining hall setup, fancy restaurant food and feel but on the cheap.
- **Willow** • 4301 N Fairfax Dr
  703-465-8800 • $$$$
  Snazzy spot helmed by Kinkhead's ex-head chef.

While many Ballston residents are lured out to Clarendon or DC on the weekends, there's still a lot to do here. **Willow**'s chefs regularly get rave reviews and **Tutto Bene** is a local spot offering casual Italian. If you don't mind bland bars ensconced in shopping malls, relive college days elbowing for happy hour specials at **Rock Bottom Brewery** or **Bailey's Pub**. For a less-packed venue, head to **The Front Page**, or to **Carpool** for billiards, or, if you must, catch the Orange Line at the Ballston metro stop to find your nightlife in the city.

Shopping

- **Arrowine and Cheese** • 4508 Lee Hwy
  703-525-0990
  Eclectic wine, gourmet cheese, and tastings of both.

- **Lebanese Taverna Market** •
  4400 Old Dominion Dr
  703-276-8681
  Area's favorite shawarma and tabouleh to go.
- **Pastries by Randolph** • 4500 Lee Hwy
  703-243-0070
  Bustling, no-nonsense bakery with killer cheesecake and pies.

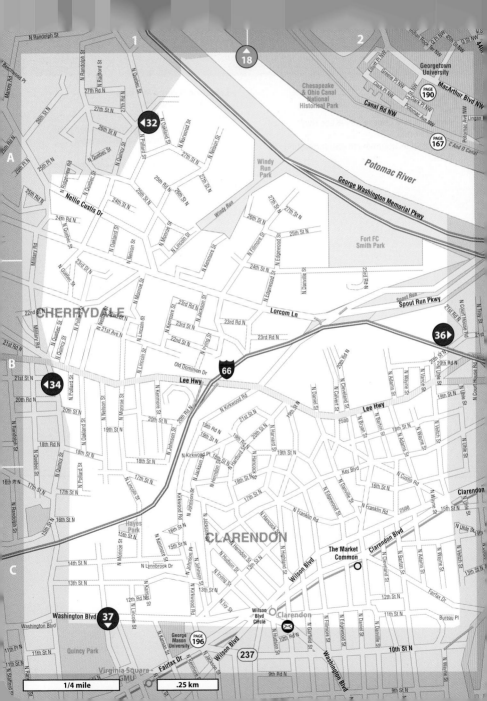

Clarendon is that remodeled community you love to hate: neat brick-lined roads with overpruned bushes and trees, matching signage, an overly sterile environment that feels like Disneyland but also feels relaxing with all its offerings: restaurants with ample outdoor seating, dance clubs, dive bars, live music, **Whole Foods**, and shopping. You could say it's a smaller, trendier, less Potomac-Rivery version of Old Town Alexandria. You could even argue it's better, since it's just as walkable but with closer access to the city.

○ Landmarks

• **The Market Common** • 2700 Clarendon Blvd
Chain retail disguised as Main Street.

☿ Nightlife

• **Clarendon Ballroom** • 3185 Wilson Blvd
703-469-2244
Head for the rooftop.
• **Clarendon Grill** • 1101 N Highland St
703-524-7455
What? Get used to saying that here.
• **Galaxy Hut** • 2711 Wilson Blvd
703-525-8646
Tiny, friendly, indie rock hangout.
• **Iota** • 2832 Wilson Blvd
703-522-8340
Great place to see a twangy band.
• **Mister Days** • 3100 Clarendon Blvd
703-527-1600
Pick-up bar disguised as a sports bar.
• **O'Sullivan's Irish Pub** • 3207 Washington Blvd
703-812-0939
Decent local Irish pub. No surprises.
• **Spider Kelly's** • 3181 Wilson Blvd
703-312-8888
Reborn as a mega-sports bar with pool, darts, and shuffleboard.
• **Whitlow's on Wilson** • 2854 Wilson Blvd
703-276-9693
A separate room for whatever mood you're in.
• **Wilson Tavern** • 2403 Wilson Blvd
571-970-5330
Simple, well crafted classic American plates.

33 34 35 36 7
37
38   40

🍴 Restaurants

- **BGR: The Burger Joint** • 3129 Lee Hwy
  703-812-4705 • $
  The quintessential burger.
- **Boccato** • 2719 Wilson Blvd
  703-869-6522 • $
  Peruvian-run gelateria. Flavors include lychee
  peachy and basil pineapple.
- **The Boulevard Woodgrill** • 2901 Wilson Blvd
  703-875-9663 • $$
  Steak and seafood.
- **Delhi Club** • 1135 N Highland St
  703-527-5666 • $$
  Good Indian. Try the salmon tandoori.
- **Delhi Dhaba** • 2424 Wilson Blvd
  703-524-0008 • $$
  Indian curries make delicious cafeteria-style dishes.
- **Earl's Sandwiches** • 2605 Wilson Blvd
  703-248-0150 • $
  Carefully crafted homemade style sandwiches.
- **East West Grill** • 2721 Wilson Blvd
  703-312-4888 • $$
  Famous kabob array featuring halal meat and naan
  perfected.
- **Eventide Restaurant** • 3165 Wilson Blvd
  703-276-3165 • $$
  Popular, polished new spot in Clarendon.
- **Faccia Luna** • 2909 Wilson Blvd
  703-276-3099 • $$
  Good pizza for a low-key night out or in.
- **Fire Works Pizza** • 2350 Clarendon Blvd
  703-527-8700 • $$
  Wood-fired pizzeria with 30-something beers on
  tap.
- **Green Pig Bistro** • 1025 N Filmore St
  703-888-1920 • $$
  A menu reminiscent of a children's palette, plus
  duck fries.
- **Hard Times Café** • 3028 Wilson Blvd
  703-528-2233 • $$
  Chili-making to a science. Home-brewed root beer
  a bonus.
- **Iota** • 2832 Wilson Blvd
  703-522-8340 •
  Live music venue serving range of sandwiches and
  breakfast.

- **La Tasca** • 2900 Wilson Blvd
  703-812-9120 • $$$
  Great Tapas and Paellas.
- **The Liberty Tavern** • 3195 Wilson Blvd
  703-465-9360 • $$$
  Make a reservation. One of Washingtonian's 100
  best.
- **Lyon Hall** • 3100 Washington Blvd
  703-741-7636 • $$
  Bohemian sausages and beers for the bourgeoisie
  of Arlington.
- **Mad Rose Tavern** • 3100 Clarendon Blvd
  703-600-0500 • $$
  Pub inspired menu, offering seafood and steak.
- **Mexicali Blues** • 2933 Wilson Blvd
  703-812-9352 • $$
  Most colorful restaurant in Arlington. First time?
  Order a burro.
- **Minh's** • 2500 Wilson Blvd
  703-525-2828 • $$
  Ten bucks goes a long way at this Vietnamese
  establishment.
- **Northside Social** • 3211 Wilson Blvd
  703-465-0145 • $$
  Coffee/wine bar…kinda like a bourgie speedball.
- **Pasha Café** • 3911 Lee Hwy
  703-528-1111 • $$
  Casual storefront café serves Middle Eastern favor-
  ites, and pizza too.
- **Pete's New Haven Style Apizza** •
  3017 Clarendon Blvd
  703-527-7383 • $$
  Simple, fresh take on classic Italian dishes.
- **Portabellos** • 2109 N Pollard St
  703-528-1557 • $$
  Contemporary American.
- **Ri Ra Irish Pub** • 2915 Wilson Blvd
  703-248-9888 • $$
  Irish pub fare, featuring traditional fish and chips.
- **Rocklands** • 3471 Washington Blvd
  703-528-9663 • $$
  Barbeque! What ho! It doesn't take long. Mercy me!
- **Silver Diner** • 3200 Wilson Blvd
  703-812-8600 • $$
  Good place for a date, or to end a relationship.
- **Zaika** • 2800 Clarendon Blvd
  703-248-8333 • $$
  Contemporary Indian restaurant, caters to young,
  urban crowd.

Wilson and Clarendon Boulevards are dotted with bars, restaurants, and music venues to suit most tastes. Get your freak on at **Clarendon Ballroom** or **Clarendon Grill**, chill and play arcade games at **Galaxy Hut**, rock out to up-and-comers (or painful open-mic performers) at **Iota**, or explore the trendy and emerging rooftop bar scene at **Whitlow's on Wilson**, **Eventide**, or **The Liberty Tavern**. Clarendon does want for parking, so walk or take the Metro. And if you don't party too hard the night before, come back and try out one of the many Sunday brunches, on your way to one of the several gyms, of course.

Map

Shopping

- **Apple** • 2700 Clarendon Blvd
  703-236-7970
  iParadise for Mac fanatics.
- **Barnes & Noble** • 2800 Clarendon Blvd
  703-248-8244
  If you can't hold out for Amazon Prime.
- **Boccato** • 2719 Wilson Blvd
  703-869-6522
  Peruvian-run gelateria. Flavors include lychee peachy and basil pineapple.
- **CD Cellar** • 2607 Wilson Blvd
  703-248-0653
  If you missed the Internet music revolution.
- **Company Flowers** • 2107 N Pollard St
  703-525-3062
  Crafted bouquets, assorted gifts, cards, and tchotchkes.
- **The Container Store** • 2800 Clarendon Blvd
  703-469-1560
  Buckets, shelves, hangers.
- **The Italian Store** • 3123 Lee Hwy
  703-528-6266
  Gourmet Italian via the old country & Brooklyn.
- **Kinder Haus Toys** • 1220 N Fillmore St
  703-527-5929
  Hooray for puppet shows.
- **Orvis** • 2879 Clarendon Blvd
  703-465-0004
  Practical clothes to match the rhino guard on your SUV.
- **Pottery Barn** • 2700 Clarendon Blvd
  703-465-9425
  Yuppie interior style.

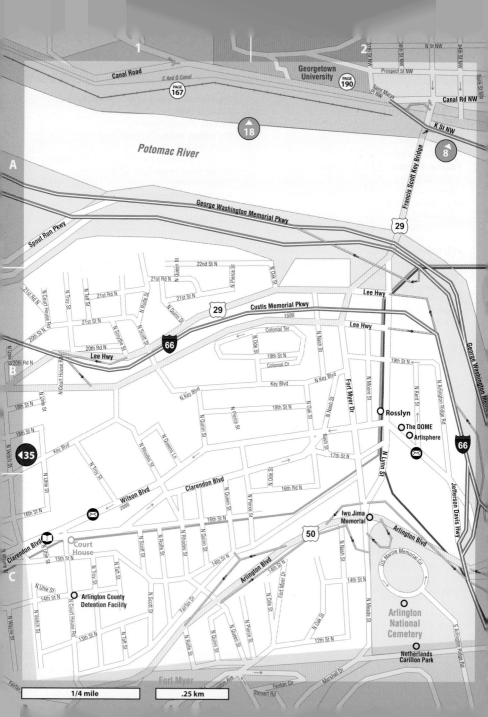

More and more high-rise dwellers are calling Rosslyn home, but amenities still tend to be subpar. You've got chain lunch spots, gyms, markets, dry cleaners, and enough parking garages to sink the heart of every living environmentalist. When the economy turns around, however, perhaps developers will pick up where they left off and bring a little more to this little Virginian 'burb-that-could.

○ Landmarks

- **Arlington County Detention Facility** •
  1425 N Courthouse Rd
  703-228-4484
  We all make mistakes.
- **Arlington National Cemetery** • 1 Memorial Dr
  877-907-8585
  Visit again and again—just not during tourist season.
- **Artisphere** • 1101 N Wilson Blvd
  703-8750-1100
  Performing arts center with free galleries and interesting events.
- **The DOME** • 1101 Wilson Blvd
  703-228-1843
  Museum space of Bodies, The Exhibition fame.
- **Iwo Jima Memorial** •
  Iwo Jima Memorial Access Rd
  Visit at night.
- **Netherlands Carillon** •
  N Meade St & N Marshall Dr
  703-289-2500
  It's all about the view.

Nightlife

- **Continental Modern Pool Lounge** •
  1911 Fort Myer Dr
  703-465-7675
  Like you stepped into the Jetsons' house.
- **Ireland's Four Courts** • 2051 Wilson Blvd
  703-525-3600
  Where beer-guzzling yuppies come to see (double) and be seen.
- **Rhodeside Grill** • 1836 Wilson Blvd
  703-243-0145
  Neighborhood bar with basement for bands.
- **Summers Restaurant** • 1520 N Courthouse Rd
  703-528-8278
  Soccer-watching bar.

Map

33 34 35 36 7
37
38 40

🍽 Restaurants

- **Bayou Bakery** • 1515 N Courthouse Rd
  703-243-2410 • $$
  Sweet and savory southern eats.
- **Cafe Asia** • 1550 Wilson Blvd
  703-741-0870 • $$$
  An after-work hot-spot for the Rosslyn set.
- **Choupi** • 1218 19th St N
  $
  Where crepe-making is a form of art. Fantastique!
- **Guajillo** • 1727 Wilson Blvd
  703-807-0840 • $$
  Don't let the strip mall fool you. It's what's inside that counts.
- **Guarapo** • 2039 Wilson Blvd
  703-528-6500 • $$$
  Chi-Cha Lounge flavor in NoVA.
- **Il Radicchio** • 1801 Clarendon Blvd
  703-276-2627 • $$$
  Quiet outdoor dining evokes *Lady and the Tramp* aura.
- **Ireland's Four Courts** • 2051 Wilson Blvd
  703-525-3600 • $$$
  Makes you forget that Ireland ever had a famine.
- **Jerry's Subs and Pizza** • 2041 15th St N
  703-312-9026 • $
  Thin, small and tasteless.

- **Piola** • 1550 Wilson Blvd
  703-528-1502 • $$
  International chain serves fresh take on Italian in vibrant setting.
- **Quarterdeck** • 1200 Fort Myer Dr
  703-528-2722 • $$$
  Brown paper covered tables, Old Bay seasoning, and fresh crabs.
- **Ray's The Steaks** • 2300 Wilson Blvd
  703-841-7297 • $$$$
  Beef. It's what's for dinner.
- **Ray's: To the Third** • 1650 Wilson Blvd
  703-974-7171 • $$
  Renowned steaks, seafood, indulgent sandwiches and alcoholic milkshakes.
- **Red, Hot, and Blue** • 1600 Wilson Blvd
  703-276-7427 • $$
  Slightly depressing atmosphere, but tasty bbq makes up for it.
- **Rhodeside Grill** • 1836 Wilson Blvd
  703-243-0145 • $$
  Hot plates on dinner tables, live music in the basement.
- **Village Bistro** • 1723 Wilson Blvd
  703-522-0284 • $$$
  Surprisingly quaint for part of a shopping strip.

Rosslyn

Nightlife around here is clustered near the Courthouse metro, though even that has been diminished with the closing of Dr. Dremo's (condo sprawl strikes again). Your choices are limited: sports pub **Summers**, Irish bar **Ireland's Four Courts**, or take advantage of weekday happy hour specials on drinks and sushi at **Café Asia**. That said, one standout is the **Continental**, where girls can get martinis, guys can grab a brew, and everyone can play shuffleboard 'til the toll of last call.

Shopping

• **Arlington Farmers' Market** •
Courthouse Rd & 14th St
703-228-6426
Farmers market, Saturday 8 am-12 pm.

• **Brooklyn Bagel Bakery** • 2055 Wilson Blvd
703-243-4442
More like Arlington Bagels. But good, doughy and big.

Map 36

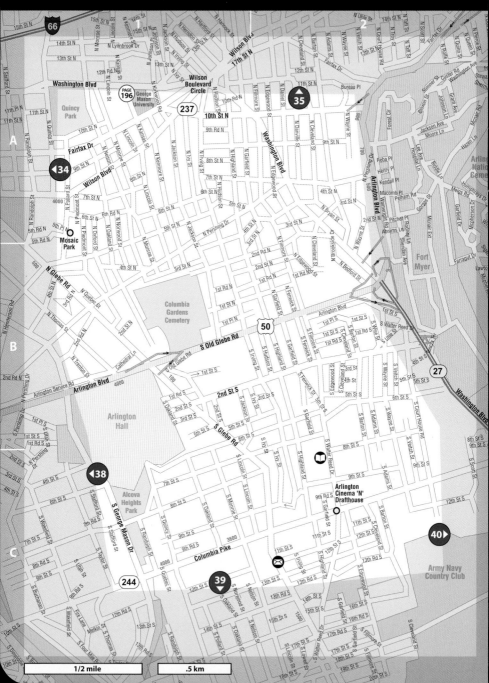

Map 37 • **Fort Myer**

Fort Myer is mostly suburban (think '40s Cape Cods with aluminum awnings) with a few commercial enclaves, which is also its appeal. There's no Metrorail stop and it's not particularly pedestrian friendly, so grab your car keys if you've got the itch to visit. Most of the fun, and essentials, are on the edges of this area, but stick around and check out the weekend **Columbia Pike Farmers Market**, just down the street from the best dive diner breakfast around at **Bob and Edith's**.

○ Landmarks

• **Arlington Cinema 'N' Drafthouse** •
2903 Columbia Pike
703-486-2345
Good movies, beer, pizza, waitresses, cigarettes. Life is good.
• **Mosaic Park** • 544 N Pollard St
703-228-6525
3D spider web for kids and climbing wall for outdoorsy types.

Nightlife

• **EatBar** • 2761 Washington Blvd
703-778-5051
Creative beers, drinks, and food with a slightly swanky atmosphere.
• **Jay's Saloon & Grille** • 3114 10th St N
703-527-3093
Down-home and friendly.
• **P. Brennan's Irish Pub & Restaurant** •
2910 Columbia Pike
703-553-1090
Corned beef & cabbage + Guinness, named after a favorite bartender.
• **Ragtime** • 1345 N Courthouse Rd
703-243-4003
No less than 2 TVs per room. Caters to WVU fans.
• **Tallula** • 2761 Washington Blvd
703-778-5051
Swanky-dank wine bar.

37 38 39 40 43
Map

Map

37
38 40
39
43

🍴Restaurants

- **Astor Mediterranean** • 2300 N Pershing Dr
  703-465-2306 • $
  Decent falafel and typical Greek fare. Free delivery!
- **Atilla's** • 2705 Columbia Pike
  703-920-8100 • $$
  Savory gyros, kabobs, salads, and more.
- **Bakeshop** • 1025 N Fillmore St
  571-970-6460 • $$
  Home-baked cookies, cupcakes, and cakes from Justin.
- **Bangkok 54** • 2919 Columbia Pike
  703-521-4070 • $$$
  Upscale Thai at downscale prices.
- **Bob & Edith's Diner** • 2310 Columbia Pk
  703-920-6103 • $
  Genuine diner, nostaglic classic for late night or breakfast.
- **The Broiler** • 3601 Columbia Pike
  703-920-5944 • $$
  Late night favorite for greasy, guilty pleasures, cheese steaks.
- **Eat Bar** • 2761 Washington Blvd
  703-778-9951 • $$$
  Don't miss the classic cartoon weekend brunch.
- **El Charrito Caminante** • 2710 N Washington Blvd
  703-351-1177 • $
  Papusas worthy of the gods.
- **El Paso Cafe** • 4253 N Pershing Dr
  703-243-9811 • $$
  True Tex-Mex, featuring fajita specials and tequila tastings.

- **El Pollo Rico** • 932 N Kenmore St
  703-522-3220 • $
  Eating this chicken is a sacramental experience.
- **L.A. Bar and Grille** • 2530 Columbia Pike
  703-685-1560 • $
  Grub and booze, dive-style.
- **Manee Thai** • 2500 Columbia Pike
  703-920-2033 • $
  True Thai treasure.
- **Mario's Pizza House** • 3322 Wilson Blvd
  703-525-0200 • $$
  Late night tradition for the bleary-eyed.
- **Mrs. Chen's Kitchen** • 3101 Columbia Pike
  703-920-3199 • $
  Chinese food before competition from Thai.
- **Pan American Bakery** • 4113 Columbia Pike
  703-271-1113 • $
  Saltenas and glistening pastries from South America.
- **Ragtime** • 1345 N Courthouse Rd
  703-243-4003 • $
  Come for the sandwiches, stay for the sports.
- **Ravi Kabob** • 250 N Glebe Rd
  703-816-0222 • $
  Top kabobs. Cash only. Long lines but worth it.
- **Rincome Thai Cuisine** • 3030 Columbia Pike
  703-979-0144 • $$
  Friendly owners, sumptuous food, neighborhood atmosphere.
- **Tallula** • 2761 Washington Blvd
  703-778-5051 • $$$
  The wine bar craze has officially hit Arlington.
- **Thai Curry** • 307 N Glebe Rd
  703-524-0711 • $$
  Specializes in Thai street food.

We use the word "entertainment" very loosely when it comes to Columbia Pike. Perhaps you're entertained being stuck in traffic jams while shopping for laundry detergent and other bulk items at one of many big-box strip malls, in which case there you go. Columbia Pike does excel when it comes to its many wonderful ethnic eateries (**Bangkok 54**), mom-and-pop pizza joints, an overlooked dive bar (**L.A. Bar & Grille**), and pawn shops. Bob and Edith's Diner will satisfy your greasy cravings 24/7 (now smoke free!), and the **Arlington Cinema 'N' Drafthouse** offers a dinner-and-a-movie option, in addition to reviving classic films with alcohol-aided viewings, hosting comics, and providing a venue to anguish over Skins losses on the big screen.

🛍 Shopping

• **Ivy Nail & Spa** • 3434 Washington Blvd
703-522-0030
Clean and reasonably priced.

• **Twisted Vines Bottleshop & Bistro** •
2803 Columbia Pike
571-482-8581
Wine priced at retail, paired with vino-friendly foodstuffs.

Map 38

A sprawling multicultural hodgepodge, two roads—Columbia Pike and Leesburg Pike—dominate this neighborhood, if you can call it that. The area isn't exactly homey (unless "chaotic" and "crammed" is what your heart desires), with its eye-paining high-rises, plethora of strip malls, and apartment communities that have seen better days. On the bright—or rather, green—side, Four Mile Run is great for riding your bike or taking your dog for a romp.

○ Landmarks
- **Ball-Sellers House** • 5620 3rd St S
703-379-2123
Will be McMansion someday.

Restaurants
- **Andy's Carry Out** • 5033 Columbia Pike
703-671-1616 • $$
Oily food cooked in woks.
- **Athens Restaurant** • 3541 Carlin Springs Rd
703-931-3300 • $$
Greek menu for everyone, even Greeks.
- **Atlacatl and Pupuseria** • 4701 Columbia Pike
703-920-3680 • $$$
Laid-back, delicious Salvadorian and Mexican cuisine with attentive staff.
- **Brick's Pizza** • 4809 1st St N
703-243-6600 • $
Order "The Ballston" for pizza with a mediterranean flair.
- **The Chicken Place** • 5519 Leesburg Pike
703-931-3090 • $
Ask for extra white sauce, and say gracias.
- **Crystal Thai** • 4819 1st St N
703-522-1311 • $$$
Moderate prices will allow you to order extra Singha.
- **Five Guys** • 4626 King St
703-671-1606 • $
THE Alexandria burger joint.
- **Flavors** • 3420 Carlyn Hill Dr
703-379-4411 • $
Just like Grandma use to make.

Shopping
- **One Two Kangaroo Toys** • 4022 S 28th St
703-845-9099
Cozy toy shop filled with old and new favorites.
- **REI** • 3509 Carlin Springs Rd
703-379-9400
Sports emporium.
- **Target** • 5115 Leesburg Pike
703-253-0021
Wal*Mart in drag.

Map 39 · **Shirlington**

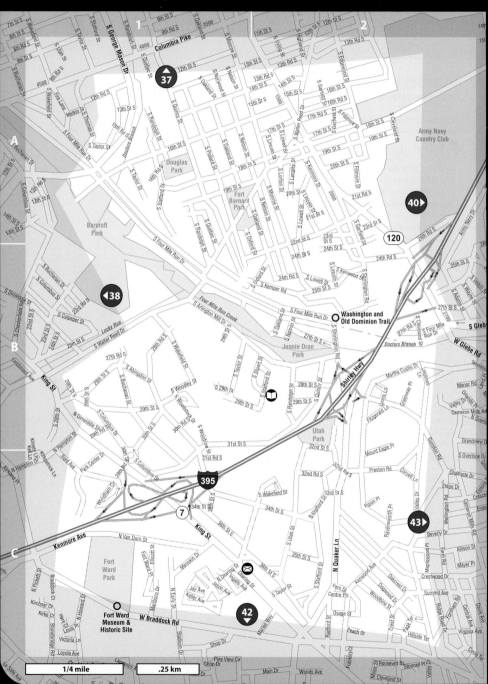

Split down the middle by 395, the major route to/from DC, more and more young professionals are shacking up in Shirlington. With luxury condos, pricey townhomes, and an abundance of shops and restaurants, the neighborhood has exploded in the past few years in that typically sterile faux-stone walls and too-neat sidewalks kind of way. But the gentrification is sharply juxtaposed with a nearby day laborer center trying to capitalize on the development, revealing the complex community dynamics in this neighborhood.

○ Landmarks

- **Fort Ward Museum & Historic Site** •
  4301 W Braddock Rd
  703-746-4848
  Eerie; we fought each other.
- **Washington and Old Dominion Trail** •
  S Four Mile Run Dr & S Shirlington Rd
  Check out the quieter Arlington section, blissfully free of any and all aerodynamic helmets.

Nightlife

- **Bungalow Sports Grill** • 2766 S Arlington Mill Dr
  703-578-0020
  Fun billiards and brews.
- **Capitol City Brewing Company** •
  4001 Campbell Ave
  703-578-3888
  Great IPA.
- **Guapo's** • 4028 Campbell Ave
  703-671-1701
  Bueno Mexican, killer margaritas.

Restaurants

- **Aladdin's Eatery** • 4044 Campbell Ave
  703-894-4401 • $
  Take-out recommended.
- **Best Buns Bread Co.** • 4010 Campbell Ave
  703-578-1500 • $
  The name says it all. The best buns in town!
- **Bonsai** • 4040 Campbell Ave
  703-824-8828 • $$
  Reliable sushi joint.
- **Busboys & Poets** • 4251 S Campbell Ave
  703-379-9757 • $$$
  A DC staple in the heart of Shirlington.
- **Cafe Pizzaiolo** • 2800 S Randolph St
  703-894-2250 • $$$
  A delight for Northerners who think good pizza in DC doesn't exist.
- **Capitol City Brewing Company** •
  4001 Campbell Ave
  703-578-3888 • $$
  Pool, beer, and really good food.
- **Carlyle** • 4000 Campbell Ave
  703-931-0777 • $$$
  Popular for Friday and Saturday dinner, arrive early.
- **Cheesetique** • 4056 Campbell Ave
  703-933-8787 •
  Buy your cheese and eat it, too, with a glass of wine!

- **Great Harvest** • 1711 Centre Plaza
  703-671-8678 • $
  A wholesome neighborhood bakery.
- **Guapo's** • 4028 Campbell Ave
  703-671-1701 • $$$
  Everyone's favorite Mexican—great margaritas.
- **Lotus Grill & Noodles** • 4041 Campbell Ave
  703-566-2173 • $$
  Pho with a French flare.
- **Luna Grill & Diner** • 4024 Campbell Ave
  703-379-7173 • $$
  Homey comfort food and breakfast served all day.
- **Medi** • 4037 Campbell Ave
  571-403-2878 • $
  A Mediterranean grill serving pitas, salads and rice bowls.
- **PING by Charlie Chiang's** • 4060 Campbell Ave
  703-671-4900 • $$$
  A definite step up from your local hole-in-the-wall Chinese.
- **Ramparts** • 1700 Fern St
  703-998-6616 • $$
  Family restaurant with true dive sports bar on the side.
- **Samuel Beckett's** • 2800 2800 S Randolph St
  703-379-0122 • $$$
  Irish hospitality, food and music in Shirlington.
- **T.H.A.I. in Shirlington** • 4029 Campbell Ave
  703-931-3203 • $$$
  Modern setting and Thai food with a twist.
- **Weenie Beenie** • 2680 S Shirlington Rd
  703-671-6661 • $
  Old-school half-smokes and burgers stand.

The Village at Shirlington, a fast-growing destination, boasts a Disney World-esque array of restaurants (one of every type, all with outdoor seating), a movie theater with a slant toward independent films, and well-designed essentials like a library with a sleek facade. Date night? For a swanky meal, try **Carlyle**. For something more low key, cozy up on a couch with your sweaty at **Busboys & Poets** or share a cupcake from **CakeLove**. Bro time? Head to **Bungalow** where you can play pool or air hockey while downing huge drafts and watching a game.

🛍 Shopping

- **Best Buns Bread Co.** • 4010 Campbell Ave
  703-578-1500
  The name says it all. The best buns in town!
- **Bloomers** • 4501 Campbell Ave
  571-970-4756
  Underwear or sleepwear; join the Panty of the Month Club!
- **Cakelove** • 4150 Campbell Ave
  703-933-0099
  High-end and tasty.
- **Cheesetique** • 4056 Campbell Ave
  703-933-8787
  Buy your cheese and eat it, too, with a glass of wine!

- **The Curious Grape** • 2900 S Quincy St
  703-671-8700
  Many wines, free tastings, great spot to stop on a date.
- **Diversions Cards and Gifts** • 1721 Centre Plaza
  703-578-3237
  Nice alternative to blah greeting cards you get at the supermarket.
- **Le Village Marche** • 2800 S Randolph Street
  703-379-4444
  Home decor and gifts with a vintage touch.
- **Unwined** • 3690 King St
  703-820-8600
  One-stop shop if you're throwing a cocktail party.

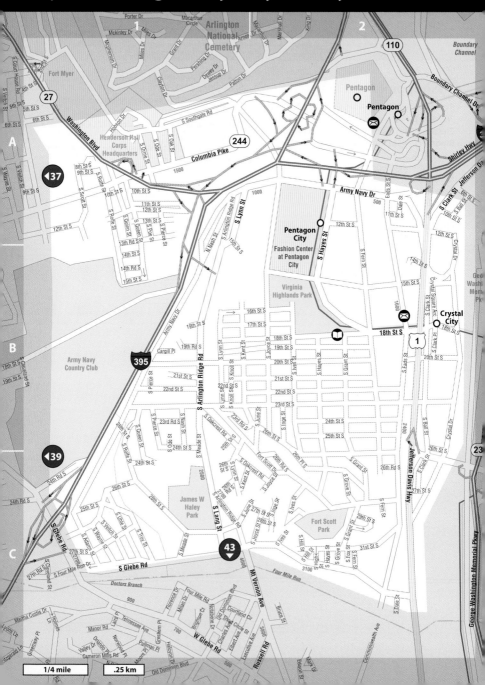

Map 18 Pentagon City / Crystal City

1

2

Arlington
National
Cemetery

Porter Dr
Macarthur
Circle

Mckinley Dr
Miles Dr

Grant Dr

Fort Myer

27

5th St S
5th St S

6th St S
6th St S

Washington Blvd

Pershing Dr
Dewey Dr
Jessup Dr

Patton Dr

110

Boundary
Channel

Boundary Channel Dr

Pentagon

Pentagon

Shirley Hwy

Jefferson Dr

A

37

S Court House Rd
S Veitch St

8th St S
9th St S

S Rolfe St

S Scott St

10th St S
11th St S
12th St S
13th St S

S Queen St
S Pierce St

S Pierce St

12th St S

S Wayne St

9th St S

S Oak St

S Ode St
S Orme St

Henderson Hall
Corps
Headquarters

S Southgate Rd

Columbia Pike

244

1500

1000

Army Navy Dr

500

Eads St S

S Clark St

8th St S
10th St S

12th St S

Crystal Dr

N Nash St
S Arlington Ridge Rd
S Lynn St
19th St S

Pentagon
City

Fashion Center
at Pentagon
City

12th St S

S Hayes St

S Fern St

14th St S

Crystal Square Ave
Crystal Dr
S Clark St

George
Washington
Memorial
Pkwy

13th St S
14th St S
14th Rd S
15th St S

Virginia
Highlands Park

15th St S

1600

Crystal Dr

B

395

Army Navy
Country Club

Cargill Pl

19th Rd S

16th St S
17th St S

18th St S
19th St S

20th St S

S Lynn St
S Kent St
S Joyce St

S Hayes St

S Grant St

18th St S

1

Crystal City

18th St S

20th St S

S Eads St

S Clark St
S Ball St

18th St S
19th St S

S Cleveland St

S Pierce St

21st St S
22nd St S

22nd St S

S Knoll St
23rd Rd S

21st St S

22nd St S

23rd St S

S June St
S Inge St

24th St S
25th St S

2400

S Ball St
Crystal Dr

23

39

24th Rd S

24th Rd S

23rd Rd S
S Ode St

24th St S
S Meade St

S Queen St
S Rolfe St

S Oakcrest Rd

26th St S

S June St
26th Pl S

26th St S

S Grant St

S Glebe Rd

25th St S

26th St S

S Little St
S Adams St
S Wayne St
S Troy St

S Lynn St

S Joyce St
Fort Scott Dr

S Oakcrest Rd

James W
Haley Park

2800

S Arlington Ridge Rd

S June St
27th St S

26th
Rd S

Jefferson Davis Hwy

S Fern St
S Grove St

27th St S

Fort Scott
Park

29th St S

C

S Glebe Rd

43

S Lang St

S Meade St
S Troy St

Mt Vernon Ave

S Joyce St
S Ives St

31st St S

S Hill St
S Hayes St
S Grove St
S Fox St
S Fern St

S Dale St

27th St S
22nd Dr S

27th Rd S
S Cleveland St

Doctors Branch

900

W Glebe Rd

Four Mile Run

3100

S Glebe Rd

Florence Dr
Four Mile Rd
Main St

Brighton Ct

Courtland Cir

Red Circle Dr

Bruce St

Elbert Ave

Commonwealth Ave

George Washington Memorial Pkwy

Martha Custis Dr
Lyons Ln
Fitzgerald Ln
Greenway Pl

Helen St

Tennessee Ave

Manor Rd

Norwood Pl
Gresham Pl
Brenton St

Holman Dr

Pullman St

Executive Ave

Russell Rd

Valley Dr
Quincy Dr
Moore St

Hutton St

700

3800

Mark Dr

Ebson Dr

Cameron Mills Rd

W Glebe Rd

500

Old Dominion Blvd

1/4 mile

.25 km

When metroing to this area listen carefully: did the conductor just say Pentagon or Pentagon City? Don't worry—the apparel of those exiting will let you know what state you're in: camouflage for the famously shaped military center, short skirts and Coach bags for the mall. Visitors to this neighborhood may be shopping for the newest prom dress, defense contract, or Costco deal.

○ Landmarks
- **The Pentagon** • 1400 Defense Pentagon
703-697-1776
SecDef's playpen.

▼ Nightlife
- **Sine Irish Pub** • 1301 S Joyce St
703-415-4420
Good beers on tap, busy happy hour. Lots of military, defense contractors.

🍴 Restaurants
- **Crystal Bonsai Sushi** • 553 23rd St S
703-553-7723 • $$$
Nowhere in the area is the white tuna as good as it is here.
- **Crystal City Restaurant** • 422 S 23rd St
703-892-0726 • $$
Kegs and legs at this diner/strip club.
- **Crystal City Sports Pub** • 529 23rd St S
703-521-8215 • $$
Rated a top ten sports bar nationwide by *Sports Illustrated*. Dozens of TVs.
- **Good Stuff Eatery** • 2110 Crystal Dr
703-415-4663 • $$
Burger, fries and shakes. It's good stuff.
- **Jaleo** • 2250 Crystal Dr
703-413-8181 • $$$$
Spanish tapas by DC's own Jose Andres.
- **Kabob Palace** • 2315 S Eads St
703-486-3535 • $
Kabobs fit for a king.
- **Legal Seafood** • 2301 Jefferson Davis Hwy
703-415-1200 • $$$$
A Boston institution. Here, it feels more. . . Institutional.
- **McCormick & Schmick's** • 2010 Crystal Dr
703-413-6400 • $$$$
If you're doing business nearby and have to woo clients.
- **Morton's the Steakhouse** • 1750 Crystal Dr
703-418-1444 • $$$$$
Gluttony with valet parking.
- **Noodles & Company** • 1201 S Joyce St
703-418-0001 • $
Ultra-fusion noodle chain.

👜 Shopping
- **Abercrombie & Fitch** • 1100 S Hayes St
703-415-4210
Quintessential college kids' clothes.
- **Apple** • 1100 S Hayes St
703-236-1550
Don't come looking for produce.
- **BCBGMAXAZRIA** • 1100 S Hayes St
703-415-3690
Cheap, trendy women's clothing.
- **bebe** • 1100 S Hayes St
703-415-2323
Sexy clothing for twentysomething women.
- **Best Buy** • 1201 S Hayes St
703-414-7090
Gadgets, gadgets, gadgets.
- **Costco** • 1200 S Fern St
703-413-2324
Exactly what you'd expect, but this one's the busiest in the country—beware!
- **Denim Bar** • 1101 S Joyce St
703-414-8202
When your butt is too good for $200 jeans.
- **The Fashion Centre at Pentagon City** •
1100 S Hayes St
703-415-2401
DC's best metro-accessible mall. Popular with tourists.
- **Harris Teeter** • 900 Army Navy Dr
703-413-7112
Pricey food mecca with a great selection.
- **Kenneth Cole** • 1100 S Hayes St
703-415-3522
Metrosexual heaven, great guys' shoes and accessories.
- **Macy's** • 1000 S Hayes St
703-418-4488
Yes, DC, department stores still exist.
- **Red Door Spa** • 1101 S Joyce St
703-373-5888
Pampered facials.
- **World Market** • 1301 S Joyce St
703-415-7575
Wine, beer, furniture, and that British candy bar you've been craving.

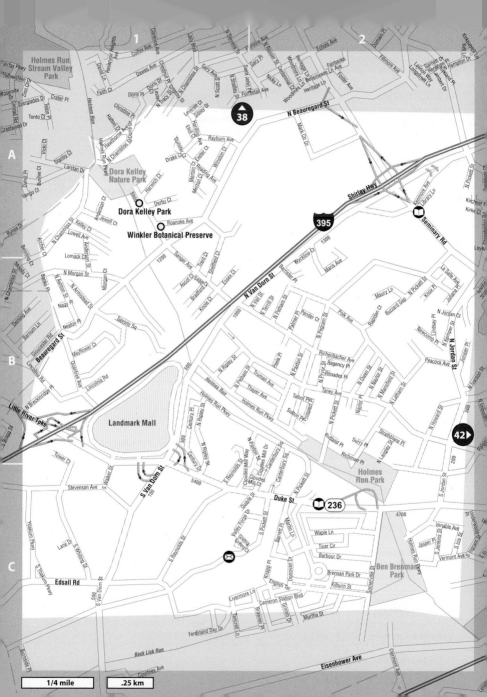

You gotta love gentrification. Suddenly, even seedy places like Landmark have golden appeal to DC commuters, who, pissed off with the traffic to their ever-farther suburbs, trade in McMansions for a piece of cheaper development closer to the city. Now, this poor relation of Old Town is beginning to shape up into a white-collar scene of new restaurants and shops, catering to the new money pouring in. The Metro is what keeps the area transitioning, and only more growth is expected.

Landmarks
- **Dora Kelley Nature Park** • 5750 Sanger Ave
  703-838-4829
  It's no Yellowstone, but it makes for a pleasant walk in the woods.
- **Winkler Botanical Preserve** • 5400 Roanoke Ave
  703-578-7888
  A 44-acre gem in the suburban rough.

Nightlife
- **Mango Mike's** • 4580 Duke St
  703-823-1166
  Pub grub from the islands, mon.
- **Shooter McGee's** • 5239 Duke St
  703-751-9266
  Another "silly first name, Irish last name" place.

Restaurants
- **Akasaka** • 514 S Van Dorn St
  703-751-3133 • $$$
  Decent sushi at decent prices.
- **Clyde's** • 1700 N Beauregard St
  703-820-8300 • $$$
  Take to the seas in this nautical-themed favorite.
- **Edgardo's Trattoria** • 281 S Van Dorn St
  703-751-6700 • $$
  Authentic wood-fired pizzas and flat breads.
- **El Paraiso** • 516 S Van Dorn St
  703-212-9200 • $$
  A slice of El Salvador on Van Dorn.
- **Finn & Porter** • 5000 Seminary Rd
  703-379-2346 • $$$$
  Yes, it's in a hotel, but it's still nice.
- **Mediterranean Bakery** • 352 S Pickett St
  703-751-0030 • $
  More market and lunch than bakery, but still a Turkish delight.
- **SakulThai Restaurant** • 408 S Van Dorn St
  703-823-5357 • $
  Wallet-friendly Thai.
- **Thai Lemongrass** • 506 S Van Dorn St
  703-751-4627 • $$
  Thai for surburbanites.

Shopping
- **BJ's** • 101 S Van Dorn St
  703-212-8700
  If you need a 24-pack of anything.

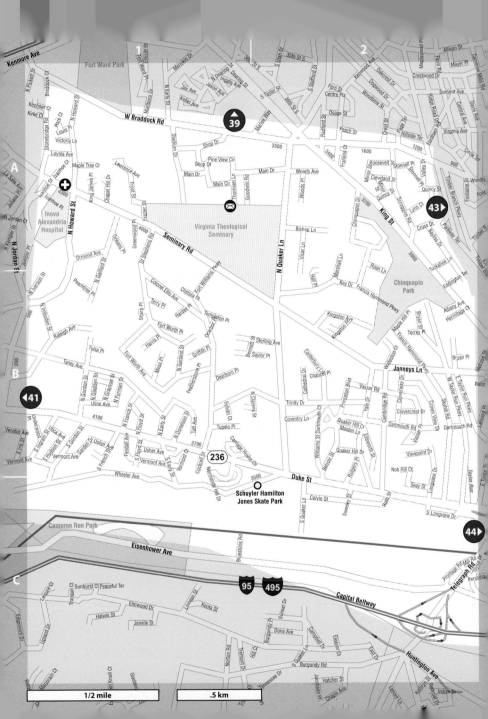

The plentiful apartments in Alexandria make it popular with 20-somethings who like urban living but can't hack the high rents in Clarendon or DC. There's also a high concentration of plaid skirts, what with all the Catholic schools around. Oh, but remember those Titans—T.C. Williams is in this area as well.

○Landmarks

• **Schuyler Hamilton Jones Skate Park** •
  3540 Wheeler Ave
  Free skateboard park. Skate at your own risk.

Restaurants

• **Rocklands** • 25 S Quaker Ln
  703-778-9663 • $$
  DC BBQ in NoVA.
• **Tempo Restaurant** • 4231 Duke St
  703-370-7900 • $$$
  French-Italian fusion.

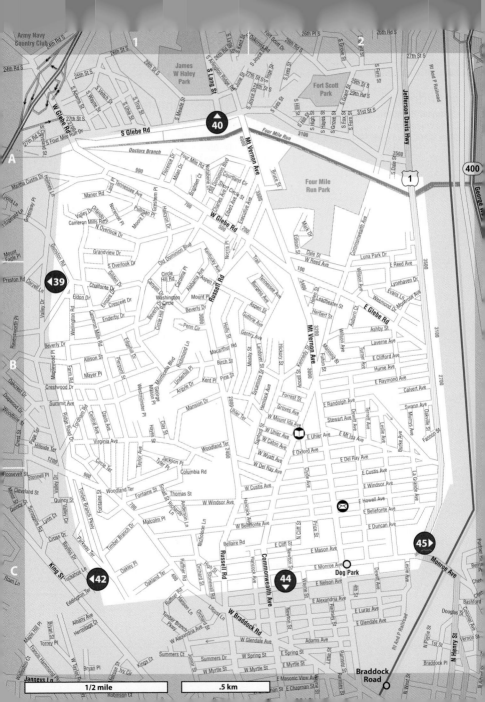

Often referred to as "the funky Old Town" by its residents, Del Ray is a place where neighbors say hello, children (and dogs) have manners, and activists fight for a better town. Thanks to its artsy, liberal residence, there's a real sense of community here—you can feel it at the Saturday **Farmers Market** or as you walk by the young families, gay couples, and fifty-something bohemians strolling "The Avenue."

○ Landmarks

- **Dog Park** • E Monroe Ave & Jefferson Davis Hwy
  The neighborhood hangout—dogs hump, people preen.

🍸 Nightlife

- **The Birchmere** • 3701 Mt Vernon Ave
  703-549-7500
  What do Kris Kristofferson and Liz Phair have in common?
- **Hops** • 3625 Jefferson Davis Hwy
  703-837-9107
  $1.29 happy hour beers, if you don't mind a cheesy chain.
- **Osteria 1909** • 1909 Mt Vernon Ave
  703-836-1212
  Wine and cocktails to go with some Italian munchies.

Map

39
41 42 43 44 45 46

🍴 Restaurants

- **Afghan Restaurant** • 2700 Jefferson Davis Hwy
703-548-0022 • $$
Bountiful $7.95 lunch buffet; reportedly a good place for spook-spotting.
- **Al's Steak House** • 1504 Mt Vernon Ave
703-836-9443 • $
Cheesesteaks worthy of Philly.
- **Bombay Curry Company** • 3110 Mt Vernon Ave
703-836-6363 • $$$
Curry that fulfills with understated authenticity.
- **Cheesetique** • 2411 Mt Vernon Ave
703-706-5300 • $$$
Buy your cheese and eat it, too, with a glass of wine!
- **Chez Andree** • 10 E Glebe Rd
703-836-1404 • $$$
When you feel like eating a different part of the pig.
- **The Dairy Godmother** • 2310 Mt Vernon Ave
703-683-7767 • $
This homemade custard cuts the mustard.
- **Del Ray Cafe** • 205 E Howell Ave
703-717-9151 • $$$
Local, organic, French fare.
- **Del Ray Pizzeria** • 2218 Mt Vernon Ave
703-549-2999 • $$
Family friendly local pizza place.
- **Evening Star Cafe** • 2000 Mount Vernon Ave
703-549-5051 • $$$
Grandma's southern soul food refined.
- **Holy Cow** • 2312 Mt Vernon Ave
703-666-8616 • $$
Gourmet burgers, fries and shakes.
- **Huascaran** • 3606 Mt Vernon Ave
703-684-0494 • $$$
Platefuls of Peruvian perfection.
- **Lilian's Restaurant** • 3901 Mt Vernon Ave
703-837-8494 • $
Plump pupusas and Spanish-language karaoke.
- **Los Tios Grill** • 2615 Mt Vernon Ave
703-299-9290 • $$
Monster margaritas in a cozy, family-friendly space.
- **Mancini's** • 1508 Mt Vernon Ave
703-838-3663 • $$
Café, carryout and catering.
- **Market 2 Market** • 116 E Del Ray Ave
571-312-3010 • $$
The best sandwich and craft beers in Del Ray.
- **Monroe's** • 1603 Commonwealth Ave
703-548-5792 • $$
Great wines and brunch.
- **Pork Barrel BBQ** • 2312 Mt Vernon Ave
703-822-5699 • $$$
It's not just a restaurant, it's a true smoked meat experience.
- **RT's Restaurant** • 3804 Mt Vernon Ave
703-684-6010 • $$
Creole and cajun before the Birchmere.
- **Taqueria El Poblano** • 2400 Mt Vernon Ave
703-548-8226 • $$
The real deal, amigo.
- **Thai Peppers** • 2018 Mt Vernon Ave
703-739-7627 • $$
Let "peppers" be a warning!
- **Waffle Shop** • 3864 Mt Vernon Ave
703-836-8851 • $
24-hour grease and caffeine.

Mount Vernon Avenue is brimming with neat little restaurants, pottery studios, and antiques shops. **The Evening Star**'s entrees always shine brightly, and are followed nicely by a stop at **The Dairy Godmother** for a creatively flavored custard. Parents visiting? Take them to one of Del Ray's more refined dining experiences, followed by a show at local institution **The Birchmere**.

Map

Shopping

- **A Show of Hands** • 2301 Mt Vernon Ave
703-683-2905
Local arts, crafts, jewelry; less highbrow than the Torpedo Factory.
- **Amalgamated** • 1904 Mt Vernon Ave
703-517-7373
Classic clothing and dry goods.
- **Artfully Chocolate** • 2003 Mt Vernon Ave
703-635-7917
All you need to know: artisinal chocolate.
- **Barnes & Noble** • 3651 Jefferson Davis Hwy
703-299-9124
Mega bookstore.
- **Bellies & Babies** • 1913 Mt Vernon Ave
703-518-8908
Consignment boutique that specializes in baby stuff.
- **Best Buy** • 3401 Jefferson Davis Hwy
703-519-0940
All sorts of electronics.
- **Cheesetique** • 2411 Mt Vernon Ave
703-706-5300
The ultimate neighborhood cheese shop.
- **The Clay Queen Pottery** • 2303 Mt Vernon Ave
703-549-7775
Throw it yourself.
- **The Dairy Godmother** • 2310 Mt Vernon Ave
703-683-7767
Make yourself comfy with homemade marshmallows and custard.

- **Exotic Planetarium and Comic & Card Collectorama** • 2008 Mt Vernon Ave
703-548-3466
Exotic plants and comics, a perfect match.
- **Let's Meat on the Avenue** • 2403 Mt Vernon Ave
703-836-6328
Neighborhood butcher featuring free-range, local meats.
- **Old Navy** • 3621 Jefferson Davis Hwy
703-739-6240
Super-cheap, super-basic clothes.
- **Planet Wine** • 2004 Mt Vernon Ave
703-549-3444
Gourmet food, craft beers, and artisan and farmhouse cheeses.
- **The Purple Goose** • 2005 Mt Vernon Ave
703-683-2918
Consignments for the kiddies.
- **Sports Authority** • 3701 Jefferson Davis Hwy
703-684-3204
The authority on sports.
- **Staples** • 3301 Jefferson Davis Hwy
703-836-9485
Everything you need for your home (or work) office.
- **Target** • 3101 Jefferson Davis Hwy
703-706-3840
Tar-zhay offers housewares, furniture and more.
- **VéloCity Bicycle Cooperative** •
2111 Mt Vernon Ave
703-835-0699
Fix your bike, hang out, donate, meet new people.

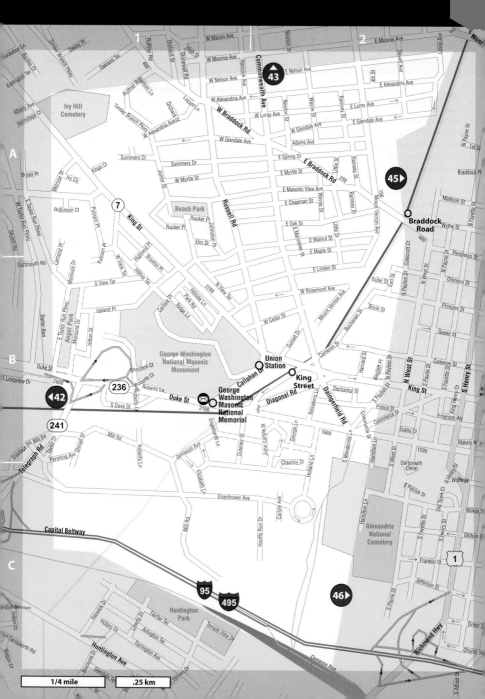

All work with little to no play, many national associations have their headquarters here in Alexandria's "downtown." Clean and professional, but short on the "wow" factor, fortunately it's located next to historic Old Town, which is bursting at the seams with character. The northern half does boast some stately homes with million dollar views, but neighboring Old Town is really where it's at.

○ Landmarks

- **George Washington Masonic Memorial** •
101 Callahan Dr
703-683-2007
Nice views from the top.
- **Union Station** • 110 Callahan Dr
The other Union Station; good people-watching post.

🍴 Restaurants

- **Brabo** • 1600 King St
703-894-3440 • $$$$
Haute Belgian cuisine from Robert Wiedmaier.
- **Café Old Town** • 2111 Eisenhower Ave
703-683-3116 • $
Variety of coffee/pastries, worth traveling off the beaten path.
- **FireFlies** • 1501 Mt Vernon Ave
703-548-7200 • $$$
Affordable eclecticism; try it at happy hour.
- **Joe Theismann's Restaurant** • 1800 Diagonal Rd
703-739-0777 • $$$
Former Redskins QB's bar and grill draws visitors and locals alike.
- **The Perfect Pita** • 1640 King St
703-683-4330 • $
Pitas and pizza, perfect for lunch on the cheap.
- **Pop's Old Fashion Ice Cream** • 105 King St
703-836-5676 • $
The way ice cream was meant to be—homemade and creamy.
- **Quattro Formaggi** • 1725 Duke St
703-548-8111 • $
Gourmet pizza options you've never dreamed of, and other Italian fare.
- **Table Talk** • 1623 Duke St
703-548-3989 • $
Terrific breakfast/lunch. Often jammed, always good.
- **Ted's Montana Grill** • 2451 Eisenhower Ave
703-960-0500 • $$$
Home, home on the chain er, range.

🛍 Shopping

- **Artfully Chocolate** • 506 John Carlyle St
703-575-8686
Gourmet chocolate confections to go with quirky cards and gifts.
- **Crate & Barrel Outlet** • 1700 Prince St
703-739-8800
Perfectly complements hyper-inflated real estate.
- **Grape + Bean** • 2 E Walnut St
703-888-0709
Wine, coffee and ice cream.
- **Whole Foods Market** • 1700 Duke St
703-706-0891
Expensive organic food chain store.

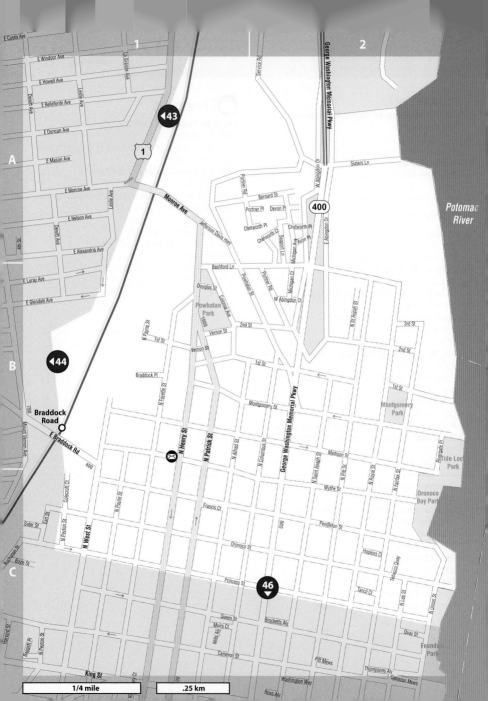

It was only a matter of time before the North began to catch up with the South—in an ironic twist of history. This area is a mix of old and new, with charming streets where residents have worked hard to update their historic townhomes with a modern edge, and modern townhomes are built with historic facades.

Restaurants

- **Buzz Bakery** • 901 Slaters Ln
  703-600-2899 • $
  Cheerful and colorful bakery/coffee spot open surprisingly late.
- **Rustico** • 827 Slaters Ln
  703-224-5051 • $$$
  Largest beer selection in NoVa (~300) and hearth-fired pizzas to boot.

Shopping

- **Trader Joe's** • 612 N St Asaph St
  703-548-0611
  If only the folks shopping there were as laid back as the décor.

Map

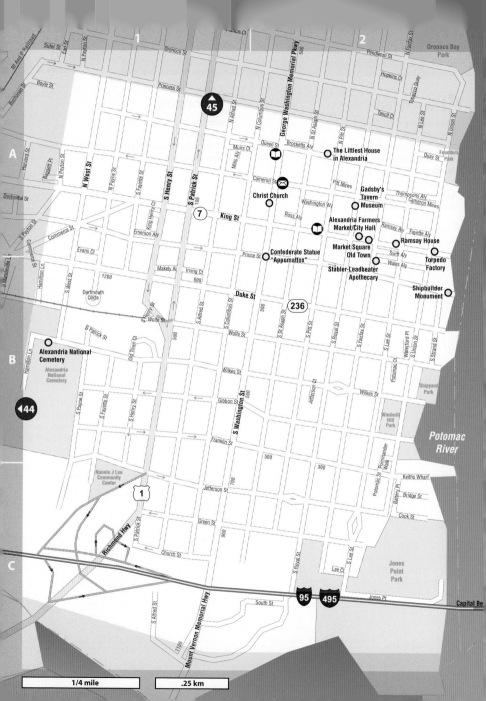

Map 46

This is arguably the most popular section of Old Town and what Arlington strives to achieve. Shops are plentiful and unique, restaurants range from high-end to pizza joints, and the streets with the million-dollar-plus townhomes (from the 18th century to centuries closer) are charming and close to the Potomac. It's a great area to perambulate, peek in on local artists at the **Torpedo Factory**, or sit for a spell by the river.

○ Landmarks

- **Alexandria City Hall** • 301 King St
  703-838-4000
  Founded in 1749.
- **Alexandria National Cemetery** • 1450 Wilkes St
  703-221-2183
  Visit the graves of buffalo soldiers.
- **Christ Church** • 118 N Washington St
  703-549-1450
  Sit in GW's pew.
- **Confederate Statue "Appomattox"** •
  S Washington St & Prince St
  This is The South, don't forget.
- **Gadsby's Tavern Museum** • 134 N Royal St
  703-746-4242
  Many US Presidents slept here.
- **The Littlest House in Alexandria** • 523 Queen St
  It's only 7 feet wide!
- **Market Square Old Town** • 301 King St
  Bring your skateboard.
- **Ramsay House** • 221 King St
  703-838-4200
  Alexandria's visitor center.
- **Stabler-Leadbeater Apothecary Museum** •
  105 S Fairfax St
  703-746-3852
  Where GW (the original) got his Viagra.
- **Torpedo Factory Art Center** • 105 N Union St
  703-838-4565
  Now it churns out art.

▼ Nightlife

- **Austin Grill** • 801 King St
  703-684-8969
  Great Tex/Mex; just outside, Janet Reno got a parking ticket!
- **Bayou Room** • 219 King St
  703-549-1141
  Lounge at historic 219 Restaurant.
- **Chadwicks** • 203 The Strand
  703-836-4442
  Tried-and-true saloon away from the King St. crush.
- **Flying Fish** • 815 King St
  703-600-3474
  Sushi and karaoke, together at last.
- **The Light Horse** • 715 King St
  703-549-0533
  Neighborhood bar, casual atmosphere.
- **Murphy's** • 713 King St
  703-548-1717
  Locals-favored pub with wonk-beloved Tuesday trivia.
- **PX** • 728 King St
  703-299-8384
  This "speakeasy" requires a blazer and lots of dough.
- **Rock It Grill** • 1319 King St
  703-739-2274
  Lowbrow and proud.
- **Union Street Public House** • 121 S Union St
  703-548-1785
  $2 happy-hour pints!!!
- **Vermilion** • 1120 King St
  703-684-9669
  No-frills lounge.

Map 46

Old Town (South)

Restaurants

- **219 Restaurant** • 219 King St
  703-549-1141 • $$$
  Interior looks like the swankiest hotel in New Orleans.
- **Bilbo Baggins** • 208 Queen St
  703-683-0300 • $$$
  Coziest tavern this side of Middle Earth. Health-conscious options.
- **Bittersweet Cafe** • 823 King Street
  703-549-2708 • $$
  Great food, Great desserts.
- **Casablanca Restaurant** • 1504 King St
  703-549-6464 • $$$
  Good deals on multi-course meals.
- **Chart House** • 1 Cameron St
  703-684-5080 • $$$$
  Chain steak and seafood restaurant.
- **Columbia Firehouse** • 109 S St Asaph St
  703-683-1776 • $$
  Old Town bistro and chophouse in a historic firehouse.
- **Eamonn's: A Dublin Chipper** • 728 King St
  703-299-8384 • $$$
  Their motto: Thanks be to cod.
- **Faccia Luna** • 823 S Washington St
  703-838-5998 • $$
  The best pizza around, locals love it.
- **Fish Market** • 105 King St
  703-836-5676 • $$$
  Just follow your nose!
- **Five Guys** • 107 N Fayette St
  703-549-7991 • $
  Best burgers in Old Town (and maybe in all of the East Coast).
- **Grape + Bean** • 118 S Royal St
  703-664-0214 • $
  It's wine! It's coffee! It's…the best of both worlds, done well.
- **The Grille at Morrison House** • 116 S Alfred St
  703-838-8000 • $$$$
  Where luxury and Alexandria collide.
- **Hard Times Café** • 1404 King St
  703-837-0050 • $$
  Nothing but chili, but plenty of it.
- **Il Porto** • 121 King St
  703-836-8833 • $$$$
  Best Italian around. Make reservations.
- **Jackson 20** • 480 King St
  703-842-2790 • $$$$
  Southern Comfort food.
- **King Street Blues** • 112 N St Asaph St
  703-836-8800 • $$$
  Not quite on King St., but great BBQ.
- **La Bergerie** • 218 N Lee St
  703-683-1007 • $$$$$
  Pay the tab if you can-can.
- **La Tasca** • 607 King St
  703-299-9810 • $$$
  Great Tapas and Paellas.
- **Las Tapas** • 710 King St
  703-836-4000 • $$$
  As almost always with tapas, hit and miss.
- **The Light Horse** • 715 King St
  703-549-0533 • $$
  Neighborhood bar, casual atmosphere.
- **Mai Thai** • 6 King St
  703-548-0600 • $$$
  Terrific Thai on Old Town's waterfront.
- **The Majestic** • 911 King St
  703-837-9117 • $$$
  American plates with killer cocktails.
- **The Pita House** • 719 King St
  703-684-9194 • $
  Intimate Middle Eastern.
- **Red Rocks** • 904 King St
  703-717-9873 • $$$
  Brick oven pizza and craft beers, and don't miss brunch.
- **Restaurant Eve** • 110 S Pitt St
  703-706-0450 • $$$$
  Reservations a must.
- **Society Fair** • 277 S Washington St
  703-683-3247 • $$$$
  Restaurant, butchery, wine bar, grocery, bakery: all your dreams come true!
- **Southside 815** • 815 S Washington St
  703-836-6222 • $$
  New Orleanean fare.
- **Virtue Feed & Grain** • 106 S Union St
  571-970-3669 • $$$$
  Modern Gastro-pub with a conscience.
- **The Warehouse** • 214 King St
  703-683-6868 • $$$
  A bit forgotten but excellent food. Plan to eat hearty.

Consider arriving into Old Town on bike, via the Mt. Vernon Trail. Stop here for lunch and a rest. Exceptional establishments include **Restaurant Eve** (four stars, so make your reservation weeks ahead) and the **Chart House** (lobster and a view). Nightlife abounds, but head to **PX** (above **Eamonn's: A Dublin Chipper**) for a unique "speakeasy" experience. On an afternoon outing grab a coffee at **Misha's** then saunter down the block and window-shop in the many area boutiques.

Map

🛍 Shopping

- **An American in Paris** • 1225 King St
  703-519-8234
  King St. goes French.
- **Apple Seed Maternity and Baby Boutique** •
  115 S Columbus St
  703-535-5446
  Why buy $50 pregnancy pants when you can spend $200?
- **Banana Republic** • 628 King St
  703-739-0888
  It is what it is.
- **Big Wheel Bikes** • 2 Prince St
  703-739-2300
  Rent one and do the Mt. Vernon Trail.
- **Candi's Candies** • 107 N Fairfax St
  703-518-1718
  Candy or something. Free samples!
- **Chinoiserie** • 1323 King St
  703-838-0520
  A sure shot for unique home décor or a gift for a hip friend.
- **Comfort One Shoes** • 201 King St
  571-257-7510
  Beyond Birkenstocks.
- **Decorium Gift & Home** • 116 King St
  703-739-4662
  Lots of pink.
- **Diva Designer Consignment** • 116 S Pitt St
  703-683-1022
  What divas wear: designer clothes.
- **The Hour** • 1015 King St
  703-224-4687
  Vintage barware for your mid-century home.
- **Hysteria** • 125 S Fairfax St
  703-548-1615
  Wearable art at museum prices.
- **The Irish Walk** • 415 King St
  703-548-0118
  Every day is St. Patrick's Day.

- **JoS. A. Bank** • 728 S Washington St
  703-837-8201
  For professional types who can't afford Brooks Brothers.
- **La Cuisine** • 323 Cameron St
  703-836-4435
  Upscale cookware.
- **The Lamplighter** • 1207 King St
  703-549-4040
  Get plugged in.
- **Montague & Son** • 115 S Union St
  703-548-5656
  Birkenstocks on cobblestone streets?
- **Notting Hill Gardens** • 446 Calvert Avenue
  703-518-0215
  A delightful urban nursery.
- **P&C Art** • 212 King St
  703-549-2525
  Original art.
- **Pacers** • 1301 King St
  703-836-1463
  Running wear, if you insist on it.
- **Paper Source** • 118 King St
  703-299-9950
  Heaven for scrapbookers and greeting card seekers alike.
- **Papyrus** • 721 King St
  571-721-0070
  Cards, gifts, and wrap.
- **The Shoe Hive** • 127 S Fairfax St
  703-548-7105
  Shooz. Nice selection.
- **Torpedo Factory Art Center** • 105 N Union St
  703-838-4565
  Giant artist compound; most of it's pretty touristy stuff.
- **Williams-Sonoma** • 825 S Washington St
  703-836-1904
  Great cooking stuff if you know how.

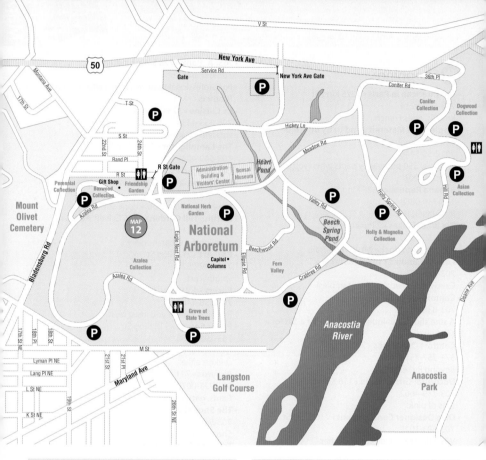

General Information

NFT Map:	12
Address:	3501 New York Ave NE
	Washington, DC 20002
Phone:	202-245-2726
Website:	www.usna.usda.gov
Hours:	Daily: 8 am–5 pm,
	except Dec 25th
Admission:	Free

Overview

Escape the hubbub of DC's urban jungle with a visit to the 446 acres of greenery at the National Arboretum, a living museum where trees, shrubs, and herbaceous plants are cultivated for science and education. Located in a remote corner of the city where few dare to venture, the Arboretum is a fresh welcome away from tourists, crowds and concrete. The Arboretum's biggest draw is the National Bonsai and Penjing Museum, where you'll find over 150 miniature trees (some hundreds of years old). A rock garden, koi pond, and ikebana exhibit (the Japanese art of fl ower arranging) surround the museum and have enough Zen to clear your head—unless you have allergies.

Other major attractions depend on the season. Spring sees the arboretum burst with the fresh pastels of daffodils, crocuses, and azaleas. In summer, the palette mellows with the arrival of waterlilies and wildflowers. Fall brings the stately crimsons and golds of fall foliage, while winter blankets the large pines and hollies with snow. In short, there's always something to see, and there's always a reason to come back. It's easy to see why so many couples get engaged and take their wedding photos on these fragrant, colorful, beautiful acres. For up-to-the-minute news on what's currently in bloom, check the "What's Blooming" page on the Arboretum's website.

While flowers may bloom and fade, the view of the Anacostia flowing quietly behind the Dogwood Collection is here to stay, as are the 22 Corinthian columns planted in a grassy field near the entrance, open to the sky. Originally part of the Capitol Building, these columns are probably the closest thing America has to the Parthenon. Picnic trips are welcomed, but must be enjoyed on the east terrace or at the picnic area in the National Grove of State Trees, leashed dogs are allowed in all areas of the park.

If you want to mix education with pleasure, visit the Economic Botany Herbarium—a collection of over 650,000 dried plant specimens classified for the studies of agriculture, medicine, science, and education. The volunteer staff also breeds plants for other locales throughout the country in a controlled greenhouse.

The National Bonsai Collection and Penjing Museum is open Monday through Friday, 10 a.m.–4 p.m.. The Arbor House Gift Shop is open Monday through Friday from 10 a.m. to 3:30 p.m., March 1 through mid-December. For the months of April through September, weekend hours are added, from 10 a.m.–5 p.m..

Activities

The 9.6 miles of paved roads serve as excellent biking and jogging paths. Picnicking is allowed in designated areas. Fishing, fires, and flower picking are all prohibited, and pets must be kept on leashes. The Arboretum offers public education programs including lectures, workshops, demonstrations, and plant, flower, and art exhibitions.

A 48-passenger open-air tram runs through the park on a 35-minute, non-stop, narrated tour covering the Arboretum's history, mission, and current highlights. Tram services are available on weekends from mid-April through October: $4 adults, $3 seniors, $2 kids 4–16 years old, and free for kids 4 and under. Private tours are also available with a 3-week advance reservation. The Arbor House hosts visitor facilities, including toilets, water fountains, snacks, and vending machines in addition to horticulturally oriented gifts. During summer months, food trucks are also located on the east terrace of the Administrative building.

Full Moon Hikes, available during the spring and fall, take participants on a somewhat strenuous five-mile moonlit trek through the grounds, with curators providing horticultural facts along the way. Hikes vary around $22–$25 (less for Friends of the National Arboretum). You'll need to register early as there is limited space and tours fill up quickly (as in, we called at the beginning of April to book a tour in May, and we were already too late). Pre-registration is required; call 202-245-4521 to make your reservation, or find the mail-in form online.

How to Get There—Driving

From northwest Washington, follow New York Avenue east to the intersection of Bladensburg Road. Turn right onto Bladensburg Road and drive four blocks to R Street. Make a left on R Street and continue two blocks to the Arboretum gates.

Parking

Large free parking lots are located near the Grove of State Trees, by the R Street entrance, and near the New York Avenue entrance. Smaller lots are scattered throughout the grounds close to most of the major collections. Several of the parking areas have been expanded recently, and a free shuttle through the park runs continuously during summer months.

How to Get There—Mass Transit

The closest Metro subway stop is Stadium Armory Station on the Blue and Orange lines. Transfer to Metrobus B-2, get off on Bladensburg Road, and walk two blocks to R Street. Make a right on R Street and continue two more blocks to the Arboretum gates.

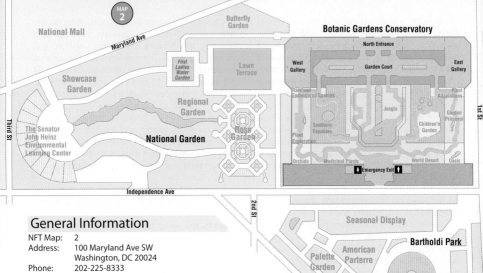

General Information

NFT Map: 2
Address: 100 Maryland Ave SW
             Washington, DC 20024
Phone: 202-225-8333
Website: www.usbg.gov
Hours: 10 am–5 pm every day, including holidays
Admission: Free

Overview

Sometimes we all feel like we're living in a concrete jungle, but if you want to experience a real jungle of the green and alive variety without blowing your budget on a trip to South America, stop into the US Botanic Garden. If you need an escape from the heat or the cold or the hustle and bustle, take a stroll through the Oasis Room or curl up with a book on a bench in the glass-ceilinged Garden Court. You'll feel like you're miles away from the sidewalks and the suits, but not necessarily the tourists, especially on weekends. Nestled in the shadow of the US Capitol Building, and known as Washington's "Secret Garden," the US Botanic Garden is one of the nation's oldest botanical gardens and home to more than 25,000 different specimens. The refurbished Conservatory features a 24-foot-high mezzanine level allowing visitors to gaze downward onto a canopied rainforest. Its distinctive glass façade now houses advanced environmental control systems that allow orchid buds to bloom in the same building as desert brush, furry cacti, and nearly 4,000 other living plants. If you're looking for a particular organism but don't know where to start, you can tap into the USBG's massive computer database and search by common name, scientific name, or geographic location, or you can simply ask one of the Garden's reputable flora-fanatic employees. Can't make it to the Gardens, but still have a pressing plant question? No worries—just call the Plant Hotline at 202-226-4785 and ask away!

The USBG offers classes, exhibits, lectures, and symposia throughout the year. Visit during the week and you might be lucky enough to land on a tour (schedules vary, so be sure to check the website for up-to-date event listings), or buy tickets in advance for events such as organic beer tastings or talks on recognizing beneficial insects.

Outside is the National Garden, a three-acre plot of land located just west of the Conservatory. The landscaped space showcases the unusual, useful, and ornamental plants that flourish in the mid-Atlantic region in areas known as the Rose Garden, Butterfly Garden, and (wait for it) First Ladies' Water Garden!

Bartholdi Park, located across Independence Avenue from the Conservatory, was created in 1932 and named for sculptor Frederic Auguste Bartholdi. In addition to creating the elegant and aptly named Bartholdi Fountain in the center of the park, he also designed the Statue of Liberty. The park is open daily from dawn until dusk. A copy of the visitor guide is available for download in multiple languages from www.usbg.gov/visit

How to Get There—Mass Transit

Taking public transportation is highly recommended. By Metro, take the Blue or Orange line to Federal Center SW or Capitol South stations. If you're using the Metro Bus, take the 30, 32, 34, 35, or 36 to Independence Avenue and First Street SW. Just walk toward the giant white dome, then look south.

General Information

NFT Map:	5
Location:	225 7th St SE
	Washington, DC 20003
Website:	www.easternmarket-dc.org
Hours:	Tues-Fri: 7 a.m.–7 p.m.
	Sat: 7 a.m.–6 p.m.
	Sun: 9 a.m.–5 p.m.
	Closed Mondays

Overview

Eastern Market, known for its farm-fresh produce, meat, local seafood and fl owers, opened in 1873 and is listed on the National Register of Historic Places. After being damaged by fi re in 2007, a completely renovated Eastern Market reopened in 2009, preserving much of the original 16,500-square-foot structure. As the surrounding Capitol Hill neighborhood continues to gentrify, more and more DC yuppies have begun fl ocking to Eastern Market on the weekends, loudly denouncing Whole Foods by fi lling their natural fiber tote bags with tomatoes, orchids and crafts from local artisans.

However, whatever your purpose, there's plenty to be seen and eaten at the Eastern Market. The lone Market Lunch counter draws a line out the door on weekends as it dishes up greasy, hit-the-spot breakfasts (we love the pancakes) and Chesapeake lunch favorites (try the softshell crab sandwich). The freshly grown produce is difficult to ignore, and you'll consider buying a giant basil plant or a beet.

On the sidewalks outside, artists, farmers, and charlatans hawk their wares. Antique and collectibles vendors fi ll the playground behind the former Hine Junior High School with piles of trinkets, textiles, furniture, bikes and trash. They call it a flea market, but don't expect bargains. It's also a good place to see if your missing bike might be for sale. A twenty minute walk from the Nat's stadium, Eastern Market also offers a pre-game diversion and ample nightlife to continue the post-game celebration, or to drown your sorrows, as the case may be. There are, however, some decent deals to be found across the street on the north side of the market, plus interesting art that might find a place in your fancy new townhouse.

How to Get There—Driving

Parking is scarce, but if you must: From the south, take I-395 across the 14th Street Bridge, bear right over the bridge onto the Southwest Expressway; exit at 6th Street SE, the first exit beyond South Capitol Street. At the bottom of the ramp, continue one block and turn left on 7th Street SE. The next major intersection with a traffic light is Pennsylvania Avenue. You'll see Hines School on the opposite corner.

From the west, take I-66 to Rosslyn, Virginia, and Route 110 to I-395 N, then follow the directions above.

From the north, take Baltimore-Washington Parkway and I-295, exiting at Pennsylvania Avenue (East). A U-turn can be made at the second light to head westbound on Pennsylvania to 7th Street SE, where you need to make a right.

From the east, take either Route 50 or I-495 to I-295, and follow the directions above.

Parking

Diagonal parking is available on 7th Street, on the alley sides of the Market, and there's some curb parking in the Capitol Hill neighborhood. On weekends, it's best to take the Metro.

How to Get There—Mass Transit

Take the Blue or Orange Metro Lines to the Eastern Market station, and walk north out of the station along 7th Street SE.

S St NW

5th St NW

R St NW

36th St NW

Reservoir Rd NW

Winfield Ln NW

S St NW

○ **Dumbarton Oaks**

Caton Pl NW

32nd St NW

Dent Pl NW

Q St NW

Volta Pl NW

Georgetown University

PAGE 190

Georgetown Recreation Center

P St NW

Wisconsin Ave NW

MAP 8

Montrose Park

Avon Pl NW

Dem Pl NW

Avon Ln NW

Cambridge Pl

Q St NW

West Ln Ky NW

P St NW

East Pl NW

26th St NW

Poplar St NW

Oak Hill Cemetery

Massachusetts

Waterside Dr

37th St NW

36th St NW

35th St NW

34th St NW

33rd St NW

Potomac St NW

Q St NW

N St NW

O ○ **The Tombs**

Canal Rd

P

Bank St NW

P

P

Prospect St NW

P

M St NW →

Congress St NW

Oak Aly NW

Blues Aly NW →

31st St NW

Dumbarton St NW

30th St NW

29th St NW

28th St NW

27th St NW

Q St NW

Old Stone ○ **House**

P

P

C&O ○ **Canal Path**

P

P

P

29

Water St NW

29

Grace St NW

Cecil Pl NW

South St NW

Thomas Jefferson St NW

K St

P

P

Potomac River

Pennsylvania

L St NW

↑

26th St NW

K St NW

Queen Anne

27th St NW

Overview

NFT Map: 8

Like a socialite fleeing the masses, Georgetown hides in a Metro-inaccessible corner of DC with the nearest Metro stop (Foggy Bottom/GWU) an 8-block walk. Hiding, however, doesn't work: the masses swarm through the tight vehicle and pedestrian traffic on M Street, Wisconsin Ave and the Key Bridge. That's only because Georgetown is so charming, with its cobblestone streets, colonial brick houses, boutique shopping and cafes, despite the commercialization of its main drags. On pleasant weekend days, tourists and locals alike flock to the neighborhood for shopping and gawking at the city's priciest residential and most desirable real estate.

Georgetown is a shopping oasis with hundreds of mainstream stores, high-end boutiques, bakeries and furnishing stores for those with discriminating taste. At night, watch out as every blueblood rich kid and those who wish they were take over the streets for a boisterous, and seemingly homogeneous, party scene. The mash of trendy restaurants, swank bars, and hole-in-the-wall pubs open their doors for the college crowd, baby boomers, and the better-coiffed see-and-be-seen crowd. Head down to the waterfront during the day for brunch and drinks while you watch yachts pull up to the harbor and crew teams row by.

Despite the area's highbrow reputation, elite schools, and garden-lined historical houses, Georgetown has a number of free events that take place throughout the year. It's still the perfect place for a leisurely stroll and window shopping, whether you're a Georgetown student or a lobbyist's wife.

History

Georgetown was formed in 1751, and the neighborhood's access to the Potomac River was a big draw to the shipping community. Originally a part of Frederick County, Maryland, Georgetown was appropriated by the City of Washington in 1871.

After the Civil War, the area became a haven for freed slaves seeking financial freedom. But a devastating flood in 1890 forced the Canal Company into bankruptcy and triggered an economic depression. By the end of World War I, Georgetown had become a total slum. In the 1930s, New Deal government officials rediscovered the convenience and charm beneath the grime, and with their help, Georgetown began its physical rehab and social climb back to its current grandeur. The reputation of the area was further boosted with the arrival of then–US Senator John F. Kennedy during the 1950s. As its most famous residents, Kennedy and his wife, Jackie, made Georgetown the hub for the fashionable elite of the District, their legendary parties drawing political heavyweights from all over DC.

Attractions

Georgetown hosts the city's most compact collection of historic, retail, gastronomic, and nightlife draws. The Old Stone House, built in 1765, is the oldest surviving building on its original lot in the federal city, and it predates the city of DC itself. The rumored-to-be-haunted-house and its gardens are both publicly strollable. The C&O Canal Path, the 184-mile leaf-shrouded park that runs alongside a murky, but historically interesting, canal. The canal was originally a water highway that linked the rapidly growing west to the east and allowed farmers to ship their goods to market. The canal path is now more of a runner and biker highway, with many a local commuting from Bethesda to Virginia on it. Locals use it to work off the one-too-manys they imbibed at bars like Georgetown University's esteemed The Tombs. For a more relaxing respite, Dumbarton Oaks is a Federal-style 19th century mansion surrounded by sublime gardens. Check out Capitol River Cruises for hourly riverboat cruises up and down the Potomac. Also catch a glimpse of the House of Sweden, a new flick at Loews Georgetown, or the United Arab Emirates Embassy. Besides being home to one of the city's most prestigious universities, Georgetown is the infamous location of a young boy's supposed exorcism during the late 1940s. The speculated exorcism spawned a bestselling novel by William Peter Blatty and one of the most well-known horror films, *The Exorcist*. Decades later, tourists and fans of the movie still visit the notorious steps where one of the characters fell to his death at the hands of the possessed Regan MacNeil. Take Jan Pottker's Celebrity Georgetown Tour to visit the remodeled house used in the film and see other locations where movies were shot.

To escape the swankiness, Key Bridge Boathouse (formerly, from 1945 until 2013, Jack's Boathouse) located under Key Bridge (3500 Water St NW) rents canoes, kayaks, and even stand-up paddle boards. Feel free to use their gas grills after working up a post-paddle hunger. The C & O canal tow path, a biker or urban runner's dream, can also be accessed along the river where Water St dead ends at the trail.

For a complete list of stores, restaurants, and attractions in Georgetown, consult the comprehensive Georgetown website: www.georgetowndc.com. For a selection of our favorite Georgetown bars, restaurants, and shopping venues, see Map 8.

How to Get There—Driving

Driving is really a terrible way to get to Georgetown unless you enjoy snarling traffic and honking at expensive cars. If you don't mind an uphill stroll, head toward the river and check out the metered street parking and garages along Water St. M Street between 27th and Francis Scott Key Bridge is where you find the action. Also venture up Wisconsin Ave. for more high-end boutiques. The area is also accessible by Canal Road NW, and Pennsylvania Avenue.

Parking

If you absolutely must take your car to Georgetown, street parking is a pain, but surprisingly not impossible if you're quick, willing to walk a little and have a small car. There is a pay-as-you go system where you have to go to a small stand on the sidewalk to obtain a parking ticket you place in the window of your car. A paid garage is your best bet, however pricey. See Map 8 for locations.

How to Get There—Mass Transit

Metrobus routes 30, 32, 34, 35, or 36 marked "Friendship Heights" run west on Pennsylvania Avenue. Buses cost $1.80 without a SmarTrip card, and $1.60 with one. Don't bother to ask for change because you won't get anything but some driver sass. Transfers are no longer available with cash, so the motivation to get a SmarTrip card only grows.

The Circulator—DC's bus for people who don't like to ride the bus—runs between Union Station and Georgetown (via K Street) and from Rosslyn to Dupont Circle (via Georgetown) every 10 minutes. This line runs up until midnight on week nights, and until 2am on weekends. Fares are $1, and again uses a paperless transfer system with SmarTrip.

There is no Metro stop in Georgetown, but on a pleasant day, if you're equipped with good walking shoes, the Foggy Bottom-GWU stop on the Orange and Blue lines is a ten minute walk from the east end of the neighborhood. The Rosslyn stop on the same line is a ten-minute walk from Georgetown's west end, but you must cross the busy Key Bridge. And finally, for those on the red line, the half-mile walk down Q St to Dupont Circle is actually quite pleasant, and beats the time you'll spend underground changing lines. Dupont Circle Metro Station, on the Red line, is also a pleasant 1.2-mile walk to Georgetown's center, M Street and Wisconsin Avenue, through its historic, well-tended neighborhood streets, and over the Dumbarton Bridge with its monumental buffalo. Biking to Georgetown is also possible from all points on the Custis, Capital Capital Crescent or C & O Canal trails. Don't have a bike? Check out www.capitalbikeshare.com to rent one by the day. To get to Georgetown, grab a bike outside the Rosslyn metro station and cross Key Bridge on two wheels.

The Monuments / Potomac Park / Tidal Basin

General Information

NFT Maps: 1, 6, and 7
Website: www.nps.gov
Phone: 202-426-6841

Overview

If there's one thing DC loves more than a free museum, it's a commemorative lawn ornament. The District is packed with monuments, statues, plaques, and fountains. This is especially apparent while strolling through the area west of the National Mall, where you'll find the Lincoln, FDR, Jefferson, and Washington memorials, as well as tributes to those who served in WWI, WWII, the Korean War, and Vietnam, all within Segway riding distance of one another (if you're a lame tourist or a lame curious-about-Segways local)—or walking/ running distance (if you're in intense local training for the sold-out, annual Cherry Blossom 10-miler race every April). If you're on foot, keep in mind that distances are not as close as they might seem. The monuments are big, but not close!

Presidential Monuments

Our forefathers were clearly larger than today's average American, as the not-so-human scale monuments of some of our more memorable predecessors can attest.

The tall, unadorned monument commemorating America's first president as recognizable a landmark as the White House or the Capitol. The giant white obelisk can be viewed from many parts of town but is more fun to experience up close, for no better reason than to hear "wow, it's tall" in 112 languages. Today, it's possible to find Dan Brown fans squinting at the pyramid tip to see if there are any Masonic references as well.

Had the Washington Monument been built in Europe, it would most likely squirt water from several places, have 12 pairs of ornately sculpted angel wings fluttering from its sides, and feature a large, bronze pair of breasts over the entranceway. The simplicity and straightforwardness of the building is a tribute to the gravitas, fortitude, and simple elegance of the man it represents. Modest George Washington never referred to this city as 'Washington,' but always 'Federal City.'

Entry to the Washington Monument is free, although your ticket is only valid during a specified entry time. Free tickets are distributed on a first-come, first-served basis at the kiosk on the Washington Monument grounds (at 15th Street and Madison Drive). Advance reservations can be made at www.recreation.gov. The ticket kiosk is open daily from 8:30 am until 4:30 pm (closed December 25th), and tickets usually run out early in the day. If you plan on visiting the monument, make it your first stop. The Monument was damaged during the 5.8 magnitude 2011 Virginia earthquake; it was closed to the public for nearly three years while repairs were made to cracks in the stone.

While many visitors use the monument as a vantage point from which to view the surrounding city, the tall structure itself is really as impressive as the view it affords. The exterior walls are constructed of white marble from Maryland; the interior walls are lined with granite from Maine. Construction began in 1848 and was only one-third complete when the Civil War broke out—hence the change in stone color a third of the way up. Construction resumed after the war, but by then, the color of stone in the quarry had changed. Today, the Washington Monument remains the tallest and most revered structure in DC, giving it alpha-monument status and deflecting the exploding metropolitan population out into surrounding farmland instead of upward into the city sky.

The Lincoln Memorial, which stands in front of the reflecting pool across from the Washington Monument, was designed to look like a Greek Temple and boasts more movie appearances than Samuel L. Jackson. The 36 pillars represent the 36 states that existed at the time of Lincoln's death. The larger-than-life sculpture of honest Abe inside underscores the man's great physical and political stature. Visitors from abroad will no doubt question why the United States saw it fit to construct a literal temple to President Lincoln, but then perhaps other countries don't embrace the towering monument the way the District does. Visiting the monument is free, and the structure is open to the public year-round.

Tidal Basin

The Tidal Basin was constructed in the late 1800s as a swimming hole in the middle of the park. It's no longer a place for a refreshing dip. Besides the questionable cleanliness of this urban pond, the ample federal security forces in the neighborhood are likely the strictest lifeguards in the country. If you're set on dipping a toe in the water, join the tourists and rent a paddle boat. For two weeks every spring, cherry blossoms bloom on some 3,000 trees around the basin and throughout the parks. Viewing the monuments through this prism of pink puffiness takes the edge off the sometimes stark grandeur of the grayish-white monuments. The original trees were a gift from Japan in 1912, and their bloom inspires an annual Japanese-influenced festival to kick off the spring. The Japanese must have heard the story of young George choppin' away (or not!); not even Bush's famed chainsaw could take down this eye-popping pastel forest.

The domed Jefferson Memorial, easily the most elegant memorial of them all, resides on the basin's edge. From tall Thomas's perch above the tidal basin, a fine view can be enjoyed of both the Washington Monument and flights leaving Reagan National across the river. The view at night is especially romantic when the marble pantheon lights up and its reflection is cast into the tidal basin. Finally, while its location is certainly beautiful, the memorial is surely but slowly sinking into the mud…Never forget that all this neoclassical grandeur sits on a giant swamp. The Martin Luther King, Jr. National Memorial, across the Tidal Basin from the Jefferson Memorial, unveiled in 2011 and designed by Chinese sculptor Lei Yixin, depicts King emerging from the granite Stone of Hope.

East Potomac Park

East Potomac Park is a long green peninsula with a golf course, tennis center, miniature golf, and a playground. Lined with cherry trees, it can be a more pleasant (read: less tourist-clogged) place to enjoy the pink cotton candy blossoms of early spring—and the sidewalk around the peninsula's perimeter is popular year-round with joggers and bikers. It's also a great place to watch the yachts from the marina across the Washington Channel carry boatloads of tourists on river tours, floating parties of drunken bachelorettes, and the rich to wherever it is they go on the weekends (Be nice, golfers!).

Hains Point sits at the confluence of the Anacostia and Potomac Rivers, with an unobstructed view of planes departing from Reagan National. Sadly the much-loved Awakening statue has moved down-river to National Harbor. But with so many available park benches, it's a popular daytime spot for fishing and picnicking, and a prime nighttime spot for making out and the discreet consumption of mind-altering substances. You'll need to drive or bike out there though because there's no public transportation for miles.

How to Get There—Driving

I-66 and I-395 run to the parks from the south. I-495, New York Avenue, Rock Creek Parkway, George Washington Memorial Parkway, and the Cabin John Parkway will get you there from the north. I-66, Route 50, and Route 29 run to the parks from the west. Routes 50, 1, and 4 are the way to go from the east.

Parking

Public parking is available along the Basin, but depending on the time of day, it's likely to be hard to find a spot. You'll end up driving around and around in circles and eventually parking far out and walking long distances.

How to Get There—Mass Transit

The Foggy Bottom, Metro Center, Federal Triangle, Smithsonian, and L'Enfant Plaza stops on the Orange and Blue lines are all within walking distance of various monuments and parks. Farragut North is also a Red Line stop. L'Enfant Plaza is also on the Green and Yellow lines. Numerous Metrobus lines and the Circulator provide access to this large swath of land.

General Information

NFT Maps:	1 & 2
National Mall Website:	www.nps.gov/nacc/index.htm
National Mall Phone:	202-426-6841
Smithsonian Website:	www.si.edu
Smithsonian Phone:	202-633-1000
U.S. Capitol Website:	www.aoc.gov
House of Reps:	www.house.gov
Senate:	www.senate.gov
Capitol Switchboard:	202-224-2131
Capitol Tour Info:	202-225-6827

National Mall

Washington DC's National Mall represents the American dream, where a melting pot of foreigners and locals gather for leisurely picnics or heated protests—without having to do any of the yard work! The layout for the sprawling grass lawn was designed by Frenchman Pierre L'Enfant in the late 18th century as an open promenade. Despite the explosive growth of the surrounding city, the Mall has remained true to L'Enfant's vision (minus the perpetual encircling tour bus brigade). Its eminent stroll-ability is a magnet for hordes of fanny-packed tourists, and its renowned marble monuments attract travel-weary schoolchildren from all over the world. The iconic marble memorials to Washington, Jefferson, Lincoln, and FDR are close by, along with the somber Vietnam and Korean war memorials and the long-needed WWII memorial. On any given day, there's also likely to be a kite festival, political rally, kickball game played by adults, or spirited Frisbee game underway. This is not the place to go if you are camera shy,

as no matter how hard you try to avoid jumping in front of lenses, you *will* end up in family albums across the nation and world.

Smithsonian Institution

If you've seen *Night at the Museum: Battle of the Smithsonians* (a shameless and successful marketing ploy by the organization), you'll know that The Smithsonian Institution is made up of 16 different museums, some of them nowhere near the Mall (one is in NYC), and a zoo. The primary museums are clustered around the Mall—here you'll find the Air and Space Museum, the Natural History Museum, and the Hirshhorn, among others, as well as several tucked-away garden areas ideal for spring-time strolling. The Smithsonian Information Center in the Castle is the best orientation point if you plan to become one of the 24 million visitors who check out one of its DC properties this year.

Like the country it caters to, the Smithsonian collection reflects a hodgepodge of experiences and backgrounds. Between its museums on the Mall, the institution's got the Hope Diamond, Japanese scrolls, and even Archie Bunker's chair. Though there is serious art at the National Portrait Gallery, the Hirshhorn, and several of the smaller museums, the "most popular" distinction goes to the Air and Space Museum, for its sheer *wowza!*-factor of dangling airplanes and shuttles. A close runner-up is the National Museum of American History, known both affectionately and derisively as "America's Attic." Besides Archie's chair, it accommodates Dorothy's ruby slippers, Muhammad Ali's gloves, George Washington's uniform, Julia Child's entire kitchen, Adlai Stevenson's briefcase, and Steven Colbert's portrait that he had hoped would hang in the Portrait Gallery. The best part about

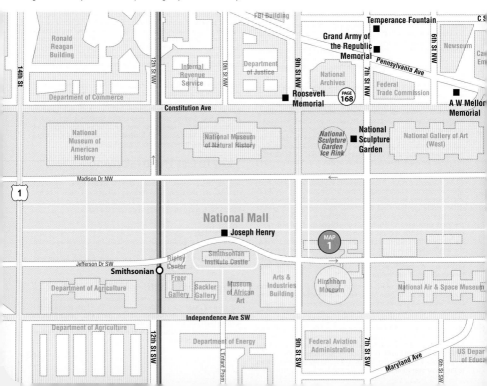

all this: admission is free! So you can come back, again and again, instead of wearing yourself out trying to cover an entire museum in one visit.

Smithsonian Institution Building (The Castle)

The first building of what has become the Smithsonian Empire was the Castle, built in 1855. The Castle was, for a time, the only Smithsonian building housing all aspects of the institution's operations, including an apartment for the first Secretary of the Smithsonian, Joseph Henry. Note to the macabre-minded: A crypt with the remains of founder James Smithson greets you just to the right of the main entrance. The Castle now serves as the seat of the Smithsonian's administrative offices, as well as a general information center. For those in DC for only a brief stay (or with chronic ADD), the Castle's common room has a mini-museum encompassing exhibits from all of the Mall's museums, which can be thoroughly viewed in approximately ten minutes. (www.si.edu/Museums/smithsonian-institution-building; 202-633-1000)

The National Museum of the American Indian

This relatively recent addition to the Mall's museum family opened in September 2004. Possibly the largest example of Greco-Anasazi architecture in DC, it includes exhibits from many of the vibrant cultures of North, Middle, and South America. After learning about the hunting and/or agricultural practices of various peoples, hungry visitors can sample native foods of the Western Hemisphere, grouped by region. Mitsitam Cafe is hands-down the best Smithsonian eats, and the cafeteria is divided by region, including the Northern Woodlands, South America, the Northwest Coast, Mesoamerica, and the Great Plains.

National Air and Space Museum

This popular museum maintains the largest collection of historic aircraft and spacecraft in the world. Hundreds of artifacts are on display, including the original Wright 1903 airplane, the *Spirit of St. Louis*, the Apollo 11 command module, the *Enola Gay*, and a lunar rock sample that visitors can touch. To avoid lines, try coming in the dead of winter during a blizzard. Otherwise don't worry; it's worth the wait. Hours: 10 am–5:30 pm (6th St & Independence Ave, SW; airandspace.si.edu)

Hirshhorn Museum and Sculpture Garden

Resembling the world's largest flan, the Hirshhorn was conceived as the nation's museum of modern and contemporary art. It has over 11,500 pieces of internationally significant art, including ample space for large-scale installation works, and an excellent line up of temporary exhibitions. This is a good one to visit to get away from the chaos of field-trippers in some of the more youth-oriented museums nearby. Hours: Mon–Sun: 10 am–5:30 pm. Sculpture Garden Hours: 7:30 am–dusk. (7th St & Independence Ave, SW; hirshhorn.si.edu) Free jazz concerts are offered in the Sculpture Garden every Friday from May 25 through August 31. Competition for space can be intense on nice nights. An eclectic food menu is available and beer and sangria may be purchased by the pitcher, but prices are a tad steep.

Arts and Industries Building

The second-oldest Smithsonian building is not in the best shape. In 2004, conditions deteriorated to a point where "diapers" had to be installed on the roof to catch falling debris and the building was closed for renovations. The good news is that a new roof is being installed, and the building will be eventually restored to

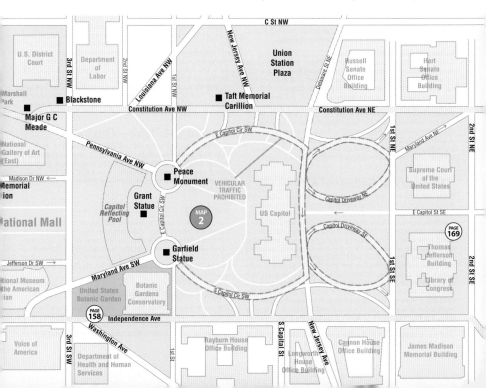

its former glory, when it opened in time for the inaugural ball of President James A. Garfield in 1881. Though renovations of the building aren't expected to be completed until summer 2014, the surrounding gardens are worth a peek (www.si.edu/Museums/ arts-and-industries-building).

National Museum of African Art

The National Museum of African Art is the only museum in the United States devoted exclusively to the display and study of traditional and contemporary arts of sub-Saharan Africa. The museum displays everything from ceramics, textiles, furniture, and tools to masks, figures, and musical instruments. Hours: Mon–Sun: 10 am–5:30 pm. (950 Independence Ave, SW; www.nmafa.si.edu)

Freer and Sackler Galleries

These twin galleries are connected via an underground passageway and house a world-renowned Asian art collection. When it opened in 1923, the Freer Gallery was the first Smithsonian museum dedicated to the fine arts. The Sackler Gallery opened in 1987. The Freer is home to one of the most extensive collections of art by American artist James McNeill Whistler. While you won't find the famous picture of his mother here, you'll find some of his other works, including his portraits and the famous Peacock Room. (Freer Gallery: Jefferson Dr & 12th St, SW; Sackler Gallery: 1050 Independence Ave; www.asia.si.edu)

National Museum of American History

This museum's mission is to collect, care for, and study the objects that reflect the experience of the American people. What better place for the Declaration of Independence Desk, Dizzy Gillespie's trumpet, or Eli Whitney's cotton gin? Two of our favorites are the original Kermit the Frog puppet and Dorothy's ruby slippers. There is also interesting displays and sections detailing the surge in American suburbs, history of technology, and of course, America's love affair with the automobile. Hours: Mon–Sun: 10 am–5:30 pm. (14th St & Constitution Ave, NW; americanhistory.si.edu)

National Museum of Natural History

Visitors come far and wide to catch a glimpse of the 45.5-carat Hope Diamond (hey, that's a lot of bling), but there's more to this museum than one rock. The National Museum of Natural History has an impressive collection of dinosaur and mammal fossils, an insect zoo (check out the daily tarantula feeding!), and an amazing array of stuffed animals (courtesy of taxidermy, not FAO Schwartz). If you're really into rocks, check out the gem collection, which includes meteorites and the Logan Sapphire; at 423 carats, it is the largest publicly displayed sapphire in the country. If you're not visually impaired from looking at the 126 million cool specimens on display, check out the IMAX shows. Hours: Mon–Sun: 10 am–5:30 pm. (10th St & Constitution Ave, NW, www.mnh.si.edu)

The National Gallery of Art

While not a part of the Smithsonian, the National Gallery still houses two buildings of art as impressive as any similar institution in the country. Everything else about Washington might get you overcooked on Greek Revival architecture, but the National Gallery shows in rich detail how DC is actually one of the key places in the world to visit for art. The Gallery's collection include everything from Byzantine art to some of today's leading artists, including Andy Goldsworthy's brilliant work, *Roof*, permanently on display on the ground level of the East Building. There is also a sculpture garden next to the West Building, which houses a "greatest hits" of post-WWII large-format sculpture—highly recommended. . Lunchtime and evening concerts are featured throughout the year, and in summer are held outside in the sculpture garden for many locals who prefer not to hike out to Wolf Trap for an equally enjoyable evening. Hours: (galleries & garden) Mon–Sat: 10 am–5 pm; Sunday: 11 am–6 pm. Note: The Sculpture Garden is open until 9:30 pm on Fridays during the summer. (Between 3rd St NW & 7th St NW at Constitution Ave; www.nga.gov)

US Capitol

The US Capitol is located on Capitol Hill, between 1st and 3rd Streets and between Constitution Avenue NE and Independence Avenue SE. Big white dome. Hard to miss.

Home to the House of Representatives and the Senate, this icon is both a museum and a functioning office where Harry Reid, John Boehner, and Nancy Pelosi are working stiffs. It's also DC's orientation point. Every city address is based on where it lies in relation to the Capitol, and all mileage markers leading to DC are measured from the Capitol. After hours, drunken Hill staffers use it as a compass to get themselves home. With security a close runner-up to the White House in terms of number of guns and cameras, this is not the place to get lost driving a delivery truck. If you've read Dan Brown's, The Lost Symbol, you'll be craning your head upward towards the dome to stare at The Apotheosis of Washington.

Construction began on the Capitol in 1793 and was more or less finished by 1813. The Capitol was burned by the British in 1814, during the War of 1812, but rain saved the structure from complete collapse. Restoration and expansion followed, the result being the building that all Americans recognize today (probably thanks to the movie *Independence Day*). If you've ever wondered who the lady on top of the dome is, she's no-one in particular. She represents freedom and was sculpted by Thomas Crawford.

The District of Columbia gets one non-voting representative in the House based on population but, like Guam and American Samoa, receives no representation in the Senate because it isn't a state. Hence the local "Taxation without Representation" license plates.

The Capitol is closed Thanksgiving and Christmas. Every other day, the public is welcome to explore the annals of the government. Tours are free (unless you count taxes, in which case they're only free if you're a foreigner). Passes are available beginning at 9 am and redistributed on a first-come, first-served basis, or advanced reservations can be made online. To see actual floor action, get in line early. Passes that are not offered in advance, and distribution is limited to one pass per person. The $621 million, 580,000-square-foot underground Capitol Visitors' Center opened in late 2008. It offers a wealth of information and activities in addition to a Capitol tour, and a surprisingly high-end cafeteria. Hours: Mon–Sat: 9:00 am–4:30 pm.

How to Get There—Driving

From the south, I-66 and I-395 will take you straight to the Mall. I-495, New York Avenue, Rock Creek Parkway, George Washington Memorial Parkway, and the Cabin John Parkway will get you there from the north. From the west, I-66, US Route 50, and 29 will take you to the Mall. US Routes 50, 1, and 4 will have you Mall-bound from the east.

Parking

There is some disabled parking at the nearby Lincoln and FDR memorials; otherwise you're dealing with regular street parking, which usually has a maximum time allocation of three hours, and more importantly, rarely exists after 9 am. On weekends, however, meters are free. There are parking garages located close to the Mall, but be prepared to pay a hefty fee for the convenience. Hint: take the metro.

How to Get There—Mass Transit

Take the Orange and Blue lines to Capital South, Federal Triangle, Smithsonian, and Federal Center SW; the Yellow and Green lines to Archives/Navy Memorial; the Red Line to Union Station and Judiciary Square; and the Yellow, Green, Blue, and Orange lines to L'Enfant Plaza.

General Information

NFT maps: 8, 18, 32, 35, 36
Website: www.nps.gov/choh
Visitor information: 301-739-4200
Fees: None outside of the Great Falls area
Open: Park is open all daylight hours

Thompson Boat Center (mile 0.1)
Address: 2900 Virginia Ave NW (Map 7)
Visitor Information: 202-333-9543
Boathouse hours: Mon–Sat 6 am–8 pm, Sun 7 am–7 pm
Rental Hours: Mon–Sun 8 am–5 pm, all rentals
                     returned by 6 pm

Georgetown Visitor Center (mile 0.4)
Address: 1057 Thomas Jefferson St NW (Map 8)
Visitor information: 202-653-5190
Open: Days and hours vary

The Boathouse at Fletcher's Cove (mile 3.1)
Address: 4940 Canal Rd NW (Map 32)
Visitor Information: 202-244-0461
Open: 7 am–7 pm

Carderock Picnic Pavilion (mile 10.5)
Visitor information: 301-767-3731 for reservations
                     and directions

The Old Angler's Inn
Address: 10801 MacArthur Blvd, Potomac, MD
Visitor information: 301-299-9097

Note: This is not part of the park. This is a pricey restaurant that has been here since 1860. This is not the place to take a rest stop with sweat stains, with a bicycle, or with ugly khaki hiking shorts.

Great Falls Tavern Visitor Center (mile 14.3)
Address: 11710 MacArthur Blvd, Potomac, MD
Visitor Information: 301-767-3714
Open: 9 am–4:30 pm (extended summer hours;
                     closed Thanksgiving,
                     Christmas, New Years Day)

Overview

Traveling 184.5 miles from Washington, DC, to Cumberland, MD, the Chesapeake & Ohio Canal parallels the Potomac River from the bustling streets of chi-chi Georgetown to the no streets of backwater Western Maryland—hugging the borders of West Virginia and Pennsylvania along the way. Back in its day, the C&O Canal was like an aquatic interstate, hauling coal, lumber, and grain from Appalachia to the nation's capital. But these days, there ain't no boats floating on the canal…apart from ones full of tourists and park rangers in period clothing. As for the canal's towpath (that's a dirt sidewalk for you urbanites), it has become one of the best ways to graciously exit this city. The Georgetown segment still feels urban, but once you walk just a mile or two along the canal, you'll soon find that the cell yellers have been replaced by singing birds. The towpath is, in effect, a flat, continuous trail sandwiched by the canal and the river, perfect for shady walks, runs, or bike rides through the beautiful Potomac River Valley. For the docile, the C&O Canal National Park offers bird watching, picnicking, fishing, and a range of flora. For the hyperactive, there is boating, hiking (read: walking for people with bad fashion sense), and camping. And for the adolescent boys—Sorry, Mr. Cheney: hunting and swimming are strictly prohibited.

Activities

Kids and corny history lovers will enjoy traveling back in time to the days of animal labor and abuse. Mules drag boats along the canal as park rangers in 1870s period dress tell stories and play music to explain what life was like in the 19th century, for both men and mules. Perhaps the coolest part is crossing one of the canal's locks, however—and feeling the water level rise/fall up to eight feet. One-hour round-trip boat rides depart from the Georgetown Visitor Center. Tickets cost $8 for adults, $6 for senior citizens, and $5 for children. Departure times vary by season and day of the week.

Biking is a good idea on all parts of the canal towpath. Those of you who don't own may rent an all-terrain or a cruiser from the Thompson Boat Center.

Boating on the river is a fabulous way to cool down on one of DC's many dog days. Canoes, kayaks, rowing shells, and sailboats are all available for rental at the Thompson Boat Center in Georgetown. Or if you'd like to float and poach, you can rent a rowboat or canoe from the Boathouse at Fletcher's Cove and cast your line on the Potomac, but be sure to also pick up a DC fishing license at Fletcher's, $10 for the year for residents, and required for every angler over the age of 16. Bait and tackle are also for sale, and anglers have been known to catch herring, striped bass, white perch, and hickory shad in these here parts (note: catch, not eat…not in this river).

For those who prefer lounging on a picnic blanket and soaking in the rays, plenty of green flanks the canal. But if you want to make it a more formal affair, Carderock Pavilion can accommodate up to 200 people on its 26—count 'em if you can, 26—picnic tables. The pavilion is available by permit only: $150 Monday–Thursday and $250 Friday–Sunday and holidays (301-767-3731). For this, though, you get electricity, water, grills, a fireplace, "comfort stations," a softball field, horseshoe pits, a volleyball court (but no net), and ample parking.

Treehuggers will be pleased to know that the park contains about 1,200 species of native plants, many of which are rare, endangered, and/or threatened. Botanists will be delighted by over 600 different species of wildflowers. For the twitchers, keep your eyes peeled and you may just spot a bald eagle.

Lastly, for those of you who are not content to spend just daylight hours with the C&O Canal, the park also has a grand total of 30 campsites—all of which (with the exception of Marsden Tract, which is reserved for do-gooder scouts) are free, free, free. You'll have to go past Great Falls Park to access these sites, but they are designed as way stations for hikers and bikers going the distance. The sites are all first come, first serve, for one night only—but offer a chemical toilet, a picnic table, a grill, and water. The closest site is 16.6 miles in at Swains Lock in Potomac, MD.

How to Get There

It's easy enough to get to the start of the canal in Georgetown. By public transportation, take the Metro to Foggy Bottom-GWU, walk north on 24th St, then turn left on Pennsylvania Ave until it merges with M St. Make a left on Thomas Jefferson St to get to the Georgetown Visitors Center. If you're in doubt, just walk south until land ends and water begins. You can also take any of the 30s buses, the D5, or the Circulator.

To get to the Boathouse at Fletcher's Cover, you can take the D3, D5, or D6 to the intersection of MacArthur Blvd & Ashby St and then walk south on Ashby St, past where the street dead ends, and then rough it through the woods until you hit Canal Rd. You should see an old stone building, the Abner Cloud House, next to the boathouse.

The rest of the C&O Canal Park is pretty much inaccessible by public transport. That's part of the reason why it's so nice.

General Information

NFT Map: 1
DC Address: 700 Pennsylvania Ave NW
               Washington, DC 20408
MD Address: 8601 Adelphi Rd
               College Park, MD 20740-6001
Web Site: www.archives.gov

DC Hours: Day after Labor Day to March 14
               Mon–Sun 10:00 am–5:30 pm
               Closed Thanksgiving Day and
               December 25th
               March 15–Labor Day
               Mon–Sun 10:00 am–7:00 pm
MD Hours: Mon–Fri, 9 am–5:00 pm

Overview

The main building of the National Archives is among the city's most impressive. Situated on Pennsylvania Avenue, it's a block's worth of stone, marble, and Corinthian columns. As impressive as it is on the outside, the inside is even better—unless, of course, you don't really *like* history. Enter from the National Mall, and you'll likely be greeted by a crowd fighting to get catch a glimpse of the Declaration of Independence, the Constitution, or Bill of Rights. Many people think that's all the National Archives has to offer, but like the proverbial iceberg, these cornerstone documents only scratch the surface. You can see these documents with a quick walk through, (enough for many, but since we aren't tourists here, we demand more!). To truly appreciate all, or even a respectable portion of what the National Archives has to offer, you need to spend a bit more time digging deeper.

Along with the United States' most treasured documents (see them soon; the Declaration is fading fast), there's an impressive collection of memorabilia, including presidential correspondence, treasured records, maps, and artwork. In the public vaults, you will find a rotating collection of items that explore different aspects of our country's history. The Lawrence F. O'Brien Gallery gives visitors a detailed journey through a select period or event in American history. There's also a children's area and a theater showing historical films on the National Archives as well as feature length documentaries. As a bonus, the DC branch of the Archives contains a document collection that is any genealogist's dream.

The Maryland location of the National Archives opened in 1994 and is geared toward research, both amateur and professional. The location has an impressive collection of documents dating from WWII including presidential papers, the Berlin Documents Center, civilian and military records, and the John F. Kennedy Assassination Collection, making this the perfect stop if you want to read up on the grassy knoll. Security at the location is high, so be forewarned; however, the staff is the epitome of helpful. See www.nara.gov for detailed information on both locations. Best of all for both spots? Entrance is free.

Getting There

By Metro take the Yellow or Green line to the Archives/Navy Memorial. A free staff shuttle runs between the DC and Maryland locations, leaving on the hour from 8 am to 5 pm and allows researchers on a space available basis. In the city, Metrobuses 30, 32, 34, 53, A42, A48, P1, P2, P4, P17 and W 13 all stop at the DC location on Pennsylvania Ave.

If you are driving, to get to the Maryland location, take I-495 toward Baltimore and exit at 28B, which will lead you to New Hampshire Ave/Route 650 South. From here, take a left at the second light onto Adelphi Road and follow the signs. The Archives is on the left. The drive will take you about 45 minutes from DC. There is limited parking provided. At the DC location, parking is on the street only.

General Information

NFT Maps: 2, 3
Address: 101 Independence Ave SE
Washington, DC 20540
Phone: 202-707-5000
Website: www.loc.gov
Hours: James Madison Building:
Mon–Fri: 8:30 am–9:30 pm; Sat: 8:30 am–6:30 pm
Thomas Jefferson Building:
Mon–Sat: 10 am–5:30 pm
John Adams Building:
Mon, Wed, Thurs: 8:30 am–9:30 pm;
Tues, Fri, Sat: 8:30 am–5:30 pm

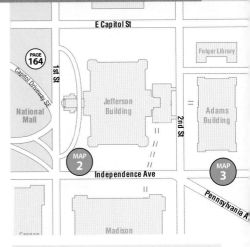

Overview

The Library of Congress doesn't own every book ever published. It IS, however, the largest library in the world. The collection includes more than 142 million items packed on 650 miles of bookshelves in a three-building complex: The Thomas Jefferson Building opened in 1897 and is home to the soaring stained glass Great Hall; the John Adams Building was built in 1939; and the James Madison Building was constructed in 1980. All three buildings are clustered together on Capitol Hill. The Declaration of Independence, the Constitution, a Gutenberg Bible, and the Giant Bible of Mainz are on permanent display.

Sounds like a bibliophile's dream, right? Harsh reality: this is no lending library. The Library of Congress, despite being a great asset to the American public, can't be used like your neighborhood library or a local bookstore. The Library's mission is to serve as a reference library and educational resource for our government *leaders*, not for us plebeians. To do more than merely wander through the ornate sections, you have to be older than 18 and register at the Reader Registration Station. The Visitors' Center (in the Jefferson Building, along with everything worth visiting) offers information, a short introductory film, and free guided tours. A system of underground tunnels connects the Library's main buildings, as well as the Cannon Office Building. The public can enter from the Adams or Madison Buildings and emerge deep within the heart of the Jefferson Building. It's easy to get lost, but worth the adventure, not to mention the time you save in line on busy tourist days. Most DC'ers have yet to look upon the catacombs of the LOC, being familiar primarily with the sculptures of Neptune and his court out front.

The Library has two theaters—the Coolidge Auditorium, located in the Thomas Jefferson Building, and the tiny Mary Pickford Theater in the Madison Building. Built in 1924, the 511-seat Coolidge Auditorium still hosts regular concerts and is known for its remarkable acoustics. Admission to all events is free; however, reservations must be made through Ticketmaster (two ticket limit per customer), which charges a $2 handling fee. The 64-seat Mary Pickford Theater screens films ranging from those of Pickford's era to modern films. Admission is free, but reservations are required. Visit the Library's web site for movie and show times.

History

The Library of Congress was first established in 1800, when the seat of government moved from Philadelphia to DC, and President John Adams approved legislation to create a Congressional law library. The first acquisition consisted of 740 volumes and three maps from London. Fourteen years later, the British army invaded the city and burned the Capitol building, including the amassed 3,000 volumes that made up the Library of Congress at the time. Thomas Jefferson offered to sell his personal library to Congress to restore its lost collection. Jefferson's 6,487 volumes, which were then the largest and finest collection of books in the country, were purchased for $23,940 (the equivalent of 958 copies of *The Da Vinci Code*). Jefferson's collection, which included works on architecture, science, literature, geography, and art, greatly expanded the Library's previously legal collection.

It was in 1870, under the leadership of librarian Ainsworth Spofford, that the collection outgrew its home. The copyright law of 1870 required all copyright applicants to send the Library of Congress two free copies of their book. The Library was flooded with pamphlets, manuscripts, photographs, and books, and eventually—16 years later—Congress authorized the construction of a new building for all their books. And today, the Library of Congress requests a complimentary copy of every publication that bears its CIP (cataloguing-in-publication) data, thus ensuring that it will stay the largest library forever… Scammers!

How to Get There—Mass Transit

The two metro stops closest to the Library are Capitol South (Orange/Blue lines) and Union Station (Red Line). Capitol South is located a block south of the Thomas Jefferson building, across Independence Avenue. From Union Station, walk south on 1st Street, NE, towards the Capitol (it's hard to miss). You'll pass the Supreme Court on your way to the Thomas Jefferson building, which will be on the east side of 1st Street—about a 15 minute walk from Union Station.

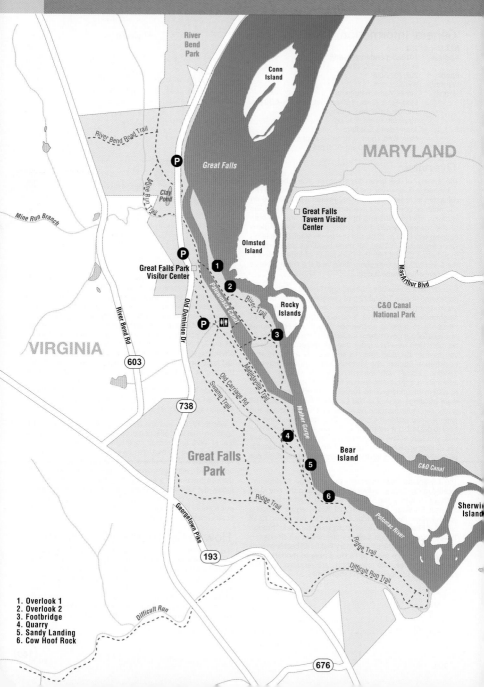

River Bend Park

Conn Island

MARYLAND

River Bend Road Trail

P

Great Falls

Mine Run Branch

Mine Run Trail

Clay Pond

Great Falls Tavern Visitor Center

P

Great Falls Park Visitor Center

Olmsted Island

MacArthur Blvd

River Bend Rd

Old Dominion Dr

Patowmack Canal

River Trail

Rocky Islands

C&O Canal National Park

VIRGINIA

1

2

3

603

P

Matildaville Trail

Mather Gorge

738

Old Carriage Rd

Swamp Trail

4

Bear Island

C&O Canal

Great Falls Park

5

6

Sherwin Island

Ridge Trail

Potomac River

Georgetown Pike

Ridge Trail

193

Difficult Run Trail

Difficult Run

676

1. Overlook 1
2. Overlook 2
3. Footbridge
4. Quarry
5. Sandy Landing
6. Cow Hoof Rock

General Information

Address:	9200 Old Dominion Dr
	McLean, VA 22101
Phone:	703-285-2965
Website:	www.nps.gov/grfa/index.htm
Fees:	
Annual Park Pass:	$20
Vehicle:	$5 for 3 days
Individual:	$3 for 3 days
	(entering by means other than
	vehicle—e.g. foot, bike)
	All passes valid on both sides of
	the falls.
Open:	7 am–dusk year-round,
	closed Christmas

Overview

Washington DC is 14 miles downriver from the aptly named Great Falls Park, where the Potomac River tears into cascading rapids and 20-foot waterfalls. The river drops 76 feet in elevation over a distance of less than a mile, and it narrows from almost 1,000 feet to 100 feet as it gushes through Mather Gorge. It's the steepest fall-line rapid of any eastern river. The best views come by the Virginia side of the river, where the viewing area expands into a massive park. There are fewer amenities on the Maryland side, but you can get there with two wheels: it's technically part of the C&O Canal National Historical Park.

History

The Great Falls weren't always so admired. In the mid-1700s, they presented a near-impossible obstacle for navigating the Potomac. One of the most significant 18th-century engineering feats in the US was the development of a canal system that lifted and lowered riverboats for over 200 miles of river. The remains of the Patowmack Canal, one of the system's largest and most difficult to create, can still be seen in the park today.

John McLean and Steven Elkins purchased the land surrounding Great Falls and built a wildly popular amusement park there in the early 1900s. Visitors traveled from Georgetown by trolley to take a spin on the wooden carousel. However, time and constant flood damage dampened the thrills until it was eventually closed. Today the land is under the authority and protection of the National Park Service.

Activities

Picnic areas with tables and grills are available on a first-come, first-served basis; ground fires are strictly prohibited. Unfortunately, there are no covered picnic tables in the event of inclement weather, so check the forecast before packing your basket. If you forget your picnic, there is a basic concession stand (open seasonally) located in the visitor center courtyard on the Virginia side.

If it's sweat-breaking activity you're after, a scenic, sometimes rocky bike trail extends between the Maryland side of the falls and downtown Washington. Hiking trails of various length and difficulty wind along and above both sides of the river, for a challenging scramble try Section A of the Billy Goat trail on the Maryland side, and for serious trek, the Virginia side's Potomac Heritage Trail provides the option for over 10 miles of hiking. Horseback riding, bird watching, rock climbing, fishing, whitewater rafting, and kayaking can be enjoyed at locations throughout the park.

If you plan on rock climbing, registration is not necessary. However, there are voluntary sign-in sheets located in the Virginia visitor center courtyard and the lower parking lot. If fishing is more your speed, a Virginia or Maryland fishing license is required for anglers over 16 years of age. Whitewater boating is recommended only for experienced boaters and, not surprisingly, you're only allowed to launch your craft *below* the falls. There are ample flat-water paddling options around Great Falls, including at adjacent Riverbend Park (8700 Potomac Hills St, Great Falls, VA 22066), stay up to date on river conditions and water levels with the National Weather Service Middle Atlantic River Forecast Center at www.erh.noaa.gov/marfc/potomac.shtml

Stop by the visitor center (open daily from 10 am–4 pm) on the Virginia side of the park or check out the National Park Service website for more information.

The Potomac River Gorge is a hotbed of biodiversity, supporting 1,400 plant species and close to 100 species of birds, and remains a national conservation priority. Wild park inhabitants include frequently encountered whitetail deer, Eastern chipmunks, more reclusive red fox, and hikers beware, the potential to encounter park's only venomous snake, the Northern copperhead. During the warmer months, beware of ticks and do a thorough tick check after your visit.

How to Get There—Driving

From I-495, take Exit 44, Route 193 W (Georgetown Pike). Turn right at Old Dominion Drive (approximately 4 1/2 miles). Drive for 1 mile to the entrance station. Parking, falls overlooks, and the visitor center are all centrally located.

To get to the visitor center on the Maryland side, take I-495 to Exit 41/MacArthur Boulevard E towards Route 189. Follow MacArthur Boulevard all the way to the visitor center.

There is no public transportation available near the park.

General Information

NFT Maps: 20, 21, 23, 24, and 28
Website: www.nps.gov/rocr
Visitor Information: 202-895-6070

Overview

Let the tourists have the National Mall; we have Rock Creek Park to call our own. This 1,754-acre forest doesn't even make it onto many tourist maps—which may explain its popularity with people who live here, and why you can bike or run for miles without braking for fanny-packers. The park, which stretches from Georgetown to Maryland, is one of the largest forested urban parks in the country, and in addition to providing habitat for urban bound outdoor enthusiasts, acts as a wildlife corridor, with high densities of opportunistic white tailed deer, and coyotes have even been observed in the park since 2004. A paved bike and running path twists alongside the creek that gives the park its name. Dozens of more secluded, rocky paths break off from the path, one of which gained notoriety in 2002 when the body of federal intern/Congressional paramour Chandra Levy was discovered nearby. The park actually has one of the lowest crime rates in the city, so long as you're not having an affair with married congressmen—but it's an urban park, nevertheless, so lugging along a cell phone or a hiking partner isn't a bad idea. There are visitors' centers advertised: the Nature Center and Planetarium and Pierce Mill, but when they're open, they're hard to reach and of limited help. For basic questions and a great map, best to check the website.

History

In 1866, federal officials proposed cordoning off some of the forest area as a presidential retreat. By the time Congress took up the plan in 1890, the vision had been democratized and the forest became a public park.

Pierce Mill, a gristmill where corn and wheat were ground into fl our using water power from Rock Creek, was built in the 1820s and is located over the bridge on Tilden Street. (Pierce Mill has been indefinitely closed to the public for repairs, but the Pierce Barn remains open.) There are also remains of several Civil War earthen fortifications in the park, including Fort Stevens, the only Civil War battle site in DC.

Activities

There are more than 30 picnic areas spread throughout the park, all of which can be reserved in advance for parties of up to 100 people for $7 (202-673-7647). A large field located at 16th and Kennedy streets has several areas suitable for soccer, football, volleyball, and field hockey. Fields can be reserved ahead of time (202-673-7449), also for $7. The Rock Creek Tennis Center has 15 clay and 10 hard-surface tennis courts that must be reserved, in person, for a small fee (202-722-5949). The outdoor courts are open from April through November, and five heated indoor courts open during winter months. Three clay courts located off Park Road, east of Pierce Mill, can also be reserved in person, May through September. The back nine was recently updated at Rock Creek's Golf Course (202-882-7332) just off Military Road and 16th Street.

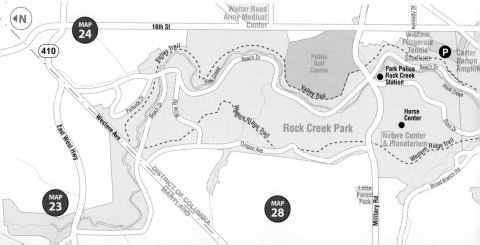

An extensive network of hiking trails runs through Rock Creek Park and the surround areas offering varied terrain for exploration, the wild and less visited northern section, the charming stream valley featured in the middle of the park, or the tree dense and residentially surrounded southern section. Blue-blazed paths maintained by the Potomac Appalachian Trail Club run along the east side of the creek, and green-blazed trails follow the park's western ridge. Tan-blazed trails connect the two systems. The paved path for bikers and roller bladers runs from the Lincoln Memorial, through the park, and into Maryland. Memorial Bridge connects the path to the Mount Vernon Trail in Virginia. Beach Drive between Military and Broad Branch roads is closed to cars on weekends and major holidays, giving bikers free range. However, bikes are not permitted on horse or foot trails at any time. If you're willing to ditch the bike for another kind of ride, horseback riding lessons and guided trail rides are available at the Rock Creek Park Horse Center (202-362-0117), located next to the Nature Center. As the horses follow the same trails described above, hikers are well advised to watch their step.

At the Rock Creek Nature Center (5200 Glover Rd, NW, 202-895-6070), you'll find the Planetarium, which features after school shows for children on Wednesdays at 4 pm and weekends at 1 pm and 4 pm. Nature Center Hours: Wed–Sun: 9 am–5 pm. Closed on national holidays.

How to Get There—Driving

To get to the Nature Center from downtown DC, take the Rock Creek/Potomac Parkway north to Beach Drive. Exit onto Beach Drive N, and follow it to Broad Branch Road. Make a left and then a right onto Glover Road, and follow the signs to the Nature Center. Note: The Parkway is one-way going south on weekdays 6:45 am–9:45 am. During this time, you can take 16th Street to Military Road W, then turn left on Glover Road. The Parkway is one-way going north 3:45 pm–6:30 pm; take Glover Road to Military Road east, then head south on 16th Street toward downtown DC. If all you're looking to do is get into the park, consult the map below—the place is so huge that no matter where you live, you're probably close to some branch of it.

Parking

Expansive parking lots are located next to the Nature Center and Planetarium. There are parking lots dotted throughout the park, but depending on your destination, you might be better off looking for street parking in nearby neighborhoods.

How to Get There—Mass Transit

Take the Red Metro line to either the Friendship Heights or Fort Totten Metro stops to get to the Nature Center. Transfer to the E2 bus line, which runs along Military/Missouri/Riggs Road between the two stations. Get off at the intersection of Glover (also called Oregon) and Military Roads and walk south on the trail up the hill to the Nature Center.

Check the map, though; the park covers so much ground in the DC Metro area that getting there may be easier than you think. There's certainly no need to start your visit at the Nature Center.

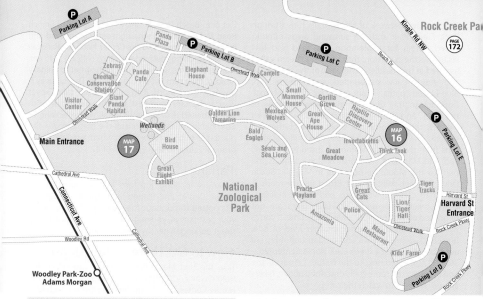

General Information

NFT Maps:	16 & 17
Address:	3001 Connecticut Ave NW
	Washington, DC 20008
Phone:	202-633-4800
Website:	www.nationalzoo.si.edu
Hours:	6 am–8 pm March 15–Oct 31; 6 am–6 pm
	the rest of the year. (Closed Christmas Day)
Admission:	Free

Overview

Nestled in Rock Creek Park, the National Zoological Park is a branch of the Smithsonian Institution (Read: It should be taken very seriously). With about 2,000 animals of 400 different species, there are more pampered foreign residents living in the National Zoo than on Embassy Row. About one-fifth of these animals are endangered, including DC's own popular pair of pandas who are on loan from the Chinese government.

The park's animal enclosures mimic natural habitats, and most exhibits strive to entertain as well as educate all those visiting school children. A popular destination in the summertime, the zoo can be just as appealing in the winter months, with so many indoor animal houses to visit—and fewer kids to elbow out of your way. The zoo is also a favorite jogging route for area residents—especially on winter snow days. (Olmsted Walk is one of the few regularly plowed paths in the city.) In the spring and summer, the zoo is packed with students on morning and early afternoon field trips. If you want to avoid them, try going before 10 am or after 2 pm. The animals tend to be more active at these times anyway, and you won't have to wait in line to see the more popular exhibits and animals.

Seasonal attractions at the zoo include the summer (mid-July) Brew at the Zoo, where environmentally friendly beer enthusiasts can sample from over 40 microbrews in the name of wildlife conservation. During the winter, brave the elements and check out Zoo Lights, a free, and festive nocturnal recreation of the zoo, complete with an environmentally friendly, synthetic ice skating rink.

Parking

Enter the zoo from Connecticut Avenue, Harvard Street, or Rock Creek Parkway. Because parking on zoo grounds is limited, public transportation is recommended. If you're set on driving, parking is $15 for the first three hours, and $20 after that. Lots fill early during the summer, so plan to arrive by 9:30 am at the latest if you expect to park.

How to Get There—Mass Transit

By Metro, take the Red Line to the Woodley Park-Zoo/Adams Morgan stop or the Cleveland Park stop; the zoo entrance lies roughly halfway between these stops and both are a short stroll away. It's an uphill walk from Woodley Park, while the walk from Cleveland Park is fairly flat.

From the Woodley Park-Zoo/Adams Morgan stop, walk north (to your left as you face Connecticut Avenue—away from the McDonald's and the CVS); and the zoo is about a twelve-minute walk from the stop. From the Cleveland Park stop, walk south toward the greater number of shops and restaurants that line Connecticut Avenue (away from the Exxon station).

If you prefer above-ground mass transit, Metrobus lines L1, L2, and L4 stop at the zoo's Connecticut Avenue entrance.

General Information

Address: 4368 Chantilly Shopping Center
           Chantilly, VA 20153
Phone: 703-378-0910
Website: www.dullesexpo.com

Overview

Dulles Expo Center should really just knock off the last two letter of "Dulles" and be done with it. "Dull" is the reigning word here—it accurately describes the area (Chantilly); the spaces in the Center itself (two separate low-slung, charmless rectangles); and most of the exhibits, exhibitors, and exhibitees. Pray to whatever gods you believe in that, if you have to attend a show or convention in DC, it'll be at the Washington Convention Center. Dulles Expo's only saving grace is that it has the best convention center parking in the universe—immediately outside the two buildings. Other than that, if it's a gun or RV show you're looking for, well, golly, this is the place!

A cab from Dulles to the Expo Center will cost about $20. A taxi from Reagan National Airport costs approximately $45. If you really want to fly into Baltimore-Washington International Airport, be prepared to cough up $85 for your 1.5-hour schlep.

Hotels

The Expo Center has an on-site Holiday Inn Select and several hotels within walking distance. Certain hotels have specials for specific conventions, so ask when you book. Or browse hotel-specific websites such as hotels.com and pricerighthotels.com.

- **Comfort Suites Chantilly-Dulles Airport,** 13980 Metrotech Dr, 703-263-2007
- **Fairfield Inn Dulles Chantilly South,** 3960 Corsair Ct, 703-435-1111
- **Hampton Inn-Dulles South,** 4050 Westfax Dr, 703-818-8200
- **Homestead Village,** 4505 Brookfield Coroporate Dr, 703-263-3361

- **Holiday Inn Select,** 4335 Chantilly Shopping Ctr, 703-815-6060
- **Courtyard by Marriott,** 3935 Centerview Dr, 703-709-7100
- **Extended Stay,** 4506 Brookfield Corporate Dr, 703-263-7200
- **Staybridge Suites,** 3860 Centerview Dr, 703-435-8090
- **TownePlace Suites by Marriott,** 14036 Thunderbolt Pl, 703-709-0453
- **Westfields Marriott,** 14750 Conference Center Dr, 703-818-0300
- **Wingate Inn Dulles Airport,** 3940 Centerview Dr, 571-203-0999

How to Get There—Driving

From DC, travel west on Constitution Avenue, and follow the signs to I-66 W to Virginia. Remain on I-66 W for about 25 miles until exit 53B, Route 28 N (Dulles Airport). Drive three miles north on Route 28, and then turn right onto Willard Road. Take the second left off into the Chantilly Shopping Center. From there, follow the signs to the Expo Center.

From Dulles Airport, follow exit signs for DC. Stay towards the right for about one mile, and take Route 28 S towards Centerville. Drive six miles and pass over Route 50. At the first light past Route 50, make a left on Willard Road. Follow signs to the Expo Center.

Better yet, don't go at all.

Parking

The Dulles Expo and Conference Center has 2,400 parking spaces on-site! (When their website has to brag about parking, you know we're not just being cynical about this place). If you arrive in your RV, you'll have to find a campsite for the night, as campers, RVs, trucks, and oversized vehicles will be ticketed if parked overnight.

How to Get There—Mass Transit

There is no public transportation to the Dulles Expo and Conference Center. Remember, this is America.

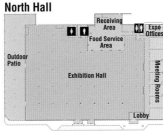

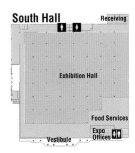

MAP 10

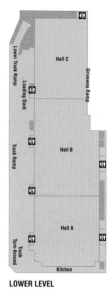

LOWER LEVEL

CONCOURSE A,B & C

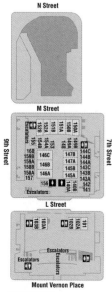

STREET LEVEL

LEVEL TWO

LEVEL THREE

General Information

NFT Map: 10
Address: 801 Mt Vernon Pl NW
Washington, DC 20001
Phone: 202-249-3000
Website: www.dcconvention.com

Overview

The Washington Convention Center is a stunning white granite and glass mammoth covering six city blocks, from 7th Street to 9th Street and N Street to Mount Vernon Place. The 2.3 million-square-foot building is the largest in DC and had the distinction of being the largest excavation site in the Western Hemisphere; 2 million tons of earth were removed during construction. Whether exhibiting or attending, you'd be well advised to wear comfy shoes to traverse the 700,000 square feet of exhibit space, 150,000 square feet of meeting space, the 52,000-square-foot ballroom (one of the East Coast's largest), and 40,000 square feet of retail space. The center hosts everything from small seminars for 80 participants to giant expos that welcome 35,000 attendees. Nonetheless, it is like every other convention center in that spending more than 15 minutes in it is a completely de-humanizing experience. Try spending three full days running a booth, and you'll know what we're talking about.

Along with the Verizon Center, the Convention Center is a pillar of revitalization for this previously seedy neighborhood. Thanks to that success, conventioneers have many more amenities to choose from in the area. The City Museum across the street used to have interesting exhibits detailing the history of Washington, but poor attendance and the shut-off of external funding spelled its demise. A string of shops, restaurants, and nightlife, especially on 7th Street NW south of Massachusetts Avenue, beckon nearby. Nevertheless, occasional panhandlers still canvass the area, hoping to profit from pedestrians with open maps making their way toward the Convention Center. The fastest and cheapest way to the Convention Center is to keep that map folded in your coat pocket and follow the platinum blonde in the plastic cowboy hat pasted with event-related bumper stickers.

If you're flying in for a convention, a cab from BWI or Dulles will cost you more than $70 to downtown DC. From Reagan, it should be no more than $16. The Metro Yellow Line runs directly from Reagan to the Mount Vernon Square/7th Street-Convention Center station.

Hotels

If you know which hotel you want to stay in, give them a call, and ask if they have any special rates for the dates you'll be attending. If you're not with any particular rewards program and don't care where you stay, try the official Washington tourism website at www.washington.org or hotel-specific websites such as www.hotels.com and www.pricerighthotels.com. The massive 1200-plus room Marriott Marquis right across 9th Street NW from the convention center is the most convenient spot to stay. See also these nearby hotels:

- **Renaissance Hotel** • 999 9th St NW, 202-898-9000
- **Henley Park** • 926 Massachusetts Ave NW, 202-638-5200
- **Courtyard by Marriott Convention Center** • 900 F St NW, 202-638-4600
- **Morrison Clark Inn** • 1101 11th St NW, 202-898-1200

- **Marriott Metro Center** • 775 12th St NW, 202-737-2200
- **Four Points by Sheraton** • 1201 K St NW, 202-289-7600
- **Hamilton Crowne Plaza** • 1001 14th St NW, 202-682-0111
- **Hilton Garden Inn** • 815 14th St NW, 202-783-7800
- **Hotel Sofitel** • 806 15th St NW, 202-737-8800
- **Washington Plaza** • 10 Thomas Cir NW, 202-842-1300
- **Wyndham Washington, DC** • 1400 M St NW, 202-429-1700
- **The Madison** • 1177 15th St NW, 202-862-1600
- **Hotel Helix** • 1430 Rhode Island Ave NW, 202-462-9001
- **Homewood Suites by Hilton** • 1475 Massachusetts Ave NW, 202-265-8000
- **Capitol Hilton** • 1001 16th St NW, 202-393-1000
- **Holiday Inn Central** • 1501 Rhode Island Ave NW, 202-483-2000
- **Comfort Inn** • 1201 13th St NW, 202-682-5300
- **Grand Hyatt Washington** • 1000 H St NW, 202-582-1234
- **Embassy Suites/Convention Center** 900 9th St, NW, 202-739-2001
- **Hampton Inn/Convention Center** 901 6th St, NW, 202-842-2500
- **Hotel Monaco** 700 F St, NW, 800-649-1202

Eating

After spending a gazillion dollars on a gleaming new Convention Center, some thought went into providing better grub than the old center's mystery meat burgers and heat-lamp fries. Here, you'll find a number of restaurants located in the Convention Center and dozens more within easy walking distance (almost all of them *south* of the Center). Executive Orders, located on the L1 Concourse, offers selections from Foggy Bottom Grill, Wolfgang Puck Express, Seafood by Phillips, Subculture, Bello Pronto, Mr. Thoi's Fine Asian Cuisine, and Latin American Cuisine. Located on Level Two off the L Street Bridge, the Supreme Court is a retail food court offering Wolfgang Puck Express, Quizno's, and Foggy Bottom Grill.

The Lobby Café, located by the main entrance, sells coffee and deluxe pastries to help exhibitors and attendees wake up in the mornings. Within each exhibit hall, there are also permanent and portable outlets/carts serving everything from coffee to Tex-Mex. For some local drinks, check out the Old Dominion Brewhouse, which has a great selection of the Virginia microbrewery's beers on tap.

Parking

The center does not have its own parking facility, and there are about 100 metered parking spaces close to the convention center, so you'll be pretty fortunate if you manage to snag one. Otherwise, be prepared to pay for one of the many parking lots within a three-block radius of the center.

How to Get There—Mass Transit

The closest Metro stop is Mt Vernon Sq/7th St-Convention Center on the Yellow or Green lines.

Overview

Baltimore's comeback streak has pretty much obliterated its former reputation as the murder capital of the nation (even if it still regularly scores well in crime rankings and visitors should still leave nothing visible in their cars). Real estate prices are booming, retail rakes it in during the tourist season, and businessmen have discovered a city where, just steps from the convention center, they can sightsee, shop for their kids, AND hoist a beer at Hooters. But the city's real treasures are hidden in its neighborhoods, where fierce local pride mixes with a local flare for the, uh, creative. (If you can't get to Café Hon or the Visionary Art Museum, ask hometown filmmaker John Waters to explain). And, yes, *The Wire* is the most amazing TV series ever. Baltimore never looked so good (and bad) on film. To see the real charm behind its nickname, "Charm City," venture into the cobblestone-and-brick-lined neighborhoods of Fells Point, Federal Hill, and Mt. Vernon. Here, you'll find Ravens fans mad-hopping in dive bars, crabs and oysters are staple menu items, artists and musicians display their work, and unpretentious locals make you feel right at home.

Getting There

For a car-free route from DC to Baltimore, take the MARC commuter train from Union Station to Penn Station Monday through Friday. Alternatively, take the Green line metro to Greenbelt, walk to the Greenbelt Station and Bus Bay D, catch bus B30 to BWI/Thurgood Marshall Airport and catch the MARC Light Rail toward Hunt Valley; stops include Camden Station for baseball fans and Pratt St for the inner harbor. For travel schedules and fare information check http://mta.maryland.gov/marc-train

Attractions

Harborplace
200 E Pratt St, 410-332-4191; www.harborplace.com
One of Baltimore's most well-known attractions is Harborplace, owned by the Rouse Company (i.e. it looks exactly the same as New York's South Street Seaport, Boston's Faneuil Hall, New Orleans's Riverwalk Marketplace, etc). The outdoor mall's retail stores and chain restaurants circle the harbor. Since most residents only hang at Harborplace when they're showing off (or cringing over the triteness of) their waterfront to out-of-towners, it becomes a mob of tourists on sunny weekends. Shop hours: Mon–Sat: 10 am–9 pm; Sun: 11 am–7 pm.

National Aquarium in Baltimore
501 E Pratt St, 410-576-3800; www.aqua.org
Baltimore's aquarium is the city's most popular tourist attraction. Entry isn't cheap, and there's bound to be a line to get in, but attractions like the Tropical Rain Forest (complete with piranhas and poisonous frogs) and the dolphin show make it worth all the hassle. General admission costs $34.95 for adults (aged 12-64), $21.95 for children (aged 3-11), and $29.95 for those 65 and over. Kids 3 and under are free. Admission prices do include unlimited time observing the daily routine of resident dolphins for those with a twinge of Flipper nostalgia. Tickets often sell out, but you can buy advance tickets through Ticketmaster. Aquarium hours: Sun–Thurs: 9 am–5 pm; Fri: 9 am–8 pm; Sat: 9 am–6 pm.

Maryland Science Center
601 Light St; 410-685-5225; www.mdsci.org
The Maryland Science Center is one of the oldest scientific institutions in the country and is full of dinosaur bones, IMAX, and all that science jazz. It's best for kids, especially ones you want to push toward Einstein-hood. The center is usually open from 10 am to 6 pm daily, although hours change by season; admission prices range from $16.95 to $20.95 for adults depending what exhibits you want to visit. Admission for children 3-12 costs between $13.95 and $17.95, and admission for members is always free.

Babe Ruth Birthplace and Museum
216 Emory St, 410-727-1539; www.baberuthmuseum.com
Visit the place where Babe was really a babe. This historic building has been transformed into a shrine to Babe, as well as to Baltimore's Colts and Orioles and Johnny Unitas (famed quarterback for the Colts). Admission costs $6 for adults, $4 for seniors and $3 for children 3–12. Hours: April–October: daily 10 am–6 pm (7:30 pm on baseball game days), November–March: daily 10 am–5 pm.

The Maryland Zoo in Baltimore
978 Druid Park Lake Dr, 410-366-LION; www.marylandzoo.org
Located in Druid Hill Park, the zoo is hidden in the middle of the city, far away from the other major tourist attractions. Kids can enjoy the number-one-rated children's zoo, while adults can look forward to the zoo's spring beer and wine festival, Brew at the Zoo (Plan on hearing lots of jokes about polar beer, penguinness, and giraffes of wine). Admission to the zoo costs $17.50 for adults (12-64), $12.50 for the kiddies (2–12), and $14.50 for seniors (65+), but parking is always free. The zoo is open daily, Mar–Dec: 10 am–4:00 pm.

Lexington Market
400 W Lexington St, 410-685-6169; www.lexingtonmarket.com
Baltimore's Lexington Market is the world's largest continuously running market. Founded in 1782, the market continues to be a rowdy place of commerce. The market prides itself for its top-quality fresh meats, seafood, poultry, groceries, specialty items, and prepared foods for take-out and on-site consumption. Visit the market during the Chocolate Festival and the Preakness Crab Derby (yes, they actually race crabs). During Lunch with the Elephants, held annually in the spring, a herd of elephants from the Ringling Bros. and Barnum & Bailey Circus marches from the Baltimore Arena to the market, where they proceed to eat the world's largest stand-up vegetarian buffet. Market hours: Mon–Sat: 8:30 am–6 pm.

National Museum of Dentistry
31 S Greene St, 410-706-0600;
www.dental.umaryland.edu/museum/index.html
After munching on goodies at the Lexington Market, swing on by the National Museum of Dentistry to learn about all the cavities you just got. This University of Maryland School of Dentistry affiliate offers interactive exhibits and the gift shop sells chocolate toothbrushes (reason enough to check it out). Plaque got you gloomy? Edgar Allan Poe's grave is just down the street. Admission to the museum costs $7.00 for adults over 18 and $6 for students and seniors, and $5 for kids. Hours: Open to visitors by appointment only. Call 410-706-7461.

The Power Plant

601 E Pratt St, 410-752-5444

Once upon a time, the Power Plant was an honest-to-goodness power plant. In 1998, it was converted into a full-fledged mall. Guess retail's just a different kind of community fuel. Inside the Power Plant, you'll find Barnes & Noble, ESPN Zone, Gold's Gym, and the Hard Rock Café.

Power Plant Live!

Market Pl & Water St, 410-727- 5483; www.powerplantlive.com

Located a block away from the Power Plant, Power Plant Live! is a dining and entertainment megaplex. You can have a full night without leaving the indoor/outdoor complex. Dinner, dancing, comedy, and stiff drinks are served up by eight bars and seven restaurants. Because of an arena liquor license, you can take your drink from one establishment to the next. During the summer, check out the free outdoor concerts. Past headliners include the Soundtrack of Our Lives, Aimee Mann, Elvis Costello, and the Wildflowers.

American Visionary Art Museum

800 Key Hwy, 410-244-1900; www.avam.org

The Visionary Art Museum exhibits works from self-taught, intuitive artists, whose backgrounds range from housewives to homeless. The museum is also home to Baltimore's newest outdoor sculptural landmark—the Giant Whirligig. Standing tall at an imposing 55 feet, this multicolored, wind-powered sculpture was created by 76-year-old mechanic, farmer, and artist Vollis Simpson. Every spring, the museum hosts a race of human-powered works of art designed to travel on land, through mud, and over deep harbor waters. Museum hours: Tues-Sun: 10 am–6 pm. Admission costs $15.95 for adults, $13.95 for seniors, and $9.95 for children over 6.

Pagoda at Patterson Park

www.pattersonpark.com

One of the most striking structures in Baltimore's Patterson Park is the newly renovated Pagoda. Originally built in 1891, the Pagoda was designed as a people's lookout tower. From the 60-foot-high octagonal tower, you can see downtown, the suburbs, and the harbor. When it ever snows, the hill next to the Pagoda is a popular sledding site. Pagoda Hours: Sun: 12 pm–6 pm, May–Oct.

Camden Yards

333 W Camden St, 888-848-2473;baltimore.orioles.mlb.com

There's more to Camden Yards than the O's. At the turn of the century, Camden Yards was a bustling freight and passenger railroad terminal. For decades, Camden Station served as a major facility for the Baltimore and Ohio Railroad (that's the B&O Railroad for Monopoly fans). The Yards were once home to thousands of commuters, and now they're home to thousands of fans who come out to see their beloved Orioles play (how we miss you, Cal Ripken Jr…).

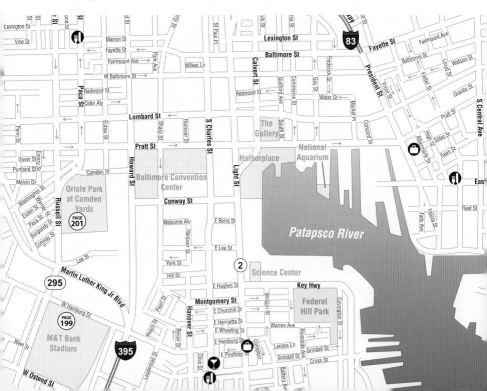

○ Landmarks
· **Baltimore Tattoo Museum** · 1534 Eastern Ave

Nightlife
· **Club Charles** · 1724 N Charles St (off map)
· **Cross Street Market** · 1065 S Charles St
· **The Horse You Came In On** · 1626 Thames St
· **Ottobar** · 2549 N Howard St

Restaurants
· **Bertha's** · 734 S Broadway
· **Boccaccio Restaurant** · 925 Eastern Ave
· **Brass Elephant** · 924 N Charles St (off map)
· **Café Hon** · 1002 W 36th St (off map)
· **The Daily Grind** · 1722 Thames St
· **Faidley's Seafood** ·
   Lexington Market, 203 N Paca St
· **Helen's Garden** · 2908 O'Donnell St
· **Ikaros** · 4805 Eastern Ave (off map)

· **Jimmy's** · 801 S Broadway
· **John Steven Ltd** · 1800 Thames St
· **New Wyman Park Diner** · 138 W 25th St (off map)
· **Pete's Grille** · 3130 Greenmount Ave (off map)
· **Rusty Scupper** · 402 Key Hwy
· **Tapas Teatro** · 1711 N Charles St (off map)
· **Ze Mean Bean** · 1739 Fleet St

Shopping
· **The Antique Man** · 1806 Fleet St
· **Cook's Table** · 1036 Light St
· **Di Pasquales Italian Marketplace** ·
   3700 Gough St (off map)
· **Karmic Connection** · 508 S Broadway
· **Mystery Loves Company** · 1730 Fleet St
· **Sound Garden** · 1616 Thames St
· **Stikky Fingers** · 802 S Broadway
· **Vaccaros Italian Pastry Shop** · 222 Albemarle St

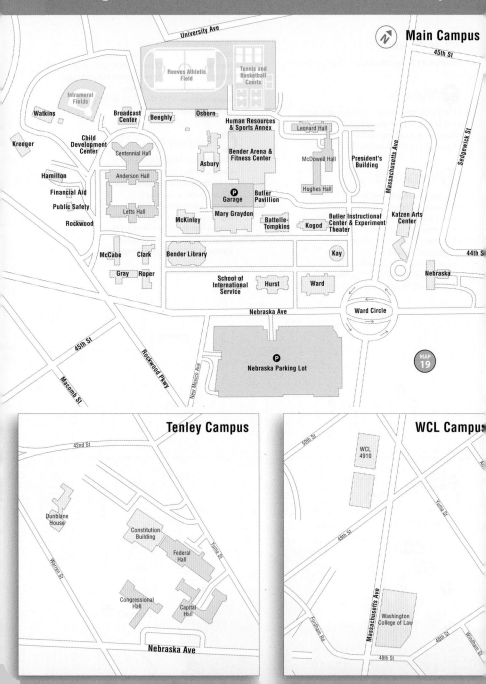

Main Campus

University Ave

45th St

Sedgewick St

Reeves Athletic Field

Tennis and Basketball Courts

Intramural Fields

Watkins

Broadcast Center

Beeghly

Osborn

Human Resources & Sports Annex

Leonard Hall

Kreeger

Child Development Center

Centennial Hall

Asbury

Bender Arena & Fitness Center

McDowell Hall

President's Building

Hamilton

Anderson Hall

Massachusetts Ave

Financial Aid

Hughes Hall

Public Safety

Letts Hall

Garage

Butler Pavillion

Rockwood

McKinley

Mary Graydon

Battelle-Tompkins

Kogod

Butler Instructional Center & Experiment Theater

Katzen Arts Center

McCabe

Clark

Bender Library

Kay

44th St

Gray

Roper

Nebraska

School of International Service

Hurst

Ward

Ward Circle

Nebraska Ave

45th St

Rockwood Pkwy

New Mexico Ave

Nebraska Parking Lot

MAP 19

Macomb St

Tenley Campus

42nd St

Dunblane House

Constitution Building

Federal Hall

Yuma St

Warren St

Congressional Hall

Capital Hall

Nebraska Ave

WCL Campus

50th St

WCL 4910

Yuma St

49th St

Massachusetts Ave

Fordham Rd

Washington College of Law

48th St

Windham St

48th St

General Information

NFT Map: 19
Main Campus: 4400 Massachusetts Ave NW
                 Washington, DC 20016
Phone: 202-885-1000
Website: www.american.edu

Overview

Congress chartered "The" American University in 1893 to fulfill George Washington's vision of a great "national university" in the nation's capital. If Washington rode the Tenleytown shuttle to campus today, he'd probably be impressed. Though it seems sometimes like half of the AU student body is from Long Island, New Jersey, or the Philly suburbs, the school's 12,000 students hail from more than 150 countries. This diversity, along with its location in the nation's capital, makes AU a popular place to study public policy and international affairs. With few Wednesday classes and a heavy internship focus, AU is something of a foreign affairs, NGO, and Hill staffer factory. AU students brag that while Georgetown's stuffed shirts end up at DC think tanks, *their* grads actually go out and get their hands dirty. Indeed, it's often the school's idealistic crowd that most resents the "brat pack" contingent of diplomat kids and OPEC heirs, who enroll more out of interest in DC's nightlife than in changing the world. AU's idealists went into full protest mode in 2005 to force former University president Benjamin Ladner to resign after improperly charging the school for more than $500,000 in personal expenses, including a personal French chef, vacations in Europe with his wife, and his son's engagement party. While searching for a less ostentatious leader, AU's board of trustees started a new fundraising drive, appropriately called "AnewAU."

Nestled in tony upper northwest DC, AU's leafy quad gives it a classic liberal-arts-school look. But its picturesque campus doesn't lack in intrigue: work on the Manhattan Project started out in AU's McKinley building, because its unusual architecture ensured that any mishap would cause the building to self-implode and therefore limit any widespread repercussions.

Tuition

In the 2013–2014 academic year, tuition and fees were $20,325 per semester, with room and board on top. Graduate student tuition, fees, and expenses vary by college.

Sports

AU's Eagles play a nice range of NCAA Division I men's and women's sports, including basketball, cross-country, soccer, swimming and diving, tennis, and track and field.

Male-exclusive sports include golf and wrestling, while women play field hockey, volleyball, and lacrosse. The men's basketball team wins every year but has trouble drumming up fan interest; it's a running joke that mid-season you'll find more students waiting for AU's shuttle to the Metro than in Bender Arena. A few years ago, the Eagles left the Colonial Athletic Association to join the Patriot League in hopes of using the league's championship as an automatic bid to the NCAA tourney. In 2008, the move finally paid off, as the Eagles' Men's Basketball team landed a number 15 seed in the Big Dance (albeit losing to number 2 seed Tennessee in their first match-up). In 2009, they won the Patriot League Tournament, and student Derrick Mercer was named the 2009 Patriot League Player of the Year and an Associated Press All-American. AU's impressive 2009 season and NCAA Tourney berth gave DC residents hope that they'll have a new perennial Tournament team to root for in the coming years.

Culture on Campus

AU operates its wildly wonkish and popular radio station, WAMU 88.5 FM, broadcasting NPR programs as well as locally produced shows like *The Kojo Nnamdi Show* and *The Diane Rehm Show*. Similarly, the University seems to score a speech a week by an inside-the-beltway celebrity, including appearances by Pulitzer Prize–winning columnist David S. Broder, Supreme Court Justice Antonin Scalia, and former President Jimmy Carter. Bender Arena appears to have lost its appetite for the big-time acts it used to feature, now hosting smaller performances by the likes of Jimmy Eat World and The Roots. The Katzen Arts Center at AU opened in late 2005, bringing all of AU's arts programs under one roof, including its Watkins collection of over 4,400 modern works of Washington-area art.

Department Contact Information

Admissions 202-885-6000
College of Arts & Sciences 202-885-2453
Kogod School of Business 202-885-1900
School of Communication 202-885-2060
School of International Service 202-885-1600
School of Public Affairs 202-885-2940
Washington College of Law 202-274-4000
Washington College of Law Library 202-274-4350
Office of Campus Life 202-885-3310
Athletic Department 202-885-3000
University Library 202-885-3232

The Catholic University of America

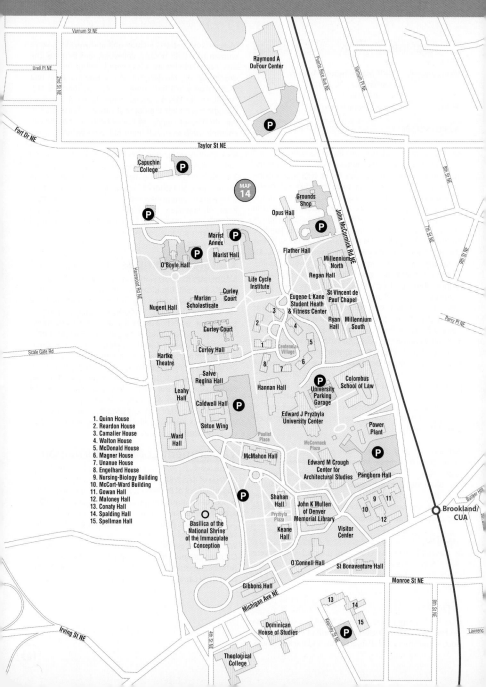

Varnum St NE

Urell Pl NE

2nd St NE

Fort Dr NE

Raymond A DuFour Center

Taylor St NE

Puerto Rico Ave NE

Varnum Pl NE

8th St NE

7th St NE

6th St NE

Capuchin College

MAP 14

Grounds Shop

Opus Hall

John McCormick Rd NE

Marist Annex

Marist Hall

Flather Hall

O'Boyle Hall

Life Cycle Institute

Millennium North

Regan Hall

Harewood Rd NE

Marian Scholasticate

Curley Court

Nugent Hall

Eugene L Kane Student Heath & Fitness Center

St Vincent de Paul Chapel

Perry Pl NE

Scale Gate Rd

Curley Court

Curley Hall

3

2

4

Ryan Hall

Millennium South

Hartke Theatre

1

Centennial Village

5

Salve Regina Hall

8

7

6

Leahy Hall

Caldwell Hall

Hannan Hall

University Parking Garage

Colombus School of Law

Ward Hall

Seton Wing

Edward J Pryzbyla University Center

Paulist Place

Power Plant

McMahon Hall

McCormack Plaza

Edward M Crough Center for Architectural Studies

Pangborn Hall

1. Quinn House
2. Reardon House
3. Camalier House
4. Walton House
5. McDonald House
6. Magner House
7. Unanue House
8. Engelhard House
9. Nursing-Biology Building
10. McCort-Ward Building
11. Gowan Hall
12. Maloney Hall
13. Conaty Hall
14. Spalding Hall
15. Spellman Hall

Shahan Hall

Pryzbyla Plaza

Keane Hall

John K Mullen of Denver Memorial Library

9 11

10

12

Visitor Center

Brookland/ CUA

Bunker Hill

Basilica of the National Shrine of the Immaculate Conception

O'Connell Hall

St Bonaventure Hall

Monroe St NE

8th St NE

Gibbons Hall

13

14

Michigan Ave NE

Irving St NE

4th St NE

Dominican House of Studies

Kearney St NE

15

Theological College

Lawrenc

The Catholic University of America

General Information

NFT Map: 14
Address: 620 Michigan Ave NE
Washington, DC 20064
Phone: 202-319-5000
Website: www.cua.edu

Overview

Lesser known than its Washington rivals but equal in academic distinction, CUA was established in 1887 as a graduate research institution where the Roman Catholic Church could do its thinking, and its undergraduate programs began in 1904. It remains the only American university founded with a papal charter. With a board of trustees still brimming with US cardinals and bishops, the school is the national university of the Catholic Church.

That said, CUA is by no means a seminary. Sixteen percent of its 3,500 undergraduates represent religions other than Catholicism, and although shadowed by the colossal Basilica of the National Shrine of the Immaculate Conception (the largest church in America), the laissez-faire campus lacks the in-your-face piousness to which other orthodox colleges subscribe. The 193-acre campus is the largest and arguably the most beautiful of the DC universities. Prominent alums include Susan Sarandon, Ed McMahon, Jon Voight, Brian Cashman (GM of the New York Yankees), and Maureen Dowd.

Though mostly religious, CUA's student body sometimes tries hard to prove otherwise. "Catholic U: Don't Let the Name Fool You" has been a popular motto of a ruddy-faced breed of students that knows how to pick the beer glasses up and put the books down. With a flourishing party scene, CUA is well-represented among DC's various watering holes. And no, Mr. Joel, Catholic girls do not always start much too late.

Tuition

Tuition for the 2013–2014 year came to $19,000 per semester. If you need a place to eat and sleep, the basic meal plan and housing costs come to approximately $5,000 and $9,000 respectively. That totals about $55,000, assuming you won't be buying any beer and books. It's college in America, what did you expect? At least a Catholic U degree can land you a job where you can actually pay off those loans.

Sports

Formerly a member of NCAA's Division I, the Catholic Cardinals (as in the little red bird, not the man with the incense and the big hat) dropped to Division III during the 1970s. Of all the school's sports, men's basketball reigns supreme. Winner of the 2000–2001 Division III National Championship, the team reeled off five consecutive Sweet Sixteen seasons before the streak came to a halt last in 2009. The women's squad, which posted a 20-win season in 2009, is also a powerhouse within CUA's Capital Athletic Conference, and in 2010, two members were awarded honors by the Landmark Conference. In 2013, both the men's and women's b-ball teams made it to postseason play. The Catholic football team may have stumbled over the last few seasons, but betting men beware: it dominated the gridiron during the nineties, ranking as high as number ten in the nation.

Culture on Campus

The Catholic U has 118 recognized student groups, and seven different leadership programs. You can sing a cappella and interact with other architecture enthusiasts, and still make it to your WCUA radio show in time to throw on that new Wale record you've been neglecting your work to listen to. Music geeks unite! Boasting an extraordinary music program—one of the top in the country—CUA's Benjamin T. Rome School of Music continuously churns out gem after gem. Thanks to a recent grant, CUA music students study with some of the most renowned composers, directors, and musicians working on Broadway today. The school stages over 200 musicals, operas, chamber concerts, and orchestral and choral performances throughout the academic year. For listings, including Department of Drama productions, visit performingarts.cua.edu.

Department Contact Information

Undergraduate Admissions 202-319-5305
Graduate Admissions 202-319-5057
Athletics 202-319-5286
The Benjamin T. Rome School of Music ..202-319-5414
The Columbus School of Law 202-319-5140
Conferences and Summer Programs 202-319-5291
Hartke Theatre Box Office 202-319-4000
Metropolitan College 202-319-5256
The National Catholic School
of Social Service 202-319-5458
Public Affairs 202-319-5600
The School of Arts and Sciences
(undergrad) 202-319-5115
The School of Arts and Sciences (grad) ...202-319-5254
The School of Business and Economics ..202-319-5236
The School of Canon Law 202-319-5492
The School of Engineering 202-319-5160
The School of Nursing 202-319-5400
The School of Philosophy 202-319-5259
The School of Theology
and Religious Studies 202-319-5683
Summer Sessions 202-319-5257

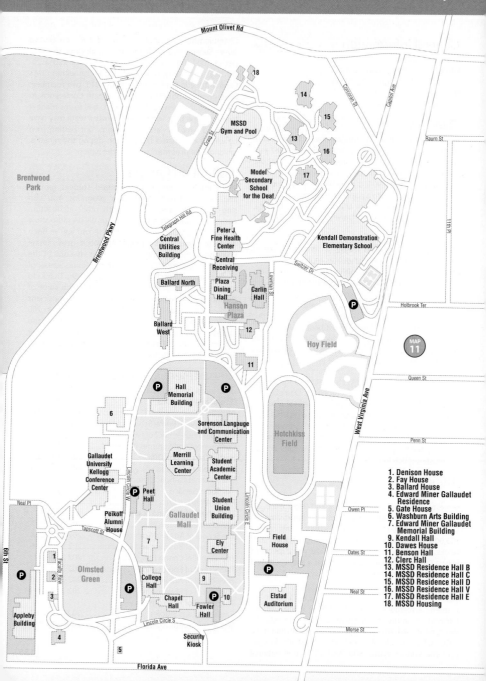

Mount Olivet Rd

Brentwood Park

Brentwood Pkwy

18

14

15

13

16

17

MSSD Gym and Pool

Model Secondary School for the Deaf

Corcoran St

Capitol Ave

Raurn St

11th Pl

Craig St

Telegraph Hill Rd

Central Utilities Building

Peter J Fine Health Center

Central Receiving

Ballard North

Plaza Dining Hall

Carlin Hall

Hanson Plaza

Ballard West

12

11

Kendall Demonstration Elementary School

Switzer Dr

Holbrook Ter

Hoy Field

MAP 11

Queen St

Hall Memorial Building

6

Sorenson Langauge and Communication Center

Merrill Learning Center

Student Academic Center

Gallaudet University Kellogg Conference Center

Peet Hall

Peikoff Alumni House

Neal Pl

Lincoln Circle W

Tapscott St

7

Gallaudet Mall

Student Union Building

Ely Center

Hotchkiss Field

West Virginia Ave

Lincoln Circle E

Field House

Penn St

Owen Pl

Oates St

1

2

3

Faculty Row

6th St

Olmsted Green

College Hall

9

Chapel Hall

Fowler Hall

10

Elstad Auditorium

Neal St

Appleby Building

4

5

Lincoln Circle S

Security Kiosk

Morse St

Florida Ave

1. Denison House
2. Fay House
3. Ballard House
4. Edward Miner Gallaudet Residence
5. Gate House
6. Washburn Arts Building
7. Edward Miner Gallaudet Memorial Building
9. Kendall Hall
10. Dawes House
11. Benson Hall
12. Clerc Hall
13. MSSD Residence Hall B
14. MSSD Residence Hall C
15. MSSD Residence Hall D
16. MSSD Residence Hall V
17. MSSD Residence Hall E
18. MSSD Housing

General Information

NFT Map: 11
Address: 800 Florida Ave NE
            Washington, DC 20002
Phone: 202-651-5050
Website: www.gallaudet.edu

Overview

Gallaudet is the premier university for the deaf and hearing-impaired, and the only university in the world where deaf students and those without hearing problems mingle. It is a campus where English and American Sign Language (ASL) coexist. Students can choose from more than 40 majors, and all aspects of the school, including classes and workshops, are designed to accommodate deaf students. Even the hearing students, who make up about 5% of each entering class, must always communicate through visual means.

Thomas Hopkins Gallaudet co-founded the American School for the Deaf in Hartford, CT, in 1817 as the first such school in the country. Forty years later, his youngest son, Dr. Edward Minor Gallaudet, established a school for the deaf in DC. In 1864, that school became the world's first and only liberal arts university for the deaf. In 1988, I. King Jordan, the University's first deaf president, was appointed after students, backed by a number of alumni, faculty, and staff, shut down the campus, demanding that a deaf president be appointed. In 2006, students took over the campus again, this time to block Jane Fernandes from being selected university president because, although born deaf, Fernandes grew up speaking and did not learn American Sign Language until she was 23. Dr. Jordan himself accused students of rejecting Fernandes because she was "not deaf enough." Gallaudet's mismanagement of the protests, as well as its low graduation rates, led the Commission on Higher Education to postpone re-accreditation, noting concerns about weak academic standards, ineffective governance, and a lack of tolerance for diverse views.

Tuition

In the 2013–2014 academic year, tuition and fees (including room and board) for US residents comes to about $15,138 for undergraduate programs and $15,813 for graduate programs. For international students from developing countries, the price of admission is $18,494 for undergraduate and $19,507 for graduate programs, and for international students from non-developing countries, it is $21,850 and 23,200, respectively.

Sports

The birth of the football huddle took place at Gallaudet. Legend has it that prior to the 1890s, football players stood around discussing their plays out of earshot of the other team. This posed a problem for Gallaudet's team; they communicated through signing and opposing teams could see the plays that were being called. Paul Hubbard, a star football player at the university, is credited with coming up with the huddle to prevent prying eyes from discovering plays.

In 2007, thanks to improved performance in club football (including an undefeated 2005 season) the Bison football team returned to NCAA Division III football for the first time since the mid-1990s. With its return to NCAA football, Gallaudet now boasts 13 NCAA Division III teams and several intramural sports teams.

In the summer, Gallaudet runs popular one-week sports camps, where teens from all over the US, as well as the local area, stay on campus and participate in basketball and volleyball activities. Check the website for details.

Culture on Campus

Gallaudet's Dance Company performs modern, tap, jazz, and other dance styles incorporating ASL. Gallaudet also produces several theater productions every year, all of which are signed, with vocal interpretation. The school is smack in the middle of a neighborhood quickly transitioning from rough to trendy. Check out the nearby theaters, coffeehouses, and farmers market before gentrification smoothes out the hard edges.

Department Contact Information

Admissions 800-995-0550
Graduate School and
    Professional Programs 800-995-0513
College of Liberal Arts, Sciences,
    and Technologies 202-651-5224
Department of ASL and Deaf
    Studies 202-651-5814
Financial Aid 202-651-5292
Gallaudet Library 202-651-5217
Registrar 202-651-5393
Visitors Center 202-651-5050

The George Washington University

1. Academic Center
   A. Phillips Hall
   B. Rome Hall
   C. Smith Hall of Art
   D. Visitor Center
2. John Quincy Adams House
3. Alumni House
4. Hortense Amsterdam House
5. Bell Hall
6. Corcoran Hall
7. Crawford Hall
8. Dakota
9. Davis-Hodgkins House
10. Abba Eban House
11. Fulbright Hall
12. Funger Hall
13. Hall of Government
14. GSEHD
15. Guthridge Hall
16. The George Washington
    University Club
17. The George Washington
    University Inn
18. Hospital, GW

19. Ivory Towers Residence Hall
20. Kennedy Onassis Hall
21. Key Hall
22. Lafayette Hall
23. Lenthall Houses
24. Lerner Hall
25. Lerner Family Health and
    Wellness Center
26. Jacob Burns Library (Law)
27. Melvin Gelman Library (University)
28. Paul Himmelfarb Health
    Sciences Library (Medical)
29. Lisner Auditorium
30. Lisner Hall
31. Madison Hall
32. Marvin Center
33. Media & Public Affairs
34. Medical Faculty Associates
    A. H. B. Burns Memorial Bldg
    B. Ambulatory Care Center
35. Mitchell Hall
36. Monroe Hall
37. Munson Hall

38. New Hall
39. Old Main
40. Quigley's
41. Rice Hall
42. International House
43. Ross Hall
44. Samson Hall
45. Schenley Hall
46. Scholars Village Townhouses
    A. 619 22nd St
    B. 2208 F St
    C. 520-526 22nd St
    D. 2028 G St
    E. 605-607 21st St
47. Smith Center
48. Staughton Hall
49. Stockton Hall
50. Strong Hall
51. Stuart Hall
52. Student Health Service
53. Support Building
54. Thurston Hall
55. Tompkins Hall of Engineering

56. Townhouse Row
57. University Garage
58. Warwick Bldg
59. The West End
60. Woodhull House
61. 700 20th St
62. 812 20th St
63. 814 20th St
64. 714 21st St
65. 600 21st St
66. 609 22nd St
67. 613 22nd St
68. 615 22nd St
69. 617 22nd St
70. 837 22nd St
71. 817 23rd St
72. 1957 E St
73. 2033-37 F St
74. 2031 F St
75. 2101 F St
76. 2109 F St
77. 2147 F St
78. 2000 G St

79. 2002 G St
80. 2008 G St
81. 2030 G St
82. 2106 G St
83. 2108 G St
84. 2112 G St
85. 2114 G St
86. 2125 G St
87. 2127 G St
88. 2129 G St
89. 2129 G St (rear)
90. 2131 G St
91. 2131 G St (rear)
92. 2136 G St
93. 2138 G St
94. 2140 G St
95. 2142 G St
96. 2129-33 Eye St (rear)
97. 2000 Pennsylvania Ave NW
98. 2100 Pennsylvania Ave NW
99. 2136 Pennsylvania Ave NW
100. 2140 Pennsylvania Ave NW
101. 2142 Pennsylvania Ave NW
102. Newman Catholic Center
103. Duques Hall/School of Business

General Information

NFT Map: 7
Address: 2121 Eye St NW
Washington, DC 20052
Phone: 202-994-1000
Website: www.gwu.edu

Overview

Once considered nothing more than a second-rate commuter school for graduate and law students, GW, like the city it inhabits, has enjoyed a massive boom in popularity over the past ten years. The school has close to 11,000 full-time undergraduate students and nearly 14,000 graduate students stomping around Foggy Bottom in search of wisdom and love. Over the last decade, the school has embarked on large-scale construction projects and has unveiled new academic buildings, a renovated fitness center, and a television studio where CNN's Crossfire was filmed until it was cancelled in 2005. The GW "campus," for lack of a better word, now stretches its tentacles far into Foggy Bottom, leaving some neighbors none too pleased.

Unlike their counterparts over at Georgetown (who smugly refer to GW as a school for the Georgetown waitlist), GW students understand the meaning of having a life outside of academics. They love their city environs; they seem surprisingly street-smart; they take full advantage of government and congressional internships; and they venture farther afield when it comes to socializing. (Tuesday nights being the exception, when local bar McFadden's is invaded by what seems to be the entire student body.) But GW students aren't all play—the libraries, which stay open 24 hours, are never empty, and each year students are selected to be Rhodes, Truman, Marshall, and Fulbright scholars.

While many undergraduates hail from similar upper-middle-class backgrounds, 139 foreign countries are represented in the student body. Collectively, students have a motley appearance, further differentiating them from the Lacoste poster children of Georgetown. Tuition-wise, GW is the city's most expensive school, and with the deep pockets comes more than a few pompous attitudes. Bigshot alums include J. Edgar Hoover, Jackie O, Kenneth Starr, General Colin Powell, as well as four presidential children.

Tuition

Tuition for the 2013–2014 school year costs $47,290, with an additional $10,850 for room and board. Add on personal expenses and books, for a whopping yearly total of around $62,250.

Sports

The university's fight song, "Hail to the buff, hail to the blue, hail to the buff and blue," provides hours of double-entendre fun for the students and it seems to work for the athletes, too. The university's 22 NCAA Division I teams, known as the fighting Colonials, usually place well in their A-10 conference, especially in basketball: in 2007 the men's team won their first Atlantic Ten Men's Basketball Championship since 1976, and over the last 19 years, GW has won nearly 75% of all games played and made the NCAA Tournament 15 times.

Culture on Campus

The Robert H. and Clarice Smith Hall of Art is a modern facility that features five floors dedicated to the study and practice of art. Students participate annually in two major shows, and faculty members also display their art on campus.

The Department of Theatre and Dance produces two dance concerts, three plays, and one musical each year. These productions are performed either in the 435-seat Dorothy Betts Marvin Theatre, or the 1,490-seat Lisner Auditorium (don't miss the Dimock Gallery of Fine Art on the first floor). If you're unaffiliated with the university, tickets to performances will probably cost between $15 and $30. For more information on performances presented by the Theatre and Dance Department, call 202-994-6178.

For information on tickets for the Dorothy Betts Marvin Theatre, call 202-994-7411. For information on tickets for the Lisner Auditorium, call 202-994-6800.

Department Contact Information

Undergraduate Admissions 202-994-6040
Athletics 202-994-6650
Campus Bookstore 202-994-6870
College of Arts & Science 202-994-6210
Elliot School of International Affairs 202-994-3002
Financial Aid 202-994-6620
Gelman Library 202-994-6558
Graduate School of Education 202-994-2194
Law School 202-994-6288
Registrar 202-994-4900
School of Business 202-994-8252
School of Medicine .202-994-3501
Student Activities Center 202-994-6555
University Police (emergency) 202-994-6111
University Police (non-emergency) 202-994-6110
Visitor Center 202-994-6602

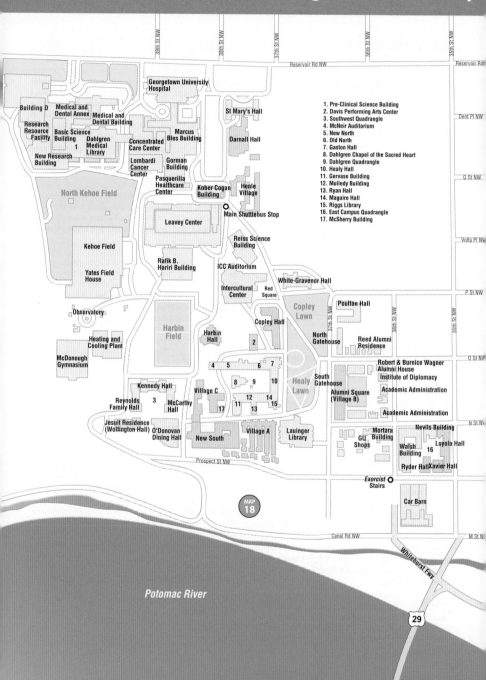

39th St NW
38th St NW
37th St NW
36th St NW
35th St NW

Reservoir Rd NW
Reservoir Rd

Georgetown University Hospital

Building D

Medical and Dental Annex

Medical and Dental Building

St Mary's Hall

Dent Pl NW

Research Resource Facility

Basic Science Building

1

Marcus Bles Building

Darnall Hall

Dahlgren Medical Library

Concentrated Care Center

New Research Building

Lombardi Cancer Center

Gorman Building

Pasquerilla Healthcare Center

O St NW

North Kehoe Field

Kober Cogan Building

Henle Village

Main Shuttlebus Stop

Leavey Center

Volta Pl NW

Kehoe Field

Reiss Science Building

Yates Field House

Rafik B. Hariri Building

ICC Auditorium

Intercultural Center

White-Gravenor Hall

P St NW

Red Square

Copley Lawn

Poulton Hall

Observatory

Copley Hall

Copley Lawn

North Gatehouse

Reed Alumni Residence

O St NW

Heating and Cooling Plant

Harbin Field

Harbin Hall

2

Healy Lawn

McDonough Gymnasium

4 5

6 7

Robert & Burnice Wagner Alumni House

Institute of Diplomacy

Academic Administration

Kennedy Hall

8 9

10

South Gatehouse

Alumni Square (Village B)

Reynolds Family Hall

3

McCarthy Hall

Village C

12 14

Academic Administration

N St NW

Jesuit Residence (Wolfington Hall)

O'Donovan Dining Hall

17

11 13

15

Nevils Building

Mortara Building

New South

Village A

Lauinger Library

GU Shops

Walsh Building

16

Loyola Hall

Prospect St NW

Exorcist Stairs

Ryder Hall

Xavier Hall

Car Barn

Canal Rd NW

M St N

Whitehurst Fwy

MAP 18

29

Potomac River

1. Pre-Clinical Science Building
2. Davis Performing Arts Center
3. Southwest Quadrangle
4. McNeir Auditorium
5. New North
6. Old North
7. Gaston Hall
8. Dahlgren Chapel of the Sacred Heart
9. Dahlgren Quadrangle
10. Healy Hall
11. Gervase Building
12. Mulledy Building
13. Ryan Hall
14. Maguire Hall
15. Riggs Library
16. East Campus Quadrangle
17. McSherry Building

General Information

NFT Map: 18
Main Campus: 37th & O Sts NW
                     Washington, DC 20057
Phone: 202-687-0100
Website: www.georgetown.edu

Overview

Georgetown University was founded the same year the US Constitution took effect, making the school not only the nation's oldest Catholic and Jesuit university, but also about the same age as most of the neighborhood's socialites. But seriously, Georgetown is the most prestigious college in town, and a "feeder school" for the federal government and foreign-policy community. Alumni include former president Bill Clinton, Supreme Court Justice Antonin Scalia, and broadcast journalist/Kennedy heir/Former Mrs. Schwarzenegger Maria Shriver. The campus sets the tone for the neighborhood around it—beautiful, old, and distinguished. A few blocks away, the endless strip of bars on M Street provide most of the Georgetown nightlife.

Georgetown's long history is not without its eerie episodes. According to campus rumor, the attic of Healy Hall is haunted by the ghost of a priest who died while winding the clock in the building's famous spire. During the Civil War, the university's buildings became bunkers and hospitals for the Yankee troops. Once the war ended, the school adopted blue and gray as its official colors to symbolize the reunification of North and South. More recently, it became part of Hollywood history by providing the setting for a scene from *The Exorcist*, a novel by alum William Peter Blatty. The creepy "*Exorcist* stairs" can be found on campus at the junction of Prospect and 36th Streets.

Tuition

Tuition for the 2013–2014 academic year for undergraduate, full-time students cost $44,280. With room and board and fees, the average total cost attendance is $60,080. Graduate tuitions vary by program.

Sports

The university's teams are known as the Hoyas because, the story goes, a student well-versed in Greek and Latin started cheering "Hoya Saxa!" which translates to "What Rocks!" The cheer proved popular and the term "Hoyas" was adopted for all Georgetown teams. Since "what rocks" did not readily translate into an animal mascot, the bulldog was chosen to represent the Blue and Gray. Georgetown is best known for its men's basketball team, a regular top-seed in the NCAA Tournament. Former Hoya athletes include Patrick Ewing, Allen Iverson, and Alonzo Mourning. Georgetown is the alma mater of more than one Ewing; son Patrick Ewing, Jr. played for the Hoyas between 2005-2008 (though he had to sit out the entire 2005-06 season). Men's sports also include crew, football, golf, lacrosse, sailing, soccer, swimming and diving, tennis, and track. Women's sports include basketball, crew, field hockey, golf, lacrosse, sailing, soccer, swimming and diving, tennis, track, and volleyball. For tickets to all Georgetown athletic events, call 202-687-HOYA. Georgetown also offers intramural sports including volleyball, flag football, racquetball, basketball, ultimate Frisbee, table tennis, softball, and floor hockey.

Culture on Campus

Although best known for its more philistine programs—government, law, and medicine—Georgetown has bolstered its fine arts program significantly in the last few years, expanding course offerings and opening the posh new Davis Performing Arts Center in 2005. The Department of Art, Music, and Theater offers majors and minors in studio art, art history, and the performing arts. Artistically inclined students can also join Georgetown's many extra-curricular arts groups, including the orchestra, band, choir, and multiple theater troupes, improv groups, and a cappella singing groups.

Department Contact Information

Undergraduate Admissions 202-687-3600
Graduate Admissions 202-687-5568
Georgetown Law Center 202-662-9000
McDonough School of Business 202-687-3851
Edmund A. Walsh School
    of Foreign Service 202-687-5696
Georgetown University
    Medical Center 202-687-5100
School of Nursing & Health Studies 202-687-2681
Department of Athletics 202-687-2435

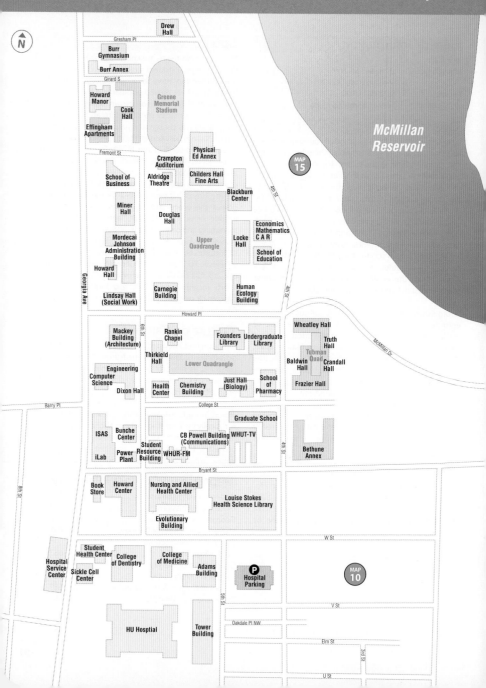

N

McMillan Reservoir

MAP 15

MAP 10

Drew Hall

Gresham Pl

Burr Gymnasium

Burr Annex

Girard S

Howard Manor

Cook Hall

Effingham Apartments

Greene Memorial Stadium

Fremont St

Crampton Auditorium

Physical Ed Annex

School of Business

Aldridge Theatre

Childers Hall Fine Arts

Blackburn Center

Miner Hall

Douglas Hall

Upper Quadrangle

Locke Hall

Economics Mathematics C A R

School of Education

Mordecai Johnson Administration Building

Howard Hall

Georgia Ave

Lindsay Hall (Social Work)

Carnegie Building

Human Ecology Building

4th St

Howard Pl

Mackey Building (Architecture)

6th St

Rankin Chapel

Founders Library

Undergraduate Library

Wheatley Hall

Truth Hall

Thirkield Hall

Lower Quadrangle

Tubman Quad

Baldwin Hall

Crandall Hall

Engineering Computer Science

Dixon Hall

Health Center

Chemistry Building

Just Hall (Biology)

School of Pharmacy

Frazier Hall

McMillan Dr

College St

Barry Pl

ISAS

Bunche Center

Graduate School

iLab

Power Plant

Student Resource Building

CB Powell Building (Communications)

WHUT-TV

WHUR-FM

4th St

Bethune Annex

Bryant St

8th St

Book Store

Howard Center

Nursing and Allied Health Center

Louise Stokes Health Science Library

Evolutionary Building

W St

Student Health Center

College of Dentistry

College of Medicine

Adams Building

P Hospital Parking

5th St

Hospital Service Center

Sickle Cell Center

V St

HU Hosptial

Tower Building

Oakdale Pl NW

Elm St

3rd St

U St

General Information

NFT Maps: 10 & 15
Main Campus: 2400 Sixth St NW
                 Washington, DC 20059
Phone: 202-806-6100
Website: www.howard.edu

Overview

Conceived in 1866 as a theological seminary for African-American ministers, Howard University remains the pre-eminent African-American university in the nation. Although no longer a seminary, it has remained nonsectarian and open to all races and genders since its founding. Today, as a Carnegie Research institution offering a full array of undergraduate and graduate programs, including medicine, law, engineering, business, and the arts, Howard continues to serve as a dominant DC intellectual, cultural, and physical presence. Distinguished Howard alumni include novelist Zora Neale Hurston, Nobel Laureate Toni Morrison, and Shirley Franklin, the first female mayor of Atlanta. Perhaps the most well known graduate was Supreme Court Justice Thurgood Marshall, who used Howard's campus to prepare himself and a team of legal scholars from around the nation to argue the landmark Brown v. Board of Education case.

Howard University once occupied a lone single-frame building and now has five campuses spanning more than 260 acres. The library system houses the largest collection of African-American literature in the nation. Despite its physical size, Howard is a relatively small school with roughly 10,500 students. Its national reputation belies its numbers, as recent graduation commencement speaker Oprah Winfrey would attest.

Howard's main campus is located just minutes away from the Capitol and the White House on "the hilltop," one of the highest elevation points in the city. The campus leads right into U Street, one of the premier catwalks of the city. The area was once the city's center of jazz and African-American nightlife before falling on rough times. But now it's back and considered the hippest of areas, with avant-garde fashion, deluxe condos, and over-priced everything.

Tuition

In the 2013–2014 academic year, undergraduate tuition for students living off-campus cost $21,450. Room and board is approximately $16,000. Graduate tuition, fees, and expenses vary by school and department.

Sports

Howard is a member of the Mid-Eastern Athletic Conference and participates in the NCAA's Division I. Annual football homecoming festivities continue to serve as a premier annual event in Washington (just listen to Ludacris' "Pimpin' All Over The World" and Notorious B.I.G.'s "Kick In The Door"). The last noteworthy sports achievement dates way back to 2003, when the women's cross-country team ran away with the MEAC championship trophy. Other teams have a less-than-stellar record. The male basketball team ranked 319th out of 326 teams in 2004. But losing (a lot) hasn't hurt their popularity on campus. Games still draw crowds. Intercollegiate men's sports include basketball, cross-country, soccer, tennis, football, swimming, wrestling, and track. Women's sports include basketball, tennis, cross-country, track, volleyball, and swimming.

Culture on Campus

The Department of Theatre Arts produces dance and drama performances throughout the school year in the Ira Aldridge Theater, which also hosts visiting professional theater troupes. Student tickets cost $8 and general admission costs $15. The season always brings in a decidedly diverse bag of productions such as the Obie Award-winning play *Zooman and the Sign* by Charles Fuller, and Nilo Cruz's Pulitzer Prize-winning *Anna in the Tropics*. The historic Howard Theatre—which hosted greats like Duke Ellington, Ella Fitzgerald and Marvin Gaye—was fully renovated and reopened in 2012 after a 32-year hiatus. The intimate space also features a museum and gift shop.

Howard University Television, WHUT-TV, is the only African-American-owned public television station in the country. It has been operating for over 30 years and reaches half a million households in the Washington metropolitan area. Howard University also runs commercial radio station WHUR-FM (96.3).

Department Contact Information

Admissions 202-806-2700
College of Arts & Sciences 202-806-6700
School of Business 202-806-1500
School of Communications 202-806-7690
School of Dentistry 202-806-0440
School of Divinity 202-806-0500
School of Education 202-806-7340
School of Engineering, Architecture,
    and Computer Sciences 202-806-6565
Graduate School of Arts & Sciences 202-806-6800
School of Law 202-806-8000
College of Medicine 202-806-5677
College of Pharmacy, Nursing, and
    Allied Health Sciences 202-806-5431
School of Social Work 202-806-7300
Student Affairs 202-806-2100
Athletic Department 202-806-7140
Founders Library 202-806-7234

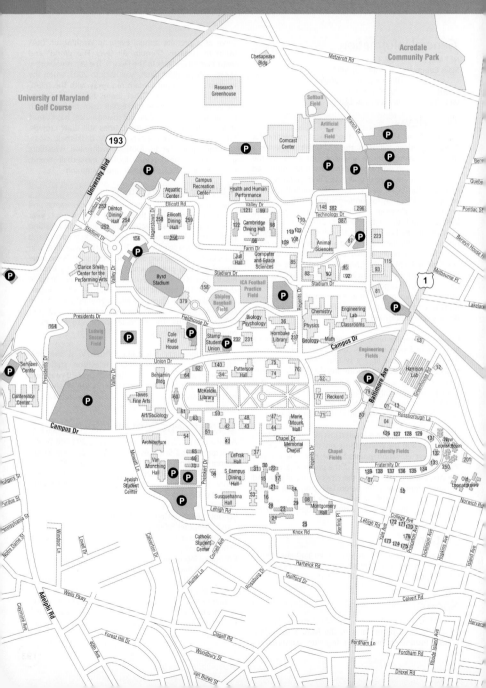

General Information

Address: College Park, MD 20742
Phone: 301-405-1000
Website: www.umd.edu

Overview

University of Maryland's gargantuan size masks its humble beginnings. First chartered as a small agricultural college in 1856, this public university now has over 37,000 students roaming its 1,500 acres. Between the 13 colleges, 111 undergraduate majors, study-abroad programs, and honors programs, there's enough excitement and intellectual rigor to keep the brightest Marylanders interested. And for students who've been surrounded by pastoral green quads for so long it makes them want to gag, the school's very own Metro stop will shuttle them into the vast city that awaits to the south. UMCP is the crème de la crème of the thirteen campuses run by The University System of Maryland and hosts a multitude of academic programs offering specialized courses and research opportunities. Of particular note are the University Honors and Gemstone programs, which continue to lure some of the brightest of Marylanders with dirty cheap (well, relatively) in-state tuition

Tuition

Undergraduate tuition for the 2013–2014 school year cost $8,900 for in-state residents and $27,228 for non-residents. Room and board averaged around $9,800.

Sports

While there's never been a real dearth of Terrapin pride, it's only skyrocketed in recent years. An ACC basketball championship win over the Duke Blue Devils, victory at college football's Gator Bowl, and a 2003 NCAA men's basketball Championship win have strengthened Marylanders' love of their winning teams. With 27 Varsity teams competing at UMD, the athletic program is widely recognized as one of the best in the country for both men's and women's sports, and the Terps are one of only six schools to have won a national championship in both football and men's basketball. Though it's usually the men's teams that hog the spotlight, 2006 ushered in the first National Championship win for the Terps women's basketball team.

Culture on Campus

The Clarice Smith Performing Arts Center hosts high-profile performers and ensembles. Past guests have included Yo-Yo Ma, the Woolly Mammoth Theater Company, and the Maryland Opera Studio. The Center is also home of the university's symphony orchestra and jazz band. Tickets are usually free or, at most, five bucks for students. You don't have to be affiliated with the university to attend events—just be prepared to shell out up to $30 if you're not a student, faculty member, or staff. 301-405-2787; www.claricesmithcenter.umd.edu.

If orchestra or jazz ensembles are not the type of entertainment you're jonesing for, the Student Entertainment Events (SEE) presents a variety of concerts featuring both headlining artists and local bands. Tickets of course are cheaper for students and range between $5 and $25, depending on the event. Tickets for larger concerts can also be purchased via Ticketmaster.

Film buffs can view an array of independent films and blockbusters at the Hoff Theater in the University's Student Union. The ample theater showcases at least one feature daily and is usually free for students, $5 for non-students.

And don't worry about things getting too boring on campus; despite the fact that sleepy College Park, Maryland is a verifiable snoozefest in comparison to nearby DC, students there are never ones to shy away from controversy. UMCP gained a bit of notoriety and quite a bit more media coverage when the student union planned in 2009 to show Pirates II: Stagnetti's Revenge, a hard-core pornographic film. The move prompted State Senator Andy Harris to threaten to rescind university funding and University President Dan Mote to cancel the event entirely. Not to be deterred, students took to the media and eventually planned another event: a "teach-in" featuring David Rocah of the ACLU which addressed free speech, academic expression, and the role of pornography in society. This scholarly speech was followed by, what else, a screening of sections of the film Pirates 2: Stagnetti's Revenge. Now that's what I call learning.

Department Contact Information

Campus Information	301-405-1000
Undergraduate Admissions	301-314-8385
Graduate Admissions	301-405-0376
Bookstore	301-314-7848
Registrar	301-314-8240
Bursar	301-314-9000
Athletic Department	800-462-8377
Ticket Office	301-314-7070
Clark School of Engineering	301-405-3855
College of Education	301-405-2344
School of Architecture	301-405-6284
School of Public Policy	301-405-6330
Smith School of Business	301-405-2189
Art and Humanities	301-405-2108
Behavioral and Social Sciences	301-405-1697
Life Sciences	301-405-2071

Building Listings

1 - Central Heating Plant
4 - Ritchie Coliseum
5 - Service Building Annex
7 - Pocomoke Building
8 - Annapolis Hall
12 - Plant Operations & Maintenance Complex
13 - Shuttle Bus Facility
14 - Harford Hall
15 - Calvert Hall
16 - Baltimore Hall
17 - Cecil Hall
18 - Police Substation
21 - Prince George's Hall
22 - Kent Hall
23 - Washington Hall
24 - Allegany Hall
25 - Charles Hall
28 - Howard Hall
29 - Frederick Hall
30 - Talbot Hall
34 - Jimenez Hall
36 - Plant Science
37 - Shoemaker Building
40 - Morrill Hall
42 - Tydings Hall
43 - Taliaferro Hall
44 - Skinner Building
47 - Woods Hall
48 - Francis Scott Key Hall

51 - Worchester Hall
52 - Mitchell Building Registration Office
53 - Dance Building
54 - Preinkert Field House
59 - Journalism Building
60 - Anne Arundel Hall
61 - Queen Anne's Hall
62 - St. Mary's Hall
63 - Somerset Hall
64 - Dorchester Hall
65 - Carroll Hall
66 - West Education Annex
69 - Wicomico Hall
70 - Caroline Hall
71 - Lee Building
74 - Holzapfel Hall
75 - Shriver Laboratory
76 - Symons Hall
77 - Main Administration
79 - Visitors Center
80 - Rossborough Inn
81 - Wind Tunnel Building
83 - JM Patterson Building
85 - Institute for Physical Science & Technology
87 - Central Animal Resources Facility
90 - Chemical and Nuclear Engineering Building

93 - Engineering Annex
96 - Cambridge Hall
98 - Centreville Hall
99 - Bel Air Hall
102 - Agriculture Shed
108 - Horse Barn
109 - Sheep Barn
110 - Cattle Barn
115 - AV Williams
119 - Blacksmith Shop
121 - Performing Arts Center, Clarice Smith
122 - Cumberland Hall
126 - Kappa Alpha Fraternity
127 - Sigma Alpha Mu Fraternity
128 - Delta Tau Delta Fraternity
129 - Sigma Alpha Epsilon Fraternity
131 - Beta Theta Pi Fraternity
132 - Phi Sigma Kappa Fraternity
133 - Pi Kappa Phi Fraternity
134 - Chi Omega Sorority
135 - Sigma Kappa Sorority
136 - Alpha Epsilon Phi Sorority
137 - Zeta Tau Alpha Sorority
138 - Sigma Phi Epsilon Fraternity
139 - Zeta Beta Tau Fraternity
140 - Health Center
148 - Manufacturing Building

156 - Apiary
158 - Varsity Sports Teamhouse
170 - Alpha Delta Pi Sorority
171 - Phi Kappa Tau Fraternity
172 - Alpha Chi Omega Sorority
173 - Delta Phi Epsilon Sorority
174 - Phi Sigma Sigma Sorority
175 - Delta Gamma Sorority
176 - Alpha Phi Sorority
201 - Leonardtown office building
223 - Energy Research
231 - Microbiology Building
232 - Nyumburu Cultural Center
237 - Geology Building
250 - Leonardtown community center
252 - Denton Hall
253 - Easton Hall
254 - Elkton Hall
256 - Ellicott Hall
258 - Hagerstown Hall
259 - LaPlata Hall
296 - Biomolecular Sciences Building
379 - Football Team Building
382 - Neutral Buoyancy Research Facility
387 - Tap Building

George Mason University

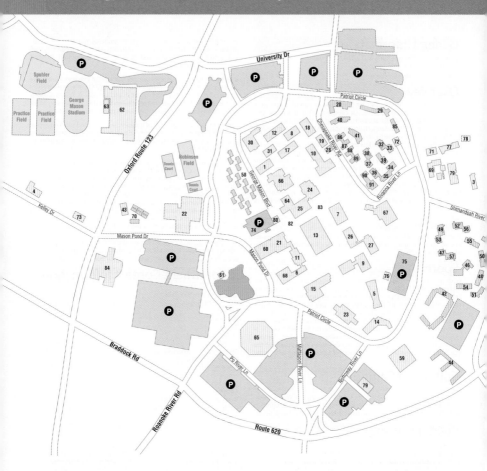

1. Aquia Building
2. Buchanan House
3. Carrow Hall
4. Carty House
5. Research I
6. College Hall
7. David King Hall
8. East Building
9. Enterprise Hall
10. Fenwick Library
11. Fine Arts Building
12. Finley Building
13. George W. Johnson Center
14. Nguyen Engineering Building
15. Innovation Hall
16. Krasnow Institute
17. Krug Hall
18. Lecture Hall
19. North Chesapeake Module
20. Northern Neck
21. Performing Arts Building
22. Recreation and Athletic Complex (RAC)
23. Art and Design Building

24. Robinson Hall A
25. Robinson Hall B
26. Science and Tech I
27. Science and Tech II
28. South Chesapeake Module
29. Hampton Roads
30. Thompson Hall
31. West Building
32. Amherst Hall
33. Brunswick Hall
34. Carroll Hall
35. Dickenson Hall
36. Essex Hall
37. Franklin Hall
38. Grayson Hall
39. Hanover Hall
40. Commonwealth Hall
41. Dominion Hall
42. Liberty Square
43. West P.E. Module
44. Potomac Housing/Housing Office
45. Adams Hall
46. Eisenhower Hall

47. Harrison Hall
48. Jackson Hall
49. Jefferson Hall
50. Kennedy Hall
51. Lincoln Hall
52. Madison Hall
53. Monroe Hall
54. Roosevelt Hall
55. Truman Hall
56. Washington Hall
57. Wilson Hall
58. Student Apartments
59. Aquatic and Fitness Center
60. Center for the Arts Concert Hall
61. Cross Cottage
62. Field House
63. Field House Module
64. Harris Theatre
65. Patriot Center
66. Student Union I/Student Health Services
67. Student Union II
68. Mason Hall
69. Central Heating and Cooling Plant

70. Patriot Village Lot
71. Facilities Administration
72. Rivanna Module
73. Kelley II
74. Parking Deck, Mason Pond (Visitors)
75. Parking Deck, Sandy Creek
76. Parking Services
77. Physical Plant/Customer Service Center
78. Recycling Center
79. University Police
80. Visitor Information
82. George Mason Statue
83. Clock Tower
84. Mason Inn Conference Center and Hotel
85. Eastern Shore
86. Blue Ridge
87. Shenandoah
88. Piedmont
89. Tidewater
90. Skyline Fitness Center
91. Southside DIning

General Information

Address: 4400 University Drive
            Fairfax, VA 22030
Phone: 703-993-1000
Website: www.gmu.edu

Overview

Named for the most obscure of the founding fathers, George Mason University began as an extension of the University of Virginia for the northern part of the state. In 1966, George Mason College became a four-year, degree-granting university. George Mason separated from UVA in 1972 and became an independent institution.

Currently the university offers more than 100 degree programs in both the undergraduate and graduate levels in three different locations in Virginia. Academically, Mason boasts award-winning faculty and offers unique curriculum, such as its biodefense graduate degree program. There are approximately 20,150 undergraduates and around 12,400 graduate students currently enrolled in the university.

Conveniently located in close proximity to Washington, DC, George Mason's picturesque main campus is centered on acres of woods in Fairfax, Virginia. In addition to its law school and campus in Arlington, GMU has recently established branches in Prince William and Loudoun countries.

Tuition

Undergraduate tuition for the 2013–2014 school year cost $9,908 for in-state students, and $28,592 for all non-residents. Room and board averaged around $9,500.

Sports

Of course we can't mention GMU without noting the successful run the men's basketball team had in 2006. While many living outside the immediate area were scratching their heads, asking, "Where the heck is George Mason?" or getting it confused with its fellow local "George" University (George Washington University), the Patriots were surpassing everyone's expectations and slowly crept into the Final Four. Although the GMU men's basketball team took a brief break from the limelight following their surprise entrance onto the national stage, the Patriots returned to the NCAA Tournament in 2008 and in 2011.

So now that we got that out of the way, there are about 19 other men's and women's Division I teams on campus including baseball, track and field, tennis, and soccer. Mason teams belong to the National Collegiate Athletic Association (NCAA) Division I, the Colonial Athletic Association (CAA), and the Eastern College Athletic Conference (ECAC).

Culture on Campus

George Mason's Center for the Arts offers a variety of musical and dance performances from celebrated entertainers like the Metropolitan Jazz Orchestra and the St. Petersburg Ballet. With several different performance spaces ranging from the larger 1,900-seat Concert Hall to the intimate 75-seat Black Box, the Center for the Arts also featured performances by its own theater company, Theater of the First Amendment, until it folded in 2012. The company had been nominated for numerous awards and was the recipient of the Helen Hayes Award.

The Film and Media Studies Program, along with University Life, show weekly films throughout the academic year in *Cinema Series*. Admission and popcorn are free for students and faculty with GMU ID.

Department Contact Information

Fairfax Campus 703-993-1000
Admissions 703-993-2400
University Services 703-993-2840
Bookstore 703-993-2666
Registrar 703-993-2441
Patriot Computer Store 703-993-4100
Academic Support Center 703-993-2470
Center For the Arts 703-993-8888
Patriot Center 703-993-3000
School of Law 703-993-8000
Arlington Campus 703-993-8999
Prince William Campus 703-993-8350
Loudoun Campus 703-993-4350

General Information

Address: 1600 FedEx Wy
                      Landover, MD 20785
Redskins Website: www.redskins.com
FedEx Field   www.redskins.com/
                      fedexfield/index.html
Website: sports/fedexfield/
Stadium Admin: 301-276-6000
Ticket Office: 301-276-6050

Overview

No city is more infatuated with its football team than Washington is with the Redskins, even in the *off*-season. Summer after summer, the team's front office has put together a line-up it claims will march straight to the Super Bowl, and year after year, the beloved 'Skins have fallen flat on their faces. Part of the problem has been Daniel Snyder, the team's unpopular owner, who knows football like Paris Hilton knows rodeo yet insists on dropping megadimes on washed-up players whom he deems messianic. (We think Deion Sanders may still be collecting Redskins paychecks.)

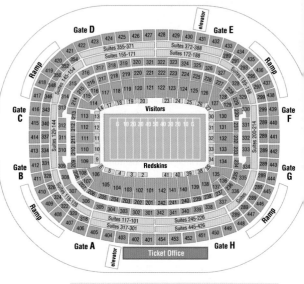

The 2007 season was probably one of the most emotional roller coaster rides any Redskins fan has taken in a decade. From a 2-0 start, to a series of injuries, to the death of 24-year-old superstar Sean Taylor, to a last-game win over Dallas to put the 'Skins in the playoffs, and finally the retirement of Hall of Fame coach Joe Gibbs, the 2007 season will not be soon forgotten by devoted Skins fans. 2008 was the inaugural season for Coach Jim Zorn, who took over for the legendary Gibbs. Zorn had never held a head coaching position, but quickly earned the trust and respect of fans. However, a series of losses left the team at 8-8 and just short of the playoffs. Despite hopes for a good 2009 season, cultivated by the high-profile acquisition of Albert Haynesworth (he came with a $100 million price tag), the year was a bleak one for Redskins fans. The Skins failed to improve upon 2008's record, which then prompted Zorn's unceremonious dismissal. In early 2010, Mike Shanahan was brought on as both coach and Executive Vice President of Football Operations, meaning he now has full control over player personnel. Fans were keeping their fingers crossed that Shanahan's guidance, and track record (he led the Broncos to two Bowl victories in both 1997 and 1998), would help turn around what had been a disappointing couple of seasons. Sadly, it was not so in 2010 and 2011, and the seasons passed with no playoff berths (and don't even get fans started on the Donovan McNabb debacle!). The 2012-13 season saw the Redskins reach the NFC wild-card playoff round, but they lost to the Seahawks. As always, hope springs eternal in DC; the 'Skins'll get 'em next season.

The stadium itself is a diamond in the middle of a very large rough known as Landover, Maryland. During the late 1980s, then-owner Jack Kent Cooke envisioned a new and sensational stadium, settling on a site deep in the Maryland suburbs just inside the Washington Beltway. Although Cooke didn't live to see the $300 million project completed, Jack Kent Cooke Stadium officially opened its gates September 14, 1997 (Snyder sold the naming rights to FedEx shortly after purchasing the team in 1999). The colossal structure is equipped to hold more than 90,000 fans, good for tops in the NFL.

How to Get There—Driving

Um, don't. The nightmares of getting in and out of FedEx Field and the myriad parking lots in the vicinity are the stuff of a Maalox moment. If you *must*, take E Capitol Street (which becomes Central Avenue at the Maryland line) to Harry Truman Drive north just outside the Beltway. Then take a right onto Lottsford Road to Arena Drive and you're there. Keep your eyes peeled for the many signs that will direct you to the field. You can also take the Capital Beltway (I-95/495) from the north or the south to Exits 15 (Central Avenue), 16 (Arena Drive, open only for FedEx events), or 17 (Landover Road). It's a barrel of laughs, especially for those Monday night games.

Parking

FedEx Field provides off-stadium parking that can cost as much as $35, with a free shuttle ride to the stadium. The team did their damnedest to prevent fans from parking for free at the nearby Landover Mall and walking to the game, but a Prince George's County judge overturned a county policy restricting pedestrian movement in the area. So you can pay up for convenience or exercise your civic rights to park free and schlep.

How to Get There—Mass Transit

Take the Blue Line to the Morgan Boulevard or Largo Town Center stops—both are close by and are a pretty short walk to the stadium. Five-dollar round-trip shuttle buses depart from these stations for FedEx Field every 15 minutes, from two hours before the game until two hours after.

How to Get Tickets

If you enjoy the prospect of languishing in a years-long line, join the Redskins season ticket waiting list by visiting www.redskins.com/tickets. If you're just looking for individual game tickets, suck up to a season ticket holder or call 301-276-6050.

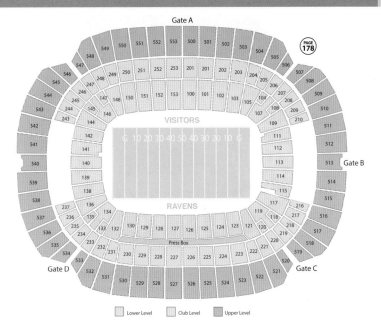

Gate A

PAGE 178

VISITORS

G 10 20 30 40 50 40 30 20 10 G

RAVENS

Press Box

Gate B

Gate C

Gate D

Lower Level   Club Level   Upper Level

General Information

Address: 1101 Russell St, Baltimore, MD 21230
Phone: 410-261-7283
Website: www.baltimoreravens.com

Overview

Dominating Baltimore's skyline from I-95, M&T Bank Stadium is a menacing structure, to say the least. Its team, the "Bol'more" Ravens, flew into town 11 years ago via Cleveland and wasted no time in capturing the 2001 Super Bowl title. 2006 was probably their next-best season, with then coach Brian Billick bringing the team to a 13-3 record and a tough playoff loss to the Baltimore—we mean Indianapolis—Colts. Harsh are the ways of the gods. But after a 3-13 finish in 2007, the Ravens made a drastic turn around–finishing with a 11-5 record and making it to the AFC Championship Game. They bowed to eventual Super Bowl champions, the Pittsburgh Steelers, but hopes were high that the Ravens would get their groove back and make a splash in years to come. And that was certainly the case in 2011, when they made it all the way to the AFC Championship game, only to lose to the Pats in a nail-biter. Even better was 2012, when the Ravens won Super Bowl XLVII (um, that's 47) against the 49ers in one of the most memorable games in Super Bowl history.

In Baltimore, as is customary with most NFL cities, the name of the game, or *pre-game*, is tailgating. For 1 pm games, the festivities usually commence at about 9 am. The parking lots slowly swell with inebriated men fashioning O-linemen bellies, confirming Baltimore's reputation as a blue-collar football town. Outsiders need not be afraid, however, because unlike fans in nearby cities (read: Philadelphia), Ravens fans are gracious hosts and typically welcome others to the party. Once inside the stadium, expect to pay through the nose for food—though the Maryland crab cakes

are definitely worth the high price, and the stadium's hot dogs are pretty damn good, too. After the game, Pickles and Sliders, two sports bars on nearby Washington Boulevard, are where weary DC-bound travelers (tired of waiting years for Redskins tickets) head to quench their thirst.

How to Get There—Driving

Take I-95 N toward Baltimore to Exit 52 (Russell Street north for immediate access to the stadium (you can't miss it) or Exit 53 (I-395 north) for better access to the downtown parking garages.

Parking

M&T Bank provides parking, for which you need to buy a permit ahead of time. Otherwise, there are 15,000 spaces-worth of public parking nearby, most of which charge a flat game day rate.

How to Get There—Mass Transit

The MTA Light Rail provides service directly to the Hamburg Street Light Rail stop, operational only on game days. Trains run every 17 minutes from Hunt Valley and Cromwell Station/Glen Burnie, and every 34 minutes from Penn Station and BWI. The stop closest to the stadium on the Baltimore Metro is Lexington Market, though you'll have to hoof it about a mile. Be sure to leave early to beat the crowds on game days. You can also take the 3, 7, 10, 14, 17, 19/19A, 27, or 31 buses, all of which stop within walking distance of the stadium.

How to Get Tickets

To purchase tickets, visit the Ravens' website, or call 410-261-7283. Tickets can also be purchased through Ticketmaster (www.ticketmaster.com).

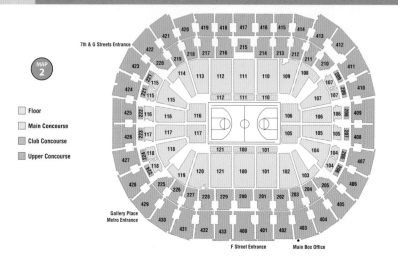

MAP 2

- Floor
- Main Concourse
- Club Concourse
- Upper Concourse

7th & G Streets Entrance

Gallery Place Metro Entrance

F Street Entrance   Main Box Office

General Information

NFT Map:	2
Address:	601 F St NW
	Washington, DC 20004
Verizon Center Phone:	202-628-3200
Verizon Center Website:	www.verizoncenter.com
Wizards Phone:	202-661-5100
Wizards Website:	www.nba.com/wizards
Capitals Phone:	202-266-2200
Capitals Website:	capitals.nhl.com
Mystics Phone:	202-661-5000
Mystics Website:	www.wnba.com/mystics
Georgetown Basketball Phone:	202-687-4692
Georgetown Basketball Website:	www.guhoyas.com

Overview

In 1997, DC's then-new MCI Center reversed a decades-old trend of arenas planting roots in the suburbs by bringing it all back to the 'hood. The block-sized complex known today as Verizon Center (which includes a 20,000-seat stadium as well as bars, restaurants, and stores) is now the centerpiece of downtown's gentrification juggernaut.

The best thing to happen to the underachieving world of DC sports since Jordan's semi-triumphant return to the hard court is the NHL winger Alexander Ovechkin, who is single-handedly making Caps games a weekend must-do activity. In addition to the Caps and the artists-formerly-known-as-the-Bullets, the Verizon Center is also home to the Washington Mystics, who boast the largest fan base in the WNBA. The Georgetown Hoyas basketball team hoops it up in the arena, as well. Beyond the ballers, Verizon Center hosts big-name concerts from the likes of Cher, Britney, Gaga and Madonna, circuses (both Ringling and Cirque de Soleil have performed here), and all sorts of other events. For post-event fun, China-alley, otherwise known as Chinatown, is a block away with plenty of eats and drinks.

How to Get There—Driving

From downtown, turn left onto 7th Street from either Constitution Avenue or New York Avenue. Verizon Center is on the northeast corner of F and 7th.

Parking

Verizon Center's parking garage is on 6th Street NW underneath the building and is open for most events at a charge of $25 for event parking. It opens 1 ½ hours before game/show time and closes 1 hour after the event. There are also several public parking garages near the building including Gallery Place's parking garage on 6th Street NW and the parking garage next to Rosa Mexicano restaurant on F Street NW.

How to Get There—Mass Transit

Verizon Center is accessible by the Metro's Red, Yellow, and Green lines; get off at the Gallery Place-Chinatown stop. It's not hard to find, just get off the Metro, and you are directly under it.

How to Get Tickets

Tickets for all Verizon Center events are available through the Ticketmaster website at www.ticketmaster.com (with the inevitable Ticketmaster markup, of course), or by calling 703-573-7328.

Level 1
Level 2
Level 3
Level 4
Level 5
Level 6
Level 7

PAGE 178

General Information

Address: 333 W Camden St
Baltimore, MD 21201
Website: baltimore.orioles.mlb.com
Phone: 888-848-2473

Overview

Oriole Park at Camden Yards opened in 1992, launching a "traditional" trend in stadium design that continues to this day. The old warehouse behind Right Field and the general look of the place give it that old-fashioned, family-friendly feel. In the face of dozens of corporations eager to smear their names across the park, the Orioles have refused to budge. All brick and history, the stately Yards stand downtown on a former railroad center, two blocks from Babe Ruth's birthplace. Center field sits atop the site where the Bambino's father ran a bar. The goods include double-decker bullpens, a sunken, asymmetrical field, and "Boog's BBQ," run by ex-Oriole Boog Powell, who is known to frequently man the grill himself during O's home games.

The Birds, unlike their stadium, haven't been much to look at in recent years. Some years back, baseball's drug problem hit the local boys of summer where it hurts—in the batter's box. In the 2012 season, the Orioles made it to postseason play only to lose to the Yankees in the American League Division Series. Still, the Birds have been playing below .500 baseball for much of the past decade and have been running through coaches like they're going outta style. The good news is there is never a shortage of all-star players to watch at Oriole Park, as both the Yankees and Red Sox inhabit the AL East with the O's, and Camden Yards offers a comfy and classic setting in which to watch your favorites swing the bats.

While their performance on the field in the recent past may have been lackluster, the O's hope to ramp up fan enthusiasm with their recently unveiled new uniforms. The team's new digs includes caps with an updated Oriole bird (which is ornithologically correct, mind you) and a new patch featuring the flag of the state of Maryland in a style

borrowed from their vintage 1960s and 1970s emblem. The hometown's name (Baltimore, baby!) also returns to the road uniforms for the first time since being removed in 1972.

How to Get There—Driving

Take MD 295 (B-W Pkwy/Russell St) to downtown Baltimore, which gets very congested on game days. You can also take I-95 North to Exits 53 (I-395), 52 (Russell St), or 52 (Washington Blvd) and follow signs to the park.

Parking

Parking at Camden Yards is reserved, but there are several public garages nearby. Prices range from $3 to $6.

How to Get There—Mass Transit

Take the MARC from Union Station in DC to Camden Station in Baltimore. It takes about an hour and ten minutes, costs $14 round trip, and the last train leaves at 6:30 pm. To return from a night game, the 701 MTA bus will get you home in 50 minutes for free with your Baltimore-bound MARC ticket.

Due to a recent court ruling, the MTA no longer allows special bus charters to run return trips to Savage, Greenbelt, and Washington D.C. after Oriole Baseball night games. The only option for car-less Orioles enthusiasts is an annoying combination of buses and MTA Light Rail. MTA Light Rail trains roll out of Camden Station at 9:38 pm and 10:08 pm, arriving at the BWI Business Station at 10:05 pm and 10:35 pm. The very last two B-30 buses leave from the BWI Business District Station at 10:15 pm and 10:44 pm, arriving at the Greenbelt Metro Station at 10:51 pm and 11:20 P.M. Keep in mind that on weekdays, the last southbound Metro train departs from Greenbelt at 11:30 pm. On weekends, the last train from Greenbelt leaves at 2:30 am.

How to Get Tickets

Orioles tickets can be purchased on their website, or by calling 888-848-2473. Individual game tickets range from $9 to $55. Group and season tickets are also available.

General Information

NFT Map: 4
Address: 2400 E Capitol St SE,
Washington, DC 20003
Websites: www.dcsec.com, www.dcunited.com
Phone: 202-547-9077

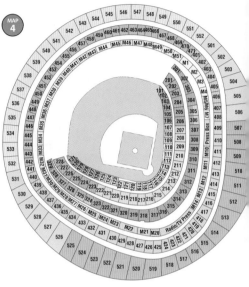

Overview

When it opened as DC Stadium in 1961, RFK was hailed as a triumph of multipurpose architecture and was one of the first of the "cookie-cutter" stadiums. Today it's a cement donut, an alien spacecraft dinosaur of the '60s vision of the future. If you want to experience this decaying jack-of-all-trades (it's hosted football, soccer, and baseball over the years), get in while you can before it crumbles into obscurity—word on the street is that RFK will be torn down as soon as an alternate location can be found for the soccer teams that use it. The stadium remains a sentimental favorite with Redskins fans, who regale us with memories of their team's 35 years there, including five Super Bowl appearances, three championships, and great gridiron personalities like Joe Gibbs, John Riggins, Joe Theisman, Vince Lombardi, Art Monk, and George Allen. In 1996, negotiations for a new football stadium in DC fell through when then-mayor Sharon Pratt Kelly, and team owner Jack Kent Cooke abandoned RFK for a new home in Landover, Maryland.

When the Redskins left, RFK stayed off life support with the arrival of Major League Soccer and the DC United in 1996. The United lost little time in gaining popularity, winning the MLS Cup Championship their inaugural season and again in 1997, 1999, and 2004. Along the sidelines, United fans bounce in the stands and chant "Ole, Ole" in hopes of rooting the team to another win. In a league where foreign-born fans cheer for players from their respective countries, United games offer a fun glimpse of Washington's international diversity. Though soccer hooliganism in DC is nothing like its counterparts in Europe (and thank god for that), DC United does boast some pretty intense fan groups, most notably Barra Brava, whose fan section covers the better part of a sideline, and a tailgating party that's almost more fun than watching the game. The Screaming Eagles and La Norte are two other popular groups, whose drumming and flag waving makes the game more fun for everyone in the stadium.

For a few brief years, RFK breathed new life with the return of Major League Baseball to DC. The vagabond Nationals (formerly the Montreal/Puerto Rico Expos) played in the confines of the roller-coaster roof from 2005 to 2007, at the time making RFK the fourth-oldest MLB stadium in use. But its glory was short-lived, as the City Council voted to build a shiny new ballpark near the Navy yard in southeast which opened just in time for the start of the 2008 season.

How to Get There—Driving

Follow Constitution Avenue east past the Capitol to Maryland Avenue. Turn left on Maryland and go two blocks to Stanton Square. At Stanton Square, turn right onto Massachusetts Avenue. Go around Lincoln Park to E Capitol Street and turn right.

Parking

Stadium parking costs between $3 and $15, depending on the event you're attending.

How to Get There—Mass Transit

Take the Metro to the Stadium-Armory Station on the Blue and Orange lines.

How to Get Tickets

For United tickets, call 703-478-6600. Tickets to United games range from $26 for north goal bleacher seats to $55 for seats on the west side. You can purchase full-season tickets or half-season tickets at various prices. Tickets can also be purchased through Ticketmaster (202-397-7328, www.ticketmaster.com).

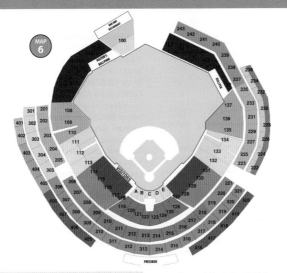

General Information

NFT Map:	6
Address:	1400 S Capitol Street SE
	Washington, DC 20003
Web site:	washington.nationals.mlb.com
Phone:	202-675-NATS

Overview

March 30, 2008 was a great day for baseball fans in DC. It marked opening day at the brand new Nationals Park, named after the original stadium for the Washington Senators. The waterfront colossus cost an estimated $611 million and seats approximately 41,000 fans, boasting views of the capitol building and the Washington Monument from certain spots in the stadium, as well as a grove of cherry blossoms and a view of the Anacostia River from outside the stadium. The stadium also features 66 suites along the infield, the "Oval Office" bar, and luxury suites, bearing the names of past US presidents.

Beyond the initial price tag, Nationals Park has a few other modern-day amenities worth noting, particularly a 4,500 square foot high-definition scoreboard—more than five times the size of RFK's. The stadium is also striving to become the first major stadium in the US accredited as a Leadership in Energy and Environmental Design (LEED) certified ballpark, a.k.a. "Green." Special attention is being paid to issues affecting the nearby Anacostia River, which more than likely will end up even more polluted with concession stand waste. But hey, at least they're trying, right?

Even though the ballpark has only been open since 2008, it is already building a little bit of history. Ryan Zimmerman's game winning walk-off home run in the ninth inning of opening day was the third walk-off home run in major-league history to be hit in the first MLB game played at a stadium. That game also set ESPN history as the most watched MLB opening night game

ever. Beyond that, the Nat's have struggled a bit trying to get attendance up, and so far they hold second-place for all-time lowest attendance for a new stadium. On the other hand, the pope gave mass there. That's cool... right.

How to Get There—Driving

Not advised. If you really feel you must, the Stadium is accessible from both I-395, and I-295. Just look for the South Capitol Street exit, and then pray for parking.

Parking

Not exactly convenient. The Nationals recently snatched up several massive parking lots in the nearby area, including at RFK and the Navy Yard, and run shuttles to and from Nationals Park. There are several reserved parking lots, many of which go to season ticket holders or anyone who wants to shell out forty bucks.

How to Get There—Mass Transit

Now you're talking! Take the Green Line to the Navy Yard station, a mere block north of the stadium entrance. A recent renovation to the Navy Yard metro entrance now allows the stop to accommodate 15,000 passengers an hour, the same as Stadium/Armory at RFK. Talks to re-route the DC Circulator buses to make a stop at Nationals Park during game nights, as well as the establishment of water taxi services are being considered as well. Other Metro buses that run close to Nationals Park include the 70, P1/P2, and V7/V8/V9.

How to Get Tickets

You can purchase Nats tickets at their web site or over the phone. From the diehard middle class fan to the suit-and-tie K Street lobbyist, there's a ticket price all economic levels. They range anywhere from $10 for a nosebleed seat to $325 for a presidential club ticket.

General Information

DC Department of Parks   dpr.dc.gov
and Recreation:
Washington Area   www.skatedc.org
Roadskaters (WAR):

Overview

Washington DC supports a surprisingly thriving skating scene, thanks in a large part to the nonprofit inline skaters' group WAR. Popular meeting places for skaters include the White House, which has a traffic-free Pennsylvania Avenue and easy Metro access; Rock Creek Park, which is mostly closed to cars on weekends; and East Potomac Park, with a recently repaved, with its 3.2-mile Ohio Drive loop.

Indoor Skating

If the weather is grim, or if you want to put in some good practice on predictably level terrain, check out **Wheels Skating Center** (1200 Odenton Rd, Odenton, MD, 410-674-9661, www.wheelsrsc.com).

Skate Parks

After years of hostile restrictions and citations against skaters grinding away outside government buildings, a skate park was finally built in the District's Shaw neighborhood in 2003. It's free and located on the corner of 11th St NW and Rhode Island Ave.
Other outdoor skate parks in the DC area include:

· **Alexandria Skate Park** ·
3540 Wheeler Ave, Alexandria
703-838-4343/4344 · Map 42

· **The Powhatan Springs Park** ·
6020 Wilson Blvd, Arlington · 703-533-2362 · Map 33
A 15,000-square-foot park, featuring 8'- and 6'-deep bowls and 4' and 6' half-pipes; opened in 2004.

Ice Skating

Finding natural outdoor ice thick enough to support skating can be difficult in Washington DC. But during particularly cold winters, the National Park Service allows ice skaters onto the C&O Canal (Maps 8, 18, 32, 35, 36) (the ice has to be more than three inches thick, so it's got to be *really* cold). The National Park Service ice skating hotline provides information on skate-safe areas: 301-767-3707.

Skating at the **National Gallery of Art's Sculpture Garden Ice Skating Rink** (Map 2) may not seem as organic as skating on natural ice, but the surrounding art exhibit rivals any natural setting in terms of beauty. The rink is open daily from mid-November through mid-March (weather permitting), Mon–Thurs 10 am to 9 pm, Sat–Fri 10 am to 11 pm, and Sun 11 am to 9 pm. Admission for a two-hour session costs $8 for adults and $7 for children, students, and seniors. Skate rental costs $3 and a locker rental costs 50¢; 700 Constitution Ave NW; 202-289-3360; Map 2. While the Sculpture Garden rink turns into a fountain once the warm weather arrives, the NHL-sized rink at **Mount Vernon Recreation Center** (2017 Belle View Blvd, Alexandria, VA, 703-838-4825.) operates year-round. The rink provides ice-hockey lessons, recreational skating lessons, and adult hockey leagues for all levels. On Friday nights, the rink brings in a DJ for teen Rock & Blade skating. Rates and fees vary nightly, so call before you go.

Other seasonal ice-skating rinks are located at:

· **Bethesda Metro Ice Center** ·
3 Bethesda Metro Ctr, Bethesda
301-657-9776 · Map 29

· **Cabin John Ice Rink** ·
10610 Westlake Drive, Rockville, MD 20852
301-765-8620, www.montgomeryparks.org/enterprise/ice/cabin_john/index.shtm

· **Herbert Wells Ice Rink** ·
5211 Paint Branch Pkwy, College Park, MD 20740
www.pgparks.com

· **Kettler Capitals Iceplex** ·
627 N Glebe Rd, Ste 800, Arlington, VA 22203
571-224-0555, www.kettlercapitalsiceplex.com

· **Pentagon Row Outdoor Ice Skating** ·
1201 S Joyce St, Arlington, VA 22202
703-418-6666, www.pentagonrowskating.com

· **Reston Town Center Rink** ·
11900 Market St, Reston, VA 20190
www.restontowncenter.com

· **Rockville Ice Arena** ·
50 Southlawn Court, Rockville, MD 20850
301-315-5650, www.rockvilleicearena.com

· **Wheaton Ice Arena** ·
11717 Orebaugh Ave, Wheaton, MD 20902
www.montgomeryparks.org/enterprise/ice/wheaton

Gear

The **Ski Center** (4300 Fordham Rd NW, 202-966-4474, Map 30)sells reasonably priced ice and inline skates. The shop, which has been serving the DC area since 1959, also rents equipment.

Sailing / Boating / Rowing

Boating enjoys a passionate following here in the District. As the weather warms, the Potomac River and the Tidal Basin swarm with sailboats, kayaks, canoes, and paddleboats.

At 380 miles long, the Potomac River ranks as the fourth longest river on the East Coast. The river also serves as a natural state border, forming part of the boundary between Maryland and West Virginia and separating Virginia from both Maryland and DC. The site of many significant battles during the American Revolution and the Civil War, the Potomac now holds an eternal place in the US history books and has earned the moniker "The Nation's River." A combination of urban sewage and run-off from mining projects upstream seriously degraded the river's water quality, but efforts by the government and citizens have made the water safe for boats and some fishing. In the summertime, motor boat enthusiasts anchor north of Key Bridge for tubing, swimming, and relaxing.

The Mariner Sailing School (703-768-0018) gives lessons and rents canoes, kayaks, and sailboats for two to six people. If a paddleboat ride is worth worming your way through swarms of sweaty tourists, the Tidal Basin is the best place to go. The boathouse, which sits among the famous cherry blossoms and tulip-bearing flower beds on the man-made inlet, rents paddleboats by the hour (202-479-2426). Two-person boats cost $12 per hour; four-person boats cost $19 per hour. If kayaking or sculling is your thing, head to Georgetown and Thompson Boat Center, which rents canoes and sailboats as well.

Sailing/Boating Centers		Phone	Map	URL
Capitol Sailboat Club	James Creek Marina, Washington, DC	202-265-3052	6	www.capitolsbc.com
DC Sail	600 Water St, Washington, DC	202-309-1115	6	www.dcsail.org
Tidal Basin Boat House	1501 Main Ave SW, Washington, DC	202-479-2426	6	www.tidalbasinpeddleboats.com
Mariner Sailing School	Belle Haven Marina, Alexandria, VA	703-768-0018	N/A	www.saildc.com
Thompson Boat Center	2900 Virginia Ave NW, Washington, DC	202-333-9543	7	www.thompsonboatcenter.com

Rowing Clubs	Address	Phone	Map	URL
Capitol Rowing Club	1115 O St SE, Washington, DC	202-289-6666	5	www.capitalrowing.org
Potomac Boat Club	3530 Water St NW, Washington, DC	202-333-9737	8	www.potomacboatclub.com
Canoe Cruisers Association	11301 Rockville Pike, Kensington, MD	301-251-2978	N/A	www.ccadc.org

Golf

Like everything else in DC, there are politics and networking involved in where you choose to tee off. Our advice—avoid the pricey rat race at the private clubs and reserve a tee time at one of the many less stuffy, and often more fun, public courses.

East Potomac Park (Map 6) offers three different course options (Red, White, and Blue, of course) as well as mini golf and a driving range. The **Langston Golf Course (Map 12)** is closest to downtown DC, making it easy to hit during lunch. The **Rock Creek Golf Course (Map 27)** can sometimes suffer from droughts and heavy play, but its great location keeps people happily putting away.

Golf Courses	Address	Phone	Fees	Type	Map
East Potomac	972 Ohio Dr SW	202-554-7660	Weekdays $12 / Weekends $19	Holes-18, Par 72; Also two 9-hole Par-3 courses	6
Langston	28th & Benning Rds NE	202-397-8638	Weekdays $21.50/ Weekends $26.50	Holes-18, Par-72	12
Sligo Creek Golf Course	9701 Sligo Creek Pkwy	301-585-6006	Weekdays $13–15/ Weekends $18	Holes-9, Par-35	25
Rock Creek Golf Course	16th & Rittenhouse NW	202-882-7332	Weekdays $19/ Weekends $24	Holes-18, Par-65	27
Greendale Golf Course	6700 Telegraph Rd, Alexandria	703-971-6170	Weekdays $18/ Weekends $22	Holes-18, Par-70	n/a
Hilltop Golf Club	7900 Telegraph Rd, Alexandria	703-719-6504	Weekdays $20/ Weekends $32	Holes-9, Par-31	n/a
Pinecrest Golf Course	6600 Little River Tpke, Alexandria	703-941-1061	Weekdays $16/ Weekends $20	Holes-9, Par-35	n/a

Driving Ranges	Address	Phone	Fees	Map
East Potomac	972 Ohio Dr SW	202-554-7660	$5.50/ 50 balls	6
Langston	28th & Benning Rds NE	202-397-8638	$4.50/45 balls	12

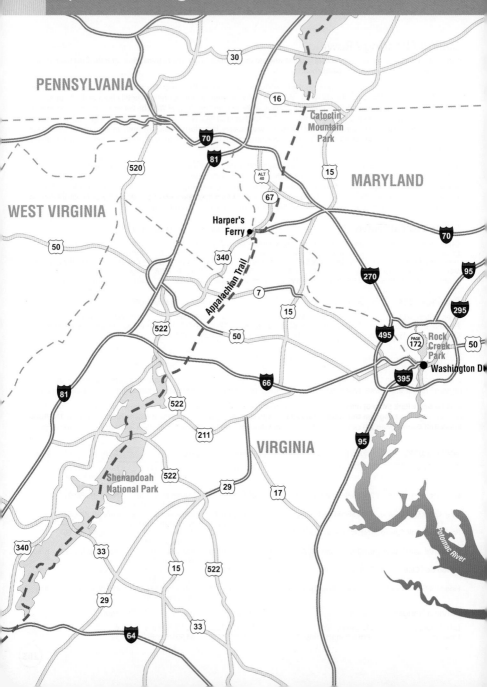

PENNSYLVANIA

30

16

Catoctin
Mountain
Park

70

81

520

ALT
40

15

MARYLAND

67

70

WEST VIRGINIA

Harper's
Ferry

340

270

95

50

Appalachian Trail

7

15

295

522

50

495

PAGE
172

Rock
Creek
Park

50

81

522

66

395

Washington D

211

VIRGINIA

95

Shenandoah
National Park

522

29

17

340

33

Potomac River

15

522

29

33

64

Overview

One of the greatest things about living in DC, a city bursting with hyper, Type-A personalities, is how easy it is to leave. The feasibility of escaping urban life for a weekend, or even just an afternoon, checks and balances the go-getting lobbying/lawyering/liaising frenzy that often seems to permeate Our Nation's Capital to the core. Rock Creek Park weaves its way through the city, and some of the best hiking routes on the east coast are just a short drive from town. The National Parks Service website is a valuable resource for planning overnight trips or day hikes (www.nps.gov), and we recommend the gem 60 Hikes within 60 Miles: Washington, DC by Paul Elliott (Menasha Ridge Press).

Shenandoah National Park

A short drive out of DC, this is one of the country's most popular national parks, mainly because of gorgeous Skyline Drive, which runs across the ridgeline of the Blue Ridge Mountains (the eastern range of the Appalachian Trail). But locals know to ditch the wheels, get out, and get dirty. There are more than 500 miles of trails in the park, including about 100 miles of the AT itself. In short, you can plan a weeklong backcountry getaway, and there'll still be more undiscovered country to come back for next time.

The Old Rag Trail, with its rock scramble and distinctive profile, is a favorite strenuous day hike. The rangers at the visitors' center will direct you to the toughest climbs, easier routes, the waterfall hikes, or the trails where you'll most likely see bears. The park is 70 miles west of DC. Take Route 66 W to Exit 13, and follow signs to Front Royal. www.nps.gov/shen; 540-999-3500.

Appalachian Trail

Forget what you've heard about lugging a summer's worth of misery along this Georgia-to-Maine trace. You don't have to hike the whole thing. Luckily, a good portion of this nationally protected 2,184-mile footpath through the Appalachian Mountains is accessible from DC. Hook up with it for a few miles at points in Maryland and Virginia, and acquire bragging rights with just a day's worth of blister-inducing pain. A good place to start is Harper's Ferry in Maryland, 65 miles from DC, where you can load up on breakfast and some history before you head out. When you return, hoist a well-deserved pint. www.nps.gov/appa; 301-535-6278.

Catoctin Mountains

While Catoctin Mountain recreation area was created in order to provide a place for federal employees to get a little bit of R&R, it has since been converted into Camp David, the famously inaccessible presidential retreat. Camp David is never open to the public, or to run-of-the-mill federal employees, but there's still the eastern hardwood forest where everyone is free to roam wild.

From DC, the Catoctin Mountains are about a two-hour drive north. Take the George Washington Memorial Parkway north to the Beltway to I-270 N. Drive 27 miles to Frederick, MD. Take Route 15 N to Route 77 W, to the Catoctin Mountain Park exit. Drive three miles west on 77, turn right onto Park Central Road, and the Visitor Center will be on the right. www.nps.gov/cato; 301-663-9388.

Sugarloaf Mountain

Sugarloaf's main appeal is that it's only an hour drive from DC. It's a modest mountain—about 1,300 feet—with nice views of the surrounding farmland, and entry into the park is free. You can choose a variety of easy and not-so-easy ways to get up the mountain, but no matter which way you choose you'll be surrounded by an impressive collection of rare red and white oak trees. To get there, drive North on Route I-270 to the Hyattstown exit, circle under I-270, and continue on Route 109 to Comus, then make a right on Comus Road to the Stronghold entrance. Or if you're looking for a beautiful Sunday drive, take the backroads: River Road is a leafy country road that hugs the Potomac from upper NW into the Maryland farmlands. www.sugarloafmd.com; 301-869-7846.

Rock Creek Park

This is the place for a quick nature fix. The historic 1,754-acre park, which reaches from Georgetown to Maryland, is laced with several hiking trails, especially in its northern reaches. The major trails along the western ridge are marked by green blazes, and the footpaths along the east side are marked with blue blazes. A tan-blazed trail connects the two trail systems. None of the trails are strenuous, but there will be moments when you can hardly believe people are outsourcing contracts and scheduling Outlook appointments only a stone's throw away. For the full effect, turn off your cell phone. See the extensive Rock Creek Park section in this book for more details. www.nps.gov/rocr; 202-895-6070.

C&O Canal

Don't think the C&O Canal towpath is just for bikers. The relatively level terrain of this 184.5-mile, Georgetown-to-Cumberland trail makes for great hiking. The entire length is dotted with scenic vistas of the Potomac that offer gentler, more natural views of the river than you're afforded when stuck in traffic on a bridge between DC and northern Virginia. History abounds along the route in the form of Civil War sites and both reconstructed and ramshackle lockhouses. Once you pass Great Falls, there are free campsites spread every five miles or so. They're simple setups of a fire pit, picnic table, water pump, and portable toilet, but after a hard day's hike they seem like the lap of luxury. For more information, visit www.nps.gov/choh or call 202-653-5190.

One of the few times it pays to be a DC resident (as opposed to a MD or VA one) is when it comes to the pool: DC residents can dip for free. Non-residents pay $3–4 (based on age) for a single admission, or can opt for a 30 or 90 day passes for greater savings. The following fees for public pools are based on county residency. Non-residents can count on paying a buck or two more.

All DC outdoor pools are open daily from June 25, with many opening from Memorial Day onwards with weekend hours. They generally close in late August or early September, on or around Labor Day. Specifics for each neighborhood pool can be found at http://app.dpr.dc.gov/dprmap/index.asp. Many of the public pools require you to register as a member at the beginning of the season and, since most fill their membership quotas quickly, it's wise to locate your nearest pool and join at the beginning of the season. You'll thank yourself on DC's dog days, when the humid air itself seems to be sweating. And speaking of dogs, they'll be thankful, too, on "Doggy Day Swim" days. DC is also home to several "spray parks," which are basically playgrounds with fountains scattered throughout. They're supposed to be for kids, but who doesn't love giant sprinkler systems?

Pools	Address	Phone	Fees	Type	Map
William Rumsey Aquatic Center	635 North Carolina Ave SE	202-724-4495	Residents free, various fees & passes for non-residents	Indoor	3
Rosedale Pool	17th St NE & Gales St NE	202-727-1502	Residents free, various fees & passes for non-residents	Outdoor	4
Barry Farm Pool	1223 Sumner Rd SE	202-645-5040	Residents free, various fees & passes for non-residents	Outdoor	5
Lincoln Capper Pool	500 L St SE	202-727-1080	Residents free, various fees & passes for non-residents	Kid's pool	5
Watkins	420 12th St SE	202-727-1504	Residents free, various fees & passes for non-residents	Outdoor	5
East Potomac	972 Ohio Dr SW	202-554-7660	Weekdays $12 / Weekends $19	Outdoor	6
Randall Pool	S Capitol St SW & I St SW	202-727-1420	Residents free, various fees & passes for non-residents	Outdoor	6
Fairmont	2401 M St NW	202-457-5070	Members and hotel guests only. Various membership fees.	Indoor	9
YMCA National Capital	1711 Rhode Island Ave NW	202-862-9622	$100 joining fee, $70 per month	Indoor	9
YMCA	1325 W St NW	202-462-1054	$50 to join, $35 per month	Indoor	10
Dunbar Pool	1301 New Jersey Ave NW	202-673-4316	Residents free, various fees & passses for non-residents	Indoor	11
Harry Thomas Sr Pool	1801 Lincoln Rd NE	202-576-5640	Residents free, various fees & passes for non-residents	Outdoor	11
Trinidad Recreation Center	1310 Childress St NW	202-727-1503	Children six and under swim ree, kids ages 6-17 $3 per day, $46 season pass	Kid's pool	12
Fort Lincoln Outdoor Pool	3201 Ft Lincoln Dr NE	202-576-6389	$4 per day, $130 season pass	Outdoor	13
Langdon Park Pool	Mills Ave & Hamlin St NE	202-576-8655	Residents free, various fees & passes for non-residents	Outdoor	13
Turkey Thicket Community Center	1100 Michigan Ave NE	202-635-6226	Residents free, various fees & passses for non-residents	Indoor	14
Banneker Pool	2500 Georgia Ave NW	202-673-2121	Residents free, various fees & passes for non-residents	Outdoor	15
Parkview Pool	639 Otis Pl NW	202-576-8658	Children six and under swim free, kids ages 6-17 $3 per day, $46 season pass	Kid's pool	15
Sport & Health Clubs	4000 Wisconsin Ave NW	202-362-8000	$20 per day, $100 per month membership	Indoor	19
Wilson Aquatic Center	Ford Dr & Albemarle St NW	202-282-2216	Residents free, various fees & passses for non-residents	Indoor	19

Pools—continued	Address	Phone	Fees	Type	Map
Upshur Outdoor Pool	14th St & Arkansas Ave NW	202-576-8661	Residents free, various fees & passses for non-residents	Outdoor	21
Bethesda YMCA	9401 Old Georgetown Rd	301-530-3725	joining fee $100, $74 per month	Indoor	22
YMCA	9800 Hastings Dr	301-585-2120	$100 joining fee, $64/month	Indoor / Outdoor	25
Piney Branch Pool	7510 Maple Ave	301-270-6093	$5 per day	Indoor	26
Takoma Outdoor Pool	300 Van Buren St NW	202-576-8660	Residents free, various fees & passes for non-residents	Outdoor	27
Sport & Health Club	4400 Montgomery Ave	301-656-9570	$25 per day ($15 per day with a member)	Indoor	29
Bethesda Outdoor Pool	Little Falls Dr	301-652-1598	$5.50 per day, $160 for year pass	Outdoor	30
Upton Hill Regional Park	6060 Wilson Blvd	703-534-3437	$5.25 per day, $72 season pass	Outdoor	33
Yorktown Swimming Pool	5201 28th St N	703-536-9739	$4 per day, $230 per year	Indoor	33
Washington-Lee Swimming Pool	1300 N Quincy St	703-228-6262	$4 per day, $230 per year	Indoor	34
YMCA Arlington	3422 N 13th St	703-525-5420	$100 joining fee, $48/month	Outdoor	35
Wakefield Swimming Pool	4901 S Chesterfield Rd	703-578-3063	$4 per day, $230 per year	Indoor	38
Chinquapin Park Rec Center	3210 King St	703-519-2160	$5 per day, $46 per month	Indoor	42
Alexandria YMCA	420 Monroe Ave	703-838-8085	$15 per day, $69 per month membership, $100 joining fee	Indoor	43
Warwick Pool	3301 Landover St	703-838-4672	$2 per day	Outdoor	43
Old Town Pool	1609 Cameron St	703-838-4671	$2 per day	Outdoor	44

Spray Parks	Address	Phone	Hours
Bald Eagle Recreation Center	100 Joliet St SW	202-645-3960	Mon–Fri, 11 am–7 pm Sat, 11 am–4 pm Sun, 10 am–2 pm
Benning Stoddert Community Center	100 Stoddert Pl SE	202-698-1873	Mon–Fri, 11 am–7 pm Sat, 11 am–4 pm
Columbia Heights Community Center	1480 Girard St NW	202-671-0373	Mon–Fri, 11 am–7 pm Sat,11 am–4 p Sun, 10 am–2 pm
Friendship Recreation Center	4500 Van Ness St NW	202-282-2198	Mon–Fri, 11 am–7 pm Sat, 11 am–4 pm
Lafayette Recreation Center	5900 33rd St NW	202-282-2206	Mon–Fri, 11 am–7 pm Sat, 11 am–4 pm
Palisades Community Center	5200 Sherrier Pl NW	202-282-2186	Mon–Fri, 11 am–7 pm Sat, 11 am–4 pm Sun, 10 am–2 pm
Petworth Recreation Center	801 Taylor St NW	202-576-6850	Mon–Fri, 11 am–7 pm Sat, 11 am–4 pm
Riggs LaSalle Community Center	501 Riggs Rd NE	202-576-6045	Mon–Fri, 11 am–7 pm Sat, 11 am–4 pm Sun, 10 am–2 pm

Sports · **Tennis**

Tennis

National Park Service: 202-208-6843, www.nps.gov
Washington, DC Department of Parks and Recreation: 202-673-7647, www.dpr.dc.gov

Public Courts at Community Recreation Centers

DC residents and visitors can play tennis at any of the public courts scattered throughout the city. All courts are available on a first-come, first-served basis. An honor code trusts that players won't hog the courts for over an hour of play-time (although you can call the Department of Parks and Recreation to obtain a permit for extended use). For more information about lessons and tournaments, visit the Athletic Programs site at dc.gov/DC/DPR/Facilities+and+Permits/Recreation+Facilities#2.

Tennis	Address	Phone	Fees	Map
South Grounds	15th St & Constitution Ave	202-698-2250	Public	1
Langston	26th St & Benning Rd NE	202-698-2250	Public	4
Rosedale	17th St NE & Gale St NE	202-698-2250	Public	4
Barry Farm	1230 Sumner Rd SE	202-698-2250	Public	5
East Potomac Tennis Center	1090 Ohio Dr SW	202-554-5962	Private	6
Jefferson	8th St SW & H St SW	202-698-2250	Public	6
King-Greenleaf	201 N St SW	202-698-2250	Public	6
Randall	1st St & I St SW	202-698-2250	Public	6
Georgetown	33rd St & Volta Pl	202-698-2250	Public	8
Montrose Park	30th St NW & R St NW	202-698-2250	Public	8
Rose Park	26th St NW & O St NW	202-698-2250	Public	8
Francis	24th St NW & N St NW	202-698-2250	Public	9
Reed	18th St NW & California St NW	202-698-2250	Public	9
Washington Hilton Sport Club	1919 Connecticut Ave NW	202-483-4100	Private	9
Shaw	10th St & Rhode Island Ave NW	202-698-2250	Public	10
Brentwood Park	6th St & Brentwood Pkwy NE	202-698-2250	Public	11
Dunbar	1st NW & O St NW	202-698-2250	Public	11
Edgewood	3rd St NE & Evart St NE	202-698-2250	Public	11
Harry Thomas Sr	Lincoln Rd & T St NE	202-698-2250	Public	11
Arboretum	24th St & Rand Pl NE	202-698-2250	Public	12
Fort Lincoln	Ft Lincoln Dr NE	202-698-2250	Public	13
Langdon Park	20th & Franklin Sts NE	202-698-2250	Public	13
Taft	19th St NE & Otis St NE	202-698-2250	Public	13
Backus	South Dakota Ave & Hamilton St NE	202-698-2250	Public	14
Turkey Thicket	1100 Michigan Ave NE	202-698-2251	Public	14
Banneker	9th St NW & Euclid St NW	202-698-2250	Public	15
Raymond	10th St & Spring Rd NW	202-698-2250	Public	15
Hardy	45th St NW & Q St NW	202-698-2250	Public	18
Newark	39th St NW & Newark St NW	202-698-2251	Public	18
Fort Reno	41st St NW & Chesapeake St NW	202-698-2250	Public	19
Friendship	4500 Van Ness St NW	202-698-2250	Public	19
Hearst	37th St NW & Tilden St NW	202-698-2250	Public	19
Forest Hills	32nd St NW & Brandywine St NW	202-698-2250	Public	20
Rock Creek Tennis Center	16th St NW & Kennedy St NW	202-722-5949	Public	21
Fort Stevens	1327 Van Buren St NW	202-698-2250	Public	27
Takoma	3rd St NW & Van Buren St NW	202-698-2250	Public	27
Chevy Chase	4101 Livingston St NW	202-698-2250	Public	28
Lafayette	33rd St NW & Quesada St NW	202-698-2250	Public	28
Bethesda Sport & Health Club	4400 Montgomery Ave	301-656-9570	Public	29
Palisades	5200 Sherrier Pl NW	202-698-2250	Public	32
Arlington Y Tennis & Squash Club	3400 N 13th St	703-749-8057	Private	35

Billiards	Address	Phone	Fees	Map
Buffalo Billiards	1330 19th St NW	202-331-7665	$12/hour	9
East Eddie's Sports & Billiards	1520 K St NW	202-638-6800	$10/hour	9
Angles Bar And Billiards	2339 18th St NW	202-462-8100	$1.25/game	16
Bedrock Billiards	1841 Columbia Rd NW	202-667-7665	$12/hour	16
Atomic Billiards	3427 Connecticut Ave NW	202-363-7665	$12/hour	17

Bowling

Sadly, bowling isn't exactly experiencing a hey-day in the DC metro area. If you're looking strictly within District lines, options are limited, especially if it's a smoking-only, mullets-abounding, Roseanne-style spot you're looking for, complete with ancient computer graphics on the score-keeping screens and a horrendous mix of music blaring over the sound system. For authentic bowling such as this, you'll have to hop in your car and cross county lines. Within DC, there's **Lucky Strike (Map 2)** for button-down shirt, black pants, bowling for the Penn Quarter crowd that will wipe out your wallet in a few short hours. Alleys like Lucky Strike and **Strike Bethesda (Map 29)** taught us that clubs aren't the only places where you can sip cleverly named cocktails and dole out phone numbers. Whether a rundown bowling alley in the 'burbs or a swanky clublike alley closer in, most area bowling alleys seem to offer up the same four wonderful B's: Bowling, Beer, Blacklights, and Beyoncé. After dark, the lights go down and the beats go up, with special "Cosmic Bowling" or "Xtreme Bowling" nights. When the DJ arrives, you can bet on the bowling fees rising accordingly with the volume of the dance traxxx.

Sunday nights are the best nights to bowl if you're looking to save money, as many alleys offer unlimited bowling after 9 pm for under $15. Show some Maryland pride, and play duckpin bowling (the sport actually originated in Baltimore) at **White Oak Bowling Lanes (11206 New Hampshire Ave, Silver Spring)** and **AMF College Park (9021 Baltimore Ave, College Park),** home to the Men's Duckpin Pro Bowlers' Association Master Tournament.

Bowling	Address	Phone	Fees	Map
Lucky Strike Lanes	701 7th St NW	202-347-1021	$5.95 per game, $3.95 for shoes	2
Bowlmor	5353 Westbard Ave	301-652-0955	$5.45–6.25 per game, $4 for shoes	29
US Bowling	100 S Pickett St	703-370-5910	$3–4.25 per game, $3.50 for shoes	41
Alexandria Bowling Center	6228A N Kings Hwy, Alexandria, VA	703-765-3633	$3.50–5 per game, $4.46 for shoes	n/a
AMF College Park	9021 Baltimore Ave, College Park, MD	301-474-8282	$4.25 per game, $4.65 for shoes	n/a
AMF Shady Grove Lanes	15720 Shady Grove Rd, Gaithersburg, MD	301-948-1390	$5–8 per game, $5 for shoes	n/a
Annandale Bowl	4245 Markham St	703-256-2211	$4.50 per game, $4.46 for shoes	n/a
Bowl America	6450 Edsall Rd, Alexandria, VA	703-354-3300	$2–5 per game, $3.40 for shoes	n/a
Bowl America - Chantilly	4525 Stonecroft Blvd, Chantilly, VA	703-830-2695	$2–5 per game, $3.40 for shoes	n/a
Bowl America - Fairfax	9699 Lee Hwy, Fairfax, VA	703-273-7700	$2–5.25 per game, $3.40 for shoes	n/a
White Oak Lanes	11207 New Hampshire Ave	301-593-3000	$3 per game, $3.50 for shoes	n/a

Yoga

Yoga	Address	Phone	URL	Map
Dahn Yoga Center	700 14th St NW	202-393-2440	www.dahnyoga.com	1
Bikram Yoga Center	410 H St NE	202-256-9156	www.bikramyoga capitolhill.com	3
Capitol Hill Yoga	221 5th St NE	202-544-0011	www.capitolhillyoga.com	3
St Mark's Yoga Center	301 A St SE	202-546-4964	www.stmarks.net	3
Dahn Yoga Center	3106 M St NW	202-298-3246	www.dahnyoga.com	8
Down Dog Yoga	1046 Potomac St NW	202-965-9642	www.downdogyoga.com	8
Georgetown Yoga	1053 31st St NW	202-342-7779	www.georgetownyoga.com	8
Spiral Flight Yoga	1826 Wisconsin Ave NW	202-965-1645	www.spiralflightyoga.com	8
Bikram Yoga Center	1635 Connecticut Ave NW	202-332-8680	www.bikramyogadc.com	9
Boundless Yoga	1522 U St NW	202-234-9642	www.boundlessyoga.com	9
DC Yoga	1635 Connecticut Ave NW	202-232-2926	www.dcyoga.com	9
Joy of Motion Dance	1643 Connecticut Ave NW	202-387-0911	www.joyofmotion.org	9
Tranquil Space Yoga	2024 P St NW	202-223-9642	www.tranquilspace.com	9
Evolution	1224 M St NW	202-347-2250	www.evolutiondc.com	10
Flow Yoga Center	1450 P St NW	202-462-3569	www.flowyogacenter.com	10
Yoga House	3634 Georgia Ave NW	202-285-1316	www.yogahousestudio.com	15
18th and Yoga	1115 U St NW	202-462-1800	www.18thandyoga.com	16
Into Afrika	1316 Adams St NE	202-797-9127	www.intoafrika.org	16
Unity Woods Yoga Center	2639 Connecticut Ave NW	202-232-9642	www.unitywoods.com	17
Hot Yoga	3408 Wisconsin Ave NW	202-468-9642	www.hotyogausa.com	18
Ashtanga Yoga Center	4435 Wisconsin Ave NW	202-342-6029	www.ashtangayogadc.com	19
Birkram's Yoga College	4908 Wisconsin Ave NW	202-243-3000	www.bikramyoga.com	19
Joy of Motion Dance	5207 Wisconsin Ave NW	202-362-3042	www.joyofmotion.org	19
Unity Woods Yoga Center	4201 Albemarle St NW	301-656-8992	www.unitywoods.com	19
Unity Woods Yoga Center	4321 Wisconsin Ave NW	301-656-8992	www.unitywoods.com	19
Bodywisdom	3701 Connecticut Ave NW	202-966-6113	n/a	20
Dahn Yoga Center	5010 Connecticut Ave NW	202-237-9642	www.dahnyoga.com	20
Balance Pilates and Yoga Studio	4719 Rosedale Ave	301-986-1730	www.balancestudio.com	22
Dahn Yoga Center	7849 Old Georgetown Rd	301-907-6520	www.dahnyoga.com	22
Unity Woods Yoga Center	4853 Cordell Ave	301-656-8992	www.unitywoods.com	22
Yoga Tales	8020 Norfolk Ave	301-951-9642	www.yogatales.com	22
Circle Yoga and Budding Yogis	3838 Northampton St NW	202-686-1104	www.buddingyogis.com	28
Fit, Inc	4963 Elm St	301-565-0885	www.robertshermansfit.com	29
Joy of Motion Dance	7315 Wisconsin Ave	301-387-0911	www.joyofmotion.org	29
Royal Fitness and Nutrician	4550 Montgomery Ave	301-961-0400	www.royfit.com	29
Try Yoga	4609 Willow Ln	240-888-9642	www.tryyoga.com	29
Unity Woods Yoga Center	4001 9th St N	301-656-8992	www.unitywoods.com	34
Sun and Moon Yoga Studio	3811 Lee Hwy	703-525-9642	www.sunandmoonstudio.com	35
Dahn Yoga Center	1630 King St	703-684-7717	www.dahnyoga.com	44

General Information

Washington Area Bicyclist Association:
www.waba.org
Bike Washington: www.bikewashington.org
Bike the Sites Bicycle Tours: www.bikethesites.com
C&O Canal Towpath: www.nps.gov/choh
Capital Bikeshare: www.capitalbikeshare.com
Capital Crescent Trail: www.cctrail.org
Mount Vernon Trail: www.nps.gov/gwmp/plan
yourvisit/mtvernontrail.htm
W&OD Trail: www.wodfriends.org

Overview

A bike in DC is as necessary as a political affiliation. The city tries to satisfy the needs of its mountain and road bikers alike with plenty of multi-terrain trails, a few good urban commuting routes, and one massive citywide bike ride in the fall. When it comes to bikes onboard mass transit, the Metrobus and Metrorail have lenient policies that also help when a bike route, or your energy, dead-ends. And now, thanks to Capital Bikeshare, an outfit that allows patrons to rent bikes right off the street, it's easier than ever to get some wheels and go!

If you're new to biking in DC, be prepared for a few wrong turns and missed trail entrances. Figuring out how various trails connect (or how to safely and easily cut through neighborhoods to move from one trail to the other) can take some time and trial and error, but the rewards are well worth it. Consult the above sites for pointers, seek out other bicyclists, and have fun!

And while commuting by bike is doable, it can get rather dicey. Bike lanes don't really exist in much of DC, and state law mandates that cyclists have to follow traffic laws—so plan on mixing it up with the cars on your way to work. Even though DC residents are an honest bunch, it's a good idea to keep your bike locked whenever it's out of your sight. A U-Lock is a necessity. For more information regarding bicycle commuting, check out the Washington Area Bicyclist Association website. The site also provides information about the annual "Bike DC."

Bike Trails

The **Chesapeake and Ohio (C&O) Canal** is probably the city's most popular bike route. The trail spans over 184 miles, and most of it is unpaved, so it's not a trail for the weak of butt. The trail begins in Georgetown and follows the route of the Potomac River from DC to Cumberland, Maryland. Biking is permitted only on the towpath. Campsites are located from Swains Lock to Seneca for bikers undertaking multi-day journeys. But be warned: because the first 20 miles are the most heavily used, conditions within the Beltway are significantly better than those outside of it. The towpath sometimes floods, so it's best to check the website, www.nps.gov/choh, for possible closures before breaking out the wheels.

The **Capital Crescent Trail** is a "rail trail"—a bike trail converted from abandoned or unused railroad tracks. The trail spans 11 miles between Georgetown and Silver Spring, Maryland. On the trail's first seven miles, from Georgetown to Bethesda, you'll encounter gentle terrain and ten foot-wide asphalt paths. On weekdays, the trail is used predominantly by commuters, and on weekends it gets crowded with recreational cyclists, rollerbladers, joggers, and dogs. Check out www.cctrail.org.

The **Mount Vernon Trail** offers a wide range of scenic views of the Potomac River and national monuments to ensure an inspiring and patriotic ride. The 18.5-mile trail stretches from Roosevelt Island through Old Town Alexandria to George Washington's house in Mount Vernon. To find out more about these and other bike trails, check out the Bike Washington web site.

The **Washington and Old Dominion (W&OD) Trail** is a highly popular paved trail that traverses the 45 miles between Arlington's Shirlington area and Purcellville, Virginia, in Loudoun County. Among the communities it passes through are Falls Church and Leesburg.

The four-mile **Custis Trail** begins in Rosslyn and parallels I-66; it serves to connect the W&OD Trail with other bike trails in the Washington area. Be ready for some inclines and curvy sections on the narrow Custis, and also be wary of bikers who may be traveling faster or slower. For more info, see both the Bike Washington site and the one maintained by The Friends of the Washington & Old Dominion Trail (www.wodfriends.org).

Bikes and Mass Transit

If you need a break while riding in the city, you can hop off your bike and take it on a bus or on Metrorail for free. All DC buses are equipped with racks to carry up to two bikes per bus. You can also ride the Metrorail with your wheels on weekends, and during non-rush hour times on weekdays (that means no bikes 7 am–10 am and 4 pm–7 pm). Also be sure to use elevators when accessing the Metrorail—blocking the stairs and escalators with your bulky bike makes officials and non-biking commuters testy.

Bike Shops

- **A&A Discount Bicycles** (sales, repair, and rental) • 1034 33rd St NW • 202-337-0254 • Map 18
- **Better Bikes** (rental and delivery) • 202-293-2080 • www.betterbikesinc.com
- **Bicycle Pro Shop** (sales, repair, and rental) • 3403 M St NW • 202-337-0311 • www.bicycleproshop.com • Map 18
- **Big Wheel Bikes** (sales, repair, and rental) • 1034 33rd St NW • 202-337-0254 • www.bigwheelbikes.com • Map 18
- **Capital Bike Share** (rentals) • 877-430-2453 • www.capitalbikeshare.com
- **Capitol Hill Bikes** (sales, repair, and rental) • 709 8th St SE • 202-544-4234 • www.capitolhillbikes.com • Map 5
- **City Bikes** (sales, repair, and rental) • 2501 Champlain St NW • 202-265-1564 • www.citybikes.com • Map 16
- **District Hardware/The Bike Shop** (sales and repair) • 2003 P St NW • 202-659-8686 • Map 9
- **Hudson Trail Outfitters** (sales and repair) • 4530 Wisconsin Ave NW • 202-363-9810 • Map 19
- **Revolution Cycles** (sales, repair, and rental) • 3411 M St NW • 202-965-3601 • www.revolutioncycles.com • Map 18

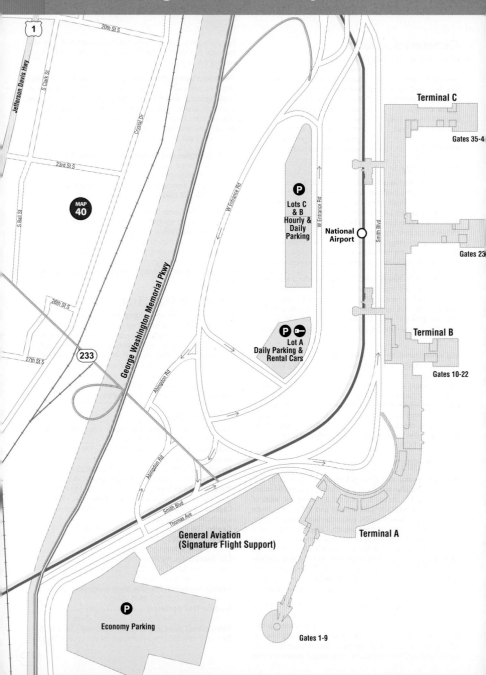

General Information

Phone: 703-417-8000
Lost & Found: 703-417-0673
Parking: 703-417-7275
Website: www.metwashairports.com/reagan/
reagan.htm

Overview

Ronald Reagan Washington National Airport (or National, to DC locals) is a small, easy-to-navigate airport located practically downtown, perfect for business travelers and politicians alike. It's also the only airport in the greater metropolitan area directly accessible by Metro. But alas, for those of us not on expense accounts or the public dole, prices can be prohibitive. If you want a discounted direct flight to Madagascar or enjoy flying on the cattle cars that charge $15 for a roundtrip to Aruba, you'll have to fly from Dulles or BWI. National is too small to host many planes or airlines, making it a short-haul airport with direct connections to cities typically no more than 1,250 miles away.

How to Get There—Driving

From DC, take I-395 S to Exit 10 ("Reagan National Airport/ Mount Vernon"). Get on the GW Parkway S, and take the Reagan Airport exit. If you're in Virginia heading north on I-395, ignore the first exit you see for the airport (Exit 8C/"to US 1/Crystal City/ Pentagon City/Reagan National Airport") and continue on to Exit 10 S. It's quicker and easier. Remember to watch out for Officer Friendly and his trusty radar gun as you enter the airport property.

Parking

Parking at Reagan is not cheap. Rates for Hourly Garages (A, B, and C) are $5 per hour (or fraction of) with a $34 maximum for 24 hours. The three Daily Garages (A, B, and C) cost $22 for 24 hours, or $5 per hour (or fraction of). The terminals are an easy walk from Garages A, B, and C and can be accessed through enclosed or underground walkways. If you're heading out for a few days, we suggest you park in the economy lot for only $14 per day. Shuttle buses run between the economy lot and garages to all terminals.

How to Get There—Mass Transit

The Blue and Yellow Lines have a Metrorail stop adjacent to Terminals B and C. If you're headed to Terminal A, a free shuttle bus will run you there or you can lug your bags on a ten-minute walk. Metro buses are also available from the base of the Metrorail station for areas not served by the rail.

How to Get There— Ground Transportation

SuperShuttle offers door-to-door served to DCA as long as you call 24 hours in advance. They also have a shuttle that goes regularly between DCA and Union Station. Call the reservation line on 800-BLUEVAN or go to www.supershuttle.com to book online. A cab ride to downtown DC will set you back less than $15. DC, Virginia, and Maryland taxis are available at the exits of each terminal. Red Top Cab - Arlington: 703-522-3333; Yellow Cab - DC: 202-TAXI-CAB; Yellow Cab - Arlington: 703-534-1111. And if you're feeling a bit flashy, stretch limousines and executive-class sedans start at approximately $35 for downtown Washington. Airport Access: 202-498-8708; Airport Connection: 202-393-2110; Roadmaster: 800-283-5634; Silver Car: 410-992-7775.

Rental Cars—On-Airport (Garage A)

Alamo • 800-462-5266   **Dollar** • 800-800-4000
Avis • 800-331-1212   **Enterprise** • 800-736-8222
Budget • 800-527-0700   **National** • 800-227-7368

Off-Airport

Advantage • 800-777-5500   **Enterprise** • 800-736-8222
Dollar • 800-800-4000

Hotels—Arlington

Crowne Plaza •1480 Crystal Dr • 703-416-1600
Crystal City Marriott • 1999 Jefferson Davis Hwy • 703-413-5500
Crystal City Courtyard by Marriott • 2899 Jefferson Davis Hwy • 703-549-3434
Crystal Gateway Marriott • 1700 Jefferson Davis Hwy • 703-920-3230
Radisson Inn • 2020 Jefferson Davis Hwy • 703-920-8600
Doubletree Crystal City • 300 Army Navy Dr • 703-416-4100
Econo Lodge • 6800 Lee Hwy • 703-538-5300
Embassy Suites • 1300 Jefferson Davis Hwy • 703-979-9799
Hilton • 2399 Jefferson Davis Hwy • 703-418-6800
Holiday Inn • 2650 Jefferson Davis Hwy • 703-684-7200
Hyatt Regency • 2799 Jefferson Davis Hwy • 703-418-1234
Ritz Carlton Pentagon City • 1250 S Hayes St • 703-415-5000
Residence Inn • 550 Army Navy Dr • 703-413-6630
Sheraton • 1800 Jefferson Davis Hwy • 703-486-1111

Hotels—Washington

Hamilton Crowne Plaza • 1001 14th & K Sts NW • 202-682-0111
Grand Hyatt • 1000 H St NW • 202-582-1234
Hilton Washington • 1919 Connecticut Ave NW • 202-483-3000
Hilton Embassy Row • 2015 Massachusetts Ave NW • 202-265-1600
Holiday Inn • 415 New Jersey Ave NW • 202-638-1616
Homewood Suites by Hilton • 1475 Massachusetts Ave NW • 202-265-8000
Hyatt Regency • 400 New Jersey Ave NW • 202-737-1234
Marriott Wardman Park • 2660 Woodley Rd NW • 202-328-2000
Red Roof Inn • 500 H St NW • 202-289-5959
Renaissance Mayflower Hotel • 1127 Connecticut Ave NW • 202-347-3000
Renaissance Washington DC • 999 9th St NW • 202-898-9000

Airline	Terminal	Airline	Terminal
Air Canada/Jazz	A	Southwest	A
Air Tran	A	Sun Country Airlines	A
Alaska	B	United Airlines	B
American Airlines	B	US Airways/Express/	C
Delta/Connection	B	/Shuttle	
Frontier	A	Virgin America	B
Jet Blue	A		

Transit · **Dulles International Airport (IAD)**

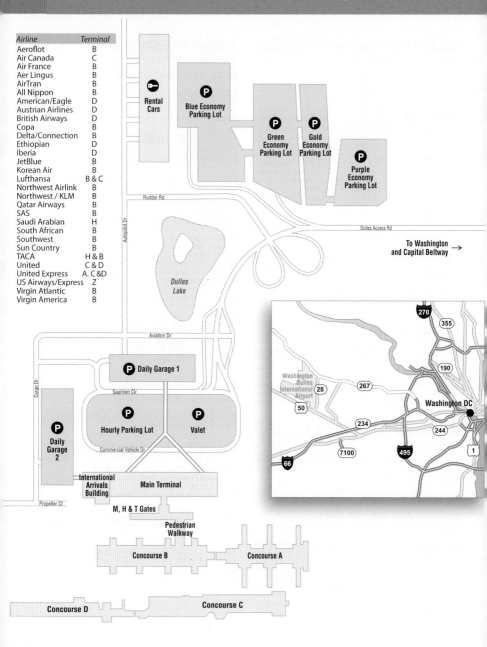

Airline	Terminal
Aeroflot	B
Air Canada	C
Air France	B
Aer Lingus	B
AirTran	B
All Nippon	B
American/Eagle	D
Austrian Airlines	D
British Airways	D
Copa	B
Delta/Connection	B
Ethiopian	D
Iberia	D
JetBlue	B
Korean Air	B
Lufthansa	B & C
Northwest Airlink	B
Northwest / KLM	B
Qatar Airways	B
SAS	B
Saudi Arabian	H
South African	B
Southwest	B
Sun Country	B
TACA	H & B
United	C & D
United Express	A. C&D
US Airways/Express	Z
Virgin Atlantic	B
Virgin America	B

Rental Cars

Blue Economy Parking Lot

Green Economy Parking Lot

Gold Economy Parking Lot

Purple Economy Parking Lot

Rudder Rd

Autopilot Dr

Dulles Access Rd

To Washington and Capital Beltway →

Dulles Lake

Aviation Dr

Daily Garage 1

Cargo Dr

Saarinen Cir

Hourly Parking Lot

Valet

Daily Garage 2

Commercial Vehicle Dr

Propeller Ct

International Arrivals Building

Main Terminal

M, H & T Gates

Pedestrian Walkway

Concourse B

Concourse A

Concourse D

Concourse C

270
355
190
28
267
Washington Dulles International Airport
50
Washington DC
234
244
66
7100
495
1

General Information

Address: 45020 Aviation Dr
Sterling, VA 20166 (not that you're going to send them anything, really)
Information: 703-572-2700
Parking: 703-572-4500
Lost & Found: 703-572-8479
Website: www.metwashairports.com/dulles/dulles.htm

Overview

The Mod Squad of airports, Dulles was born in 1958 when Finnish architect Eero Saarinen had a hankering to channel his training as a sculptor and create something groovy. His design for the terminal building and the control tower was so hip it received a First Honor Award from the American Institute of Architects in 1966. A distinctive swoosh roof over a squat building, Dulles still stands out as a stunning exhibit of modernist architecture and was the first airport in the US designed specifically for commercial jets. The "mobile lounges" that were formerly the only means of transportation between the the main terminal building and the outlying terminals were largely replaced recently by the much ballyhooed AeroTrain project, which finally made its debut in January of 2010. The stunningly old mobile lounges were considered debonair when they were engineered back in 1962, but the new Aerotrain leaves you asking "mobile what?" Sleek, shiny, and a heck of a lot less rickety, the $1.4 billion service transports passengers between the Main Terminal building and Concourses A, B and C. The Aerotrain, designed by Mitsubishi, uses rubber tires and guides large cars along a fixed underground guideway. In addition to looking pretty snazzy, the new system's trains run every two minutes, in stark contrast for the 15-minute-wait commuters spend in anticipating of the mobile lounges. But never fear, nostalgia junkies: You can still enjoy mobile lounges at the far end of Concourse A and D. In terms of ticket prices, BWI may have AirTran, but Dulles has Jet Blue and Southwest to help keep fares low, and starting in 2007, Virgin America began its attempts to hipsterize the flying experience. Note: "Washington" was officially added to the "Dulles International Airport" moniker after too many people inadvertently booked flights to Dallas, not Dulles, and vice-versa. No joke.

How to Get There—Driving

Most people get to Dulles the old fashioned way: they drive. To get to Washington Dulles Airport from downtown DC, drive west on I-66 to Exit 67. Follow signs to the airport. Be sure to use the Dulles Access Road, which avoids the tolls and traffic found on the parallel Dulles Toll Road (Rt. 267). But don't get cocky and try to use the Access Road to avoid tolls at other times—once you're on these access lanes, there's no exit until you reach the airport.

Since its inception a few years ago, the Cell Phone Waiting Area has been a smash hit. Circling around and around the airport like a hawk while waiting for friends and family to deboard and collect their baggage is blessedly a thing of the past. The waiting area is located at the intersection of Rudder Road and Autopilot Drive. Just follow the signs as you enter the airport grounds. It is free of charge and the maximum waiting time is one hour.

Parking

Hourly (short-term) parking is located in front of the terminal and costs $5 per hour and $36 per day. Daily parking is available for $4 per hour and $17 per day. There are shuttle buses and walkways (albeit lengthy ones from Garage 1) directly to the main terminal. Economist parking (long-term) is available in the four economy parking lots (Blue, Green, Gold, and Purple) located along Rudder Road. Economist parking costs $5 per hour and $10 per day. If you're short on time or energy and long on cash, valet parking is located in front of the terminal and costs $35 for the first 24 hours

and $25 per day thereafter. Parking in any lot for less than 20 minutes is free. Take your parking ticket with you as you can pay for your parking in the main terminal on your way out.

How to Get There—Mass Transit

The Metrorail doesn't go all the way to Dulles Airport...yet. The Silver Line is finally under construction, but until the dust settles you can take the Orange Line to West Falls Church Metro station and transfer to the Washington Flyer Coach service, which leaves every 30 minutes from the station. The coach fare costs $10 one-way ($18 round-trip), and the fare for the Metrorail leg will depend on exactly where you're coming from or headed to. A trip from West Falls Church to the Convention Center in downtown DC costs from $1.95 to $4.05, depending on whether or not it's rush hour. Check www.washfly.com for Flyer schedules. There are no "regular" taxis from Dulles to any destination—the Flyer is it, and you should avoid all other pitchmen. You can also take Metrobus 5A, which runs from L'Enfant Plaza to Dulles, stopping at Rosslyn Metro Station on the Orange and Blue Lines. The express bus costs $6 each way.

Ground Transportation

Super Shuttle offers service to Dulles from anywhere in the state of Maryland and runs a shuttle between the airport and Union Station. Call (800-258-3826) to book your seat. At the airport, you'll find them outside the Main Terminal. Washington Flyer Taxicabs serve Dulles International Airport exclusively with 24-hour service to and from the airport. Taxis accept American Express, Diners Club, MasterCard, Discover Card, and Visa and charge metered rates to any destination in metropolitan Washington. If you're heading to downtown DC, it will cost you between $44 and $50. For more information, or to book a car, call 703-661-6655.

Rental Cars

Alamo • 800-832-7933	**Enterprise** • 800-736-8222
Avis • 800-331-1212	**Hertz** • 800-654-3131
Budget • 800-527-0700	**National** • 800-227-7368
Dollar • 800-800-4000	**Thrifty** • 800-367-2277
Alamoot (off-airport) • 800-630-6967	

Hotels—Herndon, VA

Comfort Inn • 200 Elden St • 703-437-7555
Courtyard by Marriott • 533 Herndon Pkwy • 703-478-9400
Crowne Plaza • 2200 Centreville Rd • 703-471-6700
Embassy Suites • 13341 Woodland Park Dr • 703-464-0200
Hilton • 13869 Park Center Rd • 703-478-2900
Holiday Inn Express • 485 Elden St • 703-478-9777
Hyatt Hotels & Resorts • 2300 Dulles Corner Blvd • 703-713-1234
Marriott Hotels • 13101 Worldgate Dr • 703-709-0400
Residence Inn • 315 Elden St • 703-435-0044
Staybrdige Suites • 13700 Coppermine Rd • 703-713-6800

Hotels—Sterling, VA

Country Inn & Suites • 45620 Falke Plz • 703-435-2700
Courtyard by Marriott • 45500 Majestic Dr • 571-434-6400
Fairfield Inn • 23000 Indian Creek Dr • 703-435-5300
Hampton Inn • 45440 Holiday Park Dr • 703-471-8300
Marriott Towneplace • 22744 Holiday Park Dr • 703-707-2017
Marriott • 45020 Aviation Dr • 703-471-9500

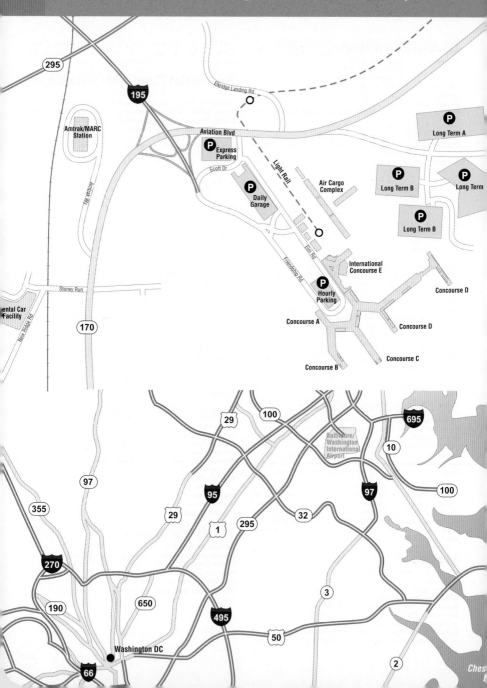

General Information

Information: 800-435-9294
Lost & Found: 410-859-7387
Parking: 800-468-6294
Police: 410-859-7040
Website: www.bwiairport.com

Overview

When Friendship International Airport opened in 1950, it was widely touted as one of the most sophisticated and advanced airports in the nation. In 1993, Southwest Airlines moved in, bringing with them their cheap, and wildly popular, cattle cars of the sky. But this bargain-basement tenant has turned BWI into a boomtown—a spanking new expanded Terminal A for Southwest only opened in 2005. Other major carriers have since joined the dirt-cheap-fares bandwagon, resulting in generally cheaper flights to and from BWI than you'll find flying into and out of Dulles or Reagan. It's a helluva haul from the city (yet pretty close for Maryland suburbanites), but sometimes time really isn't money, and cheap fares trump convenience. In October 2005, BWI was officially renamed Baltimore-Washington International Thurgood Marshall Airport in honor of native Baltimorean and first African-American Supreme Court Justice Thurgood Marshall. If you do find yourself at BWI, know that in 2007 they won the little-known "Best Overall Concessions" award in the medium-sized airport category, so you'll be well-fed before your flight.

How to Get There—Driving

From downtown DC, take New York Avenue (US 50) eastbound to the Baltimore/Washington Parkway N to I-195 E. From the Capital Beltway (I-495/95), take the I-95 N exit in Maryland (Exit 27), and then continue north to I-195 E. I-195 ends at the entrance to BWI.

Parking

Hourly parking is located across from the terminal building. The first and second 30 minutes of parking (which you may spend looking for a space) are $2 each, and the rest of your time costs $4 per hour and $22 per day. Daily parking is available for $3 the first and second hours each, $2 for each additional hour and $12 per day. Express Service Parking (ESP) is located on Aviation Boulevard across from the Air Cargo Complex and is $4 for the first hour, $2 each additional hour and $10 each day. If you're going to be gone a while, you might want to try the long-term parking lots, which is $8 per day. A new service called "Credit Card In/Credit Card Out" allows you to swipe the plastic of your choice upon entering and exiting an hourly parking facility, eliminating the fun of losing your parking ticket. The "Pay & Go" service allows you to pay your parking fee for the hourly lot in the Skywalk adjacent to the main terminal before you return to your car.

BWI also has a Cell Phone Parking lot located at the entrance to the "Daily B" parking lot on Elm Rd. You can wait there for your mother-in-law to arrive. Just remember to turn your phone on.

How to Get There—Mass Transit

Any which way you go, expect to devote a few hours to mimicking a Richard Scarry character. MARC's Penn Line and Amtrak trains service the BWI Rail Station from Union Station in DC (Massachusetts Ave & First St NE) and cost between $6 and $34. A word of caution, though: the MARC train only runs Monday through Friday, leave the more expensive Amtrak your only option. The Light Rail train now provides service between Baltimore and BWI. A free shuttle bus takes passengers from the train station to the airport. Alternatively, you can take the Metro Green Line to the Greenbelt station and catch the Express Metro Bus/B30 to BWI. The Express bus runs every 40 minutes and costs $6.

How to Get There— Ground Transportation

The Airport Shuttle offers door-to-door service within the state of Maryland. Call 800-776-0323 for reservations. For door-to-door service to BWI, Super Shuttle (800-258-3826) services all of the DC airports. The BWI taxi stand is located just outside of baggage claim on the lower level. The ride to DC usually costs about $65. 410-859-1100.

Car Rental

Avis • 410-859-1680	**Enterprise** • 800-325-8007
Alamo • 410-859-8092	**Hertz** • 410-850-7400
Budget • 410-859-0850	**National** • 410-859-8860
Dollar • 800-800-4000	**Thrifty** • 410-859-7139

Hotels

Four Points by Sheraton • 7032 Elm Rd • 410-859-3300
Amerisuites • 940 International Dr • 410-859-3366
Best Western • 6755 Dorsey Rd • 410-796-3300
Candlewood Suites • 1247 Winterson Rd • 410-789-9100
Comfort Inn • 6921 Baltimore-Annapolis Blvd • 410-789-9100
Comfort Suites • 815 Elkridge Landing Rd • 410-691-1000
Courtyard by Marriott • 1671 West Nursery Rd • 410-859-8855
Econo Lodge • 5895 Bonnieview Ln • 410-796-1020
Embassy Suites • 1300 Concourse Dr • 410-850-0747
Extended Stay America • 1500 Aero Dr • 410-850-0400
Fairfield Inn by Marriot • 1737 W Nursery Rd • 410-859-2333
Hampton Inn • 829 Elkridge Landing Rd • 410-850-0600
Hampton Inn & Suites • 7027 Arundel Mills Cir • 410-540-9225
Hilton Garden Inn • 1516 Aero Dr • 410-691-0500
Holiday Inn • 890 Elkridge Landing Rd • 410-859-8400
Holiday Inn Express • 7481 New Ridge Rd • 410-684-3388
Homestead Studio Suites • 939 International Dr • 410-691-2500
Homewood Suites • 1181 Winterson Rd • 410-684-6100
Marriott • 1743 W Nursery Rd • 410-859-7500
Microtel Inn and Suites • 1170 Winterson Rd • 410-865-7500
Ramada • 7253 Parkway Dr • 410-712-4300
Red Roof Inn • 827 Elkridge Landing Rd • 410-850-7600
Residence Inn/Marriott • 1160 Winterson Rd • 410-691-0255
Residence Inn/Marriott • 7035 Arundel Mills Cir • 410-799-7332
Sleep Inn and Suites • 6055 Belle Grove Rd • 410-789-7223
Springhill Suites by Marriott • 899 Elkridge Landing Rd • 410-694-0555
Wingate Inn • 1510 Aero Dr • 410-859-000

Airline	Terminal	Airline	Terminal
Air Canada	E	Delta	D
Air Mobility Command	E	Frontier Airlines	E
		Jet Blue	D
AirTran	A/B	Southwest Airlines	A/B
American Airlines	C	Spirit	C
British Airways	E	United Airlines	A/B
Condor	E	US Airways	D

Airline	Phone	IAD	DCA	BWI
Aer Lingus	800-474-7424	■		
Aeroflot	888-686-4949	■		
Air Canada	888-247-2262	■	■	■
Air Canada/Jazz	800-247-2262		■	
Air France	800-321-4538	■		
Air Greenland	877-245-0739			■
Air Jamaica	800-523-5585			■
AirTran	800-247-8726	■	■	■
American Airlines	800-433-7300	■	■	■
American Eagle	800-433-7300		■	
American Eagle Connection	800-433-7300	■		
ANA	800-235-9262	■		
Austrian Airlines	800-843-0002	■		
British Airways	800-247-9297	■		■
Delta	800-221-1212	■	■	■
Delta Connection	800-221-1212	■	■	
Delta Shuttle	800-933-5935		■	
Ethiopian Airlines	800-445-2733	■		
Frontier	800-432-1359		■	
Ghana Airways	800-404-4262			■
GRUPO TACA	800-535-8780	■		
Iberia	800-776-4642	■		
Jet Blue	800-538-2583	■	■	
KLM Royal Dutch	800-225-2525	■		
Korean Air	800-438-5000	■		
Lufthansa	800-645-3880	■		
Midwest	800-452-2022			■
North American Airlines	800-359-6222			■
Northwest Airlines	800-225-2525	■	■	■
SAS	800-221-2350	■		
Saudi Arabian Airlines	800-472-8342	■		
South African Airways	800-722-9675	■		
Southwest Airlines	800-435-9792	■	■	■
Spirit	800-772-7117		■	
Sun Country Airlines	800-800-6557	■		
United Airlines	800-241-6522	■	■	■
United Express	800-241-6522	■		
US Airways	800-428-4322	■	■	■
US Airways Express	800-428-4322	■		
US Airways Shuttle	800-428-4322		■	
USA3000	877-872-3000			■
Virgin	800-862-8621	■		

General Information

DC Taxicab Commission: 2041 Martin Luther King Jr Ave SE,
Ste 204
Washington, DC 20020-7024
Phone: 202-645-6018
Complaints: Must be in writing and mailed or
emailed to dctc@dc.gov
Web Site: www.dctaxi.dc.gov

Overview

After 70 years of an esoteric and antiquated zone system, the District has finally converted to time and distance meters. Following a long, drawn out dispute with area cab drivers, Adrian Fenty asserted his authority as mayor to make the switch—perhaps part of his campaign to make DC a "world-class city" by ditching its idiosyncratic system. Beginning in 2008, DC cabs shifted to a conventional metered system. The change has incited the ire of many DC cabbies who believe that the old "zone meter" allowed for fair fares and a more straightforward method of showing how that fair fare was calculated. Needless to say, Mayor Fenty disagreed. The new system has meant less money for drivers, but lower fares keep patrons happy. Still, don't be surprised if your once independent cabbie is no longer his own boss, or secretly hopes to get stuck in a traffic jam.

Calculating Your Fare

With the new meters, calculating your fare should prove a much more uncomplicated matter. The meter fare stars at $3, going up 35¢ every 1/6 mile and 40¢ for every minute of time stopped or traveling under 10 mph. There is a maximum of $25 within DC (thank goodness). In snow emergencies, an additional 25% of the total is added to the original fare. The Washington Post website has published a handy online calculator for estimating your fare: www.washingtonpost.com/wp-srv/special/local/dc-taxi-fare-calculator. Keep in mind that with time and distance meters, traffic congestion will now affect patrons. Those frequently traveling during rush hour, or to areas like Capitol Hill, will find a spike in prices as compared to the zone system.

Out of Area Cabs

Taxis from Virginia and Maryland can frequently be found in DC; however, specific rules exist that limit non-DC taxis from picking up and transporting passengers in the district and around DC. However, if a non-DC taxi is dispatched directly to DC, it can pick up passengers in DC without a dispatch fee. These non-DC cabs are often less expensive when traveling out of DC to Virginia or Maryland.

Taxi Companies

Listed below are all of the major DC cab companies as well as several from Virginia and Maryland. Remember, in DC, the dispatch will cost you an extra $2.

DC Taxis   *All area codes: 202, unless noted*

Company	Phone	Company	Phone
American	398-0529	Empire	488-4844
A-S-K	726-5430	E & P	399-0711
Atlantic	488-0609	Executive	547-6351
Automotive Care	554-6877	Fairway	832-4662
B & B	561-5770	Family	291-4788
Barwood	800-831-2323	General	462-0200
Bay	546-1818	Georgetown	529-8979
Bell	479-6729	Globe	232-3700
Best	265-7834	Gold Star	484-5555
Capitol Cab	546-2400	Hill Top	529-1212
Capital Motors	488-1370	Holiday	628-4407
Central	484-7100	HTT	484-7100
Checker	398-0532	Liberty	398-0505
City	269-0990	Lincoln	484-2222
Classic	399-6815	Mayflower	783-1111
Coastline	462-4543	Meritt Cab	554-7900
Comfort	398-0530	National	269-1234
Courtesy	269-2600	Orange	832-0436
DC Express Auto	526-5656	Palm Grove	269-2606
DC Express Cab	484-8516	Pan Am & Imperial	526-7125
DC Flyer	488-7611	Seasons	635-3498
Delta	543-0084	Sun	484-7100
Dial	829-4222	Super	488-4334
Diamond	387-6200	VIP	269-1300
Diamond Inc.	387-4011	Yellow	373-3366
Elite	529-0222	Yourway	488-0609

Maryland Taxis   *All area codes: 301*

Company	Phone	Company	Phone
Action	840-1222	Checker	816-0066
Action of Laurel	776-0310	Community	459-4454
Airport	577-2111	Greenbelt	577-2000
All County	924-4344	Montgomery	926-9300
Barwood	984-1900	Regency	990-9000
Blue Bird & Yellow	864-7700	Silver	577-4455

Virginia Taxis   *All area codes: 703*

Company	Phone	Company	Phone
Airport Metro	413-4667	Crown	528-0202
Alexandria	549-2502	Diamond	548-7505
Arlington	522-2222	King	549-3530
Blue Top	243-TAXI (8294)	Red Top	522-3333

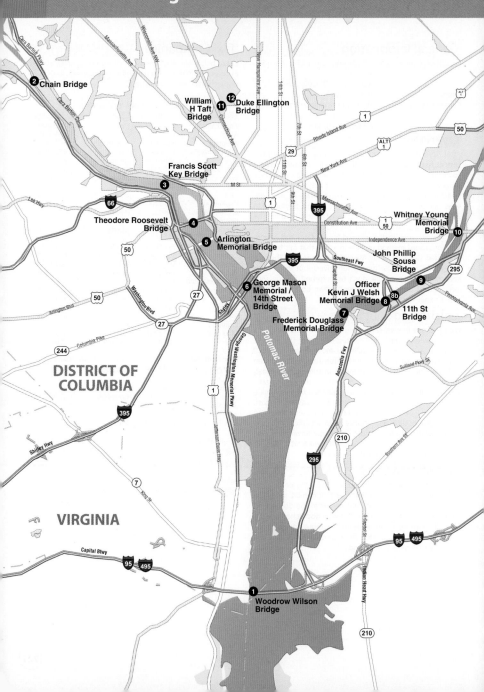

Chances are if you live in DC and you own a car, you spend a significant amount of your time sitting in traffic on one of DC's bridges. Despite constant congestion and deteriorating roadways, DC-area bridges do have one saving grace—no tolls! The city is also home to some of the most beautiful and architecturally significant spans in the country. The **Francis Scott Key Bridge** crossing the Potomac from Rosslyn, VA, into Georgetown is the best known. The **Calvert Street Bridge** between Woodley Park and Adams Morgan (officially named for native son **Duke Ellington**) and the **Connecticut Avenue Bridge** over Rock Creek Park (which must be seen from the parkway below to be fully appreciated) are other great examples. The **Connecticut Avenue Bridge**, (officially known as the **William H. Taft Bridge**) is also known as the "Million Dollar Bridge." When it was built it was the most expensive concrete bridge ever constructed in the US. And what bridge would be complete without those ornamental lions on both ends?

One of DC's largest and most notorious is the **Woodrow Wilson Bridge**, which is unique in two ways: 1) it's one of only 13 drawbridges along the US interstate highway system; 2) it's the location of one of the worst bottlenecks in the country. The Woodrow Wilson Bridge was built in 1961 with only six lanes, which was adequate at the time. Then the eastern portion of the Beltway was widened to eight lanes in the '70s, making this spot a perpetual hassle for DC drivers. In an attempt to alleviate this problem, a new 6,075-foot-long **Potomac River Bridge** was unveiled in 2008 (and was featured on an episode of National Geographic's MegaStructures). With the addition, Woodrow Wilson Bridge currently boasts 12 lanes: six are used for local traffic, four for through traffic, and two for HOV and bus traffic. The bridge's northern section also features pedestrian and bike paths. The new spans are 20 feet higher than the old and most boats and small ships are able to pass underneath without having to raise the bridge, much to the relief of weary commuters.

The **Officer Kevin J. Welsh Memorial Bridge**, which empties onto 11th Street in Southeast, was named after the police officer who drowned attempting to save a woman who jumped into the Anacostia River in an apparent suicide attempt. Note: Most people, including traffic reporters, refer to the Welsh bridge simply as the 11th Street Bridge. John Wilkes Booth escaped from Washington via a predecessor to the **11th Street Bridge** after he assassinated Abraham Lincoln in 1865.

		Lanes	Pedestrians/ Bicyclists?	Vehicles/day (thousands)	Main Span / Length	Opened to Traffic
1	Woodrow Wilson Bridge	6	no	195	5,900'	1961
2	Chain Bridge	3**	yes	22	1,350'	1939
3	Francis Scott Key Bridge	6	yes	66	1,700'	1923
4	Theodore Roosevelt Bridge	7**	yes	100		1964
5	Arlington Memorial Bridge	6	yes	66	2,163'	1932
6	14th Street Bridge	12***	yes	246		1950 1962 1972
7	Frederick Douglass Memorial Bridge	5		77	2,501'	1950
8	Officer Kevin J. Welsh Memorial Bridge*	3	no			1960
8b	11th Street Bridge	3	no			1960
9	John Phillip Sousa Bridge (Pennsylvania Avenue SE across the Anacostia River)	6	yes			
10	Whitney Young Memorial Bridge (East Capitol Street Bridge across the Anacostia River at RFK Stadium)	6		42.6	1135'	1965
11	William H. Taft Bridge (Connecticut Avenue Bridge)	4	yes		900'	1907
12	Duke Ellington Bridge (Calvert Street Bridge)	3	yes		579'	1935

* Southern span renamed in 1986
**Center lane changes so that rush hour traffic has an extra lane
***Includes dual two-lane HOV bridges in the middle which are actually open to everyone at all times. Go figure.

Overview

Driving in Washington? Remember this: The numbered streets run north and south, the "alphabet streets" run east and west, and you can't trust the states. Or the traffic circles. Or the streets that end for no reason. Or the constant construction sites. Or the potholes as big as a senator's head. Or the triple-parked delivery vans. Or the buses that will take your car and pedestrians out with one wrong move. Or the clueless tourists. Or the motorcades chauffeuring dignitaries and politicians around. Or the cabbies. Never trust the cabbies!

Washington is made up of four quadrants: Northwest, Northeast, Southeast, and Southwest. The boundaries are North Capitol Street, East Capitol Street, South Capitol Street, and the National Mall. Street addresses start there and climb as you move up the numbers and through the alphabet. Nota bene: There are no J, X, Y, or Z Streets. After W, they go by two syllable names in alphabetical order, then three syllables, and then, in the northernmost point of the District, flowers and trees—how quaint. Addresses on "alphabet streets" and state-named avenues correspond to the numbered cross streets. For example, 1717 K Street NW is between 17th and 18th streets. The addresses on "letter streets" correspond to the number of the letter in the alphabet. So 1717 20th Street NW is between R and S streets because they are the 17th and 18th letters in the alphabet, after you leave out "J." Get it?

Now, some streets on the grid are created more equal than others. North and south, 7th, 9th (one-way southbound), 12th (one-way northbound), 14th, 15th, 16th, and 23rd streets NW are major thoroughfares, as are H Street, I (often referred to as "Eye") Street, K Street, M Street, and U Street NW east and west.

The trick to driving like an insider is quick maneuvering, illegal turns, mastering the avenues named after states and knowing the highway system. Be on your best behavior when you drive near the White House (the stretch of Pennsylvania Avenue which runs outside was permanently closed to public traffic in 2001) and watch out for tourists crossing at The Mall (never has there been a group of people so ignorant of traffic signals.) If you don't, you will probably find yourself stuck behind a Winnebago with Wisconsin plates, unable to even see all the red lights you're catching. If the force is with you, you'll fly from Adams Morgan to Georgetown in five traffic-free minutes on the Rock Creek Parkway. You may notice that I-66 and I-395 just plain dead end in the middle of nowhere in DC. Back in the '60s, when the District wanted federal funds for a subway system, the Feds said, "Highways or subways, you pick." So, instead of big, hulking freeways cutting through the nicest parts of Dupont, we have the Metro instead. Traffic can be numbing, but we win out in the long run. Fair warning though, Virginia is the black hole for tickets. It's certain that speeding anywhere on I-66 and I-395 will land you one.

Young grasshopper, study the maps in this book and if you get lost, always find your way back to a lettered or numbered street and you will see the light again. For every five minutes you spend looking at the maps, you will save five hours over the next year.

Because DC is still a 9-to-5 city, many traffic patterns change to accommodate rush hours. Be careful: Some streets, such as 15th and 17th streets NW and Rock Creek Parkway, convert to one-way traffic during rush hours. A good chunk of Connecticut Avenue NW above Woodley Road and a short stretch of 16th Street NW above Columbia Road have a reversible center lane during rush hour, and it's always a hoot to watch the looks on an out-of-towner's face when a Metrobus comes barreling at them when they think it's their lane. Other routes, including most of downtown, ban parking during rush hours (a really expensive ticket and tow or a boot on your car). Also, Interstates 66, 95, and 395 in Virginia and I-270, and US 50 east of the Beltway in Maryland have high occupancy vehicle (HOV) lanes that will also earn you a big ticket and points unless you follow the rules during rush hour and have two or more people in the car.

DMV Locations

Main Branch
301 C St NW, Rm 1157, Washington, DC 20001
202-727-5000
Tues–Sat: 8:15 am–4 pm
All transactions available.

Penn Branch
3230 Pennsylvania Ave SE, Washington, DC 20020
Mon–Fri: 8:15 am–4 pm
Available services: Vehicle registration (first time and renewals) and titles; driver's license issuance and renewal; fleet transactions.
Knowledge tests are given Mon–Fri: 8:30 am–3 pm.

Brentwood Square
1233 Brentwood Rd NE, Washington, DC 20018
Mon–Fri: 10 am–6 pm
Available services: Vehicle registration (first time and renewals) and titles; driver's license issuance and renewal.
Knowledge tests are given Mon–Fri: 10 am–5 pm.

Brentwood Road Test Lot
1205 Brentwood Rd NE, Washington, DC 20018
By appointment only, call: 202-727-5000
Available services: Road test (driver's license only).

Shops at Georgetown Park
3222 M St NW, Washington, DC 20007
Mon–Fri: 8:15 am–4 pm
Available services: Vehicle registration renewal and driver's license renewal.
Knowledge tests are given Mon–Fri: 8:15 am–3 pm.

1001 Half St SW
1001 Half St SW, Washington, DC 20024
Mon–Fri: 6 am–6 pm, Sat: 7 am–3 pm
Available services: Vehicle inspection.

General Information

Department of Transportation: 202-673-6813,
(DDOT) www.ddot.dc.gov
Department of Public Works: 202-727-1000, dpw.dc.gov
Citywide Call Center: 202-727-1000
Department of Motor Vehicles: 202-727-5000,
www.dmv.dc.gov

Overview

Parking in DC can feel like buying toilet paper in communist Russia. It's incredibly hard to find, and even if you think you've lucked out, check again or it could really hurt later. Your average parking space will feature at least three or four restriction signs, sort of a parking algebra problem to solve before turning off your engine. Is your spot metered? Is it within 10 feet of a curb or a hydrant? Is it morning rush hour? Evening rush hour? Is it the weekend or a holiday? Is there street sweeping on your block? Are you in a retail district? A residential neighborhood? Is a special event going on? Is it snowing? Are you in front of a taxi stand? A delivery entrance? An embassy? And so on.

Meters

In much of DC, parking meters must be fed Monday through Friday, between 7 am and 6:30 pm. In more densely populated areas (Georgetown, convention centers, etc.), hours may extend until 10 pm and reach into Saturday. Metered parking may be prohibited on some streets during morning and rush hours. Some neighborhoods now have centralized meters that issue passes for an entire block instead of individual spots. Vehicles displaying DC-issued handicap license plates or placards are allowed to park for double the amount of time indicated on the meter. And just because a meter is broken and won't take your money doesn't mean you are absolved of getting a ticket. Please, this is DC: parking enforcement is the most profitable and efficient department in the District government.

Handicapped Permits

There was a time when the District government did not officially recognize handicapped placards from any jurisdiction outside of DC, but those days are, thankfully, over. As if to make up for years of having such a farcical law on the book, DC has added special "red top" meters throughout the city that are for the exclusive use of persons with disabilities. Washington, DC is one of the most disabled accessible cities in the world. This guide provides information about transportation, parking, access to popular attractions, scooter and wheelchair rentals, and more.

Resident Permit Parking

In the 1970s, increasing parking on residential streets by out-of-staters had locals furious; and so began the Resident Permit Parking Program. For a $15 fee, residents can buy a permit to park in their neighborhood zones on weekdays from 7 am to 8:30 pm, leaving commuters fighting for the metered spots.

If you live in a Resident Permit Parking zone and you're planning on hosting out-of-town guests, you can apply for a temporary visitor permit at your local police district headquarters. All you need is your visitor's name, license tag number, length of visit, and a few hours to kill down at the station. Temporary permits are only valid for up to 15 consecutive days—a great excuse to get rid of guests who have overstayed their welcome!

Car buyers, beware if a dealer tells you he will take care of getting you your tags. The DMV often gets so backlogged that your temporary tags might expire before you get your metal plates, especially around holidays when everyone is buying a car just as government staff is taking leave. And double check those temporary tags, too:

DC police recently issued a ban on dealer-issued temp tags when it was discovered that dealers were splitting each set of tags, giving one to a legitimate buyer and selling the other on the black market. To avoid the hassle entirely, make the trip to the DMV yourself.

Parking on Weekends and Holidays

Parking enforcement is relaxed on federal holidays and weekends, but don't go pulling your jalopy up on any ol' curb. Public safety parking laws are always in effect, even on weekends. These include the prohibition of blocking emergency entrances or exits, blocking fire hydrants, parking too close to an intersection, obstructing crosswalks, etc. Churchgoers also have to be more careful now with their long-held custom of double parking during Sunday services, as recent complaints in neighborhoods like Logan Circle have led police to start cracking down, even if it is the Lord's Day.

Tow Pound

Didn't pay your parking tickets? If your car was towed, it was taken to the District's Blue Plains Impoundment and Storage Facility at 5001 Shepherd Parkway, SW. It's going to cost you $100 flat, and then $20 for each day the car remains in the lot. To claim a towed vehicle from the Blue Plains facility, all outstanding fines and fees must first be paid at the Department of Motor Vehicles (DMV) satellite office at 65 K Streets NE. Owners should be prepared to show DMV officials proof of registration and insurance for the towed vehicle. Getting towed sure is fun, right? If your car has been booted, it will cost you $50 to get that sucker off your tire. To find the tow lot, take the Metrorail Green Line to the Anacostia station, and then ride an A4/DC Village Metrobus to Shepherd Parkway at DC Village Lane. Walk a short distance to the impoundment lot at the end of Shepherd Parkway. Any vehicle that remains unclaimed at the Blue Plains Impoundment Facility for 28 or more days is considered abandoned and may be sold as scrap or auctioned. To find out for certain where your car is, call the DMV at 202-727-5000. You can also find out through the Department of Public Works's website: www.dpw.dc.gov.

Top 21 Parking Violations

1. Expired / Overtime Meter (includes meter-feeding) $25
2. Overtime in Residential Zone $30
3. No Parking AM / PM Rush Hour $100
4. No Parking Anytime $30
5. Obstructing Building Entrance $20
6. No Standing Anytime $50
7. Parking in Alley $30
8. Expired / Missing Inspection Sticker $50
9. Expired Registration / Tags $100
10. Reserved for Zipcar / Flexcar $100
11. Parked in Loading Zone $50
12. Parked in an Embassy Space $20
13. Double Parking / Parking Abreast $50
14. Missing or Obstructed Tags $50
15. Less than 10 Feet From Fire Hydrant $50
16. Government Vehicles Only $25
17. Blocking Bus Zone $100
18. Illegally Parked in Cab Stand $20
19. No Parking / Street Cleaning $30
20. Less than Five Feet from Alley / Driveway $20
21. Ticket Indecipherable Because It Was Tacked to Your Windshield in the Rain: Priceless

Tickets must be paid within 30 days of issuance. You can pay online, by mail, in person, or by calling 202-289-2230.

Metrobus

Phone:	202-962-1234
Lost & Found:	202-962-1195
Website:	www.wmata.com
Fare:	Regular: $1.60 with SmarTrip or $1.80 using cash. For express routes, the fare is $3.65 using SmarTrip or $4 using cash. Senior/disabled regular fare is $2.

DC's bus system can be a great way to get around town, once you've figured out how to navigate its intimidating labyrinth of 176 lines, 335 routes, and 12,301 stops. New "easy-to-read" maps have been posted at stops to give riders a clue, and SmarTrip cards are now accepted on bus lines, thus avoiding the need for transfers, tokens, special fare passes, or exact change (bus drivers don't carry cash). All Metrobuses are equipped with bike racks. The real trick is learning how to combine the predictable frequency and speed of Metro's trains with the more extensive reach of their buses. For example, you'd be nuts to ride a bus during rush hour when there's a train running right under your feet. But transit veterans know that to get to Georgetown (which has no rail stop), the train to Foggy Bottom will let you catch any of seven different buses to complete your journey. Keep in mind, however, that Metrobuses, while great for getting to places the Metro doesn't run, are far from inefficient. In fact, time tables for Metrobuses are more like friendly suggestions than actual arrival times. Don't be surprised if your bus arrives ten minutes early or late for no apparent reason. Rather than giving yourself a headache by looking at maps of crazy spider-web-like bus routes, use Metro's online "TripPlanner" to find out which bus you need and estimated arrival times. In an effort to give patrons a better idea of when their darn bus is going to show up, Metro relaunched its Next Bus system in July of 2009. After numerous complaints that the system was inaccurate, it was yanked in 2007 for retooling. The new (and hopefully better) system uses GPS technology to allow riders on a limited number of routes to access real-time information about when their bus will arrive at a specific stop via phone, internet, or text message. In general, DC's buses are clean, the drivers are helpful, and they can get you almost anywhere you want to go, barring, of course, Paris and the beaches of Mexico.

DC Circulator

Phone:	202-962-1423
Website:	www.dccirculator.com
Fare:	$1; Seniors: 50¢; 50¢ with Metrorail Transfer; Free with Metrobus transfer or DC Student Travel Card

A fleet of shiny red buses sporting low doors and big windows opened two routes in 2005 and a third in 2006 to link Union Station, K Street, downtown, the Mall, the SW waterfront, and Georgetown. In March of 2009, two new routes were added: one connecting Adams Morgan and U Street and another going between Union Station and the Navy Yard. The latest newcomer is the Rosslyn—Dupont Circle route, by way of

Georgetown. The new system is funded by a partnership between DC's Department of Transportation, Metro, and a coalition of business improvement districts, convention bureaus, and tourism organizations from Capitol Hill, the Golden Triangle, and Georgetown. The Circulator's buses run from roughly 6 am to 3:30 am, depending on the day of week and route, and depart every 5–10 minutes. Riders can pay with exact change or use their SmarTrip card. Best of all, when telling your friends what bus you're going to take to meet them for happy hour, you can say "the Circ-u-lat-or" in your best robot voice.

Ride On Bus— Montgomery County, MD

Phone:	240-777-7433
Website:	www.montgomerycountymd.gov/dot-transit/index.html
Fare:	$1.60 with SmarTrip or $1.80 using cash. Seniors with valid Metro Senior ID or Medicare Card ride for free. $1.10 with Metrorail transfer.

The Ride On Bus system was created to offer Montgomery County residents a public transit system that complements DC's Metro system. Buses accept exact change, Ride On and Metrobus tokens or passes, MARC rail passes, or SmarTrip cards.

DASH Bus—Alexandria, VA

Phone:	703-370-3274
Website:	www.dashbus.com
Fare:	$1.60; free with Metrorail transfer

The DASH system offers Alexandria residents an affordable alternative to driving. It also connects with Metrobus, Metrorail, Virginia Railway Express, and all local bus systems. DASH honors combined Metrorail/Metrobus Passes, VRE/MARC rail tickets, Metrobus regular tokens, and, as of 2007, the all-powerful SmarTrip card. DASH buses accept exact change only. If you are traveling to or from the Pentagon Metrorail station, you have to pay the 25¢ Pentagon Surcharge if you don't have a DASH Pass or other valid pass.

ART—Arlington, VA

Phone:	703-228-7547
Lost & Found:	703-354-6030
Website:	www.arlingtontransit.com/
Fare:	$1.50; Seniors: 75¢; $1 with Metrorail transfer

Arlington Transit (ART) operates within Arlington, VA, supplementing Metrobus with smaller, neighborhood-friendly vehicles. It also provides access to Metrorail and Virginia Railway Express. The cheery green and white buses run on clean-burning natural gas and have climate control to keep passengers from sticking to their seats. As of 2009, you'll have to use a SmarTrip to get your rail-to-bus discount or to transfer from bus to bus free of charge.

University Shuttle Buses

GUTS: 202-687-4372
http://otm.georgetown.edu/guts/index.cfm
AU Shuttle: 202- 885-3111
www.american.edu/finance/ts/shuttle.html
GW Shuttle: 202-994-RIDE
gwired.gwu.edu/upd/transportation/
ColonialExpressShuttleBuscopy/
HUBS: 202-806-2000
www.howard.edu/ms2/campus%20shuttle/
default.htm
Fares: All fares are free for their respective university's
students
Hours: GUTS shuttle: 5 am–12 am; AU shuttle: 8
am–11:30 pm or later depending on applicable
route and day of week; GWU shuttle 7 pm–3
am; HUBS 7:20 am–12 am.

Georgetown University operates five shuttle routes, connecting the campus to the Georgetown University Law Center on Capitol Hill, to University offices on Wisconsin Avenue, to Metro stations at Rosslyn and Dupont Circle, and to stops in North Arlington, VA. Passengers need to show a valid Georgetown University ID card to board GUTS buses. AU's shuttle connects its campus with the Washington College of Law, the Katzen Arts Center, the Tenleytown Metro station, and AU's Park Bethesda apartment building. Passengers must present an AU ID Card or Shuttle Guest Pass to board. GWU's shuttle links the Marvin Center on the Foggy Bottom Campus with the Wellness Center and Columbia Plaza, as well as with Aston and the Golden Triangle business district. Howard University's HUBS line shuttles faculty and staff from the main HU campus to various parking lots, dormitories, the School of Divinity, the School of Law, and other University-based locations, as well as to and from Howard University Hospital and the Shaw/Howard University and Brookland/CUA Metro stations. All shuttles require passengers to show ID from their respective universities.

Greyhound, Peter Pan Buses

Greyhound: www.greyhound.com • 1-800-231-2222
Peter Pan: www.peterpanbus.com • 1-800-237-8747

Locations:
Washington, DC • 50 Massachusetts Ave. NE • 202-289-1908
• 24 Hrs
Silver Spring, MD • 8100 Fenton St • 301-585-8700 • 7:30
am–9 pm

Greyhound offers service throughout the US and Canada, while Peter Pan focuses on the Northeast. Both bus services offer long-distance transportation that is much cheaper than air or rail. Just keep in mind that you get what you pay for (read: traffic jams, dirty bathrooms, cramped seats, and a general feeling of unease). Booking in advance will save you money, as will buying a round-trip ticket at the time of purchase. In 2012, Greyhound and Peter Pan bus services relocated to DC's grand Union Station. The station now serves as a "bus hub" for national, regional, and intercity buses.

Chinatown Buses to New York

These buses are a poorly kept secret among the city's frugal travelers. They provide bargain-basement amenities, and the whole experience feels somewhat illegal, but they are one of the cheapest options for dashing outta town. Most companies charge $20 oneway and $35 round-trip to New York. Some drivers may not be able to tell you your destination in English, but for those prices you really can't complain. Not all are Chinese owned these days, and not all are the tiny operations you might expect. Vamoose is owned and operated by a Hassidic Jewish family, and Megabus, now operating on two continents, won a Travelzoo award in the "leading provider of outstanding car rental and bus deals" category. Megabus, BoltBus and DC2NY all provide free Wi-Fi and offer the cheapest fares—as low as $1 one way if you book early, with the price increasing the closer you get to the date of departure.

Eastern Travel
715 H St NW • www.nydcexpress.com
15 trips/day • NY Address: 28 Allen St and
430 7th Ave At 34th St

New Century Travel
513 H St NW • www.2001bus.com/
Nine trips/day • NY Address: 120 East Broadway New York,
NY

Washington Deluxe
1320 19th St NW and 50 Massachusetts Ave NE • www.washny.
com/
Four to ten trips/day

Bolt Bus
50 Massachusetts Avenue, NE • www.boltbus.com
Ten to 16 departures/day • NY Address: 33rd St & 7th Ave or
6th St between Grand & Watt Aves

DC2NY
20th St & Massachusetts Ave NW; 14th St NW between H
and I • www.dc2ny.com
Two to nine departures daily • NY Address: 215 W 34th St

Megabus
50 Massachusetts Ave NE • www.megabus.com
15 to 20 departures/day • NY Address: 7th Ave & 28th St

Vamoose Bus
1801 N Lynne St (Rosslyn) and 7490 Waverly St (Bethesda) •
www.vamoosebus.com
Five trips/day Monday – Thursday, 9 trips on Friday, 6 trips
on Saturday, and 8 trips on Sunday.• NY Address: 252 W
31st St

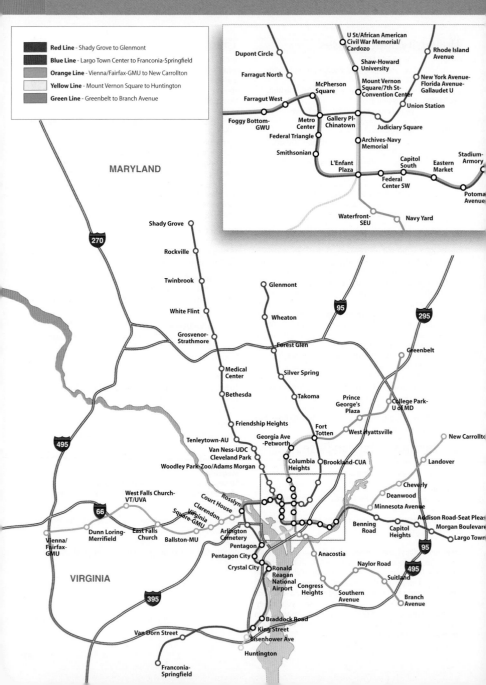

Red Line - Shady Grove to Glenmont
Blue Line - Largo Town Center to Franconia-Springfield
Orange Line - Vienna/Fairfax-GMU to New Carrollton
Yellow Line - Mount Vernon Square to Huntington
Green Line - Greenbelt to Branch Avenue

Transit • **Metrorail**

General Information

Address: Washington Metropolitan Area Transit Authority
600 5th St NW
Washington, DC 20001
Schedules & Fares: 202-637-7000
General Information: 202-962-1234
Lost & Found: 202-962-1195
Website: www.wmata.com

Overview

It's not the Subway, the "L", the "T," or the Underground. Any of these words coming from your mouth will tell everyone you're still just a tourist. Here, it's called the Metro. Metro makes locals proud, and it's so simple it seems small. It's the second busiest subway system in the country, with 904 rail cars shuttling about 206 million passengers per year between 86 stations. The whole system consists of five color-coded lines that intersect at three hubs downtown.

Scared of escalators? Get over it. And move your fanny pack, camera, color coordinated shirts, and family to the right as DC residents spit dirty looks and words to anyone standing on the left. Metro lauds the longest escalator in the Western Hemisphere at its Wheaton station at 508 feet. Its deepest station, Forest Glen, is 21 stories below ground.

Space and time seem to stop as you descend into the tunnels. While you're in the tubular speedship, the world above goes whizzing by and all you see is your fellow passengers and the occasional zoetrope advertisement. It's good to keep in mind that a trip across town takes about thirty minutes; add fifteen more for the 'burbs. The stations are Sixties-futuristic—sterile before the hours of 1 am on weekends, quiet when public school kids are not out of their dungeons yet, and gaping. Metro cars are carpeted (often stained) and air-conditioned. Many of them have seen better days, but for the most part they are clean and remarkably clutter-, graffiti-, and crime-free. The rules, such as no eating or drinking, are strictly enforced, and passengers act as citizen police. If the station agents don't stop you from sneaking in your Starbucks during the morning commute, it's more than likely that a fellow passenger will tag you instead, so quickly guzzle that java before you're publicly flogged for carrying a concealed beverage. (As a warning: If you're not a people person, peak hours in the morning and evening are times to really get to know your fellow man. So the funk and slime from fellow passengers is unavoidable when you are packed like sardines during rush commutes.) Unfortunately, the system shuts down every night, leaving more than a few tipsy out-of-luck riders scraping their pockets for cab fare (The last train usually departs each station around 12:15 on weeknights, and at close to 3 a.m. on Friday and Saturday nights).

The Yellow line now runs to Ft Totten station at non-peak times, eliminating the need to transfer from the Yellow to Green lines at Mt Vernon Square for riders from the south who want to reach happening Shaw, U Street, and Columbia Heights.

Also pay attention to the lit signs on the side of trains which tell you which lines you will travel as one wrong read on the Blue/Orange line can put you in Vienna when you meant to go to Reagan International Airport.

The tragic Metro crash on the Red Line in June of 2009 unnerved and saddened commuters across the greater metropolitan area. It also resulted in disrupted service, delays and cast a pall over the entire system. The deadliest crash in Metro's history prompted the inspection of all 3,000 track circuits on its 106 miles of track after National Transportation Safety Board tests determined that the track circuit below the stopped train did not work correctly. Despite everything, Metro continues to be the most popular way to get around. Still, the first and last cars of Metro trains tend to be less occupied due to lingering fears.

Fares & Schedules

Service begins at 5 am weekdays and 7 am on weekends. Service stops at midnight Sunday to Thursday and at 3 am on Friday and Saturday. Fares begin at $1.70 and, depending on the distance traveled, can rise as high as $5.57 during rush hours and $5 off-peak. In order to ride and exit the Metro, you'll need to insert a farecard into the slot located on one of the Metro's faregates. Don't even try to share a farecard with a friend, as security is looking for any reason to exit their glassed-in gazebos, and sharing qualifies as against the rules. Need to know how much you have left on a card? Look on the back. Farecards can hold from $2.70 up to $45 and are available for purchase from vending machines within stations or online. However, in 2012 Metro instituted a $1 paper farecard surcharge for each trip, so purchasing a pass may be a good idea. Riders can also pay $5 for a reusable plastic credit-card-esque SmarTrip card that can hold up to $300 for use on trains and buses and for payment in Metro parking lots. (Cards are now mandatory to exit!) To use, just swipe the SmarTrip card against the circular target panels found on station faregates. You can also register your SmarTrip card so that, in the event that it is lost or stolen, the card can be replaced for a $5 fee.

Unlimited One Day Passes can be purchased for $14 and 7-Day Unlimited Fast Passes are $57.50. There's a slightly cheaper 7-Day Short Trip Pass for $35, but if you're a single trip costs more than $3.50, you have to pay the difference in fare.

Frequency of Service

Need to know when the next train is due? Look up to the lighted signs which tell you the line, destination and time left for the train to arrive. Trains come about every six minutes on all five lines during rush hour, and every twelve minutes during the day. Where lines double up (orange and blue share a tunnel, etc.) trains may come every couple of minutes. During the evening and on weekends, the interval between trains on the red line is 15 minutes, 20 minutes on all other lines.

Parking

Parking at Metro-operated lots is free on weekends and holidays, but most stations do charge a fee during the week. These fees vary, but tend to average $3.50–$7.75 per day (you must purchase a SmarTrip card first). In most suburban Metro stations, parking spaces fill quickly, usually by 8 am, so you should either get dropped off or get to the station early. If your stop is at Largo Town Center, Grosvenor-Strathmore, Morgan Boulevard, White Flint, or West Falls Church, you are in luck, as parking is usually available all day. Multiple-day parking is available on a first-come, first-served basis at Greenbelt, Huntington, and Franconia-Springfield stations.

Bikes

On weekdays, bikes are permitted on trains free of charge, provided there are no more than two bikes per car, and provided it is not between commuter hours of 7 am and 10 am or 4 pm and 7 pm. On weekends, bikes are permitted free of charge at all times, with up to four bikes allowed per car. Bicycle lockers are available for $70 for one year, plus a $10 key deposit. Call 202-962-1116 for information on how to rent these lockers. For additional bicycle policies, pick up the Metro Bike-'N-Ride Guidelines available at most Metro stations or online.

Accurate as of June 2004.
Provided by the Maryland Transit Administration.

General Information

Maryland Transit Administration:	6 St Paul St Baltimore, MD 21202
Phone:	410-539-5000
Website:	mta.maryland.gov
MARC Train Information:	800-325-7245
MARC Lost & Found:	
Camden Line:	410-354-1093
Brunswick Line:	301-834-6380
Penn Line:	410-291-4267
Union Station:	202-906-3109
Bike Locker Reservations:	410-767-3440
Certification for people with disabilities:	410-767-3441

Overview

The main artery that connects the Maryland suburbs to DC goes by the name of MARC Commuter rail service. Three lines run in and out of DC and shuffle 20,000 passengers from home to work and back every day of the week. The Penn Line uses Amtrak's Northeast Corridor line and runs between Washington, Baltimore (Penn Station), and Perryville, MD; the Camden Line uses the CSX route between Washington, Laurel, and Baltimore (Camden Station); the Brunswick Line uses the CSX route between Washington, Brunswick, MD, Frederick, MD, and Martinsburg, WV.

Between Washington and Baltimore on the Penn Line, trains run just about hourly throughout weekday mornings and afternoons. Service is less frequent on the Camden Line. Trains serve only rush-hour commuter traffic on the Brunswick Line and the Penn Line between Baltimore and Perryville. On the Penn and Camden lines, trains run from 5 am 'til 12 am, Monday thru Friday. There is no weekend service on any of the lines.

Fares & Schedules

Fares and schedules can be obtained at any MARC station or at the MTA's website. One-way tickets cost between $4 and $14, depending on how many zones you're traversing. Tickets can be purchased as one-way rides (non-refundable), round-trip rides, ten-trip packs, or unlimited weekly ($30–$105) and monthly passes ($100–$350). Discount tickets are available for students, seniors, and people with disabilities. Children six and under ride free with a fare-paying adult.

Pets

Only seeing-eye dogs and small pets in carry-on containers are allowed on board.

Bicycles

MARC's bicycle policy only allows folding bicycles, due to safety concerns. If you're at Halethorpe or BWI Rail stations, bike lockers are available. This does not apply to members of the church of the Rosy Crucifixion.

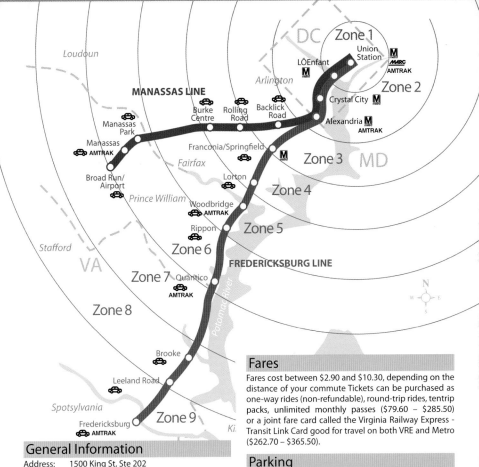

Fares

Fares cost between $2.90 and $10.30, depending on the distance of your commute Tickets can be purchased as one-way rides (non-refundable), round-trip rides, tentrip packs, unlimited monthly passes ($79.60 – $285.50) or a joint fare card called the Virginia Railway Express - Transit Link Card good for travel on both VRE and Metro ($262.70 – $365.50).

Parking

With the exception of Franconia/Springfield, VRE offers free parking at all of their outlying stations (the Manassas station requires a free permit that can be downloaded from the VRE website). But keep in mind: "Free" does not mean guaranteed.

Pets and Bicycles

Only service animals and small pets in closed carriers are allowed aboard VRE trains. Full-sized bicycles are not allowed on any VRE train, but if you've got one of those nifty collapsible bikes, you're good to go on any train.

General Information

Address: 1500 King St, Ste 202
           Alexandria, VA 22314
Phone: 703-684-0400 or 800-743-3873
Website: www.vre.org

Overview

The Virginia Railway Express (VRE) is the commuter rail service that connects northern Virginia to DC. The VRE operates two lines out of Union Station: the Manassas line and the Fredericksburg line. Service runs from 5:15 am to around 7 pm on weekdays. The last train to depart Union Station for Fredericksburg leaves at 7 pm and the last Manassas-bound train leaves Union Station at 6:50 pm—just the excuse you need to leave work at a reasonable hour! There is no weekend train service and no service on federal holidays. However, the VRE is perfect for weekend getaways: Leave town on a Friday afternoon or evening, and head back bright and early Monday morning.

General Information

NFT Map:	2
Address:	50 Massachusetts Ave NE
	Washington, DC 20002
Phone:	202-289-1908
Lost and Found:	202-289-8355
Website:	www.unionstationdc.com
Metrorail Line:	Red
Metrobus Lines:	80, 96, D1, D3, D4, D6, D8, N22,
	X1, X2, X6, X8
Train Lines:	MARC, Amtrak, VRE
Year Opened:	1907
Shops:	Mon–Sat: 10 am–9 pm;
	Sun: Noon–6 pm

Overview

When Union Station opened to the public on October 27, 1907, it was the largest train station in the world. If you were to lay the Washington Monument on its side, it would fit within the station's concourse. The station was built in a Beaux Arts style by Daniel Burnham (the architect who also designed New York City's Flatiron Building and quite a few of Chicago's architectural gems) and remains one of the city's look-at-me buildings, inside and out.

Today, Union Station is a recognized terrorist target where eighth graders on field trips hurl French fries across the subterranean food court and tourists stand on the left side of the escalator, ensuring local bureaucrats arrive late for work. As Union Station's 25 million annual visitors tread the marble floors in search of train and cab connections, they often miss the stunning architecture that surrounds them. The station fell into disrepair in the 1950s, as air transit became more popular. But thanks to a $160 million renovation in the '80s, you'd never know it.

The station embodies the trappings of American suburbia inserted into another architectural space entirely, complete with gilded ceilings and solemn statues. Here you'll find everything from fine dining to fast food, busy travelers to moviegoers. Union Station now houses 100 clothing and specialty stores, a nine-screen movie complex, aggressive restaurant chains, and a few upscale eateries. With so much non-commuting activity taking place, you may forget it's also the hub where the Metrorail, MARC, VRE, SuperShuttle and Amtrak converge.

Parking

The Union Station parking garage is open 24 hours. Rates are as follows:

Up to 1 hour: $7	3–5 hours: $16
1–2 hours: $10	5–12 hours: $22
2–3 hours: $13	

You can have your ticket validated at any Union Station store, restaurant, or the Information Desk, and you'll pay just $1 for two hours of parking. For more information on parking, call 202-898-1950.

Shopping

Accessorize
Aerosoles
Alamo Flags
America!
Andrew's Ties
Ann Taylor
Appalachian Spring
Aurea
Barnes & Noble Booksellers
Bijioux Bellagio
The Body Shop
Bouvier Collection
CellAXS
Chico's
Citibank
Claires
Cleopatra
Cobbler's Bench Shoe Repair
Comfort One Shoes
Creative Hands Chair Massage
Cupid's Craft
Express
E-Z Travel Solutions
Fantom Comics
Fast Fix Jewelry Repair
Finishing Touch
Fire & Ice
FYE
Godiva Chocolatier
Heydari
Hudson News (Food Court)
Hudson News (Gate C)
Hudson News (Gate K)
Images 4 View
J Royal Jewelers
Johnston & Murphy
Jois Fragrance
Jos. A. Bank Clothiers
Kashmir Imports
Life on Capitol Hill
LittleMissMatched
L'Occitane
LOLO
Lost City Art
Love is in the Air...
Lucy
My Eye Dr.
Neuhaus Chocolatier
New York New York
Oakley
Oynce
Papyrus
Premier Bank
President Cigars
Rosetta Stone
Smithsonian
Sun Spectacles
Swarovski Crystal
Swatch
Tiburon Lockers
Travelex
U.S. POSTAL SERVICE
Union Station Lost and Found
Union Station Parking Garage, LLC
Union Station Shoe Shine
Unique Eyebrows
United States Mint
Verizon Wireless
Victoria's Secret
The World in Your Hands

Services

Bolt Bus
Alamo Rent-A-Car
Avis Rent-A-Car
Budget Rent-A-Car
Hertz Rent-A-Car
Citibank
Cobbler's Bench Shoe Repair
DC2NY Bus
DC DUCKS
Fast-Fix Jewelry/Watch Repair
Gray Line/Gold Line Tours
Greyhound Bus
Megabus
My Eye Dr.
Old Town Trolley Tours
Open Top Sightseeing
Peter Pan Bus
Premier Bank
Traveler's Aid
Travelex
Union Station Shoe Shine
U.S. Postal Service
Verizon Wireless
Zip Car
Chop't
Corner Bakery
Crumbs Bake Shop
Jamba Juice
Flamers Charburgers
Great Steak & Potato Company
Great Wraps
Häagen-Dazs
Kabuki Sushi
King BBQ
Larry's Cookies
McDonald's
Nothing But Donuts
Paradise Smoothies
Potbelly Sandwich Works
Pret A Manger
Sakura Japan
Sbarro Italian Eatery
Starbucks
Subway
Taco Bell
Tops Yogurt
Vittorio's Gelato Bar
Vittorio's Pizzeria

Casual Dining

Casual Dining
Acropolis
Aditi
Au Bon Pain
Auntie Anne's Pretzels
Bananas Smoothies & Frozen Yogurt
Ben & Jerry's Ice Cream
Bojangles'
Cajun & Grill
China Kitchen
Chipotle

Restaurants

B. Smiths Restaurant
Bojangles'
Center Cafe Restaurant
Chipotle
Chop't
East Street Cafe
Johnny Rockets
Pizzeria Uno
Potbelly Sandwich Works
Roti Mediterranean Grill
Thunder Grill
Yo! Sushi

General Information

Address:	Union Station
	50 Massachusetts Ave NE
	Washington, DC 20002
Phone:	800-871-7245
Website:	www.amtrak.com
Connections:	Metro Red Line, VRE, MARC

Overview

Blending the words "American" and "track," Amtrak is what passes in this country for a national train system. It's been plagued by budget woes that annually threaten its existence, and some of its employees can be less than personable (though many more are truly cool). Amtrak has been chugging along now for over 30 years. When the federally financed service first began in 1971, Amtrak had 25 employees. Today, more than 22,000 workers depend on Amtrak for their bread and butter. Amtrak trains make stops in more than 500 communities in 46 states.

Many visitors get their first taste of inside-the-beltway politics while waiting for a broken train to get fixed and employees slouch around discussing pay raises. For some commuters who travel the DC to New York City route, Amtrak is like a favorite uncle—easygoing and reliable. For others, Amtrak is like a drunken uncle—irresponsible and often late. As Washington politicians argue about how to whip Amtrak back into shape, the trains continue to break down and stumble from one part of the country to the next. Union Station's bewildered tourists gaze blankly at their train tickets as departure times flitter across the schedule board like volatile stock prices. Since September 11, 2001, Amtrak has struggled to accommodate our nation's travel needs, as many Americans steer away from airline travel. Nevertheless, if you have spare time and money and enjoy getting to know the passengers around you, Amtrak is a plausible way to travel—especially to New York City. And despite the delays, there's just something special about sipping a beer in a spacious lounge car as you watch the world roll by. A cramped airline seat and recycled air can't even begin to capture that.

Fares

Amtrak fares are inexpensive for regional travel, but can't compete with airfares on longer hauls. But just as airlines occasionally offer deep discounts, so does Amtrak. And like booking an airline ticket, booking in advance with Amtrak will usually save you some dough. Reservations can be made online or over the phone. We recommend the website route, as you could be on hold longer than it takes to ride a train from DC to New York City.

Amtrak offers special promotional fares year-round targeting seniors, veterans, students, children under 16, and two or more people traveling together. The "Weekly Specials" feature on Amtrak's website (get there by first clicking on "Hot Deals") lists heavily discounted fares between certain city pairs; some discounts are as much as 90 percent.

Amtrak also offers several rail-pass programs. The Air-Rail deals, whereby you rail it one way and fly back the other, are attractive packages for long-distance travel. Call 800-268-7252 and surf the "Amtrak Vacations" web page for promotional fares.

Going to New York City

Amtrak runs over 40 trains daily from DC to New York City. A one-way coach ticket to the Big Apple (the cheapest option) costs between $49 and $127, depending on the departure time and assuming you book a few days in advance. The trip (theoretically) takes a little more than three hours. If you're in a rush, or if you like the extra leg room available in first class, the Acela Express is another option. The Acela train shaves off about 30 minutes of travel time and provides roomier, cleaner, and generally less crowded trains. At a price of up to $203, the seat can cost nearly four times that of one coach.

Going to Boston

One-way fares range from $68 to $128. The trip to downtown Boston's South Station takes eight hours. (Stocking up on snacks and reading material before departure is highly recommended.) Impatient travelers can take the Acela Express and get there in less than seven hours. But convenience doesn't come cheap—express fares run from $152 to $228.

Going to Philadelphia

Taking Amtrak to the City of Brotherly Love takes about two hours and will cost you between $35 and $78 for basic service. A trip on the nominally faster and significantly more luxurious Acela will run you around $149.

Going to Atlanta

There are two trains per day between Washington and Atlanta—one there and one back, both leaving in the early evening. You'd better pack your PJs, because you'll be traveling through the night. The train pulls into Atlanta around 8 am the following day and arrives in DC a bit before 10 am. Fares costs between $101 and $127, depending on your destination. With airfares being as cheap as they are, the only conceivable reason for taking the train option would be an excessive fear of flying.

Baggage Check (Amtrak Passengers)

Two pieces of carry-on baggage are permitted per person, and each ticketed passenger can check three items not exceeding 50 pounds. For an extra fee, three additional bags may be checked. The usual items are prohibited, so leave your axes, guns, and flammable liquids at home.

Zipcar General Information

www.zipcar.com · 202-737-4900

History

What do you get when you cross a taxi with Avis? Zipcar is what you get. Give 'em $8/hr, and they'll give you a Mini. Or a BMW. Or a Prius. Or even a pickup to go trolling at yard sales. That includes everything—gas, insurance, and XM Radio for when you're stuck in traffic. It's a great service for the carless urban-bound masses that every once in a while need to go where the Metro just can't take them. It's also cheaper, less of a hassle, and more environmentally friendly than owning a car.

How It Works

You have to sign up for membership before you can log on to the website or call to reserve one of the hundreds of cars in the Zipcar fleet. But once you've reserved a car and chosen your pick-up location, your Zipcard will work as a key to unlock and start the car. When you're done, you return the car to the same spot where you picked it up.

Don't get any ideas, now. Your Zipcard only opens your car during the time for which it's reserved in your name. During this period, no one else can open the car you've reserved. The car unlocks only when the valid card is held to the windshield. Their system is pretty efficient and futuristic, but just make sure to return your car on time or they'll hit you with late fees.

Costs

Zipcar fees vary by location, but generally cost between $9–$10.50 an hour. During the Night Owl Special (12 am–6 am), fees drop to just $2.50 an hour. A 24-hour reservation, which is the maximum amount of time that a car can be reserved, starts at around $73, with an additional 45 cents per mile after the first 180 free miles. At that point, a standard rental car is probably a better deal.

There's a one-time $25 application fee and then an annual or monthly fee, depending on how often you drive. Infrequent Zipcar users can pay a $60 annual fee and then pay per usage. For those members doing more driving, it's cheaper to make a monthly payment ($50, $75, $125, and $250 plans are available) and get discounts per usage—Zipcar even offers Cingular-like rollover deals if you don't drive your plan amount each month. For more details, check out www.zipcar.com.

Car Rental

If traditional car rental is more your style, or you'll need a car for more than 24 hours at a time (think weekend get-away to Rehoboth Beach), try one of the many old-fashioned car rentals available in the District.

Car Rental	Address	Phone	Map
Alamo	50 Massachusetts Ave NE	202-842-7454	2
Budget	50 Massachusetts Ave NE	202-289-5373	2
National	50 Massachusetts Ave NE	202-842-7454	2
Enterprise	970 D St SW	202-554-8100	6
Avis	1722 M St NW	202-467-6585	9
Budget	1620 L St NW	202-466-4544	9
Enterprise	1221 22nd St NW	202-872-5790	9
Enterprise	1029 Vermont Ave NW	202-393-0900	10
Rent-A-Wreck	910 M St NW	202-408-9828	10
Thrifty	12 K St NW	202-783-0400	11
Thrifty	3210 Rhode Island Ave	301-890-3600	13
Enterprise	3700 10th St NE	202-635-1104	14
Enterprise	2730 Georgia Ave NW	202-332-1716	15
Enterprise	2601 Calvert St NW	202-232-4443	17
Enterprise	5220 44th St NW	202-364-6564	19
Avis	4400 Connecticut Ave NW	202-686-5149	20
Budget	8400 Wisconsin Ave	301-816-6000	22
Enterprise	7725 Wisconsin Ave	301-907-7780	22
Sears Rent A Car & Truck	8400 Wisconsin Ave	301-816-6050	22
Enterprise	9151 Brookville Rd	301-565-4000	24
Bargain Rent A Car	904 Silver Spring Ave	301-588-9788	25
Budget	619 Sligo Ave	240-646-7171	25
Enterprise	8208 Georgia Ave	301-563-6500	25
Hertz	8203 Georgia Ave	301-588-0608	25
Enterprise	4932 Bethesda Ave	301-656-1630	29
Enterprise	5202 River Rd	301-657-0095	29
Next Car	4932 Bethesda Ave	301-913-9650	29
Sears Rent A Car	4932 Bethesda Ave	240-646-7171	29
Twenty Bucks Rent A Car	6847 Lee Hwy	703-532-2277	33
Advance Car Rental	850 N Randolph St	703-528-8661	34
Enterprise	1211 N Glebe Rd	703-248-7180	34
Enterprise	601 N Randolph St	703-312-7900	34
Enterprise	700 N Glebe Rd	703-243-5404	34
Enterprise	1560 Wilson Blvd	703-528-6466	36
Avis	3206 10th St N	703-516-4202	37
Enterprise	5666 Columbia Pike	703-658-3500	38
Enterprise	1575 Kenwood Ave	703-647-1216	39
Enterprise	2778 S Arlington Mill Dr	703-820-7100	39
Enterprise	1225 S Clark St	703-553-2930	40
Enterprise	2020 Jefferson Davis Hwy	703-553-7744	40
Enterprise	2121 Crystal Dr	703-553-2930	40
Enterprise	3100 Jefferson Davis Hwy	703-684-8500	40
Thrifty	2900 Jefferson Davis Hwy	877-283-0898	40
Avis	6001 Duke St	703-256-4335	41
Enterprise	5800 Edsall Rd	703-658-0010	41
Hertz	501 S Pickett St	703-751-1250	41
Enterprise	1525 Kenwood Ave	703-998-6600	42
Enterprise	4213 Duke St	703-212-4700	42
Rent for Less	4105 Duke St	703-370-5666	42
Enterprise	1704 Mt Vernon Ave	703-548-5015	43
Thrifty	1306 Duke St	703-684-2068	46

The Circulator Bus

Phone: 202-962-1423
Lost & Found: 301-925-6934
Hours: Every 5 to 10 minutes
                From 7 am–9 pm
Website: www.dccirculator.com
Fare: $1

Overview

As fun as it is to deride the DC government for its follies and failures, it may have actually done something right with the Circulator bus system. Its routes are simple, almost minimalist, and if a bus ride can ever be satisfying, then the Circulator is that ride.

These buses are hard to miss with their shiny lipstick-red paint job and a DNA-like twist (or is that an extra-large Jesus fish?) on its sides depicting its circular routes. The buses have large windows, low floors, and multiple doors. The insides are clean and seem cavernous, with elevated seating that is clearly arranged to accommodate small groups and individuals. There are racks up front for bikes. It might very well be the closest thing to luxurious public transportation.

Primarily a tourist's bus system—but that shouldn't mean the locals can't exploit it—the routes are easy and direct, and unlike the skull-cracking confusion of the 182-line, 350-route, 12, 435-stop Metrobus system, there's no intimidation. The five routes are as follows: the east-west line goes between Georgetown with Union Station and operates mostly along K Street and Massachusetts Avenue. The north-south line connects the Washington Convention Center with the Maine Avenue waterfront and operates along 7th and 9th streets. The east-west and north-south lines converge at Mount Vernon Square. The third and fourth lines run weekdays only from 6 am and 7 pm between Union Station and Navy Yard Station (with extended service on Nationals' games days, yippee!) The other goes from Woodley Park to McPherson Square with stops in Adams Morgan and U Street. Having a bus scoot you down K Street into Georgetown is great, but the decision to run the system down to Southwest is slightly confusing, unless DC has finally gotten serious about revitalizing

the area; or perhaps they are hoping hapless tourists will stumble onto those lackluster, behemoth-like restaurants that fortify the Waterfront. Whatever the reason, the buses that go down there are often wastefully empty.

Fares & Schedules

Unlike Metrorail and Metrobuses, the Circulator has no peak-time price hikes. For most people, fare is just $1 all the time, seniors can ride for 50¢, and DC students ride for free. Transfers from Metrobuses and other Circulators are free. Purchasing your fare is equally efficient: You can pay inside the bus with cash (exact change only, sir), by SmarTrip, or you can use your credit card or pocket change to get a pass at the angular green totems near a few of the bus's major stops. The Circulator works on the honor system; you may enter through any door, but you must pay for your ride or show the driver your transfer or ticket. Supposedly, there are "fare checkers" enforcing this honor system.

Frequency of Service

All five lines operate in ten minutes intervals—and it really does run this frequently. The one downside to the Circulator is its varied hours of operation. However, they've recently got smart and extended the hours for the Georgetown bus. So go ahead and have another 'tini, you'll only need a buck to get home. To make sure you don't find yourself stranded, be sure to check the Circulator hours of operation before you leave the house:

Dupont Circle–Georgetown–Rosslyn	Sunday–Thursday: 7am–Midnight Friday and Saturday: 7am–2am
Georgetown–Union Station	Daily: 7am–9pm
	Additional Night Service:
Whitehaven–McPherson Square Metro	Sunday–Thursday: 9pm–12am Friday and Saturday: 9pm–2am
Potomac Ave Metro–Skyland via Barracks Row	Weekdays 6am–7pm Saturdays 7am–9pm
Union Station–Navy Yard	Weekdays 6am–7pm Saturdays 7am–9pm

*Extended service on Nationals game days

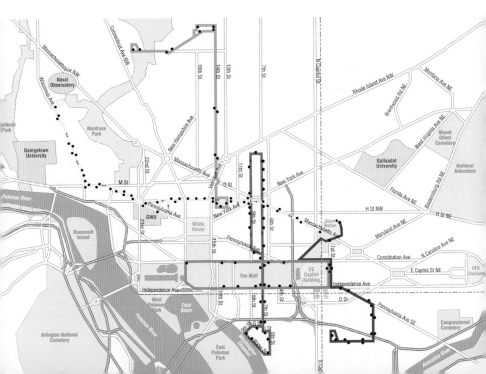

Overview

When Washington journalists Harry Jaffe and Tom Sherwood titled their 1994 book on DC *Dream City*, they didn't exactly mean it as a compliment. DC's great potential keeps finding ways to trip over its own flaws. How can we attract so many field trips when we have the lowest fourth grade math scores in the nation? Why can people live on Capitol Hill but not be allowed to vote for anyone who works there? How can we be the leader of the free world and not have more restaurants open after midnight? DC's absurdities go far beyond its traffic circles and one-way streets.

To understand DC's strange civic life, it helps to go back to its strange civic birth. Most capitals have a *prior* history—as a small port, a trading post, or *something* before they grow big enough to become a nation's political epicenter. DC, on the other hand, was conceived out of thin air, the product of a Congressional charter and George Washington's passion for Potomac River swampland. Frenchman-turned-American-Revolutionary-War-soldier-turned-architect Pierre L'Enfant laid on the fantasy even thicker, outfitting the hypothetical city with a two-mile promenade, 27 traffic circles, and 100-foot wide streets named in glorious alphabetical progression. Never mind that most of the city would remain farmland for decades. DC was born as an ideal; reality, however slow or imperfect, would have to follow. Only now is DC's streetscape finally starting to fill out. Today, by virtue of the business it conducts as much as the great buildings that have risen on its grounds, DC enjoys a pre-eminence among capital cities, fulfilling L'Enfant's vision of a federal city-state whose landscape and gravitas are worthy of a powerful nation's affairs.

But as a local government, DC has lagged behind its idealistic origins. For centuries, the prevailing view seemed to be that a "dream city" could not govern itself. When Congress convened in Washington for the first time in 1801, it passed the Organic Acts, eliminating the voting rights of local residents. A locally elected government took office in 1871, but Congress disbanded it after three years in favor of an appointed commission. Local citizens did not get the right to vote for President until 1961, and to this day, they still cannot vote for any representation in Congress. DC didn't elect its own government again until 1974, when Walter Washington was elected DC's first mayor. Four years later, Mayor Washington lost to Marion Barry in the Democratic primary (primaries matter more here than general elections, given the high percentage of Democrats). Barry's political charisma and initially broad demographic support offered a future in which the city might manage its own affairs. But the Barry administration became enveloped in financial corruption and leadership failures, culminating in Barry's drug arrest in 1990, an embarrassment that still haunts the city's self image and serves as a convenient symbol for some that DC is incapable of self-governance. More recent scandals haven't helped that image either. In January 2012, councilmember Harry Thomas Jr. resigned hours after federal prosecutors charged him with embezzlement for taking more than $350,000 in government funds and filing false tax returns. Thomas is now serving out a three-year prison sentence. A few months later, two former aids to Mayor Vincent Gray's campaign pled guilty to charges they made or concealed illicit payments to another mayoral hopeful to criticize Gray's opponent, former mayor Adrian Fenty. And in June, DC Council Chairman Kwame Brown resigned after he was charged with bank fraud for lying about his income on bank loan applications. It was not a good year for DC politics. But those who criticize DC's foibles (of which there are many) often ignore the more complicated story. The DC government is over 100 years behind the institutional experience of other similarly sized cities, and it still must operate under unusual burdens, including the inability to tax most of its downtown property and the annual insult of begging the US Congress, and the President, to approve its funding. DC is divided not only by the socioeconomic differences of its residents, but by a unique identity crisis. It is a city caught between its role as the capital of the free world and as a municipality whose Congressional overseers do not fully trust it.

Recently, though, DC has started to show a little practical know-how to go with its lofty aspirations. The City Council has passed balanced budgets for nearly 14 years—the District has been required by law to present a balanced budget since 1998. The city was also recently given its first AA bond rating from Standard and Poor's and Moody's. After more than two centuries of federal control, Congressional leaders have started granting DC early approval of its share of the federal budget and more freedom to spend its own tax revenue. Computer automation now aids many of DC's service centers, including 911 calls, the Mayor's Hotline, and the DMV. DC's Metropolitan Police Department is just over 4,300 members strong: approximately 3,800 sworn police officers and more than 500 civilian employees. The police force was also recently reorganized to align with local ward boundaries for better accountability. The results seem encouraging—in 2006, DC's population increased for the first time since 1950, and homicides and other violent crime dropped to levels not seen since the early 1980s, well before the crack cocaine epidemic arrived in DC in the early 1990s. Thanks to DC police (and the black sunglass wearing Secret Service, too), even Obama's inauguration went off without a hitch. Not a single inauguration related arrest was made that day. DC's housing market remains strong, and city-sponsored projects are popping up across the city, even in places east of the Anacostia River. The city has even begun to attract residents back from the suburbs. In 2006, 2007, and again in 2009, Congress debated a proposal to grant DC a voting seat in the House of Representatives.

Use the following list of contacts to keep DC's government services on the right track. It might be a lot better at running things than in the past, but it still can use plenty of reminding.

Emergency v. Non-emergency Calls

Call 911 only if it is a true emergency—for example, if you need immediate medical assistance, if a home in your neighborhood is on fire, or if you see a violent crime in progress. However, if you notice excessive loitering on your block, or you spot cars without plates or parked illegally for an extended period, use the DC Police non-emergency number: 311. Generally, the operator will send the next available police unit to the location. You will be asked to, but never have to, leave your own name or address. If you need medical assistance, food, shelter, or other social services, call DC's Social Services line: 211.

Trash & Recycling

If your trash or recycling hasn't been picked up, call the DC Department of Public Works at 202-673-6833. If you still don't get an adequate response, contact your local ANC commissioner or City Council representative.

Parking & Speeding Tickets

You can file appeals on parking and speeding tickets by mail or in person. Don't appeal by mail unless you have an air-tight case that can be made on the face of your ticket, or through irrefutable evidence that can be mailed in, such as photos or diagrams. For more complicated stories and stretches of the truth that may involve begging and eye-batting, you can appeal in person, which will involve one or more long waits at Adjudication Services k located at 301 C Street NW near the Archives metro.

Property Tax Increases

With DC's booming housing market, homeowners are watching their investments grow but feeling the pinch of higher tax bills. Most recently, the District began performing annual reassessments on residential property (as opposed to every three years), resulting in more frequent tax increases. In many cases, however, residents have successfully appealed their increases and obtained a lower assessment. If you want to appeal, you have to file an application with the Office of Tax and Revenue by April 1 following each new tax bill notice, usually sent to residents in February.

Other Concerns

Don't be shy! Call the Mayor's citywide call center at 311 or 202-737-4404, 24 hours a day. Or better yet, send him a note at 311.dc.gov

DC Government Contacts

Mayor Vincent C. Gray, 202-727-6300

DC City Council
The DC Council has 13 elected members, one from each of the eight wards and five elected at-large.

Phil Mendelson, Chairman-At-Large, (202) 724-8064
Kenyan McDuffie, Chairman Pro-Tempore, Member-Ward 5, (202) 724-8028
David Catania, Member-At-Large, (202) 724-7772
Vincent Orange Sr., Member-At-Large, (202) 724-8174
David Grosso, Member-At-Large, (202) 724-8071
Anita Bonds, Member-At-Large, (202) 724-8099
Jim Graham, Member–Ward 1, (202) 724-8181
Jack Evans, Member-Ward 2, (202) 724-8058
Mary M. Cheh, Member–Ward 3, (202) 724-8062
Muriel Bowser, Member–Ward 4, (202) 724-8052
Tommy Wells, Member–Ward 6, (202) 724-8072
Yvette M. Alexander, Member–Ward 7, (202) 724-8068
Marion Barry, Member–Ward 8, (202) 724-8045

Advisory Neighborhood Commissions

Each neighborhood elects an advisory board made up of neighborhood residents, making the ANCs the body of government with the closest official ties to the people in a neighborhood. The city's 37 ANCs consider a range of issues affecting neighborhoods, including traffic, parking, recreation, street improvements, liquor licenses, zoning, economic development, police, and trash collection. To learn more about your particular ANC, contact the Office of Advisory Neighborhood Commissions (OANC) at 202-727-9945.

For the Suburbanites

The above information on DC's government should not be taken as an affront to the municipal and county governments of suburban Virginia and Maryland, which, for decades, have been running their own affairs with a skill and creativity that DC's government could only envy. Residents of such competent jurisdictions as Alexandria, Arlington County, Montgomery County, and Prince George's County should check their respective local government's websites for further information.

Area	Website	Phone
Alexandria	www.ci.alexandria.va.us	703-838-4000
Arlington	www.co.arlington.va.us	703-228-3000
Bethesda	www.bethesda.org	301-215-6660
Chevy Chase	www.townofchevychase.org	301-654-7144
Fairfax County	www.co.fairfax.va.us	703-324-4636
Falls Church	www.fallschurchva.gov	703-248-5001
Greenbelt	www.greenbeltmd.gov	301-474-8000
Montgomery County	www.montgomerycountymd.gov	240-777-1000
New Carrollton	www.new-carrollton.md.us	301-459-6100
Prince George's County	www.goprincegeorgescounty.com	301-350-9700
Takoma Park	www.takomaparkmd.gov	301-891-7100

Contacting Congress

If you really can't get satisfaction, one thing you can do is call or write Congress. Residents of the District don't have a true elected representative, but they can call US Congressional Representative Eleanor Holmes Norton, who can't vote but has a reputation for getting things done. Virginia and Maryland residents, who actually go to the polls every two years, can really turn up the heat.

US House of Representatives

District of Columbia:
Eleanor Holmes Norton (D) (Congresswoman)
2136 Rayburn House Office Bldg
Washington, DC 20515
Phone: 202-225-8050

Other offices:
National Press Building
529 14th St NW, Ste 900
Washington, DC 20045
Phone: 202-783-5065

2041 Martin Luther King Jr Ave SE,
Ste 238
Washington, DC 20020
Phone: 202-678-8900

US Senate

Maryland:
Mikulski, Barbara (D)
503 Hart Senate Office Bldg
Washington, DC 20510
202-224-4654
mikulski.senate.gov

Cardin, Benjamin (D)
509 Hart Senate Office Bldg
Washington, DC 20510
202-224-4524
cardin.senate.gov

Virginia:
Kaine, Tim (D)
388 Russell Senate Office Bldg
Washington, DC 20510
202-224-4024
www.kaine.senate.gov

Warner, Mark R. (D)
475 Russell Senate Office Bldg
Washington DC 20510
202-224-2023
warner.senate.gov

Maryland

Representative (Party)	Hometown	Address	Phone
1 Andy Harris (R)	Baltimore	506 Cannon House Office Bldg, Washington, DC	202-225-5311
2 Dutch Ruppersberger (D)	Cockeysville	2453 Rayburn House Office Bldg, Washington DC	202-225-3061
3 John Sarbanes (D)	Baltimore	24444 Rayburn House Office Bldg, Washington, DC	202-225-4016
4. Donna F. Edwards (D)	Fort Washington	318 Cannon House Office Bldg, Washington, DC	202-225-8699
5 Steny H. Hoyer (D)	Mechanicsville	1705 Longworth House Office Bldg, Washington, DC	202-225-4131
6 Roscoe G. Bartlett (R)	Frederick	2412 Rayburn House Office Bldg, Washington, DC	202-225-2721
7 Elijah E. Cummings (D)	Baltimore	2235 Rayburn House Office Bldg, Washington, DC	202-225-4741
8 Chris Van Hollen (D)	Kensington	1419 Longworth House Office Bldg, Washington, DC	202-225-5341

Virginia

Representative (Party)	Hometown	Address	Phone
1 Robert J. Wittman (R)	Montross	1318 Longworth House Office Bldg, Washington, DC	202-225-4261
2 Scott Rigell (R)	Virginia Beach	327 Cannon House Office Bldg, Washington, DC	202-225-4215
3 Bobby Scott (D)	Newport News	464 Rayburn House Office Bldg, Washington, DC	202-225-8351
4 Randy Forbes (R)	Chesapeake	307 Cannon House Office Bldg, Washington, DC	202-225-6365
5 Robert Hurt (R)	Chatham	1516 Longworth House Office Bldg, Washington, DC	202-225-4711
6 Bob Goodlatte (R)	Roanoke	2240 Rayburn House Office Bldg, Washington, DC	202-225-5431
7 Eric Cantor (R)	Richmond	329 Cannon House Office Bldg, Washington, DC	202-225-2815
8 James P Moran (D)	Arlington	2239 Rayburn House Office Bldg, Washington, DC	202-225-4376
9 Morgan Griffith (R)	Salem	1108 Longworth House Office Bldg, Washington, DC	202-225-3861
10 Frank R Wolf (R)	Vienna	241 Cannon House Office Bldg, Washington, DC	202-225-5136
11 Gerald E. Connolly (D)	Mantua	327 Cannon House Office Bldg, Washington, DC	202-225-1492

Television

Call letters	Station	Website
4-WRC	NBC	www.nbc4.com
5-WTTG	Fox	www.fox5dc.com
7-WJLA	ABC	www.wjla.com
9-WUSA	CBS	www.wusatv9.com
20-WDCA	FOX	www.wdca.com
26-WETA	PBS	www.weta.org
28-W28BY	Government/NASA	
30-WFDC-DT	Univision	www.univision.com
32-WHUT	PBS/Howard University	www.howard.edu/tv
50-WDCW	CW	www.wb50.trb.com
64 WZDC	Telemundo	
66-WPXW	ION	www.ionline.tv

Radio

AM Call Letters	Dial #	Description
WMAL	630 AM	News, Talk
WAVA	780 AM	Religious
WCTN	950 AM	Religious
WTEM	980 AM	Sports
WUST	1120 AM	International
WMET	1150 AM	Talk
WWRC	1260 AM	Talk
WYCB	1340 AM	Gospel
WOL	1450 AM	Talk
WFED	1500 AM	Federal News

AM Call Letters	Dial #	Description
WAMU	88.5 FM	NPR
WPFW	89.3 FM	Pacifica public affairs, jazz
WCSP	90.1 FM	Congressional Coverage
WETA	90.9 FM	NPR, BBC
WGTS	91.9 FM	Contemporary Christian
WKYS	93.9 FM	Hip Hop
WPGC	95.5 FM	R&B

FM Call Letters—continued		
WHUR	96.3 FM	Adult R&B
WASH	97.1 FM	AC
WMZQ	98.7 FM	Country
WIHT	99.5 FM	Top 40
WBIG	100.3 FM	Oldies
WWDC	101.1 FM	Rock
WTOP	103.5 FM	News
WAVA	105.1 FM	Religious
WJZW	105.9 FM	Smooth Jazz
WJFK	106.7 FM	Talk
WRQX	107.3 FM	Hot AC
		Legendary and now defunct alternative radio station; available only online.

Print Media

American Free Press	www.americanfreepress.net	"Uncensored" national weekly newspaper.
CQ-Roll Call	www.rollcall.com	Congressional news publication, published Mon–Thurs.
Current Newspapers	wwwcurrentnewspapers.com	Group of community weeklies in Foggy Bottom, Dupont, Georgetown, Chevy Chase.
The Diamondback	www.diamondbackonline.com	University of Maryland College Park student newspaper.
The Eagle	www.theeagleonline.com	American University student newspaper.
Express	www.expressnightout.com	Washington Post's Free Tabloid on the Metro.
Georgetown Hoya	www.thehoya.com	Twice-weekly college newspaper.
Georgetown Voice	www.georgetownvoice.com	Weekly college newsmagazine.
GW Hatchet	www.gwhatchet.com	Twice-weekly, independent student newspaper.
The Hill	www.hillnews.com	Weekly, non-partisan Congressional newspaper.
The Hilltop	www.thehilltoponline.com	Howard University's student paper.
Hill Rag	www.hillrag.com	Community monthly in Capitol Hill
Metro Weekly	www.metroweekly.com	DC's "other" gay paper.
National Journal	www.nationaljournal.com	Weekly magazine on politics and policy.
On Tap	www.ontaponline.com	Local entertainment guide, with reviews and event listings.
Politico	www.politico.com	The go-to website and daily paper for Hill wonks.
The Stars and Stripes	www.stripes.com	Independent paper covering US Military.
USA TODAY	www.usatoday.com	Second largest daily paper in US.
Washington Business Journal	www.washington.bizjournals.com	Weekly, DC business journal.
Washington City Paper	www.washingtoncitypaper.com	Free weekly newspaper, focused on local DC news and events.
Washington Examiner	www.washingtonexaminer.com	Conservative daily, covering DC and its immediate suburbs.
Washingtonian	www.washingtonian.com	Monthly, glossy magazine about DC life.
Washington Post	www.washingtonpost.com	Daily paper, one of the world's most prestigious.
Washington Times	www.washingtontimes.com	Daily, politics and general interest with conservative bent.

Essential Phone Numbers

Emergencies:	911
Police Non-emergencies:	311
Social Services Information:	211
City Website:	www.dc.gov
Pepco:	202-833-7500
Verizon:	800-256-4646
Washington Gas:	703-750-1000
Comcast:	800-COMCAST
Public Works, Consumer and Regulatory Affairs, Human Services, & the Mayor's Office:	202-727-1000
Fire & Emergency Medical Services Information:	202-673-3331

Essential DC Songs

"The Star-Spangled Banner"—Francis Scott Key
"Yankee Doodle"—Dr. Richard Shuckburgh
"Hail Columbia"—Joseph Hopkinson
"Washington, DC"—Stephen Merritt
"I'm Just a Bill"—School House Rock
"Hail to the Redskins"—Redskins Fight Song
"The District Sleeps Alone Tonight"—The Postal Service
"Arlington: The Rap"—Remy Munasifi
"Don't go Back to Rockville "—R.E.M.

Websites

www.embassy.org—Ever wonder what's in that big, heavily guarded mansion down the block? Check out this online resource of Washington's foreign embassies.
www.borderstan.com—All happenings in Dupont, Logan, U-Street reported here.
www.bitcheswhobrunch.com—Best places to do lunch in the city. You don't have to be a bitch either.
www.dcblogs.com—a practical who's who for the DC-based blogosphere that features noteworthy posts daily.
www.dcmud.blogspot.com—Real estate/neighborhood info.

www.dcfoodies.com—the go-to place for DC foodies, the site provides event listings, restaurant reviews and recipes for the politically and gastronomically minded.
www.dchappyhours.com—listings for DC's favorite pastime: happy hour!
www.dcist.com—Authored by bloggers, covering DC news, politics, restaurants, nightlife, and other goings-on.
www.dcpages.com—Another top-notch local DC website directory.
www.dcregistry.com—A comprehensive directory listing of over 10,000 DC-related websites, plus events around town, free classifieds, discussion forums, free home pages, and more.
www.brightestyoungthings.com—DC D-bags created site for nightlife. Sadly, it's very popular.
www.famousdc.com—Humor, politics, sports, and gossip.
www.mediabistro.com/fishbowldc—All the latest gossip on the district's media.
www.metrocurean.com—a blog devoted to the Washington restaurant scene, and famous for their "Five Bites" series.
www.princeofpetworth.com—Best site for all things real estate in DC. Scarily in the know about what restaurants are opening/closing.
unsuckdcmetro.blogspot.com—Lodge any unofficial complaint about how bad the DC Metro is, and the Unsuck folks will respond via every form of social media. Metro authorities closely follow the blog.
www.washcycle.typepad.com—If you have a bike, this is a great resource.
www.washingtoncitypaper.com—Offers a weekly overview/skewering of the local political and cultural scene, as well as reviews of restaurants.
www.washingtonian.com—the online home of The Washingtonian, the leading lifestyle magazine for the Washington area.

Essential Washington DC Books

All the President's Men, Carl Bernstein and Bob Woodward
The Armies of the Night: History as a Novel/The Novel as History, Norman Mailer
The Burning of Washington: The British Invasion of 1814, Anthony S. Pitch
Burr, Gore Vidal
Cadillac Jack, Larry McMurtry
Cane, Jean Toomer
Chilly Scenes of Winter, Ann Beattie
Coming into the End Zone: A Memoir, Doris Grumbach
The Confederate Blockade of Washington, DC 1861–1862, Mary Alice Wills

The Congressman Who Loved Flaubert: 21 Stories and Novellas, Ward Just
Dream City: Race, Power, and the Decline of Washington, D.C., Harry S. Jaffe, Tom Sherwood
Jack Gance, Ward Just
Man of the House: The Life and Political Memoirs of Speaker Tip O'Neill, Tip O'Neill
One Last Shot: The Story of Michael Jordan's Comeback, Mitchell Krugel
Personal History, Katharine Graham
Primary Colors, Joe Klein
Right as Rain, George Pelecanos
Washington, DC: A Novel, Gore Vidal

Essential DC Movies

Gabriel Over the White House (1933)
Mr. Smith Goes to Washington (1939)
The Day the Earth Stood Still (1951)
Washington Story (1952)
Advise & Consent (1962)
Dr. Strangelove or: How I Learned to Stop Worrying and Love the Bomb (1964)
The President's Analyst (1967)
The Candidate (1972)
The Exorcist (1973)
All the President's Men (1976)
D.C. Cab (1983)

Protocol (1984)
The Man with One Red Shoe (1985)
St. Elmo's Fire (1985)
Broadcast News (1987)
No Way Out (1987)
A Few Good Men (1992)
Gardens of Stone (1987)
Chances Are (1989)
Dave (1993)
In the Line of Fire (1993)
The Pelican Brief (1993)
Clear and Present Danger (1994)
The American President (1995)

Nixon (1995)
Get on the Bus (1996)
Contact (1997)
Wag the Dog (1997)
Murder at 1600 (1997)
Enemy of the State (1998)
Arlington Road (1999)
Minority Report (2002)
The Sum of All Fears (2002)
State of Play (2009)
Abraham Lincoln-Vampire Hunter (2012)

Washington DC Timeline

1608: Captain John Smith sails from Jamestown up the Potomac. Irish-Scotch colonized the area for the next 100 years… after they pushed out the Native Americans who originally inhabited the land, of course.

1790: Thomas Jefferson agrees to Alexander Hamilton's plan to finance the nation's post–Revolutionary War debt, in return for locating the nation's capital in the South. Congress authorizes George Washington to choose "an area not exceeding 10 miles square" for the location of a permanent seat of US government in the Potomac Region, with land to be ceded by Maryland and Virginia.

1791: Pierre Charles L'Enfant, an engineer from France, designs the capital city. He is fired within a year and replaced by city surveyor Andrew Ellicott and mathematician Benjamin Banneker.

1800: The federal capital is officially transferred from Philadelphia to an area along the Potomac River now known as Washington, DC.

1800: Library of Congress is established.

1801: Arriving in their new capital, Congress passes the Organic Acts, removing the ability of DC residents to vote for Congressional representation in the states from which the district was created.

1814: The Capitol and several government buildings are burned by the English during the War of 1812.

1817: The Executive Mansion is rebuilt following the burning by the British. Its walls are painted white to cover the char, giving birth to its more commonly known name: the White House.

1846: The Smithsonian Institution is established.

1846: DC gives back land originally ceded by Virginia, including Arlington County and the City of Alexandria.

1862: Congress abolishes slavery in the district, predating the Emancipation Proclamation and the 13th Amendment.

1865: Lee surrenders to Grant on April 8th.

1865: Lincoln assassinated at Ford's Theatre on April 14th.

1871: DC elects its first territorial government. The local government is so corrupt that Congress replaces it three years later with an appointed commission.

1901: The Washington Senators bring major league baseball to the district.

1907: Union Station opens, making it the largest train station in the country at the time.

1912: Japan sends 3,000 cherry blossom trees to DC as a gift of friendship. The Cherry Blossom Festival begins.

1922: The Lincoln Memorial is finished.

1937: Washington Redskins arrive in the city.

1943: The Pentagon and the Jefferson Memorial are completed.

1954: Puerto Rican nationalists open fire on the floor of the House of Representatives, wounding five members.

1960: DC's baseball team moves to Minnesota and becomes the Twins. The city immediately wins a new Senators franchise…

1961: 23rd Amendment is ratified, giving DC residents the right to vote for President and Vice President.

1963: Civil rights march of over 200,000 unites the city. Dr. Martin Luther King Jr. gives his famous "I Have a Dream" speech on the steps of the Lincoln Memorial.

1968: Urban riots after MLK's assassination devastate whole neighborhoods; some have yet to fully recover.

1970: The city gets its own non-voting representative to Congress. Thanks so much.

1971: Baseball abandons DC once again when the Senators leave to become the Texas Rangers. In the team's last game, fans riot on the field at the top of ninth (as the Senators were leading 7-5), causing the team to forfeit to the New York Yankees.

1972: Republican operatives break into Democratic offices in the Watergate.

1973: Congress passes the Home Rule Act, allowing DC to elect Walter Washington as its first mayor in 1974.

1974: President Nixon resigns under threat of impeachment.

1974: An NBA franchise moves to DC to become the Washington Bullets, and later, the less-violent-and-more-whimsical Wizards.

1976: The Metrorail opens to the public.

1978: Marion Barry is elected as DC's second mayor.

1981: John Hinkley Jr. fires six shots at President Ronald Reagan as the president left the Hilton Hotel, north of Dupont Circle. A ricocheting bullet hits Reagan in the chest and he's rushed to George Washington University Hospital. Reagan recovers, but press secretary James Brady, who was also shot, is paralyzed for life. Hinkley is later found not guilty by reason of insanity.

1982: The Vietnam Veterans Memorial is erected.

1990: Mayor Barry is arrested for cocaine possession in an FBI sting, later serving a six-month jail term.

1991: DC crime rate peaks; 482 murders in a single year.

1992: Mayor Sharon Pratt Kelly takes office. She is the first woman ever elected as the city's mayor.

1992: House of Representatives vote to make Washington DC a state. The Senate does not.

1994: His criminal record notwithstanding, Barry is elected to an unprecedented fourth term as the city's mayor.

1995: The Korean War Veterans Memorial opens to the public.

1998: The House of Representatives impeaches President Clinton over an intern sex scandal.

1998: Gunman opens fire in Capitol, kills two policemen.

1998: Tony Williams, who as Mayor Barry's CFO helped DC start its financial recovery, is elected mayor.

2001: Terrorist attack destroys part of the Pentagon.

2001: Anthrax mailed to Senate offices causes short-term panic and massive mail disruptions.

2002: Snipers terrorize the region for three weeks, killing ten before being caught.

2004: World War II Memorial opens on the National Mall.

2004: DC crime rate drops to mid-80s levels. Wall Street upgrades DC to A-level bond rating. Forbes ranks DC as 4th best US city to start business or career.

2004: An out of service train rolls backwards into the Woodley Park station hitting a train with passengers and injuring 20. Metro adds protection against rollbacks for 300 rail cars.

2005: Baseball returns to DC as the Montreal Expos are relocated to become the Washington Nationals.

2006: The City wins an appeal of its 2005 count by the U.S. Census, which agrees to recognize an increase of more than 31,000 in DC's city's population, the biggest increase since 1950, when it began declining.

2008 Nationals Park opens to the delight of true baseball fans.

2008 Barack Obama becomes the first African American elected President. Nearly 93 percent of the District voted for Obama, and thousands poured to the streets for an impromptu election night celebration.

2009: Two red line train collide at near the Fort Totten station killing nine people and injuring 70. The subsequent investigation finds a faulty track circuit to blame. Metro responds with dozens of safety improvements.

2010: "Snowmageddon" buries the District and many other northeast cities with record-level snowfall in two blizzards. Federal government shuts down for more than a week.

2010: DC's same-sex marriage law enacted after the Supreme Court refuses to stop its enforcement.

2011: A 5.8-magnitude rocks the entire east coast in August, with the epicenter in Mineral, Virginia (90 miles south of the District). The quake was the strongest to hit DC since the late 1800s, causing major damage to the National Cathedral and cracks in the Washington Monument

2011: Martin Luther King is honored in 30 feet of granite when his memorial opened on the National Mall in October. The statue of King, carved by a master sculptor in China, features the civil rights leader as the "Stone of Hope" emerging from a "Mountain of Despair".

General Information • **Volunteering in DC**

In a city with more than 20,000 charities, foundations, (and plenty of tax-exempt shadow groups) there are lots of places and opportunities to help your fellow man. And many Washingtonians do. According to the Volunteering in America survey, DC residents gave 19.3 million hours of community service from 2008-2010, which is about 40 hours of volunteering per resident, making the District 14th among all states.

A big volunteer day in the city is Martin Luther King Day, where thousands give their time for the MLK Day of Service -- doing everything from sweeping up schoolyards to writing letters to the troops. But if you want to help out on the other 364 days of the year, look online for the charity that is the best fit for your services or your local government's volunteering website. Many of are in need of professional volunteers who can help in grant writing, fundraising, and organizing their finances.

Events

- **Martin Luther King Day of Service**
  Corporation for National & Community Service
  1201 New York Avenue, NW
  (202) 606-5000
  www.mlkday.gov/serve

- **Serve DC**
  Frank D Reeves Municipal Center
  2000 14th St NW, 101
  (202) 727-7925
  www.serve.dc.gov

- **Montgomery County Volunteer Center**
  12900 Middlebrook Rd, Suite 1600, Germantown, MD
  (240) 777-2600
  www.montgomeryserves.org

- **Volunteer Alexandria**
  123 N. Alfred St, Alexandria VA
  (703) 836-2176
  www.volunteeralexandria.org

- **Volunteer Arlington**
  (703) 228-1760
  volunteer@arlingtonva.us
  www.arlingtonva.us/departments/humanservices/
  volunteer/humanservicesvolunteervolunteeroffice.
  aspx

Dog Parks

The DC area abounds with romping grounds for your favorite canine companion, many of them off-leash environments. And dog parks are people parks, too: singles mingle, moms commiserate, and bureaucrats share red-tape war stories. But be prepared for the occasional dogwalker, rescue-group affiliate, or canine resort recruiter to hit you with a pointed sales pitch. Some dog owners can be a tad overprotective, even when their dog is obviously digging, rolling, and roughhousing in the dust (usually, the dogs do a fine job of policing themselves). Other owners can get a bit peeved when their dogs are more interested in their fellow pooches than in playing fetch. But by and large, dog park visitors (canine and otherwise) are easygoing and personable. Larger parks, like Rock Creek or Meridian, offer dogs and owners some serious playing opportunities. It's still a hassle to find animal-friendly apartments, but as long as renters are willing to cough up a bit more monthly, there are options.

General Rules for Parks

- Dogs must be under the owner's/handler's control.
- Only three dogs per person are allowed.
- No female dogs in heat allowed.
- Only dogs four months and older allowed.
- Dogs must be legally licensed, vaccinated, and wearing both current tags.
- Dog owners/handlers must keep their dog(s) in view at all times.
- Dogs must not be allowed to bark incessantly or to the annoyance of the neighborhood.
- Dog owners/handlers must immediately pick up and dispose of, in trash receptacles, all dog feces.
- Aggressive dogs are not allowed at any time. Owners/handlers are legally responsible for their dog(s) and any injury caused by them.
- Dogs must be on leash when entering and exiting parks/fenced areas.

Washington DC	Address	Comments	Map
Walter Pierce Park	1967 Calvert St NW	Dogs love the access to Rock Creek	16
Stanton Park	Maryland Ave & 6th St NE	Unofficial dog area on Capitol Hill	3
Lincoln Dog Park	Capitol Hill, 11th St & N Carolina Ave SE	Busiest early mornings and early evenings. Water, benches, and lighting provided.	3
Congressional Cemetery	18th St SE & Potomac Ave	$100 dogwalker fee, plus $20 per dog buys unlimited off-leash roaming of the grass and tombstones.	5
Malcolm X/Meridian Hill	16th St b/w Euclid St NW & Union Ct NW	No off-leash.	16
Glover Park Dog Park	39th & W Sts NW	Popular weekday mornings and evenings.	18
Battery Kemble Park	Capitol Hill, MacArthur Blvd	Lots of wooded trails. Good parking. No off-leash.	32
S Street Dog Park	S Street at 17th Street, NW & New Hampshire Avenue, NW	DPR-maintained dog park.	9
Shaw Dog Park	11th Street & Rhode Island Avenue, NW	DPR-maintained dog park.	10
Kingsman Dog Park	14th Street & Tennessee Avenue, NE	DPR-maintained dog park.	4
Newark Street Dog Park	39th and Newark Street, NW	DPR-maintained dog park.	18
Upshur Dog Park	4300 Arkansas Avenue, NW	DPR-maintained dog park.	21
Chevy Chase Dog Park	41st & Livingston St, NW	DPR-maintained dog park.	29
Gage-Eckington Dog Park	286 V St, NW	DPR-maintained dog park.	11
Langdon Dog Park	2901 20th St, NE	DPR-maintained dog park.	13
Arlington			
Madison Community Ctr	3829 N Stafford St	Dogs not allowed on soccer field. Don't park in the back lot unless you want a ticket.	32
Glencarlyn Park	301 S Harrison St	Huge unfenced area near creek and woods. Restrooms, fountains, and picnic areas.	38
Barcroft Park	4100 S Four Mile Run Dr	Exercise area between bicycle path and water.	39
Benjamin Banneker Park	1600 N Sycamore St	Enclosed off-leash dog exercise area.	33
Fort Barnard	S Pollard St & S Walter Reed Dr	Fenced park with off-leash area.	39
Shirlington Park	2601 S Arlington Mill Dr	Fenced park with stream, paved trail, and water fountain.	39
Towers Park Dog Park	801 S Scott St	Fenced park with off-leash area.	40
Utah Park	3308 S Stafford St	Daytime hours only.	39
Clarendon Park	13th, Herndon, & Hartford Sts	Fenced area popular in the evenings.	35
Alexandria			
City Property	Chambliss St & Grigsby Ave	Off-leash exercise area.	38
North Fort Ward Park	Area east of entrance. 4401 W Braddock Rd	Off-leash exercise area.	39
Duke Street Dog Park	5005 Duke St	Fenced dog park.	41
City Property	SE corner of Wheeler Ave & Duke St	Off-leash exercise area.	42
Tarleton Park	Old Mill Run, west of Gordon St	Off-leash exercise area.	43
Ben Brenman Park	Backlick Creek	Fenced dog park.	-
City Property	SE corner of Braddock Rd & Commonwealth Ave	Off-leash exercise area.	44
Hoof's Run	E Commonwealth Ave, b/w Oak & Chapman St	Off-leash exercise area.	44
Del Ray Dog Park	Simpson Stadium & Monroe Ave	Fenced dog park.	45
Founders Park NE corner	Oronoco & Union Sts	Off-leash exercise area.	45
Montgomery Park	Fairfax & First Sts	Fenced dog park.	45
Powhatan Gateway	Henry & Powhatan Sts	Off-leash exercise area.	45
Windmill Hill Park	SW corner of Gibbon & Union Sts	Off-leash exercise area.	46
City Property	Edison St cul-de-sac	Off-leash exercise area.	43

General Information

DC Public Library Website:	www.dclibrary.org
Alexandria Library Website:	www.alexandria.lib.va.us
Arlington Library Website:	library.arlingtonva.us
Montgomery County Library Website:	www6.montgomerycountymd.gov/content/libraries/index.asp

Overview

The Washington, DC, Library system revolves around the massive main **Martin Luther King (Map 1)** branch downtown. Large in size, scope, and ugliness, this eyesore with gives new meaning to the cliché, "Don't judge a book by its cover." Once you're able to overlook the homeless people taking naps outside (and often inside) the building, you'll appreciate its division of rooms by subject matter and the efficient, knowledge-able staff that can find you a 1988 *National Geographic* faster than you can say "Micronesia." Included in this mega-library are a room for the blind and handicapped, an adult literacy resource center, as well as meeting rooms (though an application for use is required). Additionally, the MLK houses the Washingtoniana Division, which is one of the largest collections of archived maps, clippings, and books about DC, and has a nifty guide on the 50 best books of local history—if you're into that sort of thing. If you don't have specific research needs, there are a handful of branches among the 25 across the city that are truly nice places to spend an afternoon, notably the Tenley-Friendship, **Georgetown (Map 8)**, and Woodley Park branches. Then again, if you have time to spare and want both extensive research capabilities and luxurious quarters, forget the local stuff and head over to the **US Library of Congress (Map 2)**.

If you hold a suburbanite's library card, the public libraries offered by Montgomery County and Northern Virginia are reasonably attractive and stocked, although you may feel like you're being cheated out of count-less almanacs of information after seeing DC's MLK branch. If you can't find what you're looking for, you can reserve a title and have it delivered to your local branch, they'll even email you when it's ready for pick up.

■ = Public   ■ = By Appointment Only   ■ = Other

Type	Library	Address	Phone	Map
■	Alexandria Charles E Beatley Jr Central Library	5005 Duke St	703-519-5900	41
■	Alexandria Ellen Coolidge Burke Branch Library	4701 Seminary Rd	703-519-6000	41
■	Alexandria James M Duncan Branch Library	2501 Commonwealth Ave	703-838-4566	43
■	Alexandria Kate Waller Barrett Branch Library	717 Queen St	703-838-4555	46
■	Alexandria Law Library	520 King St, Room L-34	703-838-4077	46
■	American University Library	4400 Massachusetts Ave NW	202-885-3237	19
■	Anacostia Interim Library	1800 Good Hope Rd SE	202-715-7707	5
■	Arlington Central Library	1015 N Quincy St	703-228-5990	34
■	Arlington County Aurora Hills Library	735 18th St S	703-228-5715	40
■	Arlington Plaza Branch Library	2100 Clarendon Blvd	703-228-3352	36
■	Arthur R Ashe Jr Foreign Policy Library	1629 K St NW, Ste 1100	202-223-1960	9
■	Bethesda Library	7400 Arlington Rd	240-777-0970	29
■	Chevy Chase Library	5625 Connecticut Ave NW	202-282-0021	28
■	Chevy Chase Library	8005 Connecticut Ave	240-773-9590	23
■	Cleveland Park Neighborhood Library	3310 Connecticut Ave NW	202-282-3080	17
■	Dibner Library	Constitution Ave NW & 12th St NW	202-633-3872	1
■	Federal Reserve Board Research & Law Libraries	20th St NW & Constitution Ave NW	202-452-3283	7
■	Federal Trade Commission Library	600 Pennsylvania Ave NW	202-326-2395	2

■ = *Public*   ■ = *By Appointment Only*   ■ = *Other*

Type	Library	Address	Phone	Map
■	Foundation Center	1627 K St NW, 3rd Fl	202-331-1400	9
■	General Services Administration Library	1800 F St NW, RM 1033	202-501-0788	7
■	Georgetown Library	3260 R St NW	202-282-0220	8
■	Jeannette Rankin Library - US Institute of Peace	1200 17th St NW, Ste 200	202-429-3851	9
■	James Melville Gilliss Library	3450 Massachusetts Ave NW	202-762-1467	17
■	Juanita E Thornton Library	7420 Georgia Ave NW	202-541-6100	27
■	Lamond-Riggs Neighborhood Library	5401 S Dakota Ave NE	202-541-6255	14
■	Martin Luther King Jr Memorial Library	901 G St NW	202-727-0321	1
■	Mt Pleasant Neighborhood Library	3160 16th St NW	202-671-0200	16
■	NASA Headquarters Library	300 E St SW	202-358-0168	6
■	National Endowment for the Humanities Library	1100 Pennsylvania Ave NW	202-606-8244	1
■	National Geographic Society Library	1145 17th St NW	202-857-7783	9
■	National Transportation Library	1200 New Jersey Ave NW	202-366-0745	11
■	National Research Council Library	500 5th St NW, Room 304	202-334-2125	2
■	NOAA Central Library	1315 East West Hwy, SSMC3, 2nd Fl	301-713-2600	25
■	Northeast Neighborhood Library	330 7th St NE	202-698-3320	3
■	Office of Thrift Supervision Library	1700 G St NW	202-906-6470	1
■	Palisades Neighborhood Library	4901 V St NW	202-282-3139	18
■	Petworth Library	4200 Kansas Ave NW	202-243-1188	21
■	Polish Library in Washington	1503 21st St NW	202-466-2665	9
■	Ralph J Bunch Library	2201 C St NW, Room 3239	202-647-1099	7
■	Robert S Rankin Memorial Library	624 9th St NW, Rm 600	202-376-8110	1
■	Silver Spring Library	8901 Colesville Rd	240-773-9420	25
■	Southeast Neighborhood Library	403 7th St SE	202-698-3377	5
■	Southwest Neighborhood Library	900 Wesley Pl SW	202-724-4752	6
■	Takoma Park Neighborhood Library	416 Cedar St NW	202-576-7252	27
■	Tenley-Friendship Library	4450 Wisconsin Ave NW	202-282-3090	19
■	Treasury Library	1500 Pennsylvania Ave NW, Rm 1314	202-622-0990	1
■	US Department of Commerce Library	1401 Constitution Ave NW	202-482-5511	1
■	US Department of Energy Library	1000 Independence Ave SW, RM GA-138	202-586-3112	1
■	US Department of the Interior Library	1849 C St NW	202-208-5815	7
■	US Housing & Urban Development Library	451 7th St SW	202-708-2370	6
■	US Library of Congress	101 Independence Ave SE	202-707-8000	2
■	US Senate Library	Russell Senate Office Bldg, B15	202-224-7106	2
■	Watha T Daniel Branch Library	1701 8th St NW	202-671-0267	10
■	West End Neighborhood Library	1101 24th St NW	202-724-8707	9
■	Westover Library	1644 N McKinley Rd	703-228-5260	33
■	Woodridge Library	1801 Hamlin St NE	202-541-6226	13

Overview

There's always some mass gathering in Washington, DC; from inauguration demonstrations to flower festivals, DC has it all. The best events are free and easily accessible by mass transit.

Event	Approx. Dates	For more info…	Comments
New Year's Eve	December 31/January 1		Celebrate the new year with music art, and bitter freezing cold.
Martin Luther King's Birthday	Observed January 15	www.whitehouse.gov/kids/ martinlutherkingjrday.html	Music, speakers, and a recital of the "I Have a Dream" speech on the Lincoln Memorial steps.
Robert E Lee's Birthday	January 19	703-235-1530	Yes, victors write the history books, but some losers' popularity endures. Robert E Lee Memorial, Arlington Cemetery.
Chinese New Year	Late January–early February	703-851-5685	Can you imagine the debauchery of a 15-day American New Year's bash? Check it out on H Street in Chinatown.
Frederick Douglas Birthday Celebration	February	www.nps.gov/frdo/index.htm	Anacostia home of the famed abolitionist celebrates his birth.
Black History Month Celebration	February	www.si.edu	African-American history at the Smithsonian.
Abraham Lincoln's Birthday	Observed February 12	202-426-6841	Reading of Gettysburg Address in front of the city's favorite marble hero.
George Washington's Birthday Parade	President's Day, February 19	800-388-9119	Parade and party in Alexandria for the city's other favorite guy.
St. Patrick's Day Parade	March 17	www.dcstpatsparade.com	Celebration of all things Irish in DC: music, food, oh, and beer, too.
Smithsonian Kite Festival	Late March–early April	www.kitefestival.org	Watch adults attack kiddie play like a combat sport.
Solar Energy Decathlon	Mid-March	www.solardecathlon.gov	Since 2002, college teams have competed to build solar-powered houses on National Mall every two years. Sponsored by the Dept. of Energy.
Washington Home & Garden Show	Mid-March	www.flowergardenshow.com	Check out the flora that actually enjoys this climate.
National Cherry Blossom Festival	Late March–mid-April	www.nationalcherryblossom festival.org	One of the can't-misses…problem is the tourists think so, too.
Filmfest DC	April	www.filmfestdc.org	For once, see a flick before it opens in NYC.
White House Spring Garden Tours	Mid-April	www.whitehouse.gov	No politics, just flowers.
Shakespeare's Birthday	April 23	202-544-4600	To go or not to go. That is the question. Folger Shakespeare Library.
White House Easter Egg Roll	Mid-April	www.whitehouse.gov	No politics, just eggs.
Department of Defense/ Joint Services Open House	Mid-May	301-981-4600	The country flexes its muscles with an air show and other military might. FedEx Field.
St. Sophia Greek Festival	Mid-May	202-333-4730	Big, fat, Greek festival.
National Symphony Orchestra 5 Memorial Day Weekend Concert		www.kennedy-center.org/nso	Easy on the ears—and wallet; it's free.
Memorial Day Ceremonies at Arlington Cemetery	Last Monday in May	www.arlingtoncemetery.org	Ceremonies at JFK's grave and the Tomb of the Unknown Soldier.
Memorial Day Ceremonies at the Vietnam Veterans Memorial	Last Monday in May	www.nps.gov/vive	Solemn memorial.
Memorial Day Jazz Festival	May 26	703-883-4686	Jazz in Alexandria.
Virginia Gold Cup	Early May	www.vagoldcup.com	Horse race on the same day as the Kentucky Derby. Someone fire the marketing department.
Dance Africa DC	Early June	202-269-1600	A feat of feet.
Dupont-Kalorama Museum Walk Weekend	First weekend in June	www.dkmuseums.com/ walk.html	Free admission to the city's smaller, quirkier, pricier exhibits.
AFI SilverDocs	Mid June	www.silverdocs.com	Hollywood takes over Silver Spring for this documentary film festival.

DC Caribbean Carnival Extravaganza	Mid June	www.dccaribbeancarnival.com	Caribbean music, food, and outrageous costumes.
Capital Pride	Early June	www.capitalpride.org	Huge, fun, funky, out, and proud.
Annual Soap Box Derby	Mid June	www.dcsoapboxderby.org	The one day parents let their kids fly down city streets in rickety wooden boxes.
National Capital Barbecue Battle	Late June	www.barbecuebattle.com	Hot and sticky BBQ on a hot and sticky day.
Smithsonian Folklife Festival	Late June – early July	www.folklife.si.edu	All the culture and crowds that can be packed into two weeks.
Independence Day Celebration	July 4	www.july4thparade.com	July 4th in America-town. Check out the parade. The fireworks are a must.
Screen on the Green	June–July	http://friendsofscreenonthegreen.org/	Summer in DC means plenty of outdoor movie viewing in several neighborhoods, but the most well known is the Screen on the Green on the National Mall. Bring a blanket and soak in season.
Virginia Scottish Games	Late July	www.vascottishgames.org	Kilts and haggis everywhere!
Capital Fringe Festival	Late July	www.capfringe.org	DC's modest attempt at cutting-edge theater.
National Army Band's 1812 Overture Performance	Mid August	www.usarmyband.com/events/overture_1812.html	No politics, just patriotic music.
Civil War Living History Day	Mid August	www.alexandriava.gov/FortWard http://alexandriava.gov/FortWard	The culmination of reenactment-stickler bickering at the Fort Ward Museum in Alexandria.
Georgia Avenue Day	Late August		Parades, music, and food from the southern US and Africa.
National Frisbee Festival	Late August		Don't fight it, join it. Rock Creek Park gets down and www.dcblues.org
DC Blues Festival	Early September	www.dcblues.org	
Kennedy Center Open House	Early September	www.kennedy-center.org	Check out the terrace and the Kennedy sculpture without shelling out for the opera.
Adams Morgan Day	Early September	www.adamsmorganday.org	Neighborhood that gets jammed nightly, gets jammed while sun's up.
National Book Festival	Mid-Late September	www.loc.gov/bookfes	Book lovers and authors collide in annual festival on the National Mall.
Hispanic Festival	Late September	www.fiestadc.org	Latin American celebration in Mt. Pleasant St. in Northeast. The parade is a huge draw.
White House Fall Garden Tour	Late October	www.whitehouse.gov	No politics, just leaf peeping.
Reel Affirmations Film Festival	Mid-October	www.reelaffirmations.org	Like Filmfest DC, except much more gay.
Marine Corps Marathon	Late October	www.marinemarathon.com	26 miles of asphalt and cheers.
Theodore Roosevelt's Birthday	October 27	www.theodoreroosevelt.org	Party for one of the other giant heads in North Dakota.
Halloween	October 31		Halloween is a top holiday in the District where bars and clubs throughout the city celebrate the chance to get drunk while wearing dumb costumes.
Veteran's Day Ceremonies	November 11	www.arlingtoncemetery.org	Military ceremony in Arlington Cemetery.
Kennedy Center Holiday Celebration	December	www.kennedy-center.org	X-mas revelry.
Kwanzaa Celebration	January	www.si.edu	Celebration at the Smithsonian. Like Filmfest DC, except much more Jewish.
Jewish Film Festival		www.wjff.org	
National Christmas Tree Lighting/ Pathway of Peace	Mid-December to January 1	www.whitehouse.gov	Trees, menorahs, & Yule logs get lit at the White House Ellipse.
Washington National Cathedral Christmas Celebration and Services	December 24–25	202-537-6247	Humongous tree from Nova Scotia.
White House Christmas Candlelight Tours	Christmastime	www.whitehouse.gov	Still no politics, just religion.

Yes, DC's a great city for lessons in history and civics, but sometimes the kids just aren't in the mood for another tutorial on the system of checks and balances. If you check out some of the destinations on this list, you'll discover there's life beyond the Mall when it comes to entertaining your mini-yous.

The Best of the Best

★ **Best Kid-Friendly Restaurant:** Café Deluxe (3228 Wisconsin Ave NW, 202-686-2233; 400 First St SE, 202-546-6768; 4910 Elm St, Bethesda, 301-656-3131). Parents breathe a sigh of relief when they walk into a restaurant and see that the tablecloth is paper and the table is littered with crayons. At Café Deluxe, your kids can perfect their masterpieces while munching on entrees like buttered noodles, PB&J, or cheese quesadillas. The prices reflect that your companions are only half-size: Children's menu prices are only $5.95 a pop.

★ **Quaintest Activity:** Canal Boat Rides (1057 Thomas Jefferson St NW, 202-653-5190). Take a boat ride along the historic C&O canal in a boat pulled by mules. Park rangers in period clothing describe what life was like for families who lived and worked on the canal during the 1870s. Tours (one hour long) are held Wednesday–Friday at 11 am and 3 pm, and Saturday and Sunday at 11 am, 1:30 pm, 3 pm, and 4:30 pm. The boats fill up on a first-come-first-served basis. $5 for visitors aged four and above. Children three and under ride for free.

★ **Funnest Park:** Rock Creek Park (5200 Glover Rd NW, 202-895-6070). An area of Rock Creek Park located on Beach Drive goes by the name of Candy Cane City—'nuf said. Leland Street is good for picnicking and has a playground, basketball courts, and tennis courts. Children's park programs include planetarium shows, animal talks, arts & crafts projects, and exploratory hikes.

★ **Best Rainy Day Activity:** Smithsonian Museum of Natural History (10th St & Constitution Ave NW, 202-633-1000). The new Kenneth E. Behring Family Hall of Mammals is open! If the kids aren't too freaked out by life-sized stuffed animals, check out the 274 new taxidermied mounts. The IMAX theater is always a hit with kids and parents alike on rainy afternoons. The timeless kid-appeal of dinosaur exhibits also keeps the little ones entertained (if they weren't recently dragged here on a school trip). Admission is free, and tickets are not required for entry. The museum is open daily 10 am–5:30 pm (and until 7:30 pm during summertime), except on federal holidays.

★ **Sunny Day Best Bet:** National Zoo (3001 Connecticut Ave, 202-673-4800, nationalzoo.si.edu). This free and easily accessible zoo is guaranteed to be the best park stroll you've ever taken. Beyond the pandas and apes, there's also a Kids' Farm with cows, donkeys, goats, chickens, and ducks. Summer camps and classes are available to Friends of the National Zoo Family Members. A $60 membership also includes free parking while visiting the zoo, a 10% discount at National Zoo stores, opportunities to attend summer camps, classes and workshops as well as discounts on tickets to popular zoo events. The zoo is open daily (6 am–8 pm April 2 to October 28, 6 am–6 pm October 29 to March 10), and admission is always free. April–October buildings are open 10 am–6 pm, November–April 10 am–4:30 pm.

★ **Neatest Store:** Barston's Child's Play (5536 Connecticut Ave NW, 202-244-3602). The store's long, narrow aisles are stocked with games, toys, puzzles, trains, costumes, art supplies, and books. It's never too early to start grooming a true shopaholic.

Parks for Playing

• **Cleveland Park** (3409 Macomb St NW). Climb a spider web, climb a wall, or catch a train. The park has separate play areas for younger and older children, picnic tables, basketball courts, a baseball field, and a rec center.

• **East Potomac Park** (Ohio Drive SW). Always a good bet with its miniature golf course, public pool, picnic facilities, and playground at the southern tip. This is an absolute must during Cherry Blossom season.

• **Turtle Park** (4500 Van Ness St NW, 202-282-2198). Plenty of slides, tunnels, swings, and climbing structures, as well as basketball and tennis courts, softball/soccer fields, and a rec center. If you need a break, there's plenty of shade and picnic tables. A.k.a. "Turtle Park."

• **Glen Echo Park** (7300 MacArthur Blvd, Glen Echo, MD) Unique Calder-esque playground, antique carousel, and two children's theaters make this restored deco-era amusement park worth the short drive for families.

• **Kalorama Park** (19th St & Kalorama Rd NW). While the shade is limited here, this is a large playground with a fence dividing big-kid from little-kid playgrounds.

• **Marie Reed Recreation Center** (2200 Champlain St NW, 202-673-7768). Plenty of shady areas to rest your old bones while the kids are devouring the jungle gym, slides, tennis courts, and basketball courts.

• **Montrose Park** (R & 30th Sts NW, 202-426-6827). For you: lots of open space, a picnicking area, and tennis courts. For your kids: swings, monkey bars, a sandbox, and a maze.

• **The Yards Park** (10 Water St, www.yardspark.org). Gorgeous new waterfront park features wooden boardwalk, tons of open grassy areas, a waterfall you can walk behind, a bridge and light sculpture, and an elevated overlook. The park is a public/private partnership between the federal government, the city and the private developer, and maybe that's why it's so cool and well made.

- **Rose Park** (26th & O Sts NW, 202-333-4946). Home to Little League games and the Georgetown Farmers Market, this park has plenty of green and a massive, wonderful sandbox.
- **Upton Hill Regional Park** (6060 Wilson Blvd. Arlington, VA 703-534-3437) Worth the short drive to Arlington for the newly renovated public pool with water slides, huge mini-golf course, batting cages, and small playground.

Rainy Day Activities

Rain ain't no big thang in the city of free museums, many of which cater to the height- and attention-challenged.

Museums with Kid Appeal

- **National Air and Space Museum** (Independence Ave & 4th St SW, 202-633-1000). Can you go wrong in a museum that sells astronauts' freeze-dried ice cream? Kids can walk through airplanes and spaceships. Check out the Einstein Planetarium and the IMAX Theater. Open daily 10 am–5:30 pm, closed Christmas Day. Admission is free but does not include special events or activities.
- **International Spy Museum** (800 F St NW, 202-393-7798, www.spymuseum.org). The sleek exhibits filled with high-tech gadgets and fascinating real-life spy stories make the hefty admissions tag totally worth it. Special family programs include making and breaking secret codes and disguise-creation workshops. Twice a year, the museum even offers a top-secret overnight "Operation Secret Slumber," which provides kids with a "behind the scenes" look at the life of spy. The museum is open daily, but hours vary according to season. Children under five enter free, adults pay $18, kids (5–11) pay $15, and seniors (65+) pay $17.
- **National Museum of American History** (14th St and Constitution Ave NW, 202-357-2700, americanhistory. si.edu). While your kids will certainly love a glimpse of Dorothy's ruby red slippers, the hands-on section of this museum is where they'll *really* want to be. The Hands-On History Room allows kids to gin cotton, send a telegraph, or say "hello" in Cherokee. The Hands-On Science Room, for children over five, lets kids take intelligence tests, separate food dyes in beverages, or use lasers to see light. Museum admission is free, but tickets (which are also free) are required for the hands-on rooms during weekends and busy hours. The museum is open daily 10 am–5:30 pm (and until 6:30 pm during summertime), except for Christmas.
- **National Museum of Natural History** (10th and Constitution Ave, N.W. 202-633-1000) This is the original kids' museum, starting with the huge stuffed mastodon in the lobby. After you take in the mandatory t-rex skeletons, head for the live Insect Zoo and Discovery Room, which have interactive, hands-on exhibits for your budding naturalist. Older kids also like the Hope Diamond and gemstone exhibits. There's a great gift shop perfect for relieving kids of their allowance money, and an IMAX theater and public cafeteria, too. Free. Open every day but Christmas, from 10 am–5:30 pm (and until 7:30 during summertime).
- **Freer Gallery** (1050 Independence Ave SW, 202-633-4880, www.asia.si.edu). Give your kids a taste of Asia with the Freer Gallery's Imaginasia program. Children from ages six to fourteen find their way through exhibitions on Japanese wood block prints or Islamic illuminated manuscripts (with the guiding hand of an activity book) then create an appropriate art project with their own two hands. No reservations required for groups smaller than eight, and Imaginasia will give your little ones a unique glimpse of the Far East on the Mall. The museum is open from 10 am to 5:30 pm, except for Christmas.

Other Indoor Distractions

- **Adventure Theatre MTC** (7300 MacArthur Blvd, Glen Echo, MD, 301-320-5331, www.adventuretheatre.org) Actors and puppets stage fables, musicals, and classic fairytales on the DC area's longest running children's stage. You can hardly ask for a nicer setting than Glen Echo Park, also home to the kid-friendly Puppet Co. Playhouse.
- **Bureau of Engraving and Printing** (14th & C Sts, SW, 202-874-3019, www.moneyfactory.com). We're all used to seeing money spent. At this museum, you can watch how money is made, although your kids will probably be most interested in watching the destruction of old money. Admission is free, but tickets are required March–August. General tours (the only way to see the museum) are given every 15 minutes from 10 am to 2 pm, Monday through Friday.
- **Discovery Theater** (1100 Jefferson Dr SW, 202-357-1500, www.discoverytheater.org). Puppet shows, dance performances, and storytelling all under one roof. Performances are given daily at 10 am and 11:30 am, Monday through Friday, and Saturday at 11:30 am and 1 pm. Shows cost $6 for adults and $5 for children, with special group rates available. Kids ages 4 to 13 can also join the Young Associates Program, where they can learn to animate clay figures or make their own puppets.
- **Imagination Stage** (4908 Auburn Ave, Bethesda, MD, 301-280-1660, www.imaginationstage.org). Help your kids enjoy the magic of theater by taking them to a show at the Imagination Stage. Your family might see anything from a hip-hop version of a favorite picture book to a fairytale musical. This non-profit organization has been putting on the hits for over twenty years now.
- **Kettler Capitals Iceplex** (627 N Glebe Rd, Arlington, VA, 703-243-8855). Vast, spanking-new ice complex on the roof of Metro-accesible Ballston Mall is area's largest, close-in ice arena. Built as a practice rink for the Washington Capitals hockey team, it offers public skate times, birthday parties, and classes.

- **Now This!** (Blair Mansion, 7111 Eastern Ave, Silver Spring, MD, 202-364-8292, www.nowthisimprov.com). The city's only improvised children's theater group entertains kids every Sunday afternoon with impromptu storytelling, songwriting, and comedy. This is a great place to take a birthday boy or girl on their special day, as the cast will write them their very own birthday tune. Lunch is served at 1 pm and the show begins at 1:30 pm.

- **Puppet Co. Playhouse** (7300 MacArthur Blvd, Glen, MD, 301-320-6668, www.thepuppetco.org). Set in the most enchanting amusement park turned arts center, the Puppet Co. Playhouse is just one piece of magic in Glen Echo. Master puppeteers wield rod puppets in front of gorgeous sets, leaving kids and adults wide-eyed and bushy-tailed.

Outdoor and Educational

Just 'cause you want to play outside doesn't mean you have to act like a hooligan! Here's a list of outdoor activities that mix culture with athleticism and offer up some surprisingly original forms of entertainment:

- **Butler's Orchard** (22200 Davis Mill Rd, Germantown, MD, 301-972-3299, www.butlersorchard.com). Teach those city slickers that apples come from trees, not Safeway! And there are Golden Deliciouses and Macintoshes and Granny Smiths and Galas! Kids and adults can pick their own crops year round (nearly) at Butler's Orchard. The berries taste sweeter when you've picked them yourself, and autumn events include hay rides and the annual pumpkin festival. Pay for what you pick by the pound.

- **Living Classrooms** (515 M St SE, Suite 222, 202-488-0627, www.livingclassroomsdc.org) Program offers hands-on educational programs on the Anacostia River and after merging with the Discovery Creek Children's Museum a few years ago runs a summer camp, birthday parties, and programs for families, schools, and scouts.

- **Fort Ward** (4301 West Braddock Rd, Alexandria, 703-838-4848, www.fortward.org). The best preserved Union fort in DC. Picnic areas are available, and the on-site museum has a Civil War Kids' Camp for ages 8 to 12 during the summer. The museum is open Tuesday through Saturday 9 am–5 pm and Sunday 12 pm–5 pm. Admission is free. The park is open daily from 9 am until sunset.

- **Leesburg Animal Park** (19270 James Monroe Highway, Leesburg, VA, 703-433-0002 www.leesburganimalpark.com). The trip across the river is worth it—particularly if you get the pleasure of riding the $4 White's Ferry ride from Maryland to Virginia. Little ones can feed baby bear cubs by bottle or pet free-ranging emus; animals are both domestic and exotic. Kids 2 to 12 gain admission for $7.95 ($9.95 for a VIP pass that includes a souvenir cup of food and a pony ride), and adults pay $9.95.

- **National Arboretum** (3501 New York Ave NE, 202-245-2726, www.usna.usda.gov). Covering 466 acres, the National Arboretum is the ultimate backyard. Picnicking is encouraged in the National Grove of State Trees picnic area, and the original columns from the Capitol dome live here at the Arb on a picturesque, grassy knoll. A 40-minute open-air tram ride is available and advised if you want to see everything. The Arboretum is open daily 8 am–5 pm, except Christmas. Admission is free, but the tram will cost you $4 for adults and $2 for children 4–16.

- **Sculpture Garden Ice-Skating Rink** (7th St & Constitution Ave NW, 202-289-3360). The Sculpture Garden's rink is specially designed to allow views of the garden's contemporary sculptures while skating. It's like subliminally feeding your kids culture while they think they're just playing. Regular admission costs $7 for a two-hour session, and children, students, and seniors pay $6. Skate rental costs $3 and a locker rental costs 50¢.

Classes

- **Ballet Nova Center for Dance** (3443 Carlin Springs Rd, Falls Church, Va, www.balletnova.org) The school offers 20,800 square foot of space, including six dance studios, five of which have Harlequin Liberty panel sprung sub flooring and non-slip vinyl overlays, walls of mirrors, double barres, 16-foot ceilings, and complete sound systems.

- **Ballet Petite** (Several throughout DC area, 301-229-6882, www.balletpetite.com). Fundamental dance instruction mixed with costumes, story telling, props, acting, and music.

- **Budding Yogis** (3838 Northampton St NW,, 202-686-1104, www.buddingyogis.com). Yoga for kids, teens, and adults. Special summer programs available.

- **Capitol Hill Arts Workshop** (545 7th St SE, 202-547-6839, www.chaw.org). Classes for children in art disciplines, tumbling, and Tae Kwon Do. If your kids are precociously cool, sign them up for the jazz/hip-hop class and watch them perform a Hip-Hop Nutcracker in December.

- **Clay Café** (101 N Maple Ave, Falls Church, VA 703 534-7600). Paint your own pottery and other hands-on crafts. Classes and summer camps for kids.

- **Dance Place** (3225 8th St NE, 202-269-1600, www.danceplace.org). Creative movement, hip-hop, and African dance instruction for kids.

- **Imagination Stage** (4908 Auburn Ave, Bethesda, MD, 301-961-6060, www.imaginationstage.org). Classes in music, dance, and theater for kids and teens. Three-week summer camps also available.

- **Joy of Motion** (1333 H St NE, Washington, 202-399-6763, Connecticut Ave, 202-387-0911, www. www. joyofmotion.org). Creative movement and fundamental dance instruction for children at locations throughout the District.

- **Kettler Capitals Ice Complex.** (627 N Glebe Rd, Arlington, VA, 703-243-8855). Year-round skating classes and even summer camps for kids trying to beat the heat.

- **Kids Moving Company** (7475 Wisconsin Ave, Bethesda, MD, 301-656-1543, www.kidsmovingco.com) Creative movement classes for children nine months to eight years in a studio with a full-sized trampoline.

- **Kumon Math and Reading Program** (6831 Wisconsin Ave, Bethesda, MD, 301-652-1234, www.kumon.com). An after-school learning program in math and reading.

- **Levine School of Music** (4 locations in NW, SE, VA, and MD, www.levineschool.org). One of the country's largest community music schools offers fundamental music instruction to toddlers through pre-professionals. Private lessons, group classes, and summer camps available.

- **Musikids** (4900 Auburn Ave, Ste. 100, Bethesda, MD, 301-215-7946, www.musikids.com) Music and movement classes for newborns and toddlers.

- **Pentagon Row Ice-Skating** (1201 S Joyce St, Arlington, VA, 703-418-6666, www.pentagonrow.com). Skating lessons and birthday parties are available November–March.

- **Rock Creek Horse Center** (5100 Glover Rd NW, 202-362-0117, www.rockcreekhorsecenter.com). Riding lessons, trail rides, summer day camp, and equestrian team training. Weekly group lessons $50/hour, private lessons $90/hour, and one-week summer camp sessions cost $500.

- **Rock Creek Tennis Center** (16th & Kennedy Sts NW, 202-722-5949, www.rockcreektennis.com). Five-week weekend tennis courses available for children at beginner and intermediate levels.

- **Round House Theatre** (4545 East West Hwy, Bethesda, MD, 240-644-1099, www.roundhousetheatre.org). The theater has a year-round drama school and an arts-centered summer day camp program.

- **Sportrock Climbing Center** (5308 Eisenhower Ave, Alexandria, VA, 703-212-7625, www.sportrock.com). Kids learn to climb. 6- to 12-year-olds have the run of the place 6:30 pm–8 pm on Fridays. $18 for adults, $10 for children (12 and under). Hours: Tues–Fri: 12 pm–11 pm; Sat–Sun: 12 pm–8 pm.

- **Sur La Table** (1101 S Joyce St, Arlington, 703-414-3580, www.surlatable.com). At Sur La Table's junior cooking classes, kids are encouraged to (gasp!) play with food. Classes are for children aged 6–12 and groups are small and well organized.

- **YMCA of Metropolitan Washington** (numerous branches, 202-232-6700, www.ymcadc.org). Youth and teen sports to spend all that hyperactive energy—particularly in the swimming pool!

- **Young Playwrights' Theatre** (2437 15th St, NW, 202-387-9173, www.youngplaywrightstheatre.org). Programs for children from fourth grade and up that encourage literacy, playwriting, and community engagement.

Shopping Essentials

- **Aladdin's Lamp Bookstore** • 2499 N Harrison St, Arlington, VA • 703-241-8281
- **Barnes & Noble** (books) • 3040 M St NW • 202-965-9880 • 555 12th St NW • 202-347-0176 • 3651 Jefferson Davis Hwy, Alexandria, VA • 703-299-9124 • 4801 Bethesda Ave, Bethesda, MD • 301-986-1761
- **Barston's Child's Play** (everything kids love) • 5536 Connecticut Ave NW • 202-244-3602
- **Children's Place** (kids' clothes) • Pentagon City, 1100 S Hayes St, Arlington, VA • 703-413-4875
- **Discovery Channel Store** (children's gifts) • Union Station, 50 Massachusetts Ave NE • 202-842-3700
- **Fairy Godmother** (toys & books) • 319 7th St SE • 202-547-5474
- **Filene's Basement** (kids' clothes) • 5300 Wisconsin Ave NW • 202-966-0208
- **Full of Beans** (kids' clothes) • 5502 Connecticut Ave NW • 202-362-8566
- **Gap Kids and Baby Gap** (kids' clothes) • 1267 Wisconsin Ave NW • 202-333-2411 • 1100 S Hayes St, Arlington, VA • 703-418-4770 • 5430 Wisconsin Ave, Chevy Chase, MD • 301-907-7656
- **Gymboree** (kids' clothes) • 1100 S Hayes St, Arlington, VA • 703-415-5009
- **Kids Closet** (kids' clothes) • 1226 Connecticut Ave NW • 202-429-9247
- **Kinderhaus Toys** • 1220 N Filmore, Arlington, VA • 703-527-5929
- **Patagonia** (clothes) • 1048 Wisconsin Ave NW • 202-333-1776
- **Piccolo Piggies** (clothes, furniture, accessories) • 1533 Wisconsin Ave NW • 202-333-0123
- **Plaza Artist Supplies** (arts & crafts) • 1990 K St NW • 202-331-0126
- **Ramer's Shoes** (children's shoes) • 3810 Northampton St NW • 202-244-2288
- **Riverby Books** (used books) • 417 E Capitol St SE • 202-543-4342
- **Sullivan's Toys & Art Supplies** • 3412 Wisconsin Ave NW • 202-362-1343
- **Sur La Table** (pint-sized cooking supplies) • 1101 S Joyce St, Arlington, VA • 703-414-3580
- **Tree Top Kids** (toys, books & clothes) • 3301 New Mexico Ave NW • 202-244-3500

Where to Go for More Information

www.gocitykids.com
www.ourkids.com
www.lilaguide.com

Dupont Circle is to DC's gay life what Capitol Hill is to the nation's politics. Just as politics seep into most aspects of city life, the gay scene reaches far beyond Dupont's gay bars. There are gay and lesbian lifestyle newspapers, clubs, bars, and community groups scattered throughout the city. In short, Dupont Circle is a geographic reference as well as a state of mind, and the city is, for the most part, sexual-orientation-blind. While there are many LGBT residents in suburbs like Takoma Park, MD, and Arlington, VA, they enjoy precious little visibility compared to their District counterparts.

We take this moment to pay our respects to Lamda Rising, the Dupont shop that was once the world's largest LGBT bookstore that closed in 2009 after 35 years of operation. We also mourn the loss of the numerous bars and clubs on O Street SE, which after a 30-year run, were shuttered forever in April 2006 to make room for the Washington Nationals' new stadium. These popular (and generally "adult-oriented") establishments were always jammed on the weekends, especially with locals taking out-of-towners to see fab-u-lous drag shows at Ziegfeld's or to see the boys bare it all at Secrets or Heat.

Websites

Capital Pride · www.capitalpride.org
Educational website dedicated to DC's LGBT community. The organization is also responsible for the planning and development of the annual Capital Pride Parade.

CAGLCC (Capital Area Gay & Lesbian Chamber of Commerce) · www.caglcc.org, Business group of 3,000 LGBT and allies.

Dykes on Bikes · www.meetup.com/Dykes-on-Bikes-Washington-DC-Chapter For the motorcycling-riding GLBTQ women of the District.

GayWdc · www.gayWdc.com
Gay and lesbian website for DC restaurant and bar listings, local news and events, classifieds, and personals.

Gay and Lesbian Activists Alliance · www.glaa.org
GLAA is the nation's oldest continuously active gay and lesbian civil rights organization.

Publications

Metro Weekly · 1012 14th St NW · 202-638-6830 · www.metroweekly.com
Free weekly gay and lesbian magazine—reliable coverage of community events, nightlife, and reviews of the District's entertainment and art scene.

Bookstores

Politics and Prose · 5015 Connecticut Ave NW · 202-364-1919 · www.politics-prose.com
Popular bookstore and coffee shop with a small selection devoted to gay and lesbian literature.

Health Center & Support Organizations

Arlington Gay & Lesbian Alliance · 703-522-7660 · www.agla.org
Monthly get-togethers for the Arlington LGBT community.

Beth Mishpachah · www.betmish.org
District of Columbia Jewish Center · 16th & Q Sts NW
DC's egalitarian synagogue that embraces a diversity of sexual and gender identities.

The Center · 1111 14th St NW · 202-518-6100 · www.thedccenter.org
A volunteer LGBT community organization in metro DC.

DC AIDS Hotline · 202-332-2437 or 800-322-7432

DC Black Pride · PO Box 77071, Washington, DC 20013 · 202-737-5767 · www.dcblackpride.org
African-American lesbian, gay, bisexual, and transgendered community group. Proceeds from Black Pride events are distributed to HIV/AIDS and other health organizations serving the African-American community.

Dignity · www.dignitywashington.org
For the LGBT Catholic community.

Food & Friends · 219 Riggs Rd NE · 202-269-2277 · www.foodandfriends.org
The organization cooks, packages, and delivers meals and groceries to over 1,000 people living with HIV/AIDS and other life-challenging illnesses in the greater DC area. Hosts annual "Chef's Best" fundraising dinner with notable volunteer chefs from around the region.

GLAAD DC · 1700 Kalorama Rd · 202-986-1360 · www.glaad.org
Gay and Lesbian Alliance Against Defamation DC chapter.

Human Rights Campaign · 1640 Rhode Island Ave NW · 800-777-4723 · www.hrc.org
Gay and Lesbian Alliance Against Defamation DC chapter.

PFLAG DC · 1111 14th St NW · 202-638-3852 · www.pflagdc.org
The headquarters of the national Human Rights Campaign opened in 2003 in the former home of B'nai B'rith, and houses the organization's Equality Center event space and the HRC Media Center, a multimedia production facility.

Sexual Minority Youth Assistance League (SMYAL) · 410 7th St SE · 202-546-5940 · www.smyal.org
Non-profit group for LGBT youth.

Whitman-Walker Clinic · 1407 S St NW · 202-797-3500 www.wwc.org
A non-profit organization that provides medical and social services to the LGBT and HIV/AIDS communities of metropolitan DC. Home to one of the oldest substance abuse programs in the US. The Lesbian Health Center at Whitman Walker's Elizabeth Taylor Medical Center, 1810 14th St NW, offers top-quality health services (202-745-6131). There is also a Legal Aid Society for information on financial assistance possibilities (202-628-1161)

Sports and Clubs

Adventuring · PO Box 18118, Washington, DC 20036 ·
202-462-0535 · www.adventuring.org
All-volunteer group organizes group hikes, bike rides, and
more for DC's LGBT community.

Capital Tennis Association · www.capital-tennis.org
Casual and organized tennis programs for the metropolitan gay and lesbian community.

Chesapeake and Potomac Softball (CAPS) ·
PO Box 3092, Falls Church, VA 22043 · 202-543-0236 ·
www.eteamz.com/caps/
A friendly place for members of the LGBT community to
play softball.

DC Aquatics Club · PO Box 12211, Washington, DC 20005 ·
www.swimdcac.org
Swimming team and social club for gays, lesbians, and
friends of the gay and lesbian community.

DC's Different Drummers ·
PO Box 57099, Washington, DC 20037 · 202-269-4868 ·
www.dcdd.org
DC's Lesbian and Gay Symphonic, Swing, Marching, and
Pep Bands.

DC Front Runners · PO Box 65550, Washington, DC 20035
202-628-3223 · www.dcfrontrunners.org
Running is so gay!

DC Lambda Squares ·
PO Box 77782, Washington, DC 20013 ·
www.dclambdasquares.org
LGBT square-dance club.

DC Strokes · PO Box 3789, Washington, DC 20027 ·
www.dcstrokes.org
The first rowing club for gays and lesbians. They row out
of the Thompson Boat Center on the Potomac.

Federal Triangles · 202-986-5363 · www.federaltriangles.org
Soccer club for the LGBT community.

Gay Men's Chorus of Washington DC:
Federal City Performing Arts Association ·
2801 M Street NW · (202) 293-1548 · www.gmcw.org

Lambda Links · www.lambdalinks.org
Gay golf.

Washington Wetskins Water Polo · www.wetskins.org
The first lesbian, gay, and bisexual polo team in the
United States.

Washington Renegades Rugby · www.dcrugby.com
A Division III club that actively recruits gays and men of
color from the DC region.

Annual Events

Capital Pride Festival/Parade · 1407 S St NW ·
202-797-3510 · www.capitalpride.org
Annual festival and parade honoring the history and heritage of the LGBT community in Washington, DC. Usually
held throughout Dupont and downtown the second week
in June.

DC Black Pride Festival/Parade · 202-737-5767 ·
866-942-5473 · www.dcblackpride.org
The world's largest Black Pride festival, drawing a crowd
of about 30,000 annually. Usually held Memorial Day
weekend.

Reel Affirmations · PO Box 73587, Washington, DC, 20056 ·
202-986-1119 · www.reelaffirmations.org
Washington DC's Annual Lesbian and Gay Film Festival.
Late October.

Youth Pride Day/Week · PO Box 33161, Washington, DC
20033 · 202-387-4141 · www.youthpridedc.org
Usually held in early April. The largest event for gay,
lesbian, bisexual, and transgendered youth in the mid-
Atlantic region.

Venues

Gay

- **The Blue Room** · 2321 18th St NW · 202-332-0800
- **Cobalt/30 Degrees** · 17th & R Sts NW · 202-462-6569 (30
  Degrees is non-smoking)
- **DC Eagle** (leather) · 639 New York Ave NW · 202-347-6025
- **Fireplace** · 2161 P St NW · 202-293-1293
- **Halo** · 1435 P St, NW · 202-797-9730 • (Non-smoking venue)
- **Titan** · 1337 14th St NW (upstairs) · 202-232-7010
- **JR's Bar & Grill** · 1519 17th St NW · 202-328-0090
- **Omega DC** · 2123 Twining Ct NW · 202-223-4917
- **Remington's** · 639 Pennsylvania Ave SE · 202-543-3113
- **Windows/Dupont Italian Kitchen (DIK) Bar** · 1635 17th
  St NW · 202-328-0100

Lesbian

- **Phase One** · 525 8th St SE · 202-544-6831

Both

- **1409 Playbill Cafe** · 1409 14th St NW · 202-265-3055
- **Apex** · 1415 22nd St NW · 202-296-0505
- **Banana Cafe** · 500 8th St SE · 202-543-5906
- **Chaos** (Wednesday, Ladies' night) · 17th & Q Sts NW ·
  202-232-4141
- **Freddie's Beach Bar** · 555 S 23rd St S, Arlington, VA ·
  703-685-0555
- **Larry's Lounge** · 1836 18th St NW · 202-483-1483

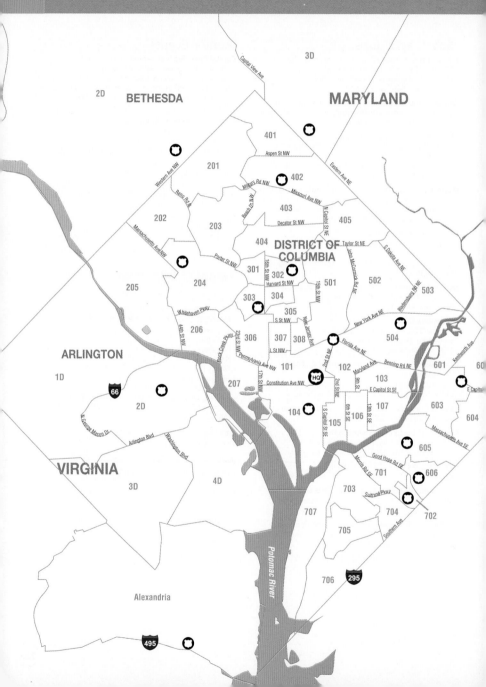

Washington DC is divided into 44 Police Service Areas (PSAs). Each PSA is staffed with a minimum of 21 MPDC officers (with the exception of PSA 707, which essentially consists of Bolling Air Force Base). High-crime neighborhoods are assigned more than the minimum number of police. For example, PSA 105 has the minimum 21 officers, while 93 officers patrol the statistically more dangerous PSA 101.

Metropolitan Police DC

All Emergencies:	911
Police Non-Emergencies:	311
Citywide Call Center:	202-727-1000
Crimesolvers Tip Line:	888-919-CRIME
Child Abuse Hotline:	202-671-7233
Corruption Hotline:	800-298-4006
Drug Abuse Hotline:	888-294-3572
Hate Crimes Hotline:	202-727-0500
Public Information Office:	202-727-4383
Office of Police Complaints:	202-727-3838
Website:	http://mpdc.dc.gov

Stations Within NFT Coverage Area

1st District Station • 101 M St. SW • 202-698-0555 • Map 6
1st District Substation • 500 E St SE • 202-698-0068 • Map 5
2nd District Station •
3320 Idaho Ave NW • 202-282-0070 • Map 18
Headquarters: 300 Indiana Ave NW • Map 2
District Stations:
Gay & Lesbian Liaison Unit •
1369 Connecticut Ave NW • 202-727-5427 • Map 9
3rd District Station •
1620 V St. NW • 202-673-6815 • Map 9
5th District Station •
1805 Bladensburg Rd NE • 202-698-0150 • Map 12
3rd District Substation •
750 Park Rd NW • 202-576-8222 • Map 15
3rd District Latino Liaison Unit •
1800 Columbia Rd NW • 202-673-4445 • Map 16

Statistics	2011	2010	2009	2008	2007
Homicide	108	132	144	186	181
Forcible Rape	174	141	134	156	142
Robbery	4,207	4,026	4,394	4,402	4,447
Assault w/ Dangerous Weapon	2,520	2,621	2,625	2,843	3,195
Burglary	3,948	4,221	3,673	3,751	3,958
Theft (Other)	10,206	9,104	9,266	9,031	8,849
Theft (from Vehicle)	7,839	6,999	9,266	8,968	7,792
Stolen Auto	3,820	4,133	4,862	8,968	6,050

Alexandria Police (VA)

All Emergencies:	911
Non-Emergencies:	703-838-4444
Community Support:	703-838-4763
Crime Prevention:	703-838-4520
Domestic Violence Unit:	703-706-3974
Parking:	703-838-3868
Property-Lost & Found:	703-838-4709
Website:	http://ci.alexandria.va.us/police

Stations Within NFT Coverage Area

Alexandria Police Department •
2003 Mill Rd • 703-838-4896 • Map 44

Statistics	2011	2010	2009	2008	2006
Homicide	1	3	5	4	7
Rape	21	20	12	30	18
Aggravated Assault	112	125	129	141	179
Burglary	308	310	347	294	366
Auto Theft	374	282	336	380	359
Larceny/Theft	2,666	2,805	2,613	2,726	2,576

Arlington County Police (VA)

All Emergencies:	911
Non-Emergencies:	703-228-3000
Rape Crisis, Victims of Violence	703-228-4848
Child Abuse:	703-228-1500
Domestic Violence Crisis Line	703-358-4848
National Capital Poison Center:	202-625-3333
Website:	www.co.arlington.va.us/police

Stations Within NFT Coverage Area

Arlington County Police Department •
1425 N Courthouse Rd • 703-228-4040 • Map 36

Statistics	2011	2010	2009	2008	2006
Homicide	0	1	2	3	2
Forcible Rape	23	24	16	21	25
Robbery	135	143	149	145	148
Aggravated Assault	143	143	157	143	151
Burglary	251	307	320	388	393
Larceny	3,439	3,944	4,120	4,115	3,522
Vehicle Theft	178	208	287	310	290

Montgomery County Police (MD)

All Emergencies:	911
Montgomery Non-Emergencies:	301-279-8000
24-Hour Bioterrorism Hotline:	240-777-4200
Takoma Park Non-Emergencies:	301-891-7102
Chevy Chase Village Police:	301-654-7302
Animal Services:	240-773-5925
Community Services:	301-840-2585
Operation Runaway:	301-251-4545
Party Buster Line:	240-777-1986
Website:	www.montgomerycountymd.gov

Stations Within NFT Coverage Area

3rd District - Silver Spring •
801 Sligo Ave • 301-565-7740 • Map25
Takoma Park Police Dept •
7500 Maple Ave • 301-270-1100 • Map 26
MPDC 4th District Station •
6001 Georgia Ave NW • 202-715-7400 • Map 27
Chevy Chase Village Police •
5906 Connecticut Ave NW • 301-654-7300 • Map28
2nd District - Bethesda •
7359 Wisconsin Ave • 301-652-9200 • Map 29

Statistics	2011	2010	2009	2008	2006
Homicide	16	17	12	21	19
Forcible Rape	112	119	124	131	129
Robbery	840	911	992	1,100	1,096
Aggravated Assault	648	911	992	1,100	1,096
Burglary	3,061	3,323	3,011	3,603	3,550
Larceny	13,505	15,261	18,356	19,027	17,534
Vehicle Theft	1,186	1,455	1,732	2,258	2,483

Post Office	Address	Phone	Zip	Map
Benjamin Franklin	1200 Pennsylvania Ave NW	202-842-1444	20004	1
National Capitol Station	2 Massachusetts Ave NE	202-523-2368	20002	2
Union Station	50 Massachusetts Ave NE	202-523-2057	20002	2
Fort McNair Station	300 A St SW	202-523-2144	20319	3
Northeast Station	1563 Maryland Ave NE	202-842-4421	20002	4
Southeast Station	600 Pennsylvania Ave SE	202-682-9135	20003	5
L'Enfant Plaza Station	437 L'Enfant Plz SW	202-842-4526	20024	6
Southwest Station	45 L St SW	202-523-2590	20024	6
McPherson Station	1750 Pennsylvania Ave NW	202-523-2394	20006	7
Watergate Station	2512 Virginia Ave NW	202-965-6278	20037	7
Georgetown Station	1215 31st St NW	202-842-2487	20007	8
Farragut Station	1800 M St NW	202-523-2024	20036	9
Temple Heights Station	1921 Florida Ave NW	202-234-4253	20009	9
Twentieth St Station	2001 M St NW	202-842-4654	20036	9
Ward Place Station	2121 Ward Pl NW	202-842-4645	20037	9
Washington Square Station	1050 Connecticut Ave NW	202-842-1211	20036	9
Martin Luther King Jr Station	1400 L St NW	202-523-2001	20005	10
T Street	1915 14th St NW	202-483-9580	20009	10
Techworld Station	800 K St NW	202-842-2309	20001	10
Le Droit Park	416 Florida Ave NW	202-635-5311	20001	11
Washington Main Office	900 Brentwood Rd NE	202-636-1972	20018	11
Woodridge Station	2211 Rhode Island Ave NE	202-842-4340	20018	13
Brookland Station	3401 12th St NE	202-842-3374	20017	14
Catholic University Cardinal Station	620 Michigan Ave NE	202-319-5225	20064	14
Columbia Heights Finance	3321 Georgia Ave NW	202-523-2674	20010	15
Howard University Post Office	2400 6th St NW	202-806-2008	20059	15
Kalorama Station	2300 18th St NW	202-523-2906	20009	16
Cleveland Park Station	3430 Connecticut Ave NW	202-364-0178	20008	17
Calvert Station	2336 Wisconsin Ave NW	202-523-2907	20007	18
Petworth Station	4211 9th St NW	202-523-2681	20011	21
Silver Spring Finance Centre	8455 Colesville Rd	301-608-1305	20910	25
Takoma Park	6909 Laurel Ave	301-270-4392	20912	26
Brightwood Station	6323 Georgia Ave NW	202-635-5300	20011	27
Chevy Chase Branch	5910 Connecticut Ave NW	301-654-7538	20815	28
Northwest Station	5636 Connecticut Ave NW	202-842-2286	20015	28
Friendship Heights Station	5530 Wisconsin Ave	301-941-2695	20815	29
Palisades Station	5136 MacArthur Blvd NW	202-842-2291	20016	32
North Station	2200 N George Mason Dr	703-536-6269	22207	34
Arlington Main Office	3118 Washington Blvd	703-841-2118	22210	35
Court House Station	2043 Wilson Blvd	703-248-9337	22201	36
Rosslyn Station	1101 Wilson Blvd	703-525-4336	22209	36
South Station	1210 S Glebe Rd	703-979-2821	22204	37
Park Fairfax Station	3682 King St	703-933-2686	22302	39
Eads Station	1720 S Eads St	703-892-0840	22202	40
Pentagon Branch	9998 The Pentagon	703-695-6835	20301	40
Trade Center Station	340 S Pickett St	703-823-0968	22304	41
Theological Seminary	3737 Seminary Rd	703-751-6791	22304	42
Potomac Station Finance	1908 Mt Vernon Ave	703-684-7821	22301	43
Alexandria Main Office	1100 Wythe St	703-684-7168	22314	45
George Mason Station	200 N Washington St	703-519-0386	22314	46

General Information · **Post Offices & Zip Codes**

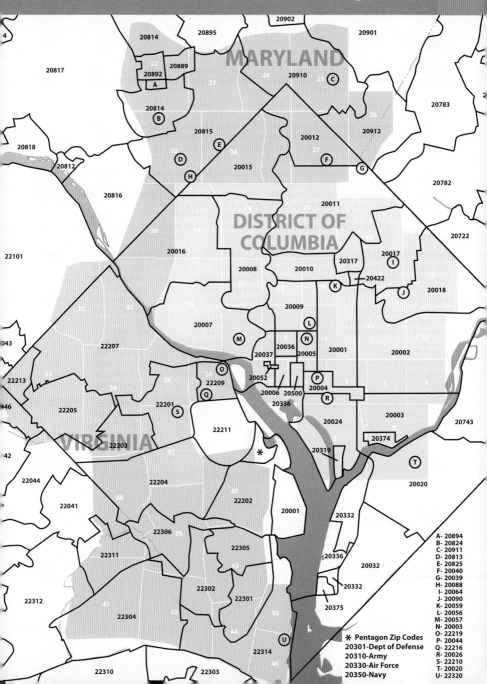

MARYLAND

DISTRICT OF COLUMBIA

VIRGINIA

A- 20894
B- 20824
C- 20911
D- 20813
E- 20825
F- 20040
G- 20039
H- 20088
I- 20064
J- 20090
K- 20059
L- 20056
M- 20057
N- 20003
O- 22219
P- 20044
Q- 22216
R- 20026
S- 22210
T- 20020
U- 20320

✳ Pentagon Zip Codes
20301-Dept of Defense
20310-Army
20330-Air Force
20350-Navy

Hospitals

As hyper-stressed, Type-A workaholics, most Washingtonians are ripe for coronary disease, so it's a good thing there are many area hospitals to offer us recourse. Although district financing snarls have led to shutdowns, such as DC General Hospital in 2001, the District nevertheless remains equipped with state-of-the-art medical facilities ready to respond to emergencies of presidential magnitude.

The area's hospitals vary in terms of the level of service they offer. Stagger into some ERs, and unless your clothes have fresh blood stains, you won't be seeing a doctor until you have memorized the theme song to *Days of Our Lives*. Other facilities treat patients like hotel guests. At the recently refurbished **Virginia Hospital Center (Map 34)**, rooms are set up to offer remarkable Arlington views, and in-patients are delivered meals by workers who sport bow ties and studs. Sibley is your average Northwest hospital, with a relatively comfortable waiting room, usually tuned to CNN, and nurses who squawk to their patients about which congressman they shot up with saline the week prior.

Many medical people assert that the region's top docs reside at **Washington Hospital Center (Map 14)**, although Washington Hospital *City* is a more appropriate title. Practically every disease you can get has its own building devoted to it, and the relatively small Irving Street becomes somewhat of a highway off-ramp just to allow access to this behemoth of medical practitioners. Allow an extra hour just to park and figure out how to navigate its labyrinthine interior structure. The best bets for residents are George Washington University Hospital and Howard University Hospital, both are teaching hospitals, so in addition to cutting-edge practices, expect to be prodded a lot unnecessarily.

Emergency Rooms	Address	Phone	Map
George Washington University Hospital	900 23rd St NW	202-715-4000	7
Howard University Hospital	2041 Georgia Ave NW	202-865-6100	10
Children's National Medical	111 Michigan Ave NW	202-476-5000	14
Providence	1150 Varnum St NE	202-269-7000	14
Washington Hospital Center	110 Irving St NW	202-877-7000	14
Georgetown University Hospital	3800 Reservoir Rd NW	202-444-2000	18
National Naval Medical Center	8901 Rockville Pike	301-295-4611	22
Suburban	8600 Old Georgetown Rd	301-896-3100	22
Washington Adventist	7600 Carroll Ave	301-891-7600	26
Sibley Memorial	5255 Loughboro Rd NW	202-537-4000	32
Virginia Hospital Center, Arlington	1701 N George Mason Dr	703-558-5000	34
Inova Alexandria	4320 Seminary Rd	703-504-3000	42

Other Hospitals	Address	Phone	Map
HSC Pediatric Center	1731 Bunker Hill Rd NE	202-832-4400	13
National Rehabilitation Hospital	102 Irving St NW	202-877-1000	14
VA Medical Center	50 Irving St NW	202-745-8000	14

One of the great things about Washington, DC, is that the Metro is safe, convenient, and affordable. That's why you don't have to be downtown to visit DC, and that's good news for those on a tight budget.

Like all big cities, though, be sure to ask around, and check blogs and listservs to get "real people" ratings on the places you are considering before you tap your credit card number into the reservations system. Ask around. Housing—no matter the rate or neighborhood—can be a mixed bag.

If you have the cash, consider the **Hotel Helix (Map 10)** in Logan Circle, which features bright, comfy, pop-art furniture and ultra-modern décor. It's trendy, has large, comfortable rooms (which are all non smoking, by the way), and is located near the US Capitol, not far from Union Station. That means public transportation is steps away. There are also some great pubs and restaurants very close by (both inside Union Station and on neighboring streets). One note of caution—this is a "pet friendly" hotel, so if you prefer only two-legged guests, this might not be for you. As far as location goes, the **Washington Hilton (Map 9)** is only a stone's throw away from Dupont Circle and everything that area has to offer. Another trendy hotel—though not good for the budget-minded—is the **Mandarin Oriental (Map 6)**. If you crave elegance with an Asian flourish, top amenities, and a possible celebrity sighting (think Bono, Beyonce and Jay-Z), this is a great choice.

If your budget is tight, there's nothing wrong with checking out a youth hostel. There are plenty of good ones to be had with room rates starting at about $25 a night. But use caution—this type of lodging varies widely in DC, from clean and secure to downright scary (think the Bronx). As with hotels, ask a number of people before you commit. **American Guesthouse (Map 40)** offers safe, clean housing. One DC youth hostel in a fairly decent neighborhood (not far from the World Bank) is the **Hilltop Hostel (Map 27)**. It is also clean, inexpensive, and near a Metro. Former guests report that the security is good, and they felt safe there. Check out hostel sites such as www.hostelworld.com and www.hostelz.com for information on hostels. Always try to book hostels in advance (they're smaller than hotels and tend to book up faster) and read user reviews online, they're often the most accurate guides out there.

As always, you should use the room rates and star ratings listed below as a guide only. You'll probably want to call or visit the hotel in question to get the most accurate room rates for the days you wish to stay. If you're booking in advance, we suggest checking out sites such as hotels.com, tripadvisor.com, and expedia.com.

Between renaming buildings, bridges, and fountains and constructing new monuments by the garden-full, DC is quickly running out of things to convert into memorials. You could spend a month visiting every official monument in DC, but you'll have a better time checking out the unofficial local landmarks that get lost in the giant shadows of the White House and the Capitol Building. As for skyscrapers… sorry King Kong, you aren't going to find them in this city. A long-standing law prohibits buildings in the District from being taller than the tip of the Capitol.

Politics, Politics, Politics

After you are done with the marble tributes to the Founding Fathers, why not tour the landmarks of other lesser politicians? Visit the Vista International Hotel (now the **Westin Wyndham (Map 10)**), where former DC Mayor Marion Barry was caught smoking crack cocaine, or The Mayflower Hotel (Map 9 – Farragut Nort) where Former New York Governor Eliot Spitzer intimately counseled a elite prostitute, or the **Washington Hilton (Map 9)**, where Ronald Reagan took a bullet from John Hinckley, Jr.

Hidden Treasures

If politics isn't your thing (then why are you here?), the District has many a grand home to admire from the inside and out. **The Heurich House (Map 9)**, also known as the Brewmaster's Castle, invites you to tour a perfectly intact Victorian home, complete with a basement Bavarian beer drinking room. Or if you're feeling more whimsical, there's the **Mushroom House (Map 30)** in Bethesda, a private residence owned by people who got a little too excited with the Smurfs. Don't forget to check out **The Littlest House in Alexandria (Map 46)**, which allows for a narrow 7-foot wide life.

Beauties of Bronze

This town also has more than its fair share of statues. Take a moment at Union Station to admire the **Columbus Memorial (Map 2)** out front. The marble fountain opened in 1912, but most visitors and commuters come and go and never take notice of it at all. The circular fountain is 44 feet deep in the middle, and Columbus himself stands at the larger-than-life height of 15 feet. Or if you're weary of oversized statues of dead white men, you can gaze up instead at the **Gandhi Statue (Map 9)** off Dupont Circle, the **Joan of Arc (Map 9)** statue at Malcolm X Park, or the beloved **Grief (Map 14)** memorial in Rock Creek Cemetery.

Those Are Landmarks?

Even more landmarks are those buildings you've seen again and again, and yet no one seems to be able to identify them. The **Temple of the Scottish Rite of Freemasonry (Map 9)** standing tall on 16th Street, the **Second Division Memorial (Map 1)** on the Mall, or **The Other FDR Memorial (Map 1)** that quietly sits outside the National Archives. Don't forget, "landmark" is a loose term, so why not throw in the still functioning **Uptown Theater (Map 17)**, DC's premiere venue for *Lord of the Rings*-type films.

Hollywood in Washington

So you think it's all happening in LA and New York? Think again, friend. If you ever find yourself on Prospect Street at night, gather up the *cojones* to visit the **Exorcist Steps (Map 8)**, the steep and narrow 97-step stairwell used in William Blatty's classic horror film, *The Exorcist*. The unassuming neighborhood of Mount Pleasant was also featured in *State of Play* starring Russell Crowe, whose character lives above local landmarks Heller's Bakery and Pfeiffer's Hardware. If that's not enough Hollywood for you, grab a beer and sit on the steps of the **Lincoln Memorial (Map 7)**, like that scene in *Wedding Crashers*.

Hometown Heroes

Every neighborhood seems to have its local landmarks—whether it be colorful mural (see: **Marilyn Monroe (Map 16)** in Woodley Park) or a frequently patronized greasy spoon (see: **Ben's Chili Bowl (Map 10)** on U Street). When in Dupont, hang out by the **Dupont Fountain (Map 9)**—the focal point of the eclectic crowd that makes up the neighborhood. In Silver Spring, head straight to the **AFI Theater (Map 25)**, where you can catch an indie American or foreign film and watch it in the stadium seats usually associated with blockbuster releases. Feeling like catching a local band but don't want to pack into a sweaty club? Hit up the family-friendly **Fort Reno Park (Map 19)** in the summer months. You can't booze, but hey, it's free.

Overview

Let's face it: The Smithsonian Museums were really cool when you were 10 years old and toured DC with your parents. But you're a cultured adult now, looking to expand your horizons a bit further than dinosaur bones and airplanes (not that dinosaur bones and airplanes aren't cool, because they are). Washington's plethora of small and independent galleries have got it all, from classical to conceptual. To top it off, you're not too likely to be bumped from behind by an unsupervised toddler whose parents wanted to see Degas's ballerinas but couldn't find a babysitter. Although crowds of young professionals aren't always much better, Washington's art galleries offer a more comfortable and casual approach to the art world. Remember that these listings fall into three categories: art museums that are free, free, free, private galleries that charge admission, and commercial galleries where if you like something enough, you might just take it home.

Dupont Circle is the traditional hub of DC's art scene, with non-Smithsonian art museums that include impressionism at the popular **Phillips Collection (Map 9)** to the shrine of rugs at the **Textile Museum (Map 9)**. Most offer interesting lectures and concert events, and are housed in historic homes, such as the Textile Museum, if you're in the market for a wedding venue. The only drawback is that, unlike the bigger museums around the mall, many galleries charge entrance fees and sometimes keep quirky hours (daytime Wednesday through Saturday is your best bet). Planning ahead will definitely pay off if you want to experience the ceramics, painting, sculpture, and other less accessible works of art that these galleries feature.

A good time to check out the Dupont art scene is on the first Friday evening (typically between 6-8 pm), of every month, when most of the galleries open their doors briefly for a free peek, and serve cheese and wine to sweeten the deal. Many of the galleries on R Street, also known as Gallery Row, are converted row houses with narrow staircases, so be careful of art enthusiast bottlenecks on Friday nights. Be sure to check out the **Kathleen Ewing Gallery (Map 9)** (great photography), **Robert Brown Gallery (Map 9)** (eclectic, varied exhibitions), and **Studio Gallery (Map 9)** (artist co-op with 30 members).

During the annual Dupont-Kalorama Museum Walk Weekend, held on the first weekend in June, galleries usually allow roaming free of charge (www.dkmuseums.com). The Dupont-Kalorama Museum Walk caters to discerning art critics, groups of children, and families alike, offering exhibits and activities that reflect a desire to inspire the art history buffs as well as the "Da Vinci who?" crowd.

Check out the *Post* and *City Paper* listings for shows at some of the other galleries that, ahead of rampant gentrification, are popping up all over the city. Another great resource for gallery information is the Going Out Guide at www.washingtonpost.com/blogs/going-out-guide, which has excellent reviews and editor picks of the art galleries in DC, as well as a list with gallery websites at http://art-collecting.com/galleries_dc.htm.

Arts & Entertainment • **Bookstores**

Washingtonians really love their books. This is a city of policy wonks, lawyers, writers, defense specialists, and activists—the one thing we all have in common, frankly, is that we're nerds. Washington, DC, and the metropolitan area is, especially recently, brimming with residents with expensive educations, lucrative government contracting jobs, and townhouses with lots of built-in bookshelves meant to house quality reads next to treasures from overseas journeys during diplomatic operations. So it seems obvious that bookstores here would get as crowded as the Beltway during rush hour. Besides the mega-chain stores like **Barnes & Noble (Map 1, Map 29, Map 35, Map 43)**, there are several local outlets in town, each with a personality of their own.

Kramerbooks & Afterwords Café (Map 9) in Dupont Circle, for instance, is something of a local landmark. Literary types will meet up here, thumbing the shelves for their next read while they wait, and then often settle into a bookish conversation at the café over a Mocha Ice and fine slice of pie, or in the restaurant for drinks and dinner. **Busboys and Poets (Map 10)** is stocked with nothing but the most progressive, left-wing literature, perfect for the U Street area. **Politics & Prose (Map 20)** is political (obviously) and also quite easily the city's

finest bookstore. It's hard to exit this upper NW gem without wishing to spend the rest of your life buried in a book, and there are authors speaking here every night of the week to further encourage you. There's also two locations of **Big Planet Comics (Map 8, Map 22)** for your inner (or outer) adolescent geek. If you have time to spare, check out the used bookstores for cheaper reads and dusty aromas. Try **Riverby Books (Map 3)** on Capitol Hill, **Second Story Books (Map 9)** in Dupont Circle, **Idle Time Books (Map 16)** in Adams Morgan, and **Book Bank (Map 46)** in Alexandria.

DC's bookstore scene also offers some of the best in specialty non-fiction. The **American Institute for Architects (Map 1)** can offer you histories of every high rise in the Chicago skyline, and the **National Gallery of Art Gift Shop (Map 2)** will provide countless coffee table books on modern art, as well as the accompanying art criticism. For religious studies, there's the **Islamic Center (Map 8)** or the **Catholic Information Center (Map 9)** (to name only two). Basically, this is a town that has national associations of pottery wheelers and international funds for left-handed clarinetists—so if there's a subject you're interested in, there's a nerd to provide you with scholarly literature on it. Go for it!

Map 1 • National Mall

American Institute for Architects	1735 New York Ave NW	202-626-7300	Architecture.
Barnes & Noble	555 12th St NW	202-347-0176	General.

Map 2 • Chinatown / Union Station

National Academies Press	500 5th St NW	202-334-2612	Science and technology, social/environment issues.
National Gallery of Art	3rd St NW & Constitution Ave NW	202-737-4215	Art books.

Map 3 • The Hill

Riverby Books	417 E Capitol St SE	202-543-4342	Used.
Trover Shop Books & Office	221 Pennsylvania Ave SE	202-547-2665	General.

Map 5 • Southeast / Anacostia

Backstage Inc	545 8th St SE	202-544-5744	Theater and performance.
Capitol Hill Books	657 C St SE	202-544-1621	Second-hand fiction, mystery, and biography.
Fairy Godmother—Children's Books & Toys	319 7th St SE	202-547-5474	Toddler to young adult fiction and nonfiction.
First Amendment Books	645 Pennsylvania Ave SE	202-547-5585	Current events, political history.
Liber Antiquus	313 12th St SE	202-546-2413	Early imprinted books.

Map 7 • Foggy Bottom

George Washington University Book Store	800 21st St NW	202-994-6870	Academic and college.
Reiter's Books	1900 G St NW	202-223-3327	
Washington Law & Professional Books	1900 G St NW	202-223-5543	Law.

Map 8 • Georgetown

Bartleby's Books	1132 29th St NW	202-298-0486	Rare and antiquarian, 18th and 19th century American history, economics, and law.
Big Planet Comics	3145 Dumbarton Ave NW	202-342-1961	Comics.
Bridge St Books	2814 Pennsylvania Ave NW	202-965-5200	General.
Islamic Center	2551 Massachussetts Ave NW	202-332-8343	Islamic books.
Lantern Bryn Mawr Book Shop	3241 P St NW	202-333-3222	Used and rare.

Map 9 • Dupont Circle / Adams Morgan

Books for America	1417 22nd St NW	202-835-2665	Books with a purpose.
Books-A-Million	11 Dupont Cir NW	202-319-1374	General.
Catholic Information Center	1501 K St NW	202-783-2062	Catholic books.
G Books	1520 U St NW	202-986-9697	Gay/lesbian discount books.
Kramerbooks & Afterwords Café	1517 Connecticut Ave NW	202-387-1400	General.
Second Story Books & Antiques	2000 P St NW	202-659-8884	Used.

Map 10 • Logan Circle / U Street

Busboys and Poets	2021 14th St NW	202-387-7638	Political, poetry and literature, multi-cultural, and independent publishers.

Map 11 • Near Northeast

Bison Shop-Gallaudet University	800 Florida Ave NE	202-651-5271	Academic and sign language.

Map 14 • Catholic U

Basilica Of The National Shrine Bookstore	400 Michigan Ave NE	202-526-8300	Catholic books.
Icon & Book Service	1217 Quincy St NE	202-526-6061	Eastern Christian books.
Newman Book Store of Washington	3025 4th St NE	202-526-1036	Scripture, theology, philosophy, and church history.

Map 15 • Columbia Heights

House Of Khamit	2822 Georgia Ave NW	202-387-4163	African History/Culture.
Howard University Book Store	2225 Georgia Ave NW	202-238-2640	Academic and Afro-centric.
Sankofa Video & Bookstore	2714 Georgia Ave NW	202-234-4755	Afro-centric.

Map 16 • Adams Morgan (North) / Mt Pleasant

AAFSW Book Room	2201 Centre St NW	202-223-5796	General used.
Idle Time Books	2467 18th St NW	202-232-4774	Used.
Potter's House Books	1658 Columbia Rd NW	202-232-5483	Spiritual/Social Justice Literature.

Map 18 • Glover Park / Foxhall

Georgetown University Book Store	3800 Reservoir Rd NW	202-687-7492	Academic.

Map 19 • Tenleytown / Friendship Heights

American University Book Store	4400 Massachusetts Ave NW	202-885-6300	Academic and college.
Kultura	4918 Wisconsin Ave NW	202-244-0224	Specializing in arts and humanities.
Red Sky Books	4318 Fessenden St NW	202-363-9147	Used and out-of-print.
Tempo Book Store	4905 Wisconsin Ave NW	202-363-6683	Language.

Map 20 • Cleveland Park / Upper Connecticut

Politics & Prose	5015 Connecticut Ave NW	202-364-1919	One of the top bookstores in DC.

Map 22 • Bethesda (North)

Big Planet Comics	4908 Fairmont Ave	301-654-6856	Superhero genealogy experts on hand.

Map 23 • Chevy Chase (North)

Audubon Naturalist Bookshop	8940 Jones Mill Rd	301-652-3606	Nature and earth.

Map 25 • Silver Spring

Alliance Comics	8317 Fenton St	301-588-2546	Comics.
Silver Spring Books	938 Bonifant St	301-587-7484	Used.

Map 29 • Bethesda (South)

Barnes & Noble	4801 Bethesda Ave	301-986-1761	General.
Writer's Center	4508 Walsh St	301-654-8664	Literature and books on writing.

Map 33 • Falls Church

Aladdin's Lamp Children's Books	2499 N Harrison St	703-241-8281	Children's.

Map 34 • Cherrydale / Ballston

Bookhouse	805 N Emerson St	703-527-7797	Scholarly history.

Map 35 • Cherrydale / Clarendon

Barnes & Noble	2800 Clarendon Blvd	703-248-8244	General.
Imagination Station at Kinder Haus Toys	1220 N Fillmore St	703-527-5929	Children's.

Map 38 • Columbia Pike

Al-Hikma Book Store	5627 Columbia Pike	703-820-7500	Arabic.
NVCC-Alexandria Campus Book Store	3101 N Beauregard St	703-671-0043	Academic and college.

Map 43 • Four Mile Run / Del Ray

Barnes & Noble	3651 Jefferson Davis Hwy	703-299-9124	General.
Book Niche & Capital Comics	2008 Mount Vernon Ave	703-548-3466	Books, comics, etc.

Map 44 • Alexandria Downtown

Already Read Used Books	2501 Duke St	703-299-8406	Used.

Map 46 • Old Town (South)

Aftertime Comics	1304 King St	703-548-5030	Comics.
Book Bank	1510 King St	703-838-3620	Used.
Books-A-Million	503 King St	703-548-3432	General.
Pauline Books & Media	1025 King St	703-549-3806	Catholic books.
Sacred Circle Books	919 King St	703-299-9309	Metaphysical.
Why Not	200 King St	703-548-4420	Children's.

This may not be NY or LA, but film buffs will find plenty to keep them busy; they just need to know where to look. **The E Street Cinema (Map 1)** and Bethesda's Landmark **Bethesda Row (Map 29)** both offer a solid roster of independent films, with some mainstream flicks mixed in. Another indie haven, **Chevy Chase's Avalon Theatre (Map 25)**, has special charm: DC's oldest movie house was shut down several years ago by then-owner Loews, but a nonprofit group calling themselves the Avalon Theatre Project took over and revamped this 1923 gem. Also visit the little known **West End Cinema (Map 7)** in Foggy Bottom for a mix of current and obscure films that are hardly ever sold out. For film fanatics, however, nothing can beat the **AFI Theater (Map 25)** in downtown Silver Spring. Like a kid in a candy store, you can pick from a few current (usually indie) films or see a flick that's part of the many film series being offered, which run the gamut from "Frankenfest: Frankenstein through the Ages" to "Rebels with a Cause: The Films of East Germany."

If you could care less about French New Wave and documentaries make you snooze, never fear, the DC area abounds with theaters showing the usual mainstream fare. For stadium-seating megaplexes, there's the **Loews Georgetown 14 (Map 8)**, which houses a brick smokestack used long ago as the Georgetown Incinerator, and the **Regal Gallery Place Stadium (Map 2)**, whose fit-for-Caesar marble atrium and 14 screens are cleverly nestled into an already crowded Chinatown. For movie-going frat boys seeking luxury (or their idea of it), the **AMC Mazza Gallerie 7 (Map 19)** offers Club Cinema with (gasp!) leather seats and (high five!) a full-service bar, but tickets cost a couple of bucks more than the rest of the auditoriums. For a different blockbuster-watching experience, one with old-school glamour and a touch of class, head to **The Uptown (Map 17)** in Cleveland Park, a magnificent art deco theater with the biggest screen (32' x 70') in town. This is a true movie "palace," complete with balcony seating and lines of people dressed like wizards for the opening of Harry Potter.

Slightly off the beaten path is the **Arlington Cinema 'N' Drafthouse (Map 37)**, an old Art Deco theater that hosts live music, stand-up comedy, wine tastings, Kentucky Derby parties, you name it. But its main gig is serving up second-run movies, dinner, and drinks for a bargain price. Keep an eye on their weekly online calendar for discount nights, special events like free advanced screenings, and midnight showings of cult favorites. Other alternative movie happenings to watch out for in the area include various film festivals, and temporary screenings every few weeks at many of the museums, schools, or historic theaters like the **Tivoli (Map 15)** in Columbia Heights and the **Lincoln (Map 10)** on U Street. In summer, there are plenty of free outdoor movie festivals like the classic "Screen on the Green" on the Mall or the NIH's "Science in the Cinema.

No matter where you choose to go, the usual print and online entertainment sources like the *Washington Post, City Paper*, and Fandango can give you show times. And remember, Netflix can't offer you movie theater popcorn, and no matter how big your flat-screen TV is, seeing a movie on the big screen is better, so get off the couch once in a while and head to one of DC's movie theaters.

Theater	Address	Phone	Map
AFI Silver Theater	8633 Colesville Rd	301-495-6720	25
AMC Courthouse Plaza 8	2150 Clarendon Blvd	703-243-4950	36
AMC Hoffman Center 22	206 Swamp Fox Rd	703-236-1083	44
AMC Loews Georgetown 14	3111 K St NW	202-342-6033	8
AMC Loews Shirlington 7	2772 S Randolph St	703-671-0912	39
AMC Loews Uptown 1	3426 Connecticut Ave	202-966-5401	17
AMC Mazza Gallerie	5300 Wisconsin Ave NW	202-537-9551	19
American City Diner & Cinema Cafe	5532 Connecticut Ave NW	202-244-1949	28
Arlington Cinema 'N' Drafthouse	2903 Columbia Pike	703-486-2345	37
Avalon Theatre	5612 Connecticut Ave NW	202-966-6000	28
Busboys and Poets	2021 14th St NW	202-387-7638	10
Carnegie Institution	1530 P St NW	202-939-1142	9
Landmark Bethesda Row Cinema	7235 Woodmont Ave	301-652-7273	29
Landmark E St Cinema	555 11th St NW	202-452-7672	1
Lockheed Martin IMAX Theater	601 Independence Ave SW	877-932-4928	2
The Regal Majestic 20	900 Ellsworth Dr	301-565-8884	25
Regal Ballston Common 12	671 N Glebe Rd	703-527-9730	34
Regal Bethesda 10	7272 Wisconsin Ave	301-718-8322	29
Regal Gallery Place Stadium	707 7th St NW	202-393-2121	2
Regal Potomac Yard 16	3575 Jefferson Davis Hwy	703-739-4054	43
Samuel C Johnson IMAX Theater	Constitution Ave NW & 10th St NW	202-633-4629	1
Wechsler Theatre	4400 Massachusetts Ave NW	202-885-2053	19
West End Cinema	2301 M St NW	202-419-3456	7

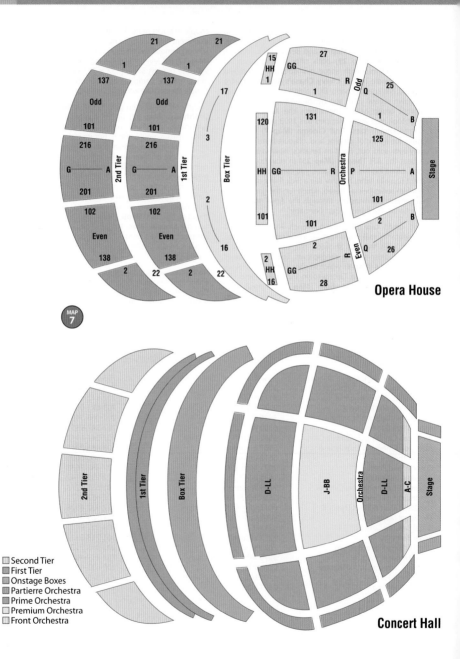

Opera House

MAP
7

Concert Hall

- Second Tier
- First Tier
- Onstage Boxes
- Partierre Orchestra
- Prime Orchestra
- Premium Orchestra
- Front Orchestra

General Information

NFT Map: 7
Address: 2700 F St NW
            Washington, DC 20566
Website: www.kennedy-center.org
Phone: 202-416-8000
Box Office: 800-444-1324 or 202-467-4600

Overview

The Kennedy Center is the city's most renowned and lavish performance art destination. While other city venues may be better at promoting cutting-edge arts, this place is where you can witness the world's best pirouette, soliloquy, and/or yodel. The Center houses the National Symphony Orchestra, the Suzanne Farrell Ballet, and VSA, the world's leading international organization on arts and disability. It also acquired the Washington National Opera in 2011. Local orchestras and performing artists showcase their work for free on various evenings as well, and the Kennedy Center also hosts auditions for future opera singers, open to the public (with tickets), who become picked for opera houses around the country. Of course, such feats come with a price tag, and the Center tends to cater to thick-of-wallet arts patrons. There are free concerts at 6 pm every day of the year on the Millennium Stage, hidden cheap seats, and occasional discounts. And there's no charge to show up and check out one of the city's most romantic dusk terrace views or the giant bust of the center's adored namesake. Dinner and a performance is a very classy DC way to spend an evening.

The Kennedy Center houses the Concert Hall, Opera House, Eisenhower Theater, Terrace Theater, Theater Lab, Film Theater, and Jazz Club. On any given night, there are concurrent music, theater, opera, and dance performances. It can be tough to keep up. If you're a confirmed culture vulture, stay afloat by becoming a Kennedy Center member. Otherwise, bookmark the websites of your favorites and check them regularly.

The Kennedy Center's history began in 1958, when President Dwight D. Eisenhower took a break from the links to sign legislation creating a National Cultural Center for the United States. President John F. Kennedy and First Lady Jackie later did much of the fundraising for what the president called "our contribution to the human spirit." Two months after President Kennedy's assassination, Congress named the center in his memory.

How to Get There—Driving

Major roadway construction near the Center makes getting there by car slightly challenging. The Center is located at the intersection of New Hampshire Ave., NW and Rock Creek Parkway. Once you get close, follow posted signs for the Kennedy Center. The website also has detailed directions for those coming from D.C. Maryland and Virginia. Also, while they may be the perfect status symbol for a night at the opera, driving an SUV taller than six feet could spell disaster – there are limited spaces available at that height with the maximum clearance of seven feet.

Parking

Kennedy Center garage parking is $22. Sixty minutes of free validated parking is available after spending $15 or more at one of the gift shops or after visiting the box office. However there's no validation for picking up free tickets.

How to Get There—Mass Transit

Take the Blue Line or Orange Line to the Foggy Bottom stop, and either walk seven minutes to the center or take a free shuttle that runs every fifteen minutes. Metrobus 80 also goes to the Kennedy Center.

How to Get Tickets

Tickets usually go on sale about two months before show announcement. Buy them online, at box office, by phone or by mail. Call 202-467-4600 for more info.

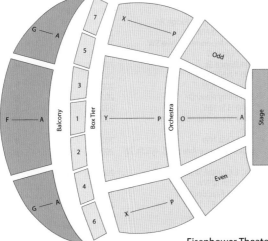

Eisenhower Theater

The Smithsonian Institution is a national system of museums, most of which are situated in a campus-like arrangement around the National Mall (other branches, like the Cooper-Hewitt National Design Museum, are located in New York City, and the Steven F. Udvar-Hazy Center, an extension of the National Air and Space Museum (Map 6), is in Chantilly, VA). The top-notch Smithsonian exhibits draw both American and international tourists by the hordes (think Mongol hordes). You could spend your whole life in Washington and still not be able to name every Smithsonian museum. But they're all free, so consider them friends who need to be checked in on from time to time.

The West Building of the **National Gallery (Map 2)** houses a world-class collection of American and Western European painting and sculpture, including the only Leonardo da Vinci painting on this side of the Atlantic. The East Building houses the museum's modern and contemporary collections. At the **Freer and Sackler Galleries (Map 1)**, sublime works of Asian art hide in unlikely corners of small and modest rooms. The **Hirshhorn Museum and Sculpture Garden (Map 2)** is, well, avant-garde—what else could you call the collection that includes Ron Mueck's eerily realistic sculpture of a naked, obese, bald man just hanging out in the corner? The **Corcoran Gallery of Art (Map 1)** is another one of DC's gems, with a solid collection of American and European art, and it also offers a wide range of classes (visit www.corcoran.org for details). The

National Museum of American History (Map 1) is more than a collection of invaluable artifacts; it addresses the history and the making of American culture. And while the American History museum might make us feel all-important, the **National Museum of Natural History (Map 1)** will deflate our egos, reminding us that we are but one mortal species among many. As depressing as it may be, the **US Holocaust Memorial Museum (Map 1)** is definitely worth visiting—an eerie but well-done reminder of the extent of man's cruelty.

DC is home to the **National Archives (Map 2)**, a government building that also contains numerous historical documents on exhibit. Stop by and pay nothing to see the *Bill of Rights* and our founding fathers' John Hancocks (even John Hancock's!). Extending out from the Mall, you'll discover the private museums. The **National Building Museum's (Map 2)** building and gift shop are interesting, even when the offbeat architectural exhibits are not. When you're in the mood for something more specific, try the targeted collections at places like the **National Museum of the American Indian (Map 2)** which has the best food court in D.C. or the **National Museum of Women in the Arts (Map 1)**. Finally the recently revamped **Newseum (Map 2)**, with its glassy patio walkway and part of the Berlin Wall, promises an interactive, multimedia experience of journalism.

Museum	Address	Phone	Map
Alexandria Archaeology Museum	105 N Union St	703-746-4399	46
Alexandria Black History Museum	902 Wythe St	703-746-4356	45
American Visionary Art Museum	800 Key Hwy	410-244-1900	n/a
Anacostia Community Museum	1901 Fort Pl SE	202-633-4820	n/a
Arlington Historical Museum	1805 S Arlington Ridge Rd	703-892-4204	40
Art Museum of the Americas	201 18th St NW	202-458-6016	7
Arthur M. Sackler Gallery	1050 Independence Ave SW	202-633-1000	1
Arts Club of Washington	2017 I St NW	202-331-7282	7
Athenaeum	201 Prince St	703-548-0035	46
Corcoran Gallery of Art	500 17th St NW	202-639-1700	1
DAR Museum	1776 D St NW	202-628-1776	7
DEA Museum & Visitors Center	700 Army Navy Dr	202-307-3463	40
Decatur House on Lafayette Square	1610 H St NW	202-842-0920	1
Discovery Creek Children's Museum- Historic Schoolhouse	4954 MacArthur Blvd NW	202-337-5111	18
Dumbarton House	2715 Q St NW	202-337-2288	8
Einstein Planetarium- National Air & Space Museum	Independence Ave SW & 4th St SW	202-633-1000	2
Folger Shakespeare Library	201 E Capitol St SE	202-544-4600	3
Ford's Theatre	511 10th St NW	202-347-4833	1
Fort Ward Museum & Historic Site	4301 W Braddock Rd	703-746-4848	39
Frederick Douglass Museum & Caring Hall of Fame	320 A St NE	202-547-4273	3
Frederick Douglass National Historic Site	1411 W St SE	202-426-5961	5

Museum	Address	Phone	Map
Freer Gallery of Art	Jefferson Drive & 12th St SW	202-633-4880	1
Friendship Firehouse Museum	107 S Alfred St	703-746-3891	46
Gadsby's Tavern Museum	134 N Royal St	703-746-4242	46
George Washington Masonic National Memorial	101 Callahan Dr	703-683-2007	44
Hillwood Museum & Gardens	4155 Linnean Ave NW	202-686-5807	20
Hirshhorn Museum and Sculpture Garden	7th St SW & Independence Ave SW	202-633-1000	2
Historical Society of Washington, DC	801 K St NW	202-383-1850	10
International Spy Museum	800 F St NW	202-393-7798	1
The Kreeger Museum	2401 Foxhall Rd NW	202-337-3050	18
The Lyceum	201 S Washington St	703-746-4994	46
The Mansion on O Street	2020 O St NW	202-496-2020	9
Marian Koshland Science Museum of the National Academy of Sciences	6th St NW & E St NW	202-334-1201	2
MOCA DC	1054 31st St NW	202-342-6230	8
Mount Vernon Estate & Gardens	3200 Mt Vernon Memorial Hwy	202-780-2000	n/a
National Academy of Sciences	500 5th St NW	202-334-2000	2
National Air and Space Museum	Independence Ave SW & 4th St SW	202-633-1000	2
National Aquarium	Constitution Ave NW & 14th St NW	202-482-2825	1
The National Archives Building	700 Pennsylvania Ave NW	202-357-5000	2
National Building Museum	401 F St NW	202-272-2448	2
National Gallery of Art	7th St NW & Constitution Ave NW	202-737-4215	2
National Geographic Museum	1145 17th St NW	202-857-7588	9
National Museum of African Art	950 Independence Ave SW	202-633-4600	1
National Museum of American Jewish Military History	1811 R St NW	202-265-6280	9
National Museum of Health and Medicine	2500 Linden Ln	301-319-3300	24
National Museum of Natural History	Constitution Ave NW & 10th St NW	202-633-1000	1
National Museum of the American Indian	4th St & Independence Ave SW	202-633-1000	2
National Museum of the US Navy (reservation required for non-military)	805 Kidder Breese SE	202-433-4882	5
National Museum of Women in the Arts	1250 New York Ave NW	202-783-5000	1
National Portrait Gallery	8th St NW & F St NW	202-633-8300	1
National Postal Museum	2 Massachusetts Ave NE	202-633-5555	2
National Zoo	3001 Connecticut Ave NW	202-633-4800	17
Newseum	555 Pennsylvania Ave NW	888-639-7386	2
The Octagon Museum	1799 New York Ave NW	202-626-7318	7
Palace of Wonders	1210 H St NE	202-398-7469	3
The Phillips Collection	1600 21st St NW	202-387-2151	9
Pope John Paul II Cultural Center	3900 Harewood Rd NE	202-635-5400	14
Renwick Gallery	1661 Pennsylvania Ave NW	202-633-7970	1
S. Dillon Ripley Center	1100 Jefferson Dr SW	202-633-1000	1
Smithsonian American Art Museum	8th St NW & F St NW	202-633-1000	1
Smithsonian Institution Building (The Castle)	1000 Jefferson Dr SW	202-633-1000	1
The Society of the Cincinnati-Anderson House	2118 Massachusetts Ave NW	202-785-2040	9
Stabler-Leadbeater Apothecary Museum	105 S Fairfax St	703-746-3852	46
Textile Museum	2320 S St NW	202-667-0441	9
The Torpedo Factory	105 N Union St	703-838-4565	46
Tudor Place	1644 31st St NW	202-965-0400	8
United States National Arboretum	3501 New York Ave NE	202-245-2726	12
US Holocaust Memorial Museum	100 Raoul Wallenberg Pl SW	202-488-0400	1
US Library of Congress	101 Independence Ave SE	202-707-8000	2
Woodrow Wilson Center for International Scholars	1300 Pennsylvania Ave NW	202-691-4000	1

DC's nightlife scene includes swank nightclubs, reliable neighborhood bars, and venues with great rooftop decks for some real summer fun. After a long day of Robert's Rules of Order for Hill staffers, exams and study sessions for the college kids, and office frustrations for the working stiffs, there is great need to release some energy. Happy hour starts in the District around 5 pm with bars and restaurants offering drinks specials, outdoor dining, and tasty eats. On weekends, the late-night fun usually begins to pick up around midnight and cruises towards the wee hours of 3 a.m. and beyond. And don't let the surplus of stiff business suits, button downs, and ballet flats fool you—this city knows how to unwind. It's a good thing they don't give out tickets for riding drunk on the Metro—expect to see your fair share of people passed out in the seat next to you. Fair warning: the Metro closes at midnight Sunday through Thursday and at 3 a.m. on Friday and Saturday, but there are always cabbies waiting on bar streets for that tipsy (but not slobbering drunk) fare. If you keep timing in mind, DC is a prime city for partying. If you have $10-$1,000 to spend every night, there is a place for you.

Nightlife revolves around the bustling K Street Corridor, Georgetown, Dupont, Adams Morgan, Columbia Heights, Cleveland Park, U Street, H-Street NE, and some of the livelier suburbs, depending on your age, music preference, and mood. Most places in DC are within walking distance of each other (or at least a short cab or Metro ride apart), providing partygoers with several options for party-hopping, and it is guaranteed that hitting up six spots in one night will become an art-form for you and yours.

Georgetown

Throw on your white loafers, pop your polo collar, and grab your designer bag for a weekend out in Georgetown. This is a hodge-podge of college students, upper-crust shop-a-holics, wayward tourists, and local residents who have managed to find nooks and crannies along bustling M Street that the out-of-towners have yet to conquer. Nothing beats watching million-dollar yachts pulling up to the pier at **Sequoia (Map 8)** while you sip outdoor drinks. Need cheap drinks and some Journey in your life? Stroll over to **Rhino Bar & Pumphouse (Map 8)**. If you're one of DC's lone Republicans (or if you're progressive when it comes to dating someone of the opposite political affiliation), head to **Smith Point (Map 8)**. Dress the part and party with Euro-trash at **Maté (Map 8)** or try to impress your date and walk into the members only **L2 (Map 8)**. Go low-key at the renowned jazz bar **Blues Alley (Map 8)** and blow your trust fund at **Mr. Smith's (Map 8)** with the other private school kids.

Dupont

Dupont, a.k.a. the gay-bor-hood, is really a mix of all types of party goers in a neighborhood that is classy, expensive, but also full of dives. Watch out as you cross the circle, not just for rats, but also for oncoming cabs. The rooftop party is at the **Eighteenth Street Lounge** and the underground beer heaven is at the **Bier Baron** (formerly the Brickskeller) **(Map 9)**. For a night of pool, check out **Buffalo Billiards (Map 9)**; for people-watching with some margarita madness, check out the deck at **Lauriol Plaza (Map 9)**. For a sports bar on crack, visit the three story tall **Public Bar (Map 9)**, which is three floors and has far too many flatscreen TVs. Shake your bum at **Café Citron (Map 9)** or grab the best mojitos in town at **Gazuza (Map 9)**. Sophisticated types abound at **Circa at Dupont (Map 9)** and the gays are grindin' at **Cobalt (Map 9)** and downing pints at **JR's (Map 9)**.

Adams Morgan

In Adams Morgan, you'll find the monetarily-challenged and the über-rich roughing it for the night. 18th Street attracts a rambunctious crowd of young kids searching for live music, local improv, and a plethora of bars with neon signs, concrete steps, and quaint awnings. The block also offers conveniently placed parking machines to cling onto when you need to vomit the last few beers before crossing the street to go dancing. Sway to reggae and Caribbean rhythms at **Bukom Café (Map 16)**, and take in blues, jazz, rock, or bluegrass at **Madam's Organ (Map 16)**. Roll up your sleeves at **Pharmacy Bar (Map 16)**, DC's best dive, which caters more to locals than visitors and has a great jukebox. And before the evening is done, soothe your late night hunger pangs at **Amsterdam Falafel (Map 16)**.

Cleveland Park

Cleveland Park's nightlife is crammed into the 3400 block of Connecticut Avenue, where Belgian mussels, basement billiards, and dimly lit enclaves serving sophisticated wines stand next to each other in a melting pot of venues. For great beer, hit up **St. Arnold's** Cleveland Park location **(Map 17)**. For something a little more low-brow, check out **Nanny O'Brien's (Map 17)**. **Atomic Billiards (Map 17)** is a good spot for guzzling beer, throwing darts, and shooting pool. Or grab a relaxing glass of wine after a long day at **Bardeo (Map 17)**, a favorite of local young urban professionals.

U Street

U Street on weekend nights is where you'll find people boozing, dancing, and taking in live music. The bars, clubs, venues have attracted everyone from sparingly-dressed college coeds to their probably-too-old-to-be-clubbing admirers who all bring cold hard cash to this formerly up-and-coming neighborhood. The revitalization has been aided by **Marvin (Map 10)** and **Local 16 (Map 9)**, with their bustling rooftop decks, the **Black Cat (Map 10)**, the **9:30 Club (Map 10)**, and **Velvet Lounge (Map 10)**, and the dance club **DC9 (Map 10)**. Get your Caribbean groove on at **Patty Patty Boom Boom (Map 10)**. Bars such as **Stetson's Famous Bar & Restaurant (Map 9)** and **Solly's U Street Tavern (Map 10)** respect the neighborhood's humble roots, while also providing a place to mingle and perhaps meet that special someone.

Columbia Heights

One of the city's first hispster enclaves, Columbia Heights is home to many down-to-earth bars, including the appropriately named **Wonderland Ballroom (Map 15)**, where PBR and Jim Beam flows like water. **Meridian Pint (Map 15)** and **The Looking Glass Lounge (Map 15)** also possess a great neighborhood vibe, while the more upscale **Room 11 (Map 15)** features a lengthy wine list and elegant meals for less elegant prices.

Capitol Hill

One of the city's biggest nightlife booms in the last five years has been the growth of H Street NE just north of Capitol Hill in the Atlas District. Here, you'll find a strip of bars and restaurants to suit any taste. There's the culturally harmonious **Star and Shamrock (Map 3)**, a great selection of German beers at **Biergartenhaus (Map 3)**, and the adorably divey **The Pug**. Hipster hangout **Rock n' Roll Hotel (Map 3)** has indie live music, you can get your Belgian fix at **Granville Moore's (Map 3)**, and for the visitors from Georgetown, there's the **H Street Country Club (Map 3)**, replete with its own indoor mini-golf course. For those in the bottom half of Capitol Hill, there's **The Dubliner (Map 2)** and **Kelly's Irish Times (Map 2)**. For some upscale wine talk, hit the upstairs lounge at **Sonoma (Map 3)** or meet up with the rest of the trendy Hill staff at The **201 Bar (Map 3)**.

Old Town Alexandria

Alexandria's Old Town may not be a regular haunt for the DC-centric, but it offers a pleasant variety of places to drink and dance, especially for the 30-plus crowd. The proximity to the water, along with the collection of art galleries, upscale boutiques, and historical sites, make Old Town a great day-to-night destination. Crank out some karaoke at **Rock It Grill (Map 46)**. You can always rub elbows with the über snotty locals (and a fair share of tourists) at **Vermilion (Map 46)**, **Murphy's (Map 46)**, or **Union Street Public House (Map 46)**. And if you're feeling really elitist, you can likely get into **PX (Map 46)**, a not-so-hidden speakeasy with no sign—just a blue light over the front door.

Everything Else

The K Street Corridor has blossomed with seven swank lounges and clubs in a two-block radius all competing for your hard-earned paycheck. Europeans and diplomat kids hop over to **Josephine Lounge (Map 10)** and **Lima (Map 10)**, while DC's power elite trek to **Proof (Map 1)**, **Tattoo Bar (Map 9)**, and **The Park at Fourteenth (Map 10)**. Turn heads at the swank **Poste Moderne Brasserie (Map 1)** in Chinatown where you can sip wine in their gorgeous monument-like courtyard space. For lower-key establishments there's also the nearby **Irish Channel (Map 2)** for a pint of Guinness, the highly-underrated **RFD (Map 1)**, and **Capitol City Brewing Company (Map 1, 39)** for the free soft pretzels provided to every table. Venture out of Northwest DC and you'll find girls from the Midwest at **Clarendon Ballroom (Map 35)** and the deepest basement bar at **Quarry House Tavern (Map 25)** in downtown Silver Spring. Drown yourself in Indie music at **Galaxy Hut (Map 35)** or **Iota (Map 35)**. **Love (Map 12)**, formerly known as Dream, a massive four-floor complex on Okie Street, is also a popular place where VIP membership will cost you just $500 a year and save you the embarrassment of being a regular person in a line that often wraps around the block.

Arts & Entertainment • Restaurants

Thanks to its unwavering economy, DC has grown into a farm of culinary delights with world renowned chefs setting up shop and über-trendy spots (with price tags to match) on every corner. It was even the setting for Top Chef Season 7 and for the subsequent restaurants opened by former contestants. But there are still plenty of eateries to patronize if you are on a tight intern-like budget, need an outdoor patio, or just want some good international comestibles. In order to provide the skinny on restaurant recommendations for every type of DC bank account, we've listed some of our favorite places under four different categories: Eating Posh, Eating Cheap, Eating Hip, and Eating Ethnic.

Eating Posh

No matter who's in office, there are still bound to be plenty of "posh" restaurants for lobbyists, lawyers, congressmen and all those transients who want the full Beltway experience. Posh in DC often means old and mahogany paneling—with C-SPAN on the bar televisions. Washington fat cats are known to chew the fat (literally) at any of a few dozen steakhouses around town, but the local favorites include **BLT Steak (Map 1)**, **Smith and Wollensky (Map 9)**, **The Palm (Map 9)**, **Prime Rib (Map 9)**, and **Charlie Palmer (Map 2)**. For French decadence, look no further than **Bistro Bis (Map 2)**, and **Marcel's (Map 9)**. If Italian is your indulgence, then mangia bene at **Ristorante Tosca (Map 1)**, or **Obelisk (Map 9)**. DC institutions **Old Ebbitt Grill (Map 1)**, **1789 (Map 8)**, **Blue Duck Tavern (Map 9)**, and **Brasserie Beck (Map 10)** are all spots to see and be seen. Finally, **Komi (Map 9)** and **CityZen (Map 6)** consistently make it onto every food critic and lay foodie's Top 10.

Eating Cheap

Cheap food is plentiful in DC—after all, nobody comes here to get rich, just controversial. The food truck craze has hit the area with all sort of gourmet delights rolling around town, but if you're looking for a restaurant that doesn't drive away, there are plenty from which to select. Two of DC's most famous joints, **El Pollo Rico (Map 37)** and **Ben's Chili Bowl (Map 10)**, will cost you between $5 and $10 a meal, and New York's burger buzz, **Shake Shack (Map 9)** has set up shop in Dupont Circle. Right down the street, hop over to **Henry's Soul Café (Map 9)** for the best soul food in the city. If pizza is your poison, the mix of thin crust/ deep dish and St. Louis flatbread style at **District of Pi (Map 1)** gives a nice representation of pizza across the country. For a unique atmosphere, check out **Mexicali Blues (Map 35)** and the Dupont institution **Kramerbooks & Afterwords Café (Map 9)**. Rounding out the cheap eats list are cod supreme joint **Eamonn's: A Dublin Chipper (Map 46)**, Greek greasy spoon **Zorba's Cafe (Map 9)**, and out-of-this-world chili machine **Hard Times Café (Maps 46, 35)**. **Tortilla Coast (Map 5)** will cure your hangover and for quick and cheap sushi head over to Dupont's **Nooshi (Map 9)** or **Kotobuki (Map 18)** in the Palisades.

Eating Hip

Everyone in DC tries to be hip, and those who can actually pull it off are flocking to the now-arrived 14th Street Corridor in Logan Circle. There, places like **Pearl Dive Oyster Bar (Map 10)** have become the newest cool kids on the block. Top Chef Mike Isabella worked at the **Zaytinya (Map 1)**, before opening his own goth-like Mexican restaurant, **Bandolero (Map 8)** in Georgetown. Zaytinya's sister restaurant **Jaleo (Maps 2, 29)** offers more fashionable eats in town. Chinatown has long lines waiting to get into **Matchbox (Maps 2, 5)**. **Proof (Map 1)** and **Cork (Map 10)** have thousands of wine bottles to choose from between them. And **Sette Osteria (Map 9)** and **Lauriol Plaza (Map 9)** make up for the food with social cache. **Busboys & Poets** is the spot for great people-watching and pleasantly left-wing conversation. **Lima (Map 10)** and **Cashion's Eat Place (Map 16)** have always been in vogue among the downtown set, and **Tryst (Map 16)** is the ultimate coffeehouse to have an indecent affair with your neighbor. If you want to be annoying organic and "responsible" in the farm-to-table trend, there's **Founding Farmers (Map 7)** with delectable Italian-leaning platters. For two of Old Town's most fabulous dining experiences, check out **Vermilion (Map 46)** and **Majestic (Map 46)**.

Eating Ethnic

All who cross our borders can find authentic international eats. In DC, the rule of thumb is that the quality of ethnic food increases proportionally to one's distance from the city's center, but there are some notable exceptions in the metro area. Check out Indian goodness at **Rasika (Map 2)**, **Indique (Map 20)**, and **Heritage India (Map 18)**. Fiesta margaritas and homemade taquitos keep em' coming back to **Haydee's (Map 16)** in Mount Pleasant. The less-common Asian cuisine represented at **Burma (Map 2)** is also worthy of your hunger and attention. The most popular Thai restaurant around is **Thai Tanic (Map 10, 15)**. For Mediterranean, savvy diners head to **Lebanese Taverna (Map 17, 25, 33)** and **Cava (Map 5)**. **Tony Cheng's Seafood Restaurant (Map 2)** and **Eat First (Map 2)** are the cream of the Chinatown crop—or at least the last men standing. For the best sushi this side of the Pacific, **Makoto Restaurant (Map 18)** and **Sushi Taro (Map 9)** are all you'll need. Experience the Middle East at **Mama Ayesha's (Map 16)** and Morocco at **Marrakesh Palace (Map 9)**. The Mexican **Mixtec (Map 16)** and the pan-Asian Spices (Map 17) each also get an A-plus in our not-so-humble opinion. And don't miss out on **Roger Miller Restaurant (Map 25)**, a gem of a purveyor of West African curry goat in suburban Silver Spring.

Historically, the District's aesthetic has leaned conservative (even while its views haven't) so it often battles the perception that you can't find the latest clothes, home furnishings, or food items in the city. Not true! There are an ample number of hip and affordable shops, chic boutiques, high-end stores, and outdoor markets that can aid and abet any shopping addiction. From stiff suits and pearls to bow-tie seersuckers and miniskirts, DC is a city with lots of spending power. But you don't have to have a fat bank account to look good; there are diamonds in the rough, if you know where to look.

Clothing/Beauty

Georgetown has long been a shopping destination despite its lack of a metro station. There's something for everyone, from designer stores like **Kate Spade (Map 8)** to mainstream mainstay **Banana Republic (Map 8)** to trendy boutiques like **Sherman Pickey (Map 8)**—if you can handle pushing your way through the mobs of flip-flop-wearing college students and Europeans preying on the weak dollar. For the best of the chains, try the palatial three-story **Anthropologie (Map 8)**. For boutiques, try **Sassanova (Map 8)** for shoes and **Wink (Map 8)** for your next party dress.

The less-crowded and more centrally located Dupont Circle/Farragut North area also offers some great chains and boutiques. The **Proper Topper (Map 9)** has been a mainstay for finding unique pieces, say a Preakness hat or a watch that everyone will notice. Just down the street, **Betsy Fisher (Map 9)** is geared toward expensive shoes and fashions from labels you've never heard of—if you can get past the buzzer that lets people into the shop. Dudes have lots of options here too, including **Thomas Pink (Map 9)** for dress shirts and **Brooks Brothers (Map 9)** for the quintessential DC uniform. For less-expensive tastes, there's always **Gap (Map 9)** and **Ann Taylor (Map 9)**. If you've had a rough week, slip into **Blue Mercury (Map 8, 9)** and treat yourself to one of their luxurious beauty products.

Metro Center has become a mecca for big box inexpensive clothing stores in the last few years. At the center of it all is the two-story **H&M (Map 1)** that offers the the latest runway copycats at affordable prices. Not to be outdone, rival **Forever 21 (Map 1)** set up shop with three-stories of head-spinning fashions and accessories right above the metro station. There's also **Zara (Map 1)** for affordable European styles, and **T.J. Maxx (Map 1)** recently opened a surprisingly huge outfit in the heart of downtown. **Macy's (Map 1)** is always good for a lunch break, and nearby there's **American Apparel (Map 1)** if you can stand its misogynist ads. For expensive hippie chic, check out **Anthropologie (Map 1)**, but try not to spend your whole paycheck.

For those in search of the fresh and funky, the U Street Corridor, Columbia Heights, and Adams Morgan are great place to shop and they are refreshingly chain-free. For truly sophisticated fashionistas, **Muleh (Map 10)** offers men's and women's über-hip designer clothing (by the likes of Rozae Nichols, Nicole Farhi, and 3.1 by Phillip Lim) as well as fabulously modern furniture, all in a NY-loft-style space. And if you're looking for something "different" (i.e. used), **Treasury Vintage boutique (Map 10)** offers some nifty vintage picks for the hopelessly trendy. U-Street boutiques **Caramel (Map 9)**, **Ginger Root (Map 10)**, **Passport Fashion (Map 10)**, and **Zina (Map 10)** have great one-of-a-kind merchandise, and **Violet Boutique (Map 16)**, tucked away in Adams Morgan, has lovely finds for the working girl.

For a taste of suburban shopping not far from the city, head to the continuously developing Friendship Heights. It has high-end shopping plus space to park. There's a selection of department stores like **Saks Fifth Avenue (Map 29)** and a smattering of other high-end and luxury designer shops lining Wisconsin Avenue and the corner of Wisconsin and Western, like **Cartier (Map 29)** that will set you back $1,000 by the bracelet. Friendship Heights keeps unveiling construction sites that then burst with new, expensive and fancy shops. If you've got label-whore tendencies, but no money to spare, there's always **Loehmann's (Map 19)** to get your fix.

Housewares and Furniture

The DC area has all the major furniture and houseware chains: **Target (Map 15, 38, 43)**, **Crate & Barrel (Map 30)**, **Pottery Barn (Map 35)**. Georgetown has a **Design Within Reach (Map 8)** store (or more appropriately, "Design Just Out Of Reach"). For those don't think anything should cost that much, there's the **Crate & Barrel Outlet (Map 44)** in Alexandria. And there's always the blue and yellow standby **Ikea** out in College Park.

If you want your living space to have a bit more character, don't lose hope, there are more options out there. **Tabletop (Map 9)** in Dupont Circle is packed with cool home décor and modern housewares. **Millennium Decorative Arts (Map 9)** will more than satisfy Danish Modern aesthetes and furnishers. Turn to **Home Rule (Map 10)** for kitschy fun. If you like a little adventure when you shop, don't miss **Ruff & Ready (Map 10)**. From the outside it looks like a decrepit old house in a horror movie. Inside it's crammed with so much used furniture, junk, and antiques that you can barely squeeze through the aisles. If vintage floats your boat, check out the **Hunted House (Map 10)**, which features more than a few quirky mid-century modern and art deco pieces and **Miss Pixie's (Map 10)** and **Bentley's (Map 21)** will meet all your picker tendencies.

Arts & Entertainment • **Shopping**

Electronics

Superstores like **Best Buy (Map 15, 19, 33, 40, 43)** and the requisite picked-on little sibling **Radio Shack (Map 1, 2, 9, 16)** can be found across the region. Die hard Mac-heads will love the high-tech **Apple Stores (Map 8, 35, 40)** in the Pentagon City mall in Arlington, in Georgetown and in Clarendon.

Food

Some will quibble, but many DC residents just love **Trader Joe's (Map 8, 29, 45)** and will voluntarily wait on the very long check-out line that wraps around the store, twice, on weekends. The location in DC sells wine and beer, too. The food stores your parents would like are also plentiful. You can't swing an empty shopping basket without hitting a **Safeway (Map 5, 6, 9, 10)**, **Giant (Map 10, 11)**, or **Harris Teeter (Map 11, 16, 33, 34, 40, 41)**.

If you live in Foggy Bottom, Dupont, or Logan Circle, likely you visit overpriced **Whole Foods (Map 7, 10, 44)** for free-ranging, organic and expensive apples and eggs. There's also **Dean & DeLuca (Map 8)** for gourmet prepared foods and coffee. If you love cheese—and who doesn't?—check out **Cheesetique (Map 43)** in Del Ray or **Cowgirl Creamery (Map 1)** in Metro Center. For less-expensive organic, local chain **Yes! Organic Market (Map 16, 17)** has several locations. Make sure you bring your own bags to stores selling food in DC, or you will be charged five cents a bag for trying to pollute the Anacostia River.

Last but certainly not least, the DC area is ripe with wonderful farmer's markets—almost every neighborhood has one. The most famous can be found at **Eastern Market (Map 5)**. Although the historic main building was gutted by fire in 2007, it has since been rebuilt, reopened, and is open for business.

Bookstores and Music Stores

After the demise of Borders, **Barnes & Noble (Map 1, 35, 43)** is the big bookstore in town, but smaller independent bookstores also abound. **Kramerbooks & Afterwords (Map 9)** is the local favorite, where people hang out checking out latest reads next to diners and after club revel-ring. There is a bar with a wine list where you can hang out 7:30 a.m. until well past midnight (all night Fridays and Saturday). Music nerds have a good chance of finding that hard-to-find album at **Crooked Beat Records (Map 16)**, a small shop that specializes in rare and independent label music. For more specialized finds, drop into DC's oldest independent bookstore, **Reiter's Books (Map 9)**. It's known for scientific, medical, and technical books, but also carries a host of games and puzzles for the less serious-minded.

Wine, Beer, Liquor

Laws regarding alcohol vary throughout the region, but as a general rule, only Virginia supermarkets and drug stores sell wine. Also, Maryland has a few grocery stores and a ton of liquor stores, especially in Silver Spring, that sell wine. In DC, you can buy alcohol at liquor stores and supermarkets. Check out **Georgetown Wine and Spirits (Map 8)**, the iconic **Barrel House (Map 10)** in Logan Circle, **Bell Wine and Spirits (Map 9)** in Farragut, and **Modern Liquors (Map 10)** in Mount Vernon, where they all stock a wide variety of wine and employ knowledgeable staff. The bourgie demographic of the District ensures plenty of gourmet alcoholic shops in most affluent neighborhoods. In Virginia, wine lovers frequent **The Curious Grape (Map 39)**. Not only is the selection great, but the staff often hosts informative—and free—classes with wine experts from France, Chile, and beyond! There's also a tasting bar, open daily. For those who like their alcohol hoppy, here's a tip: **Rustico (Map 45)**, an Alexandria restaurant with beer list of heavenly proportion (nearly 300), has a note on their menu encouraging patrons to ask about purchasing a six-pack to take home of any beer they happen to like.

Late-night revelers should keep in mind that you can't buy anything alcoholic in DC stores after 10 p.m. Most liquor stores close at 9 p.m. on weekdays and 10 p.m. on Fridays and Saturdays. On Sundays, it's beer and wine only, so make sure you stock up early if you're having people over for the Redskins game.

There's a two-tiered theater scene here: flashy, national traveling productions; and edgy, organic gems. Count on **The Kennedy Center (Map 7)** and **National Theatre (Map 1)**—members of the former group—schedule a lineup of touring productions that appeal largely to those under 12 or over 55. Look for several other playhouses, some tucked away in neighborhoods, that give new playwrights, innovative ideas, and local actors a chance. Perhaps further still, consider all the DC-based companies that don't have a theater of their own, and follow their season—not their space (…because they don't have one).

If you're interested in the uniqueness of DC's theater scene, you'll find it on the high quality, smaller stages. **Arena Stage (Map 6)** on the SW waterfront (www.arena-stage.com; 202-488-3300) has earned its reputation as a well-respected local from decades of fine productions. The **Studio Theatre (Map 10)** in Logan Circle (www.studiotheatre. org; 202-332-3300), in addition to its larger productions, is also known for developing some of Washington's best actors and directors on its **2ndStage**. But perhaps the most successful yet cutting edge club in the city is **Woolly Mammoth (Map 2)**, a company that is constantly trying to redefine the relationship between theater and the DC community. In addition to stages with their own companies, remember that this city has a thriving number of theater companies without spaces to call home—including Didactic, Catalyst, and Rorschach.

For modern takes on the classics, visit the **Folger (Map 3)** and **Shakespeare Theatres (Map 2)**. The Folger Theatre, part of the Folger Shakespeare Library, stages three plays per year in its intimate Elizabethan-style theater (www. folger.edu; 202-544-7077), The Shakespeare Theatre recently expanded, making tickets easier to come by (www. shakespearedc.org; 202-547-1122).

The theater scene changes in the summer, with most playhouses taking a break. But for real buffs, there's the popular Contemporary American Theater festival in nearby Shepardstown, West Virginia, in July. Closer to home, there's a run of free shows at the outdoor **Carter Barron Amphitheatre (Map 21)** in Rock Creek Park; 202-426-0486.

Remember: one must never have to pay full-price for a night at the theater. Whether it's a pay-what-you-can night, 25 & under, residents only, student prices, or standing room only—there's always a cheapo culture vulture solution. DC theater is not just for thespians, and the thespians like it that way.

Street Index

284

Street Index

Chevy Chase

Street Index

Takoma Park

Street Index

Street Index

Street Index

Street	Range	Page	Grid
N Irving St	(1-2299)	35	B1/C1/C2
	(11-1051)	37	A1/B1
S Irving St		37	B2/C2
N Ivanhoe St		34	B1
S Ives St		40	B2/C2
N Ivy St	(500-999)	37	A1
	(1200-1399)	35	C1
S Ivy St		37	B2
Iwo Jima Memorial Access Rd		36	C2
N Jackson St	(1-999)	37	A1/B1
	(1100-2399)	35	B1/C1
S Jackson St		37	B2
N Jacksonville St		34	C1
S Jefferson Davis Hwy		40	A2/B2/C2
N Jefferson St	(300-1205)	34	C1
	(1450-3699)	33	A2/B2
N John Marshall Dr		33	A2/B2
N Johnson St		35	B1/C1
S Joyce St		40	A2/B2/C2
S June St		40	B2/C2
N Kansas St	(900-999)	37	A1
	(1200-1299)	35	C1
S Kemper Rd		39	B2
N Kenilworth St		33	A2/B2/C2
N Kenmore St	(300-999)	37	A1/B1
	(1400-2424)	35	B1/C1
	(2425-3224)	32	B1
S Kenmore St		39	A2/B2
N Kennebec St		33	C2
N Kennesaw St		33	C2
N Kensington St	(300-1149)	34	C1
	(1250-3749)	33	A2/B2
S Kensington St		38	A1
N Kent St		36	B2
S Kent St		40	B2/C2
N Kentucky St	(845-899)	34	C1
	(960-2499)	33	B2/C2
S Kenwood St		39	B2
N Key Blvd	(1400-2149)	36	B1/B2
	(2150-3199)	35	B2/C1/C2
Key Brg		36	A2
N Kirkwood Pl		35	B1
N Kirkwood Rd		35	B1/C1
S Knoll St		40	B1
N Lancaster St		33	A2/B2/C2
S Lang St		40	C1
S Langley St		39	A2
N Larrimore St		33	C2
N Lebanon St		33	C2
Lee Hwy	(1301-2129)	36	B1/B2
	(1601-4005)	35	B1/B2
	(4006-5198)	34	A1/A2
	(5188-6999)	33	B1/B2
N Lexington St	(800-919)	34	C1
	(1000-2899)	33	B2/C2
S Lexington St		38	A1
N Liberty St		33	C2
N Lincoln St	(300-999)	37	A1/B1
	(1200-2599)	35	A1/B1/C1
	(3600-3619)	32	B1
S Lincoln St	(700-999)	37	C1/C2
	(1700-2499)	39	A2/B2
N Little Falls Rd	(4700-4919)	31	C1/C2
	(4920-6959)	33	A2/B1
N Livingston St		33	C2
N Longfellow St		33	B2/C2
N Lorcom Ln	(2600-3949)	35	A1/B1/B2
	(3950-4499)	34	A2
S Lorton St		39	A2
S Lowell St		39	A2/B2
N Lynn St		36	A2/B2/C2
S Lynn St		40	B1/C1/C2
N Lynnbrook Dr		35	C1
N Madison St		33	B2/C2
N Manchester St		33	C2
N Marcey Rd		32	C1/C2
N Marshall Dr		36	C2
N McKinley Rd		33	B2/C2
N McKinley St		33	B2
N Meade St		36	C2
S Meade St		40	C1
N Military Rd	(2100-2546)	34	A2
	(2547-3999)	32	B1/C1/C2
N Monroe St	(300-1064)	37	A1/B1
	(1065-2499)	35	A1/B1/C1
	(3000-3699)	32	B1
S Monroe St	(600-2599)	39	A1/A2/B2
	(650-1249)	37	C1/C2
N Montana St		33	C2
N Moore St		36	B2
N Nash St		36	B2/C2
S Nash St		40	A1/B1
N Nelly Custis Dr		35	A1
N Nelson St	(200-1099)	37	A1/B1
	(1100-2799)	35	A1/B1/C1
	(3100-3899)	32	B1
S Nelson St		39	A1/A2/B2
Nicholas St		33	B2/C2
N Norwood St	(400-549)	37	B1
	(550-2799)	35	A1
S Norwood St		39	A1
N Nottingham St		33	A2/B2/C2
N Oak Ct		36	A2
N Oak St		36	B2/C2
S Oak St		40	A1
S Oakcrest Rd		40	C1/C2
N Oakland St	(1-999)	37	A1/B1
	(1800-2799)	35	A1/B1
	(3000-3899)	32	B1
S Oakland St	(100-999)	37	B1/C1
	(1300-2799)	39	A1/B2
N Ode St		36	B2/C2
S Ode St		40	A1/C1
N Ohio St		33	A2/B2/C2
N Old Dominion Dr	(2407-5299)	31	C1/C2
	(3200-3299)	35	B1
	(4030-4825)	34	A1/A2
N Old Glebe Rd	(4100-4429)	31	B2
	(4430-4599)	32	A1/B1
S Old Glebe Rd		37	B1
S Old Jefferson Davis Hwy		40	A2
S Orme St		40	A1
N Ottawa St		33	A1/B2
N Oxford St	(300-699)	37	B1
	(2920-3119)	32	B1
S Oxford St		39	B1/B2
N Park Dr	(1-104)	38	A2
	(155-599)	34	C2
S Park Dr		38	A2
N Patrick Henry Dr	(840-2135)	33	B2/C2
	(2136-2198)	34	A1
N Peary St		32	B1
Pentagon Access Rd		40	A2
N Pershing Ct		38	A2
N Pershing Dr	(2250-4314)	37	A1/A2/B1
	(4315-4499)	34	C2
S Pershing Dr		38	A2
Piedmont St		37	B1
N Piedmont St	(550-799)	37	A1
	(3129-3699)	32	B1
N Pierce St		36	B1/C2
S Pierce St		40	A1/B1
N Pocomoke St		33	A1/B2
S Poe St		40	A1
N Pollard St	(512-999)	37	A1
	(1700-2749)	35	A1/B1/C1
	(2750-3199)	32	B1/C1
S Pollard St		39	A1
N Potomac St		33	A1/B2/C2
N Powhatan St		33	A1/B2/C2
N Quantico St		33	B1/B2/C2
N Quebec St	(300-399)	37	B1
	(1600-2157)	34	A2/B2
	(2158-2499)	35	A1/B1
	(2500-3519)	32	B1/C2
S Quebec St		37	C1
N Queen St		36	C1
S Queen St		40	A1/B1
N Queens Ln		36	B1
N Quesada St		33	B2/C2
N Quincy St	(800-2199)	34	A2/B2/C2
	(2200-2549)	35	A1/B1
	(2550-3149)	32	C1/C2
S Quincy St	(500-1099)	37	C1
	(1100-2899)	39	A1/B1/B2
N Quinn St		36	B1/C1
S Quinn St		40	A1
N Quintana St		33	B1/B2/C2
N Radford St		32	C2
N Randolph St	(500-2489)	34	A2/B2/C2
	(2490-4199)	32	A1/B1/C1
S Randolph St	(800-999)	37	C1
	(1300-3099)	39	A1/B1/B2
N Rhodes St		36	B1/C1
N Richmond St	(2300-2399)	34	A2
	(2620-4199)	32	A1/B1/C1
N Ridgeview Rd		35	A1
N River St		31	A2/B2
N Rixey St		31	B2
N Robert Walker Pl		32	C1
N Roberts Ln		32	B1
N Rochester St		33	A1/B1/C2
N Rock Spring Rd	(4500-4876)	31	C2
	(4877-4999)	33	A2
N Rockingham St		33	A1/B1/C2
N Rolfe St		36	B1/C1
S Rolfe St		40	A1/B1
N Roosevelt St		33	B1/C2
N Round Hill Rd		31	A2
Route 233		40	C2
N Scott St		36	B1/C1
S Scott St		40	A1
Shirlington Rd		39	A2/B2
N Smythe St		36	B1
S Somerset St		33	A1/B1
S Southgate Rd		40	A1
N Spout Run Pky		36	A1
	(2900-3099)	35	B2
N Stafford St	(900-2399)	34	A2/B2
	(2901-3854)	32	B1/C1
	(3855-4014)	31	B2
S Stafford St	(600-699)	38	A2
	(1500-3599)	39	A1/B2/C2
State Route 110		36	B2/C2
N Stuart St	(800-2399)	34	B2/C2
	(2400-4010)	32	C1
	(4011-4099)	31	A2
N Sycamore St		33	B1/C1
N Tacoma St		33	A1/B1
N Taft St		36	B1/C1
N Taylor St	(800-2498)	34	A2/B2
	(3100-3199)	32	C1
	(4000-4099)	31	B2
S Taylor St	(300-949)	38	A2
	(950-3699)	39	A1/B1/C2
N Tazewell Ct		34	A2
N Tazewell St	(600-799)	34	C2
	(3730-4099)	31	B2
N Thomas St	(1-349)	37	B1
	(350-2199)	34	A2/C2
	(3100-3499)	32	B1/C1
S Thomas St		38	B2